THE EMERGENCE OF MODERN JEWISH POLITICS

PITT SERIES IN RUSSIAN AND EAST EUROPEAN STUDIES

Jonathan Harris, Editor

THE EMERGENCE OF

Modern Jewish Politics

Bundism and Zionism in Eastern Europe

EDITED BY ZVI GITELMAN

UNIVERSITY OF PITTSBURGH PRESS

Published by the University of Pittsburgh Press, Pittsburgh, Pa., 15260
Copyright © 2003, University of Pittsburgh Press
Manufactured in the United States of America
Printed on acid-free paper
10 9 8 7 6 5 4 3 2 1

Chapter 10 has been adapted from an article by David Aberbach that first
appeared in *Nations and Nationalism* 3, no. 1 (1997): 25–44, © ASEN 1997.
Reprinted by permission of Blackwell Publishing.

Library of Congress Cataloging-in-Publication Data

The emergence of modern Jewish politics : Bundism and Zionism in Eastern
Europe / Zvi Gitelman, editor.
        p. cm. — (Pitt series in Russian and East European studies)
Chapter 10 has been adapted from an article by David Aberbach which
first appeared in Nations and Nationalism 3, no. 1 (1997): 2544, (c)
ASEN 1997.
Includes index.
    ISBN 0-8229-4188-0 (cloth : alk. paper)
    1. Zionism—Europe, Eastern—History. 2. Allgemeyner Idisher
arbeyterbund in Lita, Poylen un Rusland—History. 3. Labor
Zionism—Europe, Eastern—History. 4. Jews—Europe, Eastern—Politics
and government—20th century. 5. Jews—Europe, Eastern—Identity. I.
Gitelman, Zvi Y. II. Series.

    DS149.5.E85 E44 2003
    324'.089'924047—dc21

                                    2002011205

CONTENTS

Acknowledgments   vii

EAST EUROPEAN JEWISH POLITICS

1. A Century of Jewish Politics in Eastern Europe
   The Legacy of the Bund and the Zionist Movement   3
   ZVI GITELMAN

2. The Other Modern Jewish Politics
   Integration and Modernity in Fin de Siècle Russia   20
   BENJAMIN NATHANS

3. The New Jewish Politics and Its Discontents   35
   ANTONY POLONSKY

4. National-Minority Policy, Bundist Social Organizations,
   and Jewish Women in Interwar Poland   54
   DANIEL BLATMAN

5. The Left Poalei Tsiyon in Interwar Poland   71
   SAMUEL D. KASSOW

6. Imitation, Rejection, Cooperation
   Agudat Yisrael and the Zionist Movement in Interwar Poland   85
   GERSHON BACON

7. Jewish Politics and Youth Culture in Interwar Poland
   Preliminary Evidence from the YIVO Autobiographies   95
   MICHAEL C. STEINLAUF

POLITICS AND CULTURE

8. The Bund and Modern Yiddish Culture   107
   DAVID E. FISHMAN

9. The Political Vision of I. L. Peretz   120
   RUTH R. WISSE

10. Hebrew Literature and Jewish Nationalism in
    the Tsarist Empire, 1881–1917   132
    DAVID ABERBACH

11. Vitebsk versus Bezalel
    A Jewish Kulturkampf *in the Plastic Arts*   151
    SETH L. WOLITZ

EAST EUROPEAN JEWISH POLITICS IN EMIGRATION

12. The Bundists in America and the "Zionist Problem"   181
    JONATHAN FRANKEL

13. Genocide and Nationalism
    The Changing Nature of Jewish Politics in
    Post–World War II France   197
    MAUD MANDEL

Postscript
   East European Jewish Politics in Comparative Perspective   220
   RONALD GRIGOR SUNY

Notes   227
List of Contributors   267
Index   269

ACKNOWLEDGMENTS

The stimulus for this book was a conference called "A Century of Modern Jewish Politics: The Bund and Zionism in Poland and Eastern Europe," held at the Frankel Center for Judaic Studies at the University of Michigan in 1998. That conference was made possible by the generous support of the American Council of Learned Societies and the University of Michigan's Frankel Center for Judaic Studies and Office of the Vice-President for Research. I would like to thank James Bell and Amy Hamermesh, then of the Frankel Center, for facilitating the conference. Professors Todd Endelman and Anita Norich, both of the University of Michigan, and Professor Roman Szporluk, Harvard University, made valuable contributions to the discussions at the conference. Deborah Greene and Roseanne Magat worked assiduously to prepare the essays for publication. To these people and institutions, my profound gratitude.

THE EMERGENCE OF MODERN JEWISH POLITICS

East European Jewish Politics

ZVI GITELMAN

1

A Century of Jewish Politics in Eastern Europe

The Legacy of the Bund and the Zionist Movement

JUST OVER A CENTURY AGO, two Jewish political movements were founded. One was triumphant and the other largely forgotten, but each had a hand in bringing East European Jewry into the modern era of politics. While Zionism achieved its primary aim, the founding of a Jewish state, the Jewish Labor Bund has practically disappeared. Even its ideals of socialism and secular Jewishness based in the diaspora seem to have failed and to have been repudiated by Jews and others. Yet, perhaps more than Zionism, it was the Bund that profoundly changed the structure of Jewish society, politics and culture in Eastern Europe, and, by extension, in the Americas, much of Western Europe, and Israel. This volume analyzes the changes in Jewish political life wrought by Zionism and Bundism, examines political, social, and cultural dimensions of the two movements, and explores the relationship between politics, culture, and society among the Jews of Eastern Europe in the first half of this century.

The authors in this book differ on the degree of success and failure of the various parties and the appropriateness of their tactics. Inevitably, most address these issues through the prism of the catastrophe that ended East European Jewish politics, though some argue against such a perspective. Many contend that partisan and ideological politics did not infuse culture to the extent often assumed. There was a strong idealistic streak in both politics and culture and this may not have served the embattled Jewish minority well. The essays raise, directly and indirectly, the issue of whether ethnic minorities are best served by highly ideological or pragmatic movements in trying to defend their interests in nondemocratic, multiethnic states.

Both major modern Jewish political movements among East European Jews originated in 1897. The Bund, founded secretly in Vilna (today, Vilnius) was formally the Algemeyner Idisher Arbeter Bund in Liteh, Poiln un Rusland, or the Jewish Workers' Alliance in Lithuania, Poland, and Russia. It was a Marxist, social-democratic movement that advocated Jewish cultural autonomy based on Yiddish. It was opposed to religion, as most socialist organizations were, as well as to Zionism. The latter movement, consolidated with much fanfare into a World Zionist Organization at its founding congress in Basel, Switzerland, held that the Jews are a nation that could not survive without a state of their own. After some debate, the Zionists agreed that the Jewish state should be established in Palestine, the historic Jewish homeland. The Bundists believed that Zionism was unrealistic and that it papered over class conflicts within the Jewish population. As a "nationalist" movement, Zionism was considered "reactionary" by the Bundists as well as by the Bolsheviks and Mensheviks, members of the other major Marxist movements in Russia around 1903–1905.

In this volume, Benjamin Nathans argues that the Bund and Zionism were not the only modern political alternatives Jews had in the tsarist empire at the turn of the twentieth century. There was also a "politics of emancipation and integration," led by liberal Jewish activists, mostly lawyers, who worked for Jewish civil rights through the courts, in the Russian parliament, and finally among the Jews themselves. Whatever the Bund's achievements were, in the interwar period in Poland it operated in an authoritarian state and expended much energy on parochial and polemical activities. Antony Polonsky points out that Jews were so deeply divided ideologically in Poland that common action was "virtually impossible" even in "an increasingly perilous situation." He probes the reasons for the failure of "integrationist" politics in the Polish lands. The consequences were populist politics, mutual distrust between Poles and Jews, and the disappointment of both with the failure of assimilation or even integration. Polonsky's treatment of the failure of Jewish autonomy in neighboring Lithuania, which should have provided a contrast to Poland, raises the still relevant question of whether minority rights can be guaranteed effectively in states that define themselves as national.

Regarding political parties in interwar Poland, Daniel Blatman contends that the Bund mistakenly transferred to Poland its vision of a multinational, federative socialist state from prerevolutionary Russia. But the trade unions and women's associations it organized, the latter not very popular among working-class Jewish women, engaged in education, cultural activity, and social support. Thus, Bundist organizations filled needs that the state did not. The Left Poalei Tsiyon occupied a much smaller niche in Jewish politics than did the Bund. Samuel Kassow admits that the LPT was a marginal and quixotic group, as it stood for a binational, Yiddish-speaking Soviet Palestine. But it had a base in the trade union movement and "played a major role in the battle for secular Yiddish culture and education." Kassow explores the fascinating ideology of the LPT, its relations with the Bund, Zionists, and the USSR. He concludes that the idealism of the party "imparted hope and inspired the energy to fight back against seemingly hopeless odds" as many of its members did in Poland during World War II. At the other end of the political spectrum stood the Agudat Yisrael (Agudas Yisroel, or Aguda). A conservative, ultra-Orthodox party that rejected both socialism and Zionism, the Aguda nevertheless adopted many organizational forms that the Zionists had developed. Gershon Bacon shows how the Aguda managed a "delicate balance between imitation and rejection" of Zionism and delineates three forms of imitation and adaptation. It will come as a surprise to many that on an "everyday level," Agudat Yisrael and the Zionists "engaged in continuous cooperation."

Just before World War II, the YIVO Institute in Vilna sponsored an autobiographical essay contest for young Jews. Michael Steinlauf mines this riveting unpublished material and provides insights into family relations, the drift from tradition, economic despair, and cultural and political views and activities of Polish Jewish youth. He concludes that politics played a significant role but did not define their lives. They were part of a culture "whose core was aspiration rather than certainty," and despite extreme hardship and despair idealism survived among many.

It is often assumed that the cultural struggle between Hebrew and Yiddish not only paralleled the political struggle between Zionism and the Bund but that the two movements sponsored the cultural competition. David Fishman's research shows that the Bund did not lead the Yiddish renaissance but participated in it. "Most of the landmark events in the history of modern Yiddish culture were not sponsored by the Bund nor led by Bundists." The Bund became ideologically "Yiddishist" after 1905. "While the Bund tugged Yiddish culture to the political left, its positions did not dominate the Yiddish literary and cultural scene between 1890 and the First World War."

Perhaps the most prominent Yiddish cultural figure associated loosely with socialism was I. L. Peretz. According to Ruth Wisse, Peretz, who was critical both of assimilation and of Jewish clericalism, saw a modern Jewish culture as the best alternative. Wisse argues that this was a culture of exile and of weakness and, as it did in Peretz's own vision, ends in destruction. Wisse sees Peretz as having had a "will to powerlessness," which she defines as "the promotion of the moral ideals of exile as an end in themselves, without either true faith in the ultimate restorative justice of a just God or a political plan for national self-protection." Protecting the culture of exile, says Wisse, did not protect the Jews but led to the *khurbn* (destructive catastrophe) that Peretz himself had envisioned.

In contrast to the perhaps tenuous relationship between Yiddish literature and Bundism, David Aberbach argues that Hebrew literature in the tsarist empire was an integral part of the rise of Jewish nationalism, creating literary norms that were transplanted to Palestine. Like the Russian literature of the time, by which it was heavily influenced, Hebrew literature subverted tsarist authority and depicted the failings of society with the aim of reforming it. The pogroms of 1881–1882 politicized Hebrew literature and linked it explicitly to the Zionist movement. Chaim Nachman Bialik's "poems of wrath" express the radicalization of the post-1881 generation and the revolt against powerlessness.

In a sweeping survey of Jewish art, a term he explores thoroughly, Seth Wolitz discerns two schools of that art a century ago. The "Vitebsk" school was oriented to the diaspora and was loosely associated with secular socialism, whereas the "Bezalel" school was explicitly Zionist, propagandistic, and strove to be inspirational. The Vitebsk school, founded by Yehuda Pen, included such artists as Marc Chagall, El Lissitsky, and Salomon Yudovin. Boris Shatz and E. M. Lilien were among those in the Bezalel group. The Vitebsk artists stressed class consciousness and the rich particularity of present East European Jewish life, whereas the Bezalel artists tried explicitly to link the Hebraic past to a heroic Zionist future. Marc Chagall, however, a product of the Vitebsk school, remained fiercely independent, carving out for himself a unique place in the history of art.

This introductory essay attempts to demonstrate that the Bund contributed to the democratization and modernization of Jewish political life, perhaps to a greater extent than the Zionist movement. The Bund's contribution should be acknowledged despite the failure to sustain itself beyond the catastrophe of European Jewry and the apparent bankruptcy of the movement's political and economic positions.

The major political ideals of the twentieth century have been nationalism, socialism, and democracy. Nationalism and socialism, like the Bund and Zionism, emerged in the nineteenth century but came to full flower in the twentieth. Zionism combined versions of nationalism and socialism. Most versions of Zionism have also been democratic, though there have been nondemocratic and antidemocratic strains in some versions of socialist Zionism, Zionist Revisionism, and religious Zionism.[1] There remain unresolved issues of democracy in Zionist thought and certainly in the Zionist state. One of these is whether Israel can be both an "ethnic" state, that is, a Jewish state, and a "civic" state, one for all of its citizens, including the nearly 20 percent who are not Jews.[2] A second issue is how citizens can best be represented in a postcollectivist age. This involves largely structural questions of proportional representation, party lists, geographic constituencies, and the direct election of the prime minister. Third, the issue of civil rights continues to be contentious, and is compounded by the absence of a written constitution. Nevertheless, over a century after it was envisioned as a goal, and over a half-century after its founding, the Jewish state seems firmly established, though its very existence is still challenged by some and its borders remain a matter of dispute.

If Zionism is the great winner among rival Jewish ideologies, the Bund—although it, too, combined elements of nationalism, socialism, and democracy—is the great loser. All the major critics of Zionism except Bundism survive. Reform Judaism, which condemned Zionism on the grounds that Jews were no longer a nation, but only a religious group, and therefore did not warrant a state of their own, became pro-Zionist in the middle of the twentieth century. Most Orthodox authorities also condemned Zionism on the grounds that it sought to do what God and the Messiah would do—return the Jews to their ancestral homeland. There was, however, an Orthodox Zionist minority as early as the mid-nineteenth century. After the Holocaust, most anti-Zionist Orthodox movements and leaders shifted to a position of neutrality toward Zionism. Assimilationism, the belief that the solution to the "Jewish problem" lay in the assimilation of the Jews into the peoples and cultures among whom they lived to the point where Jews would cease to be a distinct entity rather than in strengthening Jewish consciousness and recreating a Jewish nation, is no longer much of an explicit ideology. However, very high rates of intermarriage in all of the diaspora and almost total Jewish linguistic acculturation proclaim its success. Territorialism, which sought to settle Jews in compact areas in the diaspora, has failed completely, but it was never as large a movement as Bundism.

Though the Bund is now but a memory, its appeal to social and economic justice, its advocacy of ethnic and civic equality, and its militancy in struggling for labor and Jewish rights made it a powerful movement, especially among younger workers. After 1936 the Bund won more votes than any other Jewish party in *kehilla* (organized Jewish community) and municipal elections in the major Polish cities. In the municipal elections in Warsaw in December–January 1938–1939, the Bund won seventeen of twenty Jewish seats, and in Lodz it gained eleven of seventeen seats.[3] These were the cities with the largest Jewish populations in Poland. One estimate is that in seven major cities with a total Jewish population of about 840,000, some 40 percent of Jewish voters cast their ballots for the Bund, though in twenty-six cities with Jewish populations of under 10,000, about 20 percent voted for the Bund and some 45 percent for Zionist lists. In all, the Bund probably received 38 percent of the Jewish vote, Zionist lists 36 percent, and Agudat Yisrael and middle-class groups about 23 percent.[4] The Bund had a flourishing press, youth organizations, summer camps and sanatoria, sports clubs, and powerful trade unions. It had allies in the Polish Socialist Party (PPS) and sister parties in other East European countries, as well as influential sympathizers in North and South America and France. Yet, today, if one were to ask Israeli or American Jews under the age of sixty to identify the Bund, probably over 90 percent would be unable to do so. Even in academia, after a brief flurry of scholarly interest in the Bund in the 1960s, few scholars in Israel, the United States, or Eastern Europe have paid it any attention.[5] How can one explain the disappearance from consciousness and even memory, both individual and collective, of this once powerful movement?

The simple answer is, of course, that the Bund was murdered. That is, almost all its European members fell victim to the Nazis. But millions of Orthodox Jews and Zionists were also murdered, members of Agudat Yisrael and Poalei Tsiyon (Socialist Zionists), of Mizrachi (religious Zionist) and Betar (Zionist Revisionist). Why do their ideologies and movements survive when the Bund's does not? True, the other movements had members and adherents outside of Europe, but so did the Bund, albeit to a lesser extent. I believe the answer is that the Nazis and the Soviets, each in their own way, destroyed not only the Bundists but also the appeal of the Bund's ideology, and at the same time strengthened the appeal of Zionism. The deeds of the two totalitarian powers convinced many Jews that Jewish life in the diaspora, as a minority everywhere, was fragile, tenuous, or altogether not viable. Second, the assumption of the Bund that socialism would solve the "Jewish problem," along with all other ethnic problems, was contradicted by the failure of the states that called themselves socialist, most notably the Soviet Union, to solve not only the "Jewish problem" but those of other peoples and cultures. Third, socialism was an appealing doctrine while there was a substantial Jewish proletariat. But once Jewish urban workers in England and the United States became suburban professionals and businessmen, the doctrine seemed at best quaint and at worst directly inimical to their own interests. How many Jews after 1950 read or sang the working-class poetry of Morris Rosenfeld or Dovid Edelshtat?

That brings us to perhaps the fourth and most fatal flaw of Bundism. Jews eschew proletarian poetry partly because it stands outside of their experiences, but also because they cannot read it; it is written in a language, Yiddish, they have abandoned. The Bund argued that Yiddish was the everyday language of the Jewish people and that it was no less legitimate and worthy than any other language. Hebrew, said the Bundists, was a language that only rabbis, scholars, and highly educated *maskilim* (enlightened ones) could understand, and they did not easily use it as an *umgangssprache*. But making Yiddish and its culture the basis of Jewish ethnicity turned out to be a fatal error. Unlike other peoples, Jews are notoriously pragmatic in their approach to any language other than Hebrew, which they long ago elevated to the status of *lashon ha-kodesh*, the holy tongue. Yiddish did not survive transplantation from the East European soil in which it had grown to the new lands of Jewish immigration in the Americas and Western Europe. In Israel, Zionists fought against Yiddish as a product of the *galut* (diaspora). It would interfere with the crucial task of *mizug galuyot*, the integration of diaspora Jews from Europe with those from Africa and Asia not only in a new state but also into a new and united nation. The prevailing understanding of national unity was homogenization, a simplistic, but perhaps necessary, understanding. Just as Americans had sought to forge a nation out of successive waves of immigrants by amalgamating them in the celebrated "melting pot," so too did the Zionists believe that the only way to achieve national unity was through ethnic and cultural fusion. This strategy led to the emergence of a vibrant Hebrew culture and, indeed, a distinctly Israeli culture shared by the great majority of Jews —and some non-Jews—in Israel. However, the cost has been the loss of languages and cultural traditions from Eastern Europe and every region and culture from which Israelis originated. As in the United States, which has moved from the "melting pot" theory to "cultural pluralism" (or "multiculturalism"), once Hebrew culture emerged unchallenged, people began to rethink the strategy of assimilation. Israelis have begun to make gestures in the direction of multiculturalism.

Language is not merely a neutral instrument of communication. For many of its users, a particular language evokes associations, memories, and emotions, thereby affirming, strengthening, and, in some cases, even creating, allegiances. In some instances, language is contentious and crucial because it is an instrument of state-building, as in Tanzania and the former USSR; for others, it is the primary symbol of the nation rather than of the state.[6] In Israel, Hebrew has been an instrument of both state- and nation-building.

Language can also be a defining characteristic, but is not always so. In Quebec, Belgium, and Estonia, language is a central issue. In contrast, the recent war in Bosnia involved one group of people who speak Serbian and Croatian against two others speaking the same languages; in addition, the Palestinian/Israeli conflict is not at all about language. In India, where language issues were often at the root of ethnic conflicts, those issues receded once internal state boundaries were drawn to coincide roughly with linguistic boundaries. And language does not appear to have been a very powerful nexus for Jewish ethnicity. An ethnic group is one that has a "real or putative common ancestry, memories of a shared historical past and a common focus on one or more symbolic elements defined as the epitome of their peoplehood."[7] Clearly, language has not been the "distinctive characteristic" or "epitome of peoplehood" for Jews. They have picked up and dropped languages with impressive frequency, though abandoned languages have left their traces on successive Jewish languages. Thus, Hebrew gave way to Aramaic with the Babylonian exile, but Hebrew remained the language of the holy and classic texts, and through the medium of Talmudic study, Aramaic has left its imprint on modern Yiddish and Hebrew. Judeo-Greek, Judeo-Español (Ladino), Judeo-Arabic, Judeo-Persian, Tat, and, of course, Yiddish are examples of the languages Jews have fused with elements drawn from Hebrew, Aramaic, and local vernaculars.

In many instances, even the most traditional and highly conscious Jews have adopted non-Jewish languages. Georgian has long been the dominant vernacular of Jews in Georgia, though they are a very traditional, religious group, as Italian was the common language of all kinds of Jews in Italy, and Arabic or French the languages of North African and Middle Eastern Jews. Whereas many strictly Orthodox Jews in Poland, Liteh (roughly, present-day Lithuania, Belarus, and northeastern Poland), and Ukraine shunned the use of "*goyish*" (what they saw as the peasant patois around them) and even the "higher" languages of Polish or Russian, culturally isolated and religiously fervent Szatmar Hasidim and other

Hungarian Jews seem to have no hesitation in using Magyar. More recently, English has gained wide acceptance among Hasidim in communities such as Boro Park in New York and Stamford Hill in London.

A hypothesis that might explain these variations is that where Jews regarded the culture of peoples as "higher" than theirs, they adopted that language, if not the culture in its entirety. Where they regarded surrounding cultures as inferior to their own, they did not adopt it. Secondly, they tended to adopt the imperial language or the language of social and economic power, rather than the languages of surrounding, but subjugated, peoples. Thus, in the Austro-Hungarian Empire, Jews who spoke Yiddish earlier—even the traditionalists among them —could switch to Hungarian and/or German. In the Russian Empire, while some may have switched to Russian or Polish, few adopted Lithuanian, Ukrainian, or Belorussian, languages of the "benighted" peasantry. On the other hand, few traditionalists crossed over to the language of power, Russian, so that there must be some other variable at work here. In Quebec, where English and French were equally foreign to the East European immigrant Jew, he or she generally adopted English, the language of the then socially and economically dominant minority.[8] The important point for our purpose is the lack of language loyalty among Jews, their readiness to move from one tongue to another.

This fluidity may be explained by several factors. First, since Hebrew was enthroned as *lashon ha-kodesh* (*loshn koidesh* in the Yiddish pronunciation) all other languages were relegated to the status of purely instrumental vernaculars. Second, the great mobility of Jews, moving from one country to another and then from one continent to another, meant that a particular language would lose its usefulness rather quickly. Many Jews never learned a single language properly because of their own, sometimes forced, mobility. Finally, language did not become a subject of ideology among Jews until early in the nineteenth century when West European *maskilim* proposed that Jews learn local languages as a prerequisite to their political and social emancipation. Later in the century, East European *maskilim* demanded that Jews both learn local languages and revive Hebrew as an *umgangssprache*.

Among Jews, the battle between Yiddish and Hebrew was politicized when Bundists and other socialists adopted the cause of Yiddish, and Zionists waved the flag of Hebrew. An ideology of Yiddishism developed.[9] One of the architects of this ideology, Chaim Zhitlovsky, claimed that a "complete revolution . . . the secularization of Jewish national and cultural life" had taken place. "The

Yiddish language form becomes for us a content of great weight, a fundamental."[10] Thus, for the first time, language was identified as the "distinctive characteristic" of or "epitome of peoplehood" for the Jews.

This was a serious miscalculation. Once East European Jewry was destroyed, Yiddish had no chance to substitute for religion as the "distinctive characteristic" or "epitome of peoplehood" of the Jews. The Soviet experience confirms this. The USSR was the only country in the world to invest heavily in Yiddish—by 1930, there were 1,100 Yiddish schools and dozens of Yiddish newspapers and theaters paid for by the state—but Yiddish declined rapidly there, not only because the state withdrew its support by the late 1930s but because the Jews themselves opted for what they saw as the higher, urban, Russian culture. In 1926, three-quarters of Soviet Jews claimed Yiddish as their mother tongue (*rodnoi iazyk*); by 1989, only 11 percent did so. Today most Jews in the diaspora speak English, Russian, French, and Spanish, rather than a Jewish language.

Jewish Ideologies and Democracy

If the Bund's focus on socialism and Yiddish left no lasting imprint on world Jewry, its lasting contribution was to democratize Jewish public life. Years ago, American rabbis preached the doctrine that Judaism and democracy were not only compatible, but that democracy was the Jewish tradition. We can understand why this theme was emphasized at a time when Jews were struggling for acceptance in democratic America, but factually, this was off the mark. Lacking sovereignty, Jewish politics in Europe before the late nineteenth century was a combination of *shtadlones* (intercession, pleading) vis-à-vis the outer world and oligarchic communal politics. The Vilna *Kahal* (communal board, governing body), for example, consisted of 196 members in 1787, 13 of whom were officers, all males, and all of whom had to have been married for at least ten years. In order to be officers they had to give a special contribution to the *Kahal's* treasury. Israel Cohen has noted that "Family relationship played an important and rather unfortunate part in the composition of the *Kahal*, as father, son, and other relatives sometimes held office together and exercised a prejudicial influence."[11] Office-holders had to pay fees, "and since the *Kahal*, owing to its frequent financial difficulties, was obliged to make these fees a substantial source of revenue, only rich men could aspire to office."[12] The *Kahal* was far ahead of the polities in which it operated, providing a broad range of welfare services, but it was oligarchic, unrepresentative, and undemocratic. Soviet Jewish historians, whose ideological motivations are clear, assembled rich materials on social tensions and "class struggle" within the Jewish communities of Russia and Poland in the eighteenth and nineteenth centuries, but these materials are largely ignored by historians today.[13]

Jewish politics began to change in the middle of the nineteenth century with the sharpening of social conflict and the emergence of both the Haskalah (enlightenment) movement among Jews and radical politics in the larger society. As noted earlier, the *maskilim* advocated Jewish acculturation to the dominant cultures in the places they lived, but without giving up their own culture and identity. The changes culminated in the founding of the Zionist and Bundist movements in 1897, and included a shift from the oligarchic politics of the *kehilla* to the mass politics of parties and movements, as well as a move from religious politics, such as the clash between Hasidim and Misnagdim (their opponents), to secular and ideological politics. In addition, Jewish politics, which had once been concerned only with Jewish issues, began to take up general issues such as economics, political rights, and civil rights. Finally, the *shtadlones*, or pleading, that once characterized Jewish politics gave way to assertiveness and demands for rights. These changes naturally led to the emergence of a new kind of leadership; alongside the traditional leaders of the community, the wealthy and the learned, a new type of leader emerged whose credentials were knowledge of the larger world, the ability to organize, and the ability to mobilize the masses. Knowledge of non-Jewish languages and mores is what enabled acculturated and even assimilated figures such as Vladimir Medem of the Bund and Zionists such as Theodor Herzl, Leon Pinsker, and Vladimir Zhabotinsky, to assume the mantle of leadership.

The class tensions of *kehilla* politics were paralleled by tensions between acculturated elites and more ethnically conscious and loyal masses. Thus, for example, in the Zionist movement the East European masses, motivated as much by traditional yearnings for Zion as by modern romantic nationalism or the calculations of realpolitik, rejected the Uganda plan the British had offered and which Herzl was prepared to entertain. In the Bund, it was the rank-and-file Yiddish speakers who pushed the Bund's Russified leadership to demand national-cultural autonomy and to press for Jewish cultural rights.[14] As one of those early, Russified leaders acknowledged, "We were for assimilation; we did not even dream of a special Jewish mass movement . . . Our task was developing cadres for the Russian revolutionary movement."[15]

Compared to their sometimes socialist allies and sometimes enemies, Robert Brym points out, "The Bundists never reached the same heights of intelligentsia elitism as the Mensheviks and Bolsheviks."[16] The shift from mass to elite politics and the broadening of the political agenda democratized Jewish politics. Many more people were now involved and the issues of economic welfare, cultural development, national defense, and collective and individual rights were the kind that most people could understand on some level.

Modern democracy is a system of government that meets three essential conditions: meaningful, extensive and nonviolent competition for power at predictable intervals; the opportunity for all to participate in politics; and civil and political liberties "sufficient to ensure the integrity of political competition and participation."[17] What differentiates democratic governments or organizations from others is that anyone can aspire to leadership or dissent from leadership, and leadership is responsive to the rank and file.

Democracy, like other forms of government, should not be seen as an absolute, but as a spectrum. There are more and less democratic governments and organizations. The Bund was far from a perfectly democratic organization, but it was far more democratic than the *kehilla*, certainly more so than the East European regimes, and even more democratic than other socialist movements such as the Bolsheviks. Since it never came to power, the first criterion of democracy—free competition for power—is not relevant. The Bund fought for the civil and political liberties that are essential to democracy, but that fight was unsuccessful in Russia and Poland. Therefore, the Bund's achievement in democratization was broadening the political arena to include women and people who were not wealthy or learned, and establishing more democratic forms of decision making. The former became a permanent change in Jewish politics and has survived the demise of the Bund, which has not been credited with this revolutionary change that affected all of Jewish political life, in Israel and in the diaspora. Whether more democratic forms of decision making have become a permanent feature of Jewish life is far less clear.

It might be argued that Zionism shares in having made these changes, but in regard to the broadening of the social base of Jewish public life, it is not clear how far the Russian Zionist movement went. Surprisingly, there seem to be almost no studies of the social bases of the Zionist movement and how and by whom its constituency was formed. There are voluminous writings on Zionism and its origins, but all concentrate on ideological issues. Few tell us very much about what kind of people became Zionists: intelligentsia or *amcha* (plain folk), men or women, more educated or less educated?[18] An initial search turned up a fascinating article on the social composition of the "second *aliyah*" (the second wave of Jewish immigrants to Palestine, 1904–1914) who were still in Palestine in the late 1930s. But of the 35,000–40,000 *olim* (immigrants) in this period, the great majority had left Palestine by this time. Of the sample of 937, about 95 percent were from territories in the Russian Empire (Russia, Lithuania, and Poland excluding Galicia and Bessarabia). Sixty-nine percent (644) were men, whereas men constituted only slightly more than half of the Jewish immigrants to America from the Russian Empire. Most revealing are the social class origins of the *olim*. Whereas in 1897–1900, 29 percent of the Jews of Congress Poland and 34 percent of the Jews of Russia were classified as merchants (including small traders), over 55 percent of the parents of the *olim* were of this middle-class background. Only 19 percent of the *olim* came from working-class families, while 34 percent of Jews in the Russian Empire were in this category. Commenting on this discrepancy, Yosef Gorny surmises that the Zionists were rebelling not only against the diaspora, "but also against the occupation or the profession of their parents," since the *olim* were dedicated to manual, agricultural labor.[19]

Of course, the *olim* may not have been representative of the social class origins of the rest of the Zionists, and only further research could uncover the social composition of the Zionist movement. However, it seems that at least before World War I, the Zionist movement drew more heavily from the middle class and the intelligentsia than it did from the proletariat. There was a proletarian Zionist party, Poalei Tsiyon, which had been founded in 1906. The Zionist-Socialist Workers Party (Ts.S.) and the Jewish Socialist Workers party (SERP) were also formed at this time, though how accurately their names reflected their social composition is not clear.[20] An analysis of seventy leaders of Russian Zionism in 1897–1904 concludes that they came from the "Russian[ized] Jewish intelligentsia," which was generally more sympathetic to the Russian radical and liberal movements than to Zionism. They were men who came from "enlightened" families and had received traditional Jewish educations, but then studied in *gymnazii* and in universities, becoming professionals. The wave of pogroms in the early 1880s turned them from passive supporters of revolutionary parties to active Zionists.[21] Yosef Goldshtain notes:

> In sum, Zionism attracted the middle class Jews who were open to new tendencies but sought to maintain Jewish tradition. . . . The intelligentsia and the working class . . . did not join the movement in its early days, despite the fact that the leadership came from the intelligentsia. . . . The Jewish proletariat was not attracted to the Zionist movement because the latter offered it no immediate social, economic and

cultural solutions. Only when a radical change toward *'gegenwartsarbeit'* (work in the present in the diaspora) was made, did proletarians and young intelligentsia stream into the movement. . . . But even then the number of people who joined from these social strata was tiny . . . A major portion of the Jewish proletariat was drawn to the Bund and the Jewish intellectual sought more to be integrated into the surrounding society than to join the Zionist movement.[22]

While the Zionist movement did not exclude people on the grounds of their class origins, it did not represent the lower strata of the Jewish population commensurate with their proportion in the population as a whole. Analyzing the Zionist movement in geographic terms, Goldshtain finds that it was weak in the Polish areas of the Russian Empire, where Hasidism, militantly opposed to Zionism, was strong. Zionism was especially popular in Ukraine, Liteh, and cities outside the Pale of Settlement. In Poland, it was only in the interwar period that Zionism became a serious rival to Bundism.

The participation of women in public affairs seems not to have been as prominent an issue then, nor is it today in the former Soviet Union, as it is in the United States. Nevertheless, the fact that women began to participate in politics did not go unnoticed. One religious polemic against Zionism, noting women's increased participation in the movement objected, "Public affairs must never be the subject of idle chatter of the crowd or of women. There is no greater disaster for the nation than the transfer of its business from the private domain of individual leaders to the public domain, where youngsters and even girls are free to meddle."[23] I have no data on the gender composition of the Zionist movement as a whole, but it is obvious that women participated less than men in this, as in every, political movement. Using the photographs of delegates to the congresses of the Hovevei Tsiyon, the earliest Russian Zionists, and the national congresses of Russian Zionists (1896–1909), I calculate that of 1,249 delegates, 79, or 6.3 percent, were women.[24]

A historian of the Bund notes that by the 1890s, "Women formed a substantial segment of both the intelligentsia and the kase-organized working force. . . . It was not unusual by now for the daughters of the assimilated bourgeoisie to attend state schools and universities. But among lower-class Jewish families the very idea of educating women beyond the minimum needed for prayer was out of the question. In these families the break with the older generation was excruciating. It is easy to imagine the shock of parents on learning that their daughters had attended secret meetings late at night or on the Sabbath. . . . The gradual move toward the emancipation of women shook the very foundation of Jewish social life."[25]

Since the Bund was a clandestine organization, its earliest records are incomplete. Using the data available, I examined the lists of delegates to Bundist national conferences and congresses (1897–1922), and of the members of the Bund's Central Committees. Of 201 delegates/members, 20 were women. This is a higher percentage (10 percent) than among the Zionists. Moreover, women were prominent in the Bund's leadership from its inception, though, curiously, their role in the leadership seems to have declined over time. Among the seven "Vilna Pioneers" of the Bund were two women, and at its founding congress, two of the thirteen delegates were women. By 1919–1922, however, only one woman— Esther Frumkin, who later became a leading figure in the Jewish Sections of the Communist Party and who died in a Soviet labor camp—was in the three Central Committees elected in that period.[26] One of the early Bundist women leaders suggests that women were more prominent in the illegal period of the Bund because "illegal work demanded a great deal of faith, devotion, self-sacrifice," whereas the legal movement needed "speakers, writers, political activists and organizers with a broad horizon. Life did not prepare a large number of women of this type. Women adjusted slowly, with difficulty, to the new forms of the movement."[27] A cursory examination of the composition of subnational conferences and executive bodies of the Bund gives one the impression that more women were active on the regional and local levels than on the national. In any case, it is clear that it was through both the Zionist and especially the Bundist movements that women entered Jewish public life and political activism.

How democratic the Bund was in its internal workings is a matter of debate. One historian points out that Bund leadership was always collective and that "The Central Committee did not dictate decisions, but instead referred important problems to conferences."[28] Another argues that this occurred only after 1906 and that democratic procedures "in the prewar period constituted the exception rather than the rule."[29] In any case, as compared to the politics of the pre-1897 period, political life in the Bund, and likely in the Zionist movement as well, was conducted in a far less oligarchic and more inclusive manner. In fact, the internal procedures of both movements probably were no less democratic than those in political parties in Western democracies today.

The last political innovation of the Bund and the Zionists was that they cooperated with non-Jewish political movements and parties. In the case of the Bund, interethnic cooperation did not just serve the needs of the Jews, but was a fundamental ideal of the organization. For most Zionists, cooperation with other peoples and their political spokesmen seems to have been largely a matter of pragmatic alliances of convenience. In each case, collaboration and cooperation were difficult enterprises, whether we speak of the Bund's relationship to the Russian Social Democratic Labor Party and, later, the Polish Socialist Party, or Zionist cooperation with Ukrainian nationalists or the British government. Nevertheless, the principle was established that Jews were no longer always the supplicants begging for political handouts from more powerful political bodies, but could be partners in mutually beneficial arrangements.

Modern Politics and Modern Culture

Both the Bund and the Zionists modernized Jewish life in another major respect. Both made it clear, to their own constituencies and to the outside world, that culture is a political issue. Each movement built schools, published newspapers, sponsored theaters, inspired music, and undertook other cultural activities, all of which were designed to articulate, promote, and disseminate the ideals of the movement. Religious Judaism had done the same thing in many respects, but whereas it continued culture and traditions, Zionism and Bundism created or at least supported new institutions and cultural undertakings, whether it was the secular Yiddish school or the modern Hebrew school, the Yiddish theater or the Hebrew theater.

Both movements made a second kind of cultural innovation. Each created a kind of counterculture and countercommunity to the historically dominant religious culture and communities of Eastern Europe, just as the *narodniki* (populists) and later the Marxists created not just a political movement but a counterculture. This was especially true of the Bund because its break with the past was sharper than that of the Zionists. Zionists had their own, alternative, synagogues, but Bundists had no synagogue at all. Beyond promoting a literature and language, the movements created cultural and social communities within which one could lead one's social and cultural life. Parallel to the life of the Orthodox Jew, one's every activity could be carried out within the movement, which, like *halacha* (Jewish law), had its prescriptions and proscriptions, its traditions and mores. As with religion, there were the more and less observant, the more and less involved, but Zionism and Bundism each offered an all-encompassing, intensive, largely secular alternative to the traditional way of life, unlike Jewish life in America which, for most, is a sometime activity, pursued at leisure and by choice, and limited to well-defined spheres of activity.

Conclusion

All these changes taken together constitute a shift to modernity. They lasted throughout the twentieth century in some form. They were the basis for the Israeli political system and for some diaspora communal institutions, though many of the latter are based on *kehilla* models. Both the "winner" and "loser" of twentieth-century Jewish politics made enormous and decisive changes in Jewish life. Those of Zionism are obvious: it created a state with all the implications thereof. It is a source of pride and identity for Jews and it provides them with the capability of self-defense. It has been a haven for European "displaced persons," North African and Middle Eastern, Soviet, Iranian, and Ethiopian Jews. In the view of some, it provides the only viable alternative to religion for those Jews who seek to preserve and transmit Jewish ethnicity.

The Bund's contributions are less obvious, and the movement is largely forgotten. Yet it profoundly changed the structure of Jewish society, politics, and culture. While its two main aims, socialism and a secular Yiddish culture, failed or are out of fashion, the process of struggling for them left an indelible mark on Jewish life. Any scientist knows that we often learn as much from failed experiments as we do from successful ones. The tragedy of the Bund is not just that its experiment failed, but that the murder of most of its adherents deprived it of the chance to compete.

BENJAMIN NATHANS

2

The Other Modern Jewish Politics

Integration and Modernity in Fin de Siècle Russia

IN 1991, DURING A RESEARCH TRIP to archives in what was then Leningrad, I had the pleasure of meeting Valerii Iulevich Gessen. The descendant of a distinguished Russian-Jewish family, Gessen counted among his once well-known relatives the prerevolutionary lawyer and deputy of the Constitutional Democratic Party to the State Duma, Iosif V. Gessen. Valerii's own father was the noted turn-of-the-century historian Iulii I. Gessen, whose many works on the history of the Jews in Russia are still of great value. As we sat in his apartment in a dilapidated Soviet high-rise on the outskirts of Leningrad, Gessen—then in his sixties—shared with me his personal archive of photographs, unpublished letters, and other family documents. He was an amateur genealogist and historian, and at the end of our conversation he suddenly presented me with a proposal: that we jointly organize a conference marking the 125th anniversary of the first and longest-lived public Jewish organization in Russia, the Society for the Spread of Enlightenment among the Jews.[1] Founded in 1863 under the regime of the "Tsar-Liberator" Alexander II, the Society survived until 1929, when it was liquidated as part of the general assault on "bourgeois" institutions. After all, Gessen reminded me, Mikhail Gorbachev's policy of *glasnost'* was opening up Soviet society, and it was now possible to publicly commemorate the important institutions of Russian-Jewish life, and indeed the entire lost world that his father had inhabited.

As Gessen's parting words rang in my ears—*"ishchite sponsorov!"* (find sponsors!)—I was thinking how odd this whole scheme sounded. Did the Society for the Spread of Enlightenment really deserve a conference? Hadn't it become obsolete before the antibourgeois campaign of 1929, before even the Bolshevik Revolution of 1917, as far back as 1882? That, after all, was the year when the entire edifice of the Haskalah, the Jewish Enlightenment movement with a naive ideology of integration as the Jews' sole path to modernity, was allegedly reduced to rubble by a wave of violent anti-Jewish pogroms. The best thing, it seemed to me at the time, was to let Gessen's proposal for a commemorative conference die a quiet death—not unlike the Society for the Spread of Enlightenment itself.

I have taken the liberty of beginning with this vignette because it raises two important problems, namely, the legacy of what one might call the "other" modern Jewish politics, the politics of emancipation and integration, and the relationship of that politics to Zionism and the Bund. In grappling with what is *modern* about modern Jewish politics, I propose that we should widen the circle of inquiry beyond Zionism and the Bund, beyond solutions that relied on *aliyah* (emigration to the Land of Israel) or revolution. We would thereby broaden our understanding of what modernity has meant for Jewish political thought and practice.

The Modernization of East European Jewish Politics

Like Europe itself, Ashkenaz (European Jewry) since the second half of the eighteenth century has typically been conceptualized as containing roughly two diverging zones, East and West. The dominant framework for the study of Jewish politics in the Russian Empire has been the contrasting historical experience of these Jewish communities. For Jews in Europe west of the Russian Empire (including Poland), the central narrative has been the dissolution of traditional Jewish autonomy and the effects of the resulting contact with European societies and cultures, usually encapsulated under the themes of "emancipation and assimilation" or "the encounter with modernity." In the historiography of Russian Jewry, by contrast, such themes have found only limited resonance. With a top-heavy, authoritarian regime and an overwhelmingly peasant society, the Russian Empire appears to have offered an environment inimical to emancipation, assimilation, or, for that matter, modernity.

As a result, historians of Jewish politics in Russia have focused largely on the turn away from the European pattern and on the various attempts—by Zionists and Bundists in particular—to reconstitute Jewish autonomy in new, secular forms. As Jonathan Frankel put it in his magisterial *Prophecy and Politics: Socialism, Nationalism, and the Russian Jews, 1862–1917*, Russian Jews moved "directly

from a pre-liberal to a post-liberal state of development, from medieval community to projects for national revival, from a religious to a social and secular messianism."[2] Although there has been a good deal of debate about when and why
this "skipping of phases" occurred among Russian Jews, few have questioned its
actual occurrence.[3] Consequently, historians have tended to locate authentic modern Jewish politics in the radical movements whose twin centenaries were marked
in 1997. Interestingly, modern Yiddish writers displayed a parallel tendency, as
Dan Miron has recently shown, by casting the *shtetl* as the locus of authentic national Jewish life at a time when, in reality, it was by no means the dominant form
of Jewish collective existence, even in Eastern Europe.[4] Something similar could
be said about the *kibbutz*, which, until fairly recently, symbolized Israel, though
less than 5 percent of Israelis lived on *kibbutzim*.

What *is* modern about modern Jewish politics? This question requires some
sort of clarity about the nature of modern politics itself. Ever since the French
and American Revolutions, self-consciously innovative (which is to say, modern)
political systems have displayed a remarkable range of characteristics, from liberal republicanism to social democracy to totalitarianism of both the left and the
right. To exclude our century's authoritarian mass movements from the category
of the modern would amount to accepting a narrow liberal-democratic teleology.
At the same time, certain common denominators do link the various expressions
of political modernity, if only (in some cases) on the level of rhetoric and symbol.
These include commitments to the idea that sovereignty ultimately resides in the
population, or part of the population, of a given state, rather than in the state itself
or its rulers; to the notion that the state exists to further the welfare of its subjects,
however defined; and to the project of mass political participation, though in a
wide variety of formats.

Eli Lederhendler's insightful book, *The Road to Modern Jewish Politics*, contains an excellent definition of modern politics in an East European Jewish setting.
Lederhendler contends that in its premodern mode, Jewish politics is fundamentally derivative, that is, it depends upon access to the gentile state as the ultimate
guarantor of the social and political order. In an ingenious move, Lederhendler
suggests that if, as Max Weber posited, the monopoly on the legitimate use of
violence is the defining characteristic of the state, then the *kehilla*'s monopoly on
legitimate recourse to the state is the defining characteristic of premodern Jewish
politics. Consequently, the modernity of Jewish politics can be measured by the
degree to which it has freed itself from state tutelage and shifted the locus of authority to the Jewish people.[5]

This definition is notable in several respects. Apart from a general commitment to popular sovereignty, it leaves open the specific content of modern Jewish politics—left, right, Zionist, diasporic. But by defining premodern Jewish politics as fundamentally derivative, Lederhendler implies that to be modern, Jewish politics must emancipate itself from the gentile state, that is, it must strive for maximum self-reliance. In the case of Zionism, that implication more or less holds true, since that has been the basic tenet of Zionism from its beginnings. But no Jewish politics committed to life in the diaspora could afford to disengage itself from gentile power structures—especially in Russia, where the tsarist autocracy (and later the Soviet partocracy) loomed so large in public life. If anything, emancipation and integration inevitably increased Jewish dependence on gentile institutions—schools, the army, the professions—regardless of the kind of Jewish politics emancipationists and integrationists produced. In order to be truly inclusive, therefore, the yardstick of Jewish political modernity ought to measure not simply the extent to which Jews freed themselves from dependence on gentile institutions, but the ways in which their collective engagement with those institutions changed over time.

In the political polemics of the early twentieth century, the "other" modern Jewish politics was known primarily under the highly unflattering label of "assimilation." Few, if any, of those to whom this epithet was applied, however, accepted it. If by assimilation one means the erasure of a public Jewish identity, then it certainly did not apply to Jewish activists like Horace Gintsburg, Maxim Vinaver, Genrikh Sliozberg, Menashe Morgulis, Mikhail Sheftel, and others most closely identified with liberal Jewish politics. In the Jewish case, the "assimilationist" label was wielded with particular ferocity in part because many of those who used it had themselves previously subscribed to the goals of emancipation and integration, only to repudiate these views in favor of more radical solutions. One thinks of people such as Moshe Leib Lilienblum, the would-be cosmopolitan turned Zionist and author of the influential autobiography *Hate'ot Ne'urim* (Sins of youth, 1876); Leon Pinsker, a major figure in the Society for the Spread of Enlightenment in Odessa before writing the famous pamphlet *Autoemancipation!* (1882) and helping found the *Hibat Tsiyon* (Love of Zion) movement; Shimon Dubnov, an integrationist par excellence before turning to Jewish nationalism and the doctrine of autonomism; Vladimir Medem, baptized by his (converted) Jewish parents and educated in Russian schools, only to become a leader of the Bund; and Sh. An-sky, a *narodnik* (populist) consumed by the plight of the Russian peasantry who eventually returned to the Jewish national cause. Countless figures in the Zionist and Bundist movements "returned" to the Jewish people in one form or another. By definition, to return, one must first leave, and leaving usually involved an initial faith in the possibility or necessity of integration. In describing their opponents as "assimilationists," therefore, representatives of the radical Jewish movements were often engaged in an ongoing act of purging themselves of their own former identities.

It is time now to have a closer look at the object of these polemics, the torchbearers of Jewish integration in fin de siècle Russia who have too often been consigned to the dustbin of modern Jewish politics. The first striking fact about Jewish liberals, or at least their leaders, from Sliozberg and Vinaver on down, is that a very high proportion had received a university or other postsecondary education.[6] While the educational and other social characteristics of competing Russian-Jewish political elites need further research, scattered evidence suggests that Bundist leaders were less likely to hold postsecondary degrees (especially in the movement's early years) and that Zionist leaders in Russia, while often highly educated, were much more likely than their integrationist counterparts to have studied abroad, as in the cases of David Ben-Gurion, Chaim Weizmann, Shmarya Levin, and Ze'ev Zhabotinsky. In addition, liberal Jewish leaders in late Imperial Russia were overwhelmingly lawyers by training, much like their counterparts in Jewish organizations in Europe such as the Berlin-based *Central-Verein deutscher Staatsbürger judischen Glaubens* and the Paris-based *Alliance Israelite Universelle*. Legal training and legal concepts profoundly shaped the politics of Jewish integrationists, as well as their relationship with Zionists and Bundists.

Jewish lawyers, and lawyers in general, appeared in Russia in the wake of the Judicial Reform of 1864, which created for the first time a modern, independent judiciary in the Russian Empire. A significant proportion of the Jews who flocked to Russian universities in the 1870s and 1880s studied law. In some universities more than half the Jewish student body was enrolled in the law faculty.[7] Indeed, at Novorossiiskii University in Odessa in the mid-1880s, 41 percent of all law students were Jews.[8] Jewish lawyers such as Ilya Orshanskii and Menashe Morgulis were the first to subject the so-called "Jewish Question" in Russia to a juridical analysis from a Jewish standpoint. They were also the first to respond to collective violence against Jews—always a powerful catalyst for modern Jewish politics —in a thoroughly modern way. Immediately following the Odessa pogrom of May 1871, Orshanskii, Morgulis, and their fellow lawyers Alexander Passover and Mikhail Kulisher conducted a systematic, neighborhood-by-neighborhood survey of the violence. They identified victims, perpetrators, and eyewitnesses, and then prepared a report critical of the feeble responses by city authorities. Their next, wholly unprecedented step was to turn to the recently reformed courts, where trials were open and uncensored testimony could be printed in the newspapers, in order to seek official compensation for damages inflicted on the city's Jewish population.[9] The government, however, insisted on trying those arrested in closed-door military courts. Evidence gathered by Orshanskii and others went unheeded and was barred from publication.[10]

At roughly the same time, that is, in the 1870s, the juridical approach to advancing Jewish interests began to penetrate the *maskilic* (enlightened) circles surrounding Baron Horace Gintsburg, the *shtadlan*, or unofficial spokesman, of Russian Jewry in St. Petersburg. Briefly put, the juridical approach maintained that while non-Jews in Russia were subject to the classic legal doctrine that "everything not forbidden is permitted," the Jews were treated according to the principle that "everything not permitted is forbidden." It was precisely this anomalous and inferior legal status, claimed Orshanskii and others, that fostered popular hostility toward Jews, by making them appear as a group that could be attacked with impunity. Only the abolition of legal discrimination against Jews would put an end to Jewish isolation and victimization and turn Jews into useful citizens of Russia. Or, to quote Orshanskii, "The ideal toward which we strive consists precisely of expelling the Jews once and for all from the legal codes."[11] Returning to Lederhendler's definition of modernity in Jewish politics, we can see that Orshanskii and other Jewish lawyers, in classic nineteenth-century liberal fashion, sought to harness the power of the Russian state not so much to manipulate the internal affairs of Jewish communities, but to reform and regulate relations between Jews and Russians, whether as groups or as individuals.

By the late 1870s, these ideas were making their way into the Russian-Jewish press, and into the numerous petitions and memoranda sent to government officials by Gintsburg and other Jewish notables.[12] They formed the core of the response by Jewish elites in St. Petersburg when a new and far broader wave of pogroms spread across southern Russia in 1881 and raged for over a year. Whereas nearly all elements of Russian society and government viewed the pogroms as a protest against Jewish economic exploitation, liberal Jewish spokesmen insisted on a different interpretation. As an 1882 conference of Jewish notables wrote in its final report on the pogroms, "The whole problem lies in the restrictive legislation against Jews. The mob instinctively understands that the Jews are singled out in the law and that those who attack them will not be punished according to the normal pattern. . . . If the current restrictive legislation against Jews were to fall on another class of the population—the merchantry, the nobility, etc.—it would elicit the same horrifying pogroms against that class."[13] A similar analysis was given by the state rabbi of Moscow, Zalkind Minor, who emphasized that the emancipation of the serfs in 1861 had left the Jews as the only group with restricted rights, and that therefore the masses "had every reason to suppose that there was no need to stand on ceremony with the Jews."[14]

This is the first stage in the emergence of a modern Jewish politics in Russia —a politics grounded in liberalism and the rule of law. True, it was not a mass movement. But in the 1880s there were no Jewish mass political movements in Russia, and Jewish liberals employed the most modern and effective means then available for advancing their cause: the courts and the press. True, they retained some of the political naivete of the Haskalah, as demonstrated by their reliance on petitions from individuals and their faith in the power and reasonableness of the tsarist state, or at least its judicial system. But the judicial approach broke decisively with the myth of the "royal alliance" between state and *maskilim*. First, this strategy located the root of the problem—discrimination against Jews—in the state itself (or its laws) rather than in the Jews, and second, it appealed to state authority not in order to force internal reforms in Jewish life, but to normalize relations between Jews and non-Jews. Finally, it is true that Jewish lawyers were unsuccessful in their attempts to use Russian courts to compensate victims of pogrom violence. This certainly did not enhance their public standing on the Jewish street. But was any Jewish group successful in countering pogrom violence?

While the pogroms of 1881–1882, and the government's decision to punish the Jews in response, were important catalysts in the emergence of Zionism and the Bund, these events in no way put an end to the emerging liberal Jewish politics. The influence of the juridical approach on the strategies of the Petersburg Jewish elite took an important turn in 1893, when Emmanuel Levin retired at seventy-three from his post as secretary to the Gintsburgs after nearly four decades of service, during which he had drafted countless petitions and memoranda. A typical *maskil*, Levin was largely an autodidact, had published one of the first textbooks on Russian grammar for Jewish students in the 1840s, and was the first secretary of the Society for the Spread of Enlightenment among the Jews.[15] He was succeeded as the Gintsburgs' right-hand man by Genrikh Sliozberg, who had recently graduated with the gold medal in law from Petersburg University.[16] One could hardly wish for a better symbol of the transformation of *shtadlanut* (*shtadlones*): the *maskil* replaced by the lawyer.

Driven by his profession's ideal of replacing autocratic arbitrariness (*proizvol*) with the rule of law (*zakonnost'*), Sliozberg shifted the emphasis of Gintsburg's efforts from personally petitioning various high-placed officials (although this certainly continued) to systematically defending Jewish rights in the reformed courts, and at the highest levels. "I became convinced," Sliozberg wrote, "that the time had come for a determined struggle to retain those few rights which had been granted the Jews, that arbitrariness threatened to destroy the very possibility of existence for the Jewish masses, if those rights were not defended point for point by means of those legal resources which were still at our disposal."[17]

Through professional contacts, Sliozberg gained access to hundreds of Jewish appeals in advance of their consideration by the State Senate, the highest court in the land. In many cases he would arrange, with Horace Gintsburg's financial support, to serve as attorney for the plaintiffs.[18] In a legal system that relied heavily on precedent, he wrote, "defending the interests of a plaintiff in the Senate served as a defense of the Jewish population in general."[19] By the turn of the century, Sliozberg's reputation had spread throughout the Pale.[20] A fellow Jewish lawyer wrote that "[Sliozberg's] continuous client over the course of many years was the Jewish people."[21]

At the turn of the century, Sliozberg and other Jewish lawyers teamed up to create what they called the Defense Bureau, an organization that offered free legal services to victims of anti-Jewish discrimination. They also enlisted prominent members of the Russian intelligentsia as well as Jewish groups abroad in a campaign to publicly condemn official anti-Semitism in Russia.[22] The Defense Bureau grew out of the criminal trial of David Blondes, accused of ritual murder in 1900. Like pogroms, accusations of ritual murder had a quickening effect on the Jewish political mood. From the 1878 blood libel in Kutaisi (Georgia)—the first ritual murder trial held in the new, open courts—to the notorious trials of Blondes in Vilna and Mendel Beilis in Kiev in 1911, Jewish lawyers pioneered a new approach. They sought to exploit the openness of Russia's courts not only to refute the charge of murder, but also to discredit the entire notion of ritual intent. Without exception, they succeeded in the former and failed in the latter. Russian juries could be persuaded to acquit individual Jews accused of ritual murder, but not to disavow the charge itself.

Regardless of outcome, ritual murder and pogrom trials transformed lawyers such as Oskar Gruzenberg, Sliozberg, and Vinaver into household names on the Jewish street. Civil trials following the wave of pogroms in Kishinev, Gomel, Odessa, and Bialystok between 1903 and 1906 created opportunities, for the first time, for public indictments against tsarist officials and others suspected of complicity in anti-Jewish violence. The Defense Bureau coordinated the preparation of lawsuits as well as the legal defense of Jews who had taken up arms against the *pogromshchiki* (perpetrators of pogroms) and now faced criminal charges. And once again, results were mixed: some low-level perpetrators were convicted, but not a single tsarist official was made to stand trial.

Unlike previous pogroms, however, those of 1905 and 1906 were linked to a much larger political upheaval that erupted in the first Russian Revolution and culminated in the establishment of Russia's first popularly elected parliament. The year 1905 was to prove no less decisive in the history of modern Jewish politics than in the history of modern Russian politics. To be sure, Zionists abroad and Bundists in Russia had formed political parties well before the revolution of 1905. But this should not obscure the fact that it was Jewish liberals, including the very same lawyers who had turned to the courts and the press in the struggle for Jewish rights, who took the lead in advancing Jewish interests through parliamentary— which is to say quintessentially modern—politics. It was the liberals who prevailed upon Count Witte and the Council of Ministers to grant Jews the right to vote on an equal basis in elections to the Duma. Without this effort, Jews might easily have been excluded from Russia's constitutional experiment altogether. The fact that they were not excluded had immediate and profound consequences for both Zionists and Bundists: both were forced by the liberals' successful lobbying to take a stand on the thorny question of whether and/or how to participate in Russian parliamentary politics. As is well known, the sudden prospect of open political contestation in Russia led to the formation of a panoply of Jewish parties, and by the second Duma elections in 1907 even those Jewish parties, such as the Bund, that had initially boycotted elections had little choice but to follow the lead of the integrationists and of Jewish voters who were flocking to the polls in extraordinarily high numbers.[23]

The by now well-rehearsed debate over *gegenwartsarbeit* demonstrates the extent to which the Jewish relationship to the non-Jewish state continued to be a central fault line even in modern Jewish politics. If, as Lederhendler suggests, the defining issue of premodern Jewish politics was the *kehilla's* monopoly on legitimate recourse to the gentile state, the question now was whether and/or how Jews should participate in the emerging political life of the surrounding gentile society. The Bund struggled with this question vis-à-vis the Russian Social Democrats; integrationists struggled with it vis-à-vis the Kadets (Constitutional Democrats); and Zionists vis-à-vis the Foreign Ministries of the Russian, British, and Ottoman empires. But the integrationists were the first to enter the Russian political arena as Jews, and comprised a majority of the twelve Jewish delegates elected to the first Duma. In effect, they—together with hundreds of thousands of Jewish voters— made it impossible for Bundists and Zionists to stay out of Russian parliamentary politics. Their influence, moreover, went beyond the mere fact of participation and extended to the level of political programs. The Fourth Party Congress of the Bund in Bialystok and the Third All-Russian Zionist Conference in Helsinki (Helsingfors) each adopted platforms explicitly endorsing the goal of civic emancipation, the centerpiece of the integrationist agenda, despite severe ideological resistance to emancipation as a bourgeois, assimilationist project that could only retard revolution and/or *aliyah*.

Influence ran in the other direction too. One of the most striking qualities of Russian-Jewish integrationists was the degree to which they took up the struggle not just for civil and political rights but for national rights and certain forms of communal autonomy. This was much more than mere "flirting" with Jewish nationalism, as one historian has described it.[24] Although integrationists such as Sliozberg and Vinaver disagreed with their Bundist, Zionist, and Autonomist (those who advocated Jewish autonomy in the diaspora) rivals over the relative tactical priority of civil versus national rights, they consistently included national rights in their agenda—including obligatory membership by Jews in communal organizations and a communal income tax to replace taxes on Sabbath candles and kosher meat.[25] In this they distinguished themselves from their counterparts in the *Central-Verein* and the *Alliance Israelite Universelle*, for whom national rights were virtually meaningless. A roughly analogous shift occurred among the Kadets, Russia's liberals par excellence, who advocated forcible expropriation of land for Russia's peasantry with compensation below market value, something no European liberal party would have done.[26] In Russia, it seems, even liberals could not help but breathe the air of collectivism.

In fact, Jewish integrationists were the *klal-yisroelniks* (advocates of unified Jewry) of the Russian-Jewish political scene, in the sense that they insisted on creating an umbrella organization open to all Jewish political groupings in favor of civic emancipation, rather than yet another Jewish political party. This was true of the Union for the Attainment of Equal Rights, which by 1907 had over forty local branches, as well as of its successor, the Jewish People's Group.[27] Like Russia's reformed courts, however, the Duma proved a bitter disappointment to Jewish liberals. Only four Jews were elected to the Second Duma and two to the Third, which, thanks to manipulation of the suffrage laws, had shifted considerably to the right. Given the centrality of parliamentary politics to liberal hopes, this was a devastating development.

After Piotr Arkadevich Stolypin's June 1907 coup d'etat, as Christoph Gassenschmidt has shown, Jewish liberals turned their energies almost entirely to grassroots reform within Jewish communities, above all in the areas of education and economic reform.[28] Here they joined forces with and revitalized two Russian-Jewish organizations dating from the era of *shtadlanut*, namely, the Society for Artisan Labor (better known under its Russian acronym ORT), and the Society for the Spread of Enlightenment among the Jews. But this was in no way a retreat to a premodern politics. Between 1908 and 1916, the Society for the Spread of Enlightenment opened new branches in over forty cities, from Balta to Irkutsk, and raised its membership to over seven thousand.[29] Its energies and its 1.3-million-ruble budget were no longer targeted only to elite Jewish university students, but were devoted to a new network of Jewish primary and secondary schools whose curriculum reflected the national-Jewish climate of the day.[30] Along with the establishment of Jewish savings and loan cooperatives, credit unions, and vocational schools, these were the "small deeds," the day-to-day works that sought to bring not just Jewish politics but the Jewish people into the modern age.

Genrikh Sliozberg and the Synthesis of Jewish and Russian Identities

Genrikh Sliozberg, an exemplary Jewish integrationist in late Imperial Russia, wrote in his memoirs, "We considered ourselves *Russian Jews*," giving deliberate emphasis to a term that neither he nor other liberal Jewish intellectuals at the turn of the century could take for granted.[31] Such emphasis conveys, subtly but unmistakably, the sense that the combination of Russian and Jew was as much an aspiration as a self-description. To articulate one's identity as a Russian Jew, as an integrationist, in fin de siècle Russia meant not only swimming against a tide of official and social anti-Semitism, but also bearing the additional weight of the Zionist polemic against the "spiritual slavery" of assimilation. More than once, Sliozberg, Vinaver, and other Jewish integrationists were dismissed by Zionist opponents as "Russians of the Mosaic faith," a term they never applied to themselves. On the contrary, Sliozberg explicitly distanced himself from self-described "Poles of the Mosaic faith": "There was a huge divide between Poles of the Mosaic faith and non-Zionist Russian Jews, conditioned not only by the attitudes of the Jews themselves, but by the general conditions of Russian and Polish life. We, [even as] non-Zionists, recognized the Jewish nationality. . . . In the life of the all-Russian (*rossiiskoe*) state we, Jews by nationality, were not an alien element, since in Russia there resided many nationalities, united in Russian statehood."[32] The invocation of Russia's ethnic pluralism as a bulwark against assimilation is familiar enough. Although with hindsight it appears utopian, this is no longer the

Haskalah utopia that Jacob Katz aptly characterized as the "neutral society."[33] The particular multinational setting of the Russian Empire, together with the density of Jewish settlement there, insured that Sliozberg and others sought to secure both a neutral society (Russian and therefore supranational) and a non-neutral community (Jewish and national). Other ethnic minorities entertained similar hopes.

But the dream of ethnic pluralism is not the only or even the main context of Sliozberg's identity as a Jewish integrationist. In a famous passage in his memoirs, he wrote: "To be a good Jew does not prevent one from being a good Russian citizen, and vice-versa, to be a proper Russian citizen does not at all interfere with one's remaining a good Jew, believing in Jewish national culture, being devoted to one's people and serving them according to one's strength. Acquisition of Russian culture . . . is entirely consistent with faithfulness to Jewish national culture."[34] The asymmetries in this passage were carefully chosen. Not only is "Jew" paired with "Russian citizen," but Jewish culture is specifically described as national, while Russian culture is not. These distinctions appear more than once in Sliozberg's memoirs.[35] Similarly, in his eulogy of Maxim Vinaver, the lawyer Moisei Gol'dshtein described him as "the greatest Russian Jew and a great Russian citizen."[36]

It is impossible to read Sliozberg's call to be "a good Jew and a good Russian citizen" without hearing a clear, if unintended, echo of the poet Yehudah Leib Gordon (1831–1892), whose earlier Haskalah maxim, "Be a man in the streets and a Jew at home," was interpreted by many to mean that Jewishness should not be publicly displayed. But it is important to appreciate the distance separating the two declarations, as well. To begin with, while Gordon appealed to the ideal of a universal "man," for Sliozberg this entity has descended somewhat from the stratosphere and taken the more limited form of a transnational "Russian citizen." Furthermore, Gordon's division of identity into public and private components —his virtual domestication of its Jewish aspect ("be a Jew at home")—finds no parallel in Sliozberg and other integrationists, who insisted on a public, national Jewishness.

In the worldview of Jewish liberals, Russianness served as the medium for a civic, legal relationship to the gentile society and the state, while Jewishness expressed a national allegiance based on faith and tradition. Since the dominant values of educated Russian society, according to Sliozberg, were imported from Europe, and since the "Russian national idea" was almost exclusively the creation of the state in opposition to the multinational character of the country, what passed for "Russian" culture was in fact more pan-European, or universal, than national. Even acculturated Jews, Sliozberg insisted, "became 'Russians,' at best, only in the official (*gosudarstvennyi*) sense, not in the national sense."[37] The liberal lawyer Solomon Pozner expressed similar views: "While guarding their national-cultural independence, Jews should take part in the civic life" of Russia.[38] Vinaver, too, was wont to distinguish between two types of nations: those grounded in law and the state (Russia), and those formed by culture and history (the Jews).[39]

There is much in the distinction between a Jewish national identity and a Russian civic identity that fits the typology developed by Ferdinand Tönnies of *Gemeinschaft* (traditional community) and *Gesellschaft* (modern society)—in this case, Jewish community and Russian society.[40] Unlike Tönnies, however, Russian-Jewish liberals conceived of community as coexisting within, rather than being destroyed by, society. The particular Russian identity articulated by Sliozberg and the other lawyers who dominated the integrationist camp was grounded in the idea of a citizenship defined juridically rather than ethnically.[41] By making possible the articulation of a civic identity, the legal profession's ideals of the rule of law and the contractual nature of public relationships exercised a profound influence on Jewish lawyers' sense of their place as Jews in Russian society. Whatever one's criticisms of this approach, which proved unable to secure Jewish collective interests, it would be difficult to argue that it failed because it was not sufficiently "modern." On the contrary: it failed largely because it was too modern for its time and place.

It should be clear by now that lack of success was one of the hallmarks of liberal Jewish politics in prerevolutionary Russia, though it shared this distinction with virtually every other brand of Jewish politics at the time, as well as with Russian liberalism. Speaking at Sliozberg's funeral in Paris in 1937, the renowned lawyer and fellow integrationist Oskar Gruzenberg eulogized the liberal struggle for civic emancipation and Sliozberg's step-by-step, law-based approach to that struggle:

> Only those who themselves have trod the tortuous path of the *everyday* struggle for justice and for the interests of individual *people*, who have fought on their behalf in courts, in ministries, against the mighty of this world—only they know the price of giving out one's heart in small pieces. [Sliozberg] understood perfectly well that "history" remembers the names only of those who fight on behalf of the distant, not the nearby. And nonetheless the pain and suffering of *isolated individuals* compelled him to decline the entrance ticket to history.[42]

These words reflect more than just bitterness at the fact that the Bolshevik Revolution derailed the integrationists' hopes for a European-style civic emancipation in Russia. They rebuke the seemingly adventurist politics of Bundists and Zionists, with their far-off utopian dreams of a workers' paradise or a return en masse to Zion. Finally, Gruzenberg's speech responds to countless charges of elitism, anachronism, and naivete leveled at Sliozberg and other partisans of integration.

It is therefore all the more surprising to discover a rather different assessment of Sliozberg's career by none other than the militant Zionist, Ze'ev Zhabotinsky. Describing a typically chilly encounter at a meeting of the Union for the Attainment of Equal Rights in 1905, Zhabotinsky began his account with a remark Sliozberg made to him:

> "I envy you—for you the Jewish Question is a dream about the future. But for me a clause in this or that statute concerning the liquor trade is also a big part of the Jewish Question." Sliozberg probably had no idea that that night, after the meeting, we, his opponents, the young people of our camp, had a long conversation among ourselves about this statement. Prosaic, as if issued from a chancellery, and pronounced without passion, it struck us like a thunderbolt. It reminded us of the terrible tragedy of everyday existence (*obydenshchina*), of the fact that in three lines of an official text there was sometimes contained a nearly fatal verdict for hundreds of thousands of people. It reminded us of the enormous idealistic value of realism.[43]

One cannot help but note the curious fact that so little attention has been paid by American Jews to liberal Jewish politics in tsarist Russia, despite American Jewry's close identification with the ideals of liberalism and integration, not to mention the spirit of realism and pragmatism that moved Zhabotinsky. It may be that, for many American Jews, "modern Jewish politics" in the sense of parties and elections and public contestation for power is experienced largely vicariously, via Israel, where the major parties trace their lineage back to the radical Jewish movements launched in Russia and Eastern Europe a century ago. One may certainly question whether the Society for the Spread of Enlightenment warrants a conference all its own, as Valerii Gessen insisted during that memorable conversation in Leningrad a decade ago. But even at its epicenter in Eastern Europe, modern Jewish politics has, from its very inception, included an important liberal current. Jewish liberalism in tsarist Russia originated within the Jewish "Old Regime," that is, within the tradition of *shtadlanut*. It transformed the modus operandi of that regime, adapting it to the civil society that was emerging within the framework of Russia's rigidly authoritarian state. Rather than being rendered an anachronism by anti-Jewish violence, or by the socialist and Zionist movements that arose in its wake, Russian-Jewish liberals took their struggle first to the reformed Russian courts, then to the Russian Parliament, and, finally, to the Jewish street itself.

ANTONY POLONSKY

3

The New Jewish Politics and Its Discontents

How did we come to this? How did we lose ourselves
In this vast world, strange and hostile to us?

Julian Tuwim, 1926

IN RECENT YEARS, LARGE CLAIMS have been made for the General
Jewish Workers' Alliance (the Bund) in the late 1930s. In his history of the party,
written in 1967, Bernard Johnpoll wrote that political developments in the 1930s
"handed the Bund the leadership of Polish Jewry. Because the Bund was an *ec-
clesia militanta* [*sic*], it was able to defy the threats from within and without and
to lead the Jewish people during a period of despair."[1] These views have been
widely echoed. According to Majer Bogdanski, a former Bundist activist in Lodz,
"Because the Bund led—yes, led—the struggle of life and death for the whole
Jewish population in Poland, the population put its complete trust in it."[2]

It is certainly true that the Bund grew greatly in political influence in the late
1930s. Its break with revolutionary socialism, entry into the Second International,
strengthened ties with the Polish Socialist Party (PPS), and willingness to take
up Jewish issues—as in its defense of Jews against anti-Semitic violence and its
participation in *kehilla* and local government elections—gave it a new prestige
on the Jewish street. This was translated into real support in the local government elections of 1938 and 1939, in which a very significant proportion of the
Jewish population of Poland cast its vote for the Bund. According to one estimate, 38 percent of Jewish votes went to the Bund, 36 percent to the Zionists, 23

percent to middle-class groups (in many cases Agudat Yisrael), and 3 percent to others (mainly Poalei Tsiyon).[3] The showings in the bigger towns demonstrated the real sources of Bundist strength. In Warsaw the Bund received nearly 62 percent of votes cast for Jewish parties, as opposed to 19 percent for the Zionists, 16.7 percent for the Aguda, and 2.6 percent for the Left Poalei Tsiyon. In Lodz, the Bund won 57.4 percent of the votes cast for Jewish parties, while 22.2 percent went to the Democratic Zionist bloc and 20.4 percent to the Aguda. In Vilna, of 17 Jewish councilors, 10 represented the Bund, 5 the Zionist bloc, and 2 Right Poalei Tsiyon. In Grodno, 9 of 11 councilors were Bundists, in Bialystok 10 of 15, in Radom 9 of 11, in Lublin 10 of 15, and in Zamosc 5 of 6. Only in Galicia, where the Bund had never been strong, did traditional political loyalties hold fast. In Kraków, of 13 Jewish councilors, 9 were Zionist, 2 Bundist, and 2 represented other Jewish groups, while in Lwow (Lviv), all 16 Jewish councilors were elected on the Zionist bloc list.[4]

Yet these impressive successes could not be translated into real political influence. Poland was a semiauthoritarian state and the government was, for the most part, not interested in sharing power. Thus, although the Polish Socialist Party won a majority, together with its allies, the German Social Democratic Party and the Bund, in the municipal elections in Lodz in September 1936, the government very quickly dissolved the new council and ran the city through an appointed commissioner.[5] Similarly, when the Bund won a majority in the Warsaw *kehilla* in 1936, the government refused to let it take power and put in office a group of politicians (including Adam Czerniakow) with whom it was more comfortable.

It could be argued that another reason for the Bund's limited political influence was that its alliance with the PPS, which was one of the reasons for its growing electoral support, was never as firm as it appeared. The Bund's foreign connections with the Second International and the Jewish Labor Committee in the United States, impressive on paper, could not be used to defend the Jews of Poland in their increasingly desperate situation. How desperate this situation was —with the government pressed by the persistence of the economic crisis and the encouragement anti-Semites derived from the success of the Nazis in disenfranchising and expropriating one of the best integrated and prosperous Jewish communities in Europe—is reflected in the comment of a very cautious historian of the period, Jerzy Tomaszewski. After pointing out that mass emigration was not a feasible possibility at this time for dealing with the "Jewish question," he comes to the following conclusion: "A lasting solution of the social and economic problems of the Jews had thus to be sought in Poland, in close association with the whole range of problems faced by the country. It is difficult today to reach a conclusion on the chances of finding such a solution, because the outbreak of the war made a breach in the normal evolution of the country. If one takes into account the situation that prevailed at the end of the 1930s, the prospects for lasting solutions must seem doubtful."[6]

More seriously, even given the Bund's success in the elections of 1938–1939, it was very clear that the Bund was only one of the political groups vying for the leadership of Polish Jewry. The Bund certainly could not claim to have the "complete trust" of the Jewish population of Poland. In fact, its intransigent refusal to cooperate with other Jewish parties, whether in responding to the economic crisis or to the growth of anti-Semitism in Poland, merely weakened the Jewish community. The contrast with Romania on this point is striking. Although Romania, too, was falling prey to rampant anti-Semitism, there, Wilhelm Filderman was able to create an effective Jewish pressure group. Shimon Dubnow, father-in-law of one of the Bundist leaders, Henryk Erlich, aptly described the consequences of the Bund's stubbornness. In an open letter to the Bundist daily paper, he castigated the party for "withdrawing from *klal yisroel*." He was not a Zionist, he stated, and had often criticized the mistakes of the Zionists. Yet he felt obliged to express astonishment at the hostility of the Bund to Zionism at a time of such critical danger for the Jewish people. The Zionists had achieved great things in *Erets Yisroel*. "The majority of the Jewish people is impressed by these achievements and is Zionist. The error of the Bund," he claimed, "is that it does not see itself as part of the Jewish people, but of the Jewish proletariat. The Bund will ensure its future only if it abandons its separation and works together with all democratic and progressive forces within the Jewish people."[7] This reproach certainly stung and provoked a reply from Erlich under the heading "Is Zionism a democratic and progressive force?" The Bund, he asserted, was the largest political force in Jewish Poland and not merely a temporary phenomenon:

> The Bund is an organic part of the Jewish people and represents its true interests. It is concerned for all Jews in Poland and not only for the workers. Yet the concept of *klal yisroel* cannot involve co-operation with reactionaries, with the Aguda or with the Revisionists. Zionism has become an ally of anti-Semitism. The worsening situation of the Jews throughout the world is exploited by the Zionists. The Zionists regard themselves as second-class citizens in Poland. Their aim is to be first-class citizens in Palestine and make the Arabs second-class citizens. The Bund, therefore, cannot see the Zionists as partners in the struggle against the reactionary forces in Poland.[8]

This exchange illustrates the main theme of this chapter, which could be summed up as, "The New Jewish Politics and Its Discontents." The fact that, in an increasingly perilous situation, Jews were so deeply divided ideologically that common action was virtually impossible, was not new. In his story, "Samo-oborona," written in 1907, Israel Zangwill describes a Polish *shtetl*, to which he gives the ironic name Milovka (agreeable). A young man, David Ben Amram, arrives to organize the local Jews in the face of the anti-Jewish violence sweeping the tsarist empire. He is unable to accomplish his mission because of the deep ideological divisions that have developed even in this remote backwater. The Jews are split between the integrationists and assimilationists (of which there were several varieties), the religious (divided into Hasidic and Misnagdic), several varieties of socialist Zionism, Zionist Zionism, cultural Zionism, Mizrachi, Sejmism, territorialism, socialist territorialism, and Bundism. The young idealist is brought to the brink of despair:

> He had a nightmare vision of bristling sects and pullulating factions, each with its councils, Federations, Funds, Conferences, Party-days, Agendas, Referats, Press-Organs, each differentiating itself with meticulous subtlety from all the other Parties, each defining with casuistic minuteness its relation to every contemporary problem, each equipped with inexhaustible polyglot orators speechifying through tumultuous nights.[9]

It is clear that the principal reason for the fractious and querulous character of the "new Jewish politics" was the increasingly desperate situation of the Jews, first before 1914 and then, even more, in the darkening world scene of the 1930s. Politics has a number of functions, including mobilizing opinion, changing social consciousness, and comforting groups in difficult times. But if it is above all the "art of the possible," then what is to be done in "impossible" situations, in what Dubnow characterized in a 1939 essay as "Haman's times . . . the epoch of the counter-emancipation"?[10] It is also clear that the deep ideological rifts and inability to compromise were deeply embedded in the "new Jewish politics." This new politics was the politics of "peoplehood." It first emerged in the decade of the 1880s in the tsarist empire and, from there, transformed Jewish politics in the Kingdom of Poland and in Galicia. Because it was seen a response to the perceived failure of the "politics of integration," it also affected, though less fundamentally, the whole of the Jewish world. The attempt, initiated in Europe from the middle of the eighteenth century, to transform the Jews from a religious and cultural community linked by a common set of values and culture into citizens of their respective nations—Englishmen, Frenchmen, and even Germans or Poles "of the Mosaic faith"—had a different impact in the different parts of Europe. In the states of Western Europe—England, France, the Netherlands, and in some ways Italy—the Jewish communities were small, the progress toward constitutional government fairly rapid, and the emergence of an industrial society with a large middle class more or less accomplished by the beginning of the twentieth century. Jews were rapidly integrated, both politically and socially, into the rising middle class.

In German-speaking Central Europe, the progress toward constitutional government was slower (it was never complete before 1914), industrial development began later, and the middle class was much weaker. In this area, as in Hungary, the Jews formed a large part of the commercial middle class and, in the eyes of many, were responsible for the ills of capitalism. Political integration was not, by and large, followed by social integration. It was in the lands of the former Polish-Lithuanian Commonwealth, where the bulk of European Jews lived, that integration was least successful. Only in the area incorporated by Prussia were the Jews transformed into citizens, in this case of Prussia itself. In Galicia, the Kingdom of Poland—whose autonomy, established at the Congress of Vienna, was almost entirely done away with after the Polish insurrection of 1863—and in the tsarist empire, the slow development of constitutional norms, weakness of the middle class, small size and conservatism of the Jewish community, and strength of hostility to the Jews, both governmental and popular, impeded the granting of civil rights. Jews achieved civil equality in the Kingdom of Poland in 1862, in Galicia in 1868, and in the tsarist empire only after the revolution of February 1917. Outside a small, Polonized elite in Galicia and the Congress Kingdom and a not much larger Russified elite in the tsarist empire, there was very little social integration.

This was the situation when, after the pogroms of 1881, the tsarist government came to the conclusion that the integration of the Jews was not a desirable goal. Two separate Jewish communities had developed in the area acquired by the tsarist empire in the partitions of Poland and, in particular, the division of the Polish lands at the Congress of Vienna: that in the Kingdom of Poland, which included one-quarter of the Jews under tsarist rule, and that in the Pale of Settlement, where the remaining three-quarters lived. The historiographies of the two areas, which have developed rapidly in recent years, often seem to be written in almost complete isolation from each other. In the Pale of Settlement the tsarist government had, in the first half of the nineteenth century, pursued aggressive policies designed to break up Jewish "separatism," conscripting the Jews and attempting to Russify them through special schools. Although in the 1860s these harsh measures had been rescinded, the promised abolition of the restrictions on Jewish civil rights had never been introduced. With the wave of pogroms that followed the assassination of Alexander II, the tsarist authorities made it clear that they had no intention of granting citizenship to their Jewish subjects. Thus, it was within the Russian Jewish community that autonomous concepts of Jewish self-identity, the basis of the new Jewish politics, were first articulated. With the development of modern Hebrew and of Yiddish as a literary language, this Russian Jewish community increasingly formed a protonation, like the other emerging nations of the area—the Ukrainians, the Lithuanians, and the Belorussians.

In the Kingdom of Poland, the pattern of Jewish politics was rather different. In the first half of the nineteenth century, the Polish nobility, the dominant force in the area even after the failure of the revolution of 1830–1831, took the view that Jewish emancipation was conditional on the Jews abandoning their religious and social separateness. This development was regarded as rather unlikely, or, at best, likely to take a very long time. The prelude to the insurrection of 1863 changed this situation as a competition developed between the Viceroy of the Kingdom, and the Pole, Alexander Wielopolski, who was trying to introduce a measure of self-rule that would be acceptable to the tsarist authorities and to the growing national movement. As a result, the Jews of the Kingdom received their emancipation on May 23 / June 4, 1862 from Wielopolski. This was not rescinded after the failure of the uprising and the Jewish elite remained committed to an integrationist view of the Jewish future, which they propagated through the newspaper *Izraelita*. Their position was weakened by the slow progress of acculturation, because the educational system was in the hands of the Russian authorities who were determined to prevent another Polish uprising. It was further undermined by the impact of the new Jewish politics developing in the Pale of Settlement. This new politics was brought to the Kingdom both by pamphlets and newspapers and by the immigration of considerable numbers of Jews (the so-called "Litvaks") from the Pale to the Kingdom. The growth of anti-Semitism further increased the attractiveness of the new politics, suggesting that the hope of converting the Jews into "Poles of the Mosaic faith" was nothing more than an illusion.

It is obvious that one of the main tasks of historians of East European Jews is to integrate these two historiographies, one that stresses the character of tsarist government policy toward the Jews and the Jewish response, and one that is especially concerned with the failure of the attempt to transform the Jews in the Kingdom of Poland and in Galicia into "Poles of the Mosaic faith." This is a task far beyond the scope of this chapter. However, it may be helpful to examine in more detail the reasons for the failure of integrationist politics in the Polish lands and the consequences of this failure. At the same time, developments in the different areas of the former Polish-Lithuanian Commonwealth cannot be treated in isolation. The Jews in the area had formed one community before the partitions and, in spite of the different effects of governmental policy in different regions, they remained in many senses, one community. Indeed, one of the goals of the new Jewish politics was to strengthen that sense of unity. In addition, even in the "Polish sphere of influence" Poles and Jews were not the only players. The late nineteenth century saw the emergence of increasingly strong national sentiments among the Lithuanians, Ukrainians, and even Belorussians and saw the entry into political life of groups like the peasantry and industrial working class that had not formed part of the Polish noble nation. It is also clear that the policies pursued toward the Jews in the tsarist empire itself and the growing strength of anti-Semitism there had a considerable impact on the situation in the remaining Polish lands.

Initially, the granting of full legal equality to the Jews in the Kingdom of Poland was accompanied by high hopes. In emancipating the Jews, Wielopolski had hoped that they could form a significant element in an emerging Polish middle class, which could carry out the capitalist transformation of the Kingdom of Poland and give it a much more balanced and western social structure. This was also the hope of the Polish liberals, who called themselves positivists because of their admiration for the secular and pro-industrial ideas of Auguste Comte, Alexander Swietochowski, and Eliza Orzeszkowa. This capitalist ideal was also supported by the Jewish commercial and financial elite, who benefited from the economic boom in the Congress Kingdom that followed the opening of the Russian market in 1858 and the abolition of un-free cultivation in 1864. The transformation of the Jews was always likely to prove long and difficult. The increasingly repressive character of tsarist rule after the crushing of the insurrection of 1863, and the absence of a Polish-controlled educational system impeded it further. Most importantly, a large and self-confident Polish bourgeoisie did not emerge, and from the 1890s onward there was a growing revulsion against the excesses and injustices that accompanied the progress of capitalism. According to the turn-of-the-century critic, Ignacy Matuszewski:

Alas! The golden age remained a dream, the heroic engineers, praised by contemporary writers, were transformed in legal bandits. [Organic] work, which was to raise the spirits of the individual and of the collective, changed into a nightmare which preyed on the sweat of the poor and the brains, nerves and hearts of the rich and those determined to become rich.[11]

This change in attitude inevitably had an adverse effect on attitudes to the Jews who were widely blamed for the defects of capitalism. There is a whole series of fin de siècle Polish novels that describe the unsuccessful attempts of Polish characters to free themselves from the capitalist cobwebs that entangle them. "In all cases, the 'flies' are ultimately strangled and become the prey of a swarm of Jewish 'spiders.'"[12] Around the same time, the revival of nationalism across Europe led to the emergence in Poland of the National Democratic movement. Its chief ideologist, Roman Dmowski, was a social Darwinist who believed that if Poland were to survive as a nation it would have to abandon the naive belief in international brotherhood that had characterized the gentry revolutionaries of 1830, 1848, and 1863. "Struggle and . . . oppression are a reality and universal peace and universal freedom are a fiction," he asserted.[13] In these conditions, Dmowski believed, the Poles should create an organic national movement that would defend their national interests. In such a movement, there could be no place for the Jews, a disruptive force who could never be integrated into the national substance.

These developments both caused and were stimulated by the transformation of the Jewish consciousness that spread from tsarist Russia to the Kingdom of Poland in the last two decades of the nineteenth century. Increasingly, the assimilationist solution was rejected as unrealistic and involving a series of compromises which had proved both humiliating and fruitless. Autonomist Jewish political movements now emerged, of which the most important were Zionism, Bundism, and folkism. All of these groups believed that Jewish national autonomy should be sought within the framework of the socialist millennium, and were underpinned by the development of a modern Hebrew and Yiddish literature. The new politics—characterized by a more strident and anti-Semitic form of Polish nationalism, a socialist challenge to the tsarist empire, and Jewish autonomist claims—was both more populist and more demagogic.

In Galicia, too, the politics of integration was increasingly seen as bankrupt. The Polish nobility, which gained control of the province in the 1860s, had accepted the granting of full legal equality for the Jews under pressure from Vienna. In the last decades of the nineteenth century, an alliance developed between the

Polish governing stratum in the province and the Jewish leadership. This worked very successfully for quite a long time—the alliance between the Jews, Ukrainians, and German liberal centralists in the national election of 1873 was the only occasion when it failed to operate before the beginning of the twentieth century. But in the years before 1914, a number of developments worked to undermine it. One was the increasingly democratic character of Galician politics (universal male suffrage was granted in 1907), which brought the Polish peasantry into politics and disrupted the noble-Jewish alliance. Another was the increasingly bitter character of the Polish-Ukrainian conflict, which created particular problems for the Jews, since most of them lived in areas in which Ukrainians were the majority. The growth of political anti-Semitism and the influence of Dmowski's National Democrats in East Galicia also stimulated the emergence of autonomous Jewish politics.[14]

The new Jewish politics is usually described as shifting the marker for Jewish identity from "religion" to "peoplehood," and as rejecting the old Jewish elite's claim to a monopoly on the entry of new elements into political life, above all the intelligentsia. There is another element that should be stressed. The new politics emerged at a time when previously passive political groups were mobilizing toward participation in electoral politics, with all the demagogy this seemed to entail. This mobilization compelled the practitioners of the new politics to look for allies in the wider political scene. Certainly, the search for allies had been a feature of Jewish politics from the beginning of the process of Jewish integration (and probably before). The *maskilim* had looked to enlightened autocrats to aid with the transformation of the Jews, while Jewish integrationists had sought liberal and democratic allies, seeing Jewish emancipation as part of the wider process of the establishment of constitutional government. The practitioners of the new Jewish politics rejected the liberals (or felt rejected by them). Theodor Herzl was even prepared to negotiate with V. K. Plehve, the Russian minister of the interior. Herzl also sought the support of reactionary governments to assist in the creation of the Jewish state. This was also, later, the policy of Zionist Ze'ev Zhabotinsky. The more radical Zionist groups, particularly after the Helsingfors Conference in 1906, sought to ally themselves with groups struggling for constitutional rule in the tsarist empire or with rising national groups in the western parts of the empire, especially the Lithuanians. For the Bund, the only possible allies could be other revolutionary socialist parties like itself. Even the neo-Orthodox parties, first the Mahzikei Hadas in Galicia and then the Agudat Yisrael in interwar Poland, sought allies, preferably conservative or government parties.

They could be won over by assurances that the Orthodox were not interested in participating in the wider political scene, but sought only to ensure conditions in which they could practice their religion.

When the new Jewish politics began to make its impact in the Kingdom of Poland in the 1890s, Polish political life was in a state of flux. At this time, the Polish intelligentsia was divided between conservatives and positivist liberals, with a tiny group of socialists on the fringe of one side and radical anti-Semites on the other. Anti-Semitism had already struck root in all parts of dismembered Poland, but had not yet gained respectability in the mainstream of Polish culture. As early as 1883, Jan Jelenski, in his book *Zydʑi, Niemcy i my* (The Jews, the Germans and We), had attacked the Jewish and German "domination" of Poland, a view he also propagated in his weekly, *Rola*, founded in the same year. In 1891, *Glos*, another anti-Semitic weekly, founded in 1886, had declared the assimilation was a "harmful fantasy." Yet these views, particularly in their obsessive incarnation best exemplified by *Rola*, were still a marginal ideology of the extreme right. The positivists took the growing strength of Zionism in the Kingdom of Poland as a rejection of their offer of integration by a significant section of the Jewish elite. The transformation in attitudes here can best be charted in the views expressed by the doyen of Polish liberalism, Alexander Swietochowski. Confronted by the phenomenon of Zionism, he wrote in his journal *Prawda* in April 1902 that he did not believe that the Jews possessed the "cultural material needed to create their own homeland or to build a separate nation." If, however, they were to pursue such an ideal, then friendly coexistence with such an alien and separate nation would become impossible for the Poles. In a second article in February 1903, significantly entitled "Take Care with Fire," he claimed that the spread of Zionism would result in the rise of hostility to the Jews in segments of society that until then had been free of hatred. Anti-Zionism would quickly turn into anti-Semitism and would destroy all hope of Polish-Jewish reconciliation.

The 1905 revolution saw an unprecedented mobilization of political opinion in the Polish lands. Integral nationalism, Zionism, and socialism—Polish, Jewish, and revolutionary—had been previously largely theoretical ideologies, but now emerged as parties with large followings. The revolution was crushed with corresponding disillusionment, but the rights granted by the Manifesto of October 1905 were not rescinded. Thus, Poles now enjoyed a whole range of benefits that they had long been denied—education in the national language, voluntary associations, trade unions, increased freedom of the press, voting rights. All these rights

were also granted to the Jews, thus immediately widening the area of conflict between the two groups. For Dmowski and his National Democrats, conflict with
the Jews now became a central part of their political ideology and strategy. More
seriously, within the liberal camp, shocked by the signs of Jewish collective action
and the new self-esteem it engendered, talk of the "bankruptcy" of assimilation
became increasingly fashionable. The Warsaw Duma election of October 1912
engendered a conflict in which the Jewish majority of the very restricted elec-
torate voted for a socialist candidate, rather than a liberal who refused to give any
clear assurances on Jewish rights. In response, Swietochowski adopted a clearly
anti-Semitic position:

> The jelly-like mass of Polish society is now becoming crystallized as a nation. And
> the Jewish nation has for the first time stood squarely against the Polish nation. This
> is no longer an ignorant "ghetto" crowd . . . or an amorphous mass, which we need
> to digest and absorb. We have spotted this enemy late, but fortunately he has now
> emerged from the fog into our view.[15]

In his memoirs, written somewhat later (in the 1920s), he explained:

> I admit only to the name of evolutionist in philosophy and national humanist in so-
> ciology. Because of my views, I defended the Jews fifty years ago, when they wished
> to be Poles, and, because of the same views, I do not defend them today, when they
> wish to be Jews, enemies of the Poles.[16]

Not all Polish responses were as extreme as this. There were those who opposed the chauvinist tide. Some were Marxists, like Ludwik Krzywicki and Julian
Marchlewski. Others were liberals, like Sempolowska, Lubinska, and others, who
were motivated primarily by ethical revulsion at the reversion to the politics of
the jungle and filled with apprehension at the future of a society in which relations between Poles and Jews were poisoned by mutual hatred. Jan Baudouin De
Courtenay was the most consistent opponent of the spreaders of racial hatred;
he saw its roots in the national idea itself and staunchly defended the inalienable
right of every individual to choose his own way of life. The socialist ideologue
Kazimierz Kelles-Krauz had also somewhat earlier expressed his support for
Jewish national aspirations.[17]

The Ukrainians in Galicia saw the emergence of autonomous Jewish politics
as a tool that could be used to undermine Polish hegemony. Ivan Franko thus
welcomed Herzl's Judenstaat, and in 1906, in a speech in the Austrian Reichsrat,

the Ukrainian leader Iulian Romanchuk advocated that the Jews be recognized as a separate nationality. In the Austrian elections of the following year, a Zionist-Ukrainian electoral alliance was established, which led to the election of three Jewish national candidates in Galicia and the creation of a Jewish Club in the Reichsrat. A similar situation developed in Lithuania, where the emerging Lithuanian national movement felt more threatened by Poles than by Jews and where a degree of cooperation developed in the Duma elections of 1906 and 1907.

The First World War fundamentally transformed the situation of the Jews in Eastern Europe. It was accompanied by appalling devastation and the worst anti-Jewish massacres since the uprising of Ukrainians, led by Bohdan Khmelnytsky in 1648–1654. On the ruins of the tsarist empire a revolutionary state emerged, committed to a new and more extreme version of the policy articulated by the French Count Stanislaus de Clermont-Tonnerre in 1791—that of giving the Jews everything as individuals and taking away from them all semblance of communal autonomy. At the same time, as a transitional step to aid Jewish integration, a specific form of socialist Jewish autonomy, expressed through a sovietized Yiddish language, was established. From today's perspective, we know how the Soviet Utopia turned out, both in general and in its specifically Jewish aspects. But in the 1920s, it exerted a considerable attraction to many in the Jewish world. At the same time, the collapse of the tsarist, Austro-Hungarian, and German states made possible the creation of Polish and Lithuanian national states. The peacemakers at Versailles were determined to safeguard the rights of the national minorities in these states, and these guarantees were not only inserted in the respective Polish and Lithuanian constitutions, but were guaranteed by the Allied and Associated Powers in the peace settlement. This also gave international reinforcement to the British promises in the Balfour Declaration to establish a Jewish national homeland in Palestine. The Jewish delegations at Versailles were an uneasy mix of old-style integrationists, like Lucien Wolf and Louis Marshall, and proponents of the new politics. But the final settlement seemed to fulfill the highest dreams of those who thought in terms of Jewish peoplehood, both by underpinning Zionist aspirations and by establishing conditions for the creation of a system of non-territorial national autonomy in Eastern Europe.

The autonomists focused their highest hopes for the creation of such a system on Lithuania. According to Leo Motzkin, who represented the World Zionist Organization at the Second Jewish National Assembly in Lithuania held in Kaunas in February 1922, "Fifteen million Jews are watching your experiment in the struggle for national rights." In response, Dr Max Soloveitchik, minister for Jewish affairs in the Lithuanian government, affirmed, "Lithuania is the source from which will flow ideas which will form the basis for new forms of Jewish life."[18]

Lithuanian Jewry had a very specific character, derived from a formidable knowledge of the Haskalah and of Zionism, a low level of acculturation, and the strength of Misnagdic and Musar traditions. It appeared to be the ideal soil on which to establish a system of Jewish autonomy, a system that both Jews and Lithuanians felt were in their interests. The two groups had cooperated before the war in elections to the Duma, and after the war the Lithuanians hoped that the Jews would support their claims to Vilnius (Vilna). There was no apparent fundamental economic conflict between the emerging Lithuanian intelligentsia and the Jews, and the Lithuanian nationalists were more comfortable with specifically Jewish cultural manifestations than with Jewish acculturation to Russian, Polish, or German culture. Given the multiethnic character of the area, Jewish national autonomy would also make the state more attractive to Belorussians and Germans who might be incorporated into it.

The origins of the autonomous system lay in the period of Lithuania's emergence. In September 1918, as German rule was collapsing, a Zionist Central Committee was established in Vilnius that supported the Lithuanian claims to the town. Shortly afterwards, the German authorities set up a Lithuanian parliament (*taryba*) and called on it to respect minority rights. Three Jews represented the Jewish community in the new Lithuanian government, Dr. Samson Rosenbaum, vice minister for foreign affairs; Dr. N. Rachmilevich, vice minister for trade and industry; and Dr. Jacob Wygodzki, minister for Jewish affairs. This government was forced to move to Kaunas when the Poles captured the city on January 1, 1919, and was followed five days later by the Bolsheviks—who were expelled by the Polish legionaries again on April 19. Dr. Max Soloveitchik replaced Wygodzki in the Lithuanian government.

What the Jews understood by autonomy was clearly set out in point five of the memorandum submitted by the Committee of Jewish Delegations to the Paris Peace Conference. It demanded that the Jewish minority be recognized as an autonomous and independent organization with the right to direct its own religious, cultural, philanthropic, and social institutions. In Lithuania, the Jews asked for full rights for Jews in politics, economics, and language, as well as representation in parliament, administrative bodies, and courts to be based on the Jewish proportion of the population. They also requested that autonomy be based on three sets of institutions: local *kehillot*, a National Jewish Council, and a Ministry for Jewish Affairs.[19]

The Lithuanians responded positively. On August 5, 1919, Augustas Volde-maras, the Lithuanian foreign minister, presented a memorandum to the Committee of Jewish Delegations to the Paris Peace Conference. It had four main points. It conceded proportional representation in parliament, the administration, and the judiciary. It established a ministry to deal with Jewish affairs. Jews were to be granted full rights as citizens, the right to use the Yiddish language in public life and in governmental institutions, and autonomy in all internal matters including religion, social services, education, and cultural affairs. The *kehillot* and the Jewish Council were to constitute the operating agencies of Jewish autonomy. They were to be governmental bodies, organized on a territorial basis, with the right to issue ordinances that would bind both Jews and the agencies of the Lithuanian government.

In October 1919, seventy-eight *kehillot* were organized. Their first Jewish National Assembly took place in Kaunas on January 4, 1920, with the participation of 139 delegates. A Va'ad Haarets (National Council) of thirty-four members was elected. On this occasion, the prime minister, Ernestas Galvanauskas, and the foreign minister, Voldemaras, affirmed their support for autonomy. On January 10, 1920, the representatives of the Jewish minority joined the Lithuanian Council of State, and the President of Lithuania issued a declaration of Jewish national autonomy.

On 4 March 1920, the Law on *Kehillot* was published. A *kehilla* was defined as a body recognized by public law with the right to impose taxes and to issue ordinances dealing with religious matters, education, and philanthropy. It was responsible for the registration of Jewish births, deaths, marriages, and divorces. Every citizen who was registered as a Jew in public documents (birth certificate, family listing, school registration) was to be considered a Jew. One could leave the Jewish community only through conversion or submission of proof that the documentation showing that one was a Jew was incorrect.

In the next months the basic structures of the system were established. Yet problems soon appeared. One was the fissiparous character of Jewish politics. At the second Jewish National Assembly, the minister for Jewish affairs, Dr. Max Soloveitchik, felt compelled to warn the delegates: "If we are unable to demonstrate a minimum of tolerance and trust, we will be unable to build up the system of national autonomy. If that is the situation, let us give up the experiment immediately."[20] More importantly, the Lithuanian authorities were now markedly less enthusiastic. In April 1922, Soloveitchik felt compelled to resign as minister in protest at the failure of the proposed constitution to provide for the constitutional entrenchment of the Ministry of Jewish Affairs and the autonomous structure. He was replaced first by Dr. J. Brutzkus and then by Bernard Friedman, who was distrusted by the supporters of autonomist politics. On May 12, 1922, the Lithuanian ambassador in Washington, D.C., stated that Lithuania was not obligated to provide national autonomy to minorities, but only to guarantee them citizenship rights and the rights to schools where children could be educated in their own language. However, the new constitution did make some provision for national autonomy. According to paragraph 73, "Citizens of national minorities, which make up a substantial part of the population, have the right to carry on autonomously the affairs of their national culture, politics, education, social services and mutual aid and to elect representative institutions for the direction of these affairs in a manner provided for in special laws." Paragraph 74 reads: "The minorities mentioned in paragraph 73 have the right to tax their members for cultural purposes and to receive both from the government and the municipal bodies their rightful share of the funds assigned for popular education."

What really undermined the system was the way its maintenance became linked with the increasingly bitter Lithuanian political conflict. In March 1923, a vote of no confidence in the Christian Democratic government was supported by Jewish members of parliament, which caused some bitterness among parliament members on the right. Three months later, in June, the presidium of parliament stopped the use of Yiddish in parliamentary speeches.

By the time the third Jewish National Assembly met in November 1923, there was growing opposition to the whole system in the Jewish community from the religious right (the Akhdes) and the left. The new conservative government of Lithuania was also determined to bring the system to an end, partly since the census of 1923 had revealed that the number of Jews in Lithuania was considerably less than had been expected (150,000 instead of 250,000). Thus, no budget was approved for the Ministry of Jewish Affairs, and the minister accordingly resigned in February 1924. The new cabinet of June 1924 did not include a minister of Jewish affairs. In September 1924, the Jewish National Council was dissolved and new laws on *kehillot* were introduced in accordance with which registration of births, deaths, and marriages was handed over to the rabbinate and more than one *kehilla* was permitted in each community. In March 1926, the *kehillot* were stripped of their autonomous powers and control of religious matters was handed over to the Orthodox.

Any attempt to reestablish the system was forestalled by the growing political crisis. In May 1926, a new, leftist government came to power and made important concessions to national minorities. This and general dissatisfaction with the functioning of the democratic system led to a December 1926 coup led by a right-wing nationalist, Antanas Smetona. The political system was becoming increasingly autocratic and no longer had any place for Jewish—or indeed any sort of minority—autonomy. The highly developed Jewish private school systems and the Jewish cooperative banking system, however, survived.

The reasons for the collapse of the autonomous experiment in Lithuania are clear. The two sides had unrealistic expectations of each other. The Lithuanians believed that the Jews would aid them in acquiring Vilnius and the port city of Memel (Klaipeda) and in attracting Belorussians to a multinational Lithuania. They had much less need of the Jews in the fairly homogeneous Lithuania that actually emerged, while it soon became clear that Jews would not be a significant factor in acquiring Vilnius. For their part, the Jews took far too seriously assurances made by the leading Lithuanian politicians, whose commitment to Jewish autonomy was always contingent on larger goals. There were other reasons for the failure of the experiment. It fell prey to Lithuanian party conflict, and the degree of consensus necessary for its success was absent in the Jewish community. It may be, too, that there is an inherent contradiction between the basic principles of the liberal state and the guaranteeing of group rights.

The attempt to establish Jewish autonomy in Lithuania explains some of the otherwise puzzling features of interwar Jewish politics in Poland. The bitter dispute between the Galician Zionists, led by Leon Reich, and those in the Kingdom of Poland, led by Yitzhak Grunbaum, has to be understood in the context of what seemed like the successful achievement of Jewish national autonomy in Lithuania. Grunbaum, coming from an area where ethnic antagonisms had become quite pronounced, stressed the need for a vigorous and uncompromising defense of Jewish national rights, especially as the Polish Constitution and the National Minorities Treaty had guaranteed them. The Jews, in his view, would find a reasonable place for themselves only when Poland had been transformed from a national state into a state of nationalities, in which the various ethnic groups enjoyed a wide measure of autonomy. Grunbaum's ideas led him to advocate for a united front of the minorities—Jews, Germans, Ukrainians, and Belorussians—which resulted in the establishment of the National Minorities Bloc in the elections of November 1922. Only someone who set unrealistic goals in politics and who had no practical political experience could have pursued this policy. It bitterly antagonized the Poles, already hostile to the Jews because of their support for the Lithuanian claim to Vilnius and their neutrality in the Polish-

Ukrainian conflict in Lwow. Moreover, the Jews' objectives were quite different from those of the other minorities with whom they sought an alliance. The Jews wanted only the implementation of rights they were guaranteed, the Germans were openly revisionist, and the Slavic minorities wanted at least territorial autonomy and, at most, secession.

Reich, coming from Galicia where ethnic tensions were much less acute, rejected Grunbaum's maximalism and favored a direct approach to the Polish authorities. This resulted in the May 1925 agreement with Premier Wladyslaw Grabski, which soon collapsed amidst a welter of accusations and counteraccusations of bad faith by the parties involved. Yet, after the May 1926 coup, Reich (who died in 1929) and his associates, who dominated the Jewish Parliamentary Club, still hoped to establish lines of communication with the government. They were generally satisfied with government behavior in the twenties and, although uneasy about the impact of the depression, still regarded the government as far better than the alternatives, whether on the right or the left. In August 1929, they felt particularly justified by the actions of the government. The National Democrats attempted to exploit an alleged Jewish profanation of a Corpus Christi procession in Lwow by initiating a campaign of anti-Jewish disturbances. The prime minister, Felicjan Slawoj Skladkowski, who was later to make himself notorious by his encouragement of the economic boycott in parliament in April 1936, acted firmly and swiftly to restore order and stop attacks on the Jews.

The main Orthodox political organization, Agudat Yisrael, in accordance with its understanding of the talmudic principle *dina de malkhuta dina* (the law of the state is law), had quickly established friendly relations with the regime of Jozef Pilsudski after his military coup of May 1926.[21] The Aguda was rewarded by a decree in 1927 extending and reorganizing the *kehillot*, which were now granted wide powers in religious matters, including the maintenance of rabbis, synagogues, ritual baths, religious education, and kosher slaughtering. Some welfare for poor members of the community was also to be provided. The Aguda, in return, supported the government in the elections of March 1928 and November 1930. In 1928, one of the Aguda's leaders, Eliasz Kirszbraun, was even elected on the government (BBWR) list.

Grunbaum's followers, Reich's supporters, and Agudat Yisrael all found their political positions drastically undermined after 1935 by the increasingly anti-Semitic stance of the government and the national minorities, particularly the Germans and Ukrainians. Grunbaum moved to Palestine in 1929. But for his followers, the idea of transforming Poland into a state of nationalities was now merely a pipe dream. Reich's attempt to find a modus vivendi with the Polish authorities that would guarantee both Polish national interests and Jewish group rights had also clearly failed. In addition, the hope of large-scale emigration to the Middle East was now chimerical, and that undermined the position of the more moderate Zionist groupings. The position of the Aguda was also crumbling. It had continued to regard the government as sympathetic in the early 1930s, and in these circumstances it came as a particularly cruel blow when, in April 1936, the government introduced a law effectively banning ritual slaughter. This move was justified on hygienic and humanitarian grounds, but it was clear to all that its main objectives were to make life difficult for Jews and to damage the Jewish slaughterers who also sold meat to Christians.[22] These circumstances brought the Bund to the center of Jewish politics in Poland. Its links with the PPS seemed to tie it to a group that had a real chance of taking power and was more sympathetic to Jewish aspirations than most other political movements in Poland. The political and economic crises also explain the support for radical Zionist groups (especially the Revisionists) and leftist movements (primarily the Communists). These are all examples of the politics of desperation. The politics of the possible had been abjured because it did not exist. One cannot ultimately determine whether Tomaszewski's judgment, expressed in more extreme terms by Jabotinsky in the 1930s, that the Jews had no future in Poland, or indeed anywhere in Eastern Europe, is correct. Earlier dire predictions of a "Polish-Jewish war," frequently uttered on the eve of 1914, had proved misplaced (an even earlier "Polish-Jewish war" in 1859 had been followed by the Polish-Jewish rapprochement which preceded the insurrection of 1863), and under German occupation from 1915, Polish-Jewish tensions abated. On the eve of a second German occupation, during which the Nazis murdered over ninety percent of Polish Jewry, Polish-Jewish relations were certainly envenomed. But it is only with the benefit of hindsight that we know that in 1939 the bulk of Polish Jewry was doomed. Assertions, like that of Celia Heller, that the Poles had pushed the Jews to "the edge of destruction" so that all that was required for the Nazis to complete this work was a small shove, are, by their nature, unprovable.[23] It could equally be argued that the bark of Polish anti-Semitism was rather worse than its bite, and that had the Polish regime moved back, as seemed possible in 1938–1939, to some form of liberal democracy, some new Polish-Jewish modus vivendi would have become possible. What is clear is that the creation of an appropriate arrangement for nationally conscious Jews in national states is a highly complex matter. The failure of the attempt to establish Jewish autonomy in Lithuania, where there was considerable goodwill on both sides at the outset, should lead to serious reflection. So too should the involvement of a significant number of Lithuanians, previously regarded by many Jews as not particularly prone to anti-Semitism, in the Nazi anti-Jewish genocide. The fundamental problems posed by the "new Jewish politics" remain and their implications go far beyond the Jewish world. How is one to guarantee minority rights, particularly those of a nonterritorial minority, in a national state? How much do Jews have to give up to live securely as Jews in the diaspora? Is it only in a Jewish national state that Jewish national rights can be guaranteed?

DANIEL BLATMAN

4

National-Minority Policy, Bundist Social Organizations, and Jewish Women in Interwar Poland

THE NATIONAL-MINORITIES PROBLEM was one of the most conspic-
uous points of tension and instability in interwar Eastern Europe. At issue were
groups of people that lacked the role and status of the ethnic groups who were
included in the countries' governments and power centers. No such group was
more strongly identified with the minorities problem than the Jews, who stood out
as a national-minority group in all European countries. Other large minorities
were Germans, Ukrainians, Lithuanians, Greeks, Tatars, and Gypsies, to name
only a few.[1]

Interwar Poland found itself with one of the most complicated and daunting
national-minorities problems of the new states in Eastern Europe. Polish historiography has dealt extensively with the national-minorities problem and the ways
in which the Polish state and society confronted it. One of the main questions
asked is how to define membership in the Polish nation. Who is a Pole? Is he or she
a person born to Polish parents, one whose language is Polish, and / or one who
has become Polish through assimilation—a Jew, a Ukrainian, or a Belorussian—
that is, one who joined the Polish nation by choice?

Extensive research into these questions has failed thus far to elicit an acceptable answer in determining the main criterion of Polish nationality. In the interwar
period, the issue revolved around two possibilities: defining Polish nationality as
a "political nation" or as an "ethnic nation." The political and constitutional
structure of the state militated in favor of the political-nation definition, whereas

very powerful social forces—the Catholic Church, intellectual circles, various politicians, and most of public opinion—favored ethnic-Catholic criteria. The nexus of borders, territories, and nationalities in the Second Republic is also complicated. The borders of Poland as it was reconstituted in 1918 corresponded neither to those of the territory inhabited by the Polish nation until the first partition in 1772 nor to the territory populated by ethnic Poles in 1918. Thus, the indefinite nature of the borders of the Polish state and their incongruence with the territorial distribution of the Polish nation aggravated the tensions that already surrounded the issue of Polish identity and its relation to the national territory.[2]

Nearly all historians who have dealt with the national-minority question generally, and the problem of the Jewish minority specifically, agree that the policies of Polish governments in the 1920s and 1930s favored Polish exclusivity as opposed to national and cultural pluralism. Poland eventually adopted a nation-state definition of nationhood.[3] It is also worth bearing in mind that the development of the national-minorities policy corresponded closely to economic issues, since the formation of a national economy was an explicit policy goal. For example, the presence of non-Poles in provinces of major economic importance, such as the industrial and mining areas of Upper Silesia (inhabited by a large German population), or farming regions in the eastern border area (Kresy), settled by Belorussians and Ukrainians, affected the regime's national-minorities policy at the inception of the Second Republic.[4] Radicalization in the government's attitude toward the Jewish minority, one Polish historian asserts, became perceptible only in the late 1920s. In the first years of independence, in contrast, the problem of the Jewish minority attracted no special attention. The transition occurred because changes in economic conditions in Poland modified attitudes toward the Jews' economic role in the lower middle-class urban economy, in which they were conspicuous.[5]

Development of the Bund's National Platform in Independent Poland

At the beginning of World War I, the question of national minorities in Poland, including the status of Polish Jewry, was not high on the Bund's agenda of current problems. The Polish Bund and the Russian Bund parted ways in the midst of war, separated by mutually inaccessible occupation zones and the fact that the party could operate more freely in Congress Poland—the German-occupied areas —than in the areas under Russian rule.[6] The final separation came with the 1917

Russian Revolution. According to the veteran Bund historian J. S. Hertz, the attitude of the Polish Bund toward the national issue at the beginning of the war was based on Vladimir Medem's "neutralism" doctrine. In this concept, the Jewish labor movement neither encourages nor resists the assimilation of Jews. The Jewish labor movement should not interfere with Jews' wishes to develop a culture of their own, but it opposes the creation of a national culture that serves the interests of those who espouse a Jewish national policy.[7]

In the Russian Bund, the dispute over national culture and national-cultural autonomy ended around the year 1910. Practical actions toward building a system that would nurture the Jewish national culture began shortly before World War I. Several Bund leaders, including one of the founders of the movement, Vladimir Kossovsky, had already rejected "neutralism" on the national issue.[8] In Poland, however, the formation of the Bund's national platform was influenced by different factors.

The Polish Bund seems first to have adopted a particularistic approach toward the status and national organization of the Jews (outside the contours of the accepted ideological conception in the Russian Bund) in response to actions taken by the German regime. In December 1916, after the authorities issued new regulations on the status of the *kehilla* (the semiautonomous Jewish community organization), Vladimir Medem argued vehemently against intervention in what he considered the "religious labor" of a specific population group. In no enlightened country, he stated (citing France and Switzerland as examples), does the state interfere in its citizens' beliefs and views. Medem criticized not only intervention in religious practices but also the control the state had imposed on an activity that, in his estimation, belonged solely to the private domain. This turned the *kehilla* into a framework that meddled in a jumble of matters—provision of religious needs, help for the needy, care for the ill—all of them under government control. To put it differently, the *kehilla* had become an entity corresponding to a municipal authority, but for Jews only. Not only was it government controlled, but it also created a buffer between Jews and non-Jews on the basis of religious definition. This, Medem ruled, was not the way to attain "genuine self-management of Jewish national life in Poland."[9]

However, objections to the powers and status of the *kehilla* did not craft a definition of the mechanisms of the "genuine self-management of Jewish national life" to which Medem referred. The Bund had to answer this question within a broader ambit—to address the problem of the status and entitlements of the Jewish national minority in the multinational reality of the new Poland.

Even before 1918 and the reinstatement of Polish independence, the Bund found it difficult to establish cooperative relationships with its political counterparts, the parties of the Polish Left. It disagreed with the Social Democratic Party of the Kingdom of Poland and Lithuania (SDKPiL) and with the Polish Socialist Party–Lewica on the status and separate organization of the Jewish proletariat, although it cooperated with the latter on the municipal level. The Bund clashed with the Polish Socialist Party–Frakcja, the national wing of Polish socialism, on issues related to the war and the future of Poland as a nation-state.[10] The disputes with the Polish socialists prompted the Bund to search its soul again on the national question.[11]

In the formative years of the transition to renewed Polish independence, the Polish Socialist Party (PPS) was the most important political player that continued to predicate Polish statehood on the old myth of a Polish "league of nations," composed of different nationalities.[12] However, in view of the political and national reality they confronted at the dawn of Polish independence, Polish socialists quickly revised the ideological stance on the structure of the Polish state that they had championed since the late nineteenth century. In 1919, the PPS came out in favor of "the right to self-determination of the Peoples of the East" (*samostanowienia narodow kresowych*). The Polish socialists, headed by Mieczyslaw Niedzialkowski—editor of the PPS journal, *Robotnik*—favored national territorial autonomy for Ukrainians in Eastern Galicia. This attitude created a linkage between the right to autonomy and the territorial element, and it was also based on the wish of the PPS to mitigate the tension between the Ukrainians and the newly formed Polish state. According to the traditional stance of the PPS, the Jews were definitely not entitled to such autonomy privileges, for they were neither a territorial minority nor, in all probability—from the perspective of the Polish Left—a nation. The party staunchly opposed a linkage between collective religious identity and autonomy rights for national minorities. The Jews, perceived as a religious group, were entitled to civil equality. In no way, the Polish socialists argued, should the solution to the Jewish problem be sought by isolating the Jews, discriminating against them, or forcing them to emigrate—nor by giving them the privilege of national autonomy.[13]

Although some in the Bund expressed doubt about the necessity of establishing a Polish nation-state and the sincerity of Poland's intentions to safeguard the rights of its minorities, and although the PPS criticized these voices vehemently, the Bund did not categorically reject Polish independence during those years.[14] Even before World War I, there were several activists, foremost among the second generation of party leaders, whose education and cultural world were largely Polish. These young leaders, the most prominent of whom was Bronislaw Grosser, believed that Jews and Poles could cooperate on behalf of their shared homeland and sought to base the integration of the Jews into the Polish state not on assimilationist yearnings but on recognition of the separate existence of a Jewish nation, endowed with national and cultural rights within the framework of a broad Polish nation-state. Henryk Erlich also expressed support of the idea of Polish independence at the Petrograd Soviet in March 1917.[15] Therefore, the dispute with the PPS in 1918–1920 seems not to have been about the question of "national Poland." Rather, it pertained to the wishes of Bund leaders in Poland —foremost among them Medem—that the Polish state would grant Jews the status of a national minority endowed with assured entitlements in the area of cultural autonomy.

The national question was also raised in response to the wave of anti-Semitism and pogroms that swept Poland during its first two years of independence. In November 1918, Polish soldiers who had taken Lwow (Lviv) from the Ukrainians killed more than seventy Jews in a pogrom there, burning synagogues, destroying Jewish property, and leaving hundreds of Jewish families homeless. In April 1919, during the Polish-Russian War, thirty-five Jews whom the Polish army accused of supporting the Communists were murdered in Pinsk. These were but extreme cases in a countrywide series of anti-Jewish attacks and violence.[16] The PPS condemned the violence without hesitation. It seems, however, that the Polish socialists did not wish to make the treatment of the Jews into a major issue amidst the thicket of problems that beset Poland in its formative years.[17] The Bund strenuously criticized the Polish socialists' hesitancy on this account, charging that it stemmed from their reluctance to come to grips with the need to combine the struggle against anti-Semitism with a principled stance in favor of the right of the Jewish proletariat to organize separately, foster its culture, and use its language.[18]

Historians and researchers of the Bund stress the internal disputes within the party during those years—between the Left (the *"tsveyers"*) and the Right—as the main issue on the party's agenda.[19] This fractiousness not only threatened the integrity of the party but also affected the attitude of the PPS toward it, especially after the Polish Communist Party (KPP) was established in 1920. The dominance of proponents of the Bolshevik Revolution in the Bund leadership during those years, which prompted the party's most prominent leader in Poland, Vladimir Medem, to withdraw from activity and immigrate to the United States, gave the Bund a pro-Bolshevik image. This internal dispute largely marginalized discussion of the national question and focused attention on the Bund's place within the socialist camp after the Soviet regime had come into being.[20] This dispute obviously affected the attitude of the Polish Left, and of the other Jewish parties, toward the Bund. However, the Bund's real problems were not theoretical, as Medem stated in late 1918. The choice was not between support of democracy and support of the dictatorship of the proletariat, but between democracy and reaction.[21] Did the Bund have the ability to integrate itself into a Polish framework that would allow the party to promote Jewish workers' occupational and cultural rights? Or would the Bund be relegated to the political sidelines of the Polish state and become irrelevant to the existential realities of the Jewish masses in Poland? To resolve the question, the Bund had to take a stance on internal Jewish controversies and the dispute with Polish socialism. However, by early 1919 the party had already defined its goal and mission as "fulfilling the [Jewish proletariat's] entitlements to national and cultural autonomy."[22] After its convention in Danzig [Gdansk] in 1921 and its third conference in Warsaw in 1924, the party steadily united around the policy that rejected the dictates of the Comintern in Moscow.[23] Despite the threat of schism that hovered over it, it chose a path that stressed its singularity in Jewish political life.

Notwithstanding its decisions in the early 1920s, in order to distinguish itself from other Jewish political organizations the Bund had to explain the difference between the national autonomy that it favored and the autonomist frameworks advocated by other Jewish parties and entities. In other words, the Bund had to explain what distinguished its national perspective from that of the Zionist movement beyond the vision of Eretz Yisrael, which meant little to the Jewish masses in Poland. What was singular about Bundist nationalism and the organizations that the movement had established for the Jewish public?

Beinish Michalewicz, one of the most important Bund theoreticians in the 1920s, took up this issue after the internal party crisis blew over. In a series of articles published in 1927–1928, he differentiated between a nationalism based on national materialism, national mysticism, or national utopias, and a nationalism that placed cultural reality at the forefront. He argued that the Jewish nation was neither an economic nor an ethnic organism, but a cultural organism that joined with other cultural organisms to make up the economic and political superstructure, such as the state. The national idea of the Bund, said Michalewicz, was not based on the premise that every nation needs a separate state and that every state should be inhabited by one nation. The modern state was an instrument to use in meeting the requisites of social development; the more flexible it was, the better it could serve this cause. "A state of nations," Michalewicz asserted, was the way of the Bund—not a separatist, clerical state, but a large, open state accommodating diverse nationalities.[24]

Having defined the proper state structure, Michalewicz then elaborated on the Bund's views of national autonomy in independent Poland. As he put it, the autonomy presented by the Zionists was an anachronistic replica of the autonomy the Jews experienced under the Council of the Four Lands—an autonomy based on internal management of religious needs or welfare services. Such autonomy, which kept Jews isolated from society at large, was manifested most saliently in the *kehilla* and its institutions. It is no wonder that the Zionists advocated this "autonomy," he said, for in this way they reinforced the xenophobic Judeocentrism on which their entire political theory rested. The Bund's purpose in struggling for Jewish autonomous rights was not to segregate Jews from society but to integrate them.[25]

Michalewicz's statements indicate that the Bund leadership had made peace with political realities in Poland; furthermore, this was after the 1926 "May Revolution" and the stabilization of the Pilsudski camp in the state leadership. The multinational state and the need to act on behalf of the Jewish national minority had become irrefutable facts. They coincided with a goal that transcended ideology—prodding Poland in the direction of becoming a democratic, pluralistic, and socialist state. Although the Bund shared this goal with the progressive Polish forces, it considered itself the main standard-bearer in the struggle for Jews' occupational, cultural, and national rights.

It is clear that the Bund's ideological discourse in its formative years in independent Poland derived from political and ideational concepts it had developed in tsarist Russia. It attempted to adapt, almost unaltered, the vision of a multinational federative socialist republic, in which the Jews were one piece in a broad multinational jigsaw puzzle, to the reality of the Polish state with its proliferation of national minorities. Yet the latter was a complicated reality that had nothing in common with that of the turn of century. This transposition also dictated the complexion of several party-affiliated organizations.

Workers, Artisans, and Women in the Bund

The Jewish trade unionism that took shape in Poland during World War I was a new phenomenon in the history of the Jewish labor movement in Eastern Europe. Establishment of Jewish trade unions was part of the consolidation of the Jewish labor movement in the German-controlled parts of Poland and, subsequently, in independent Poland. This unionization drive, however, presented ideological questions to Bund activists in Poland. Foremost among them was the very need for separate organizational action for Jewish workers. This was one of the main bones of contention between the Bund and the PPS. When the unionization of Jewish workers first began during World War I, Bund spokesmen went out of their way to stress that this was prompted not by separatist or nationalist aims but by an obvious class and cultural need. Jewish workers regarded their unions as trade organizations that saw to their specific needs as Jewish workers. At that time, too, party spokesmen began to make overt use of the term "national culture" as the marker that distinguished Jewish workers from the rest of the proletariat—a culture based on the Yiddish language.[26]

This debate between the Bund and the Polish Left lasted until the mid-1920s. Szmuel Zygielbojm, one of the most prominent Jewish union activists in the interwar period, wrote about this matter in 1941 from New York, where he had settled, noting that maintaining relations with the country's general trade unions was a necessity for the Jewish labor movement.[27] However, this did not rule out creating an infrastructure of cultural and educational settings for Jewish workers to address their special needs. For example, an activist from Lublin reported in May 1916 about activity undertaken at the "workers' house" (*arbayter haym*) in that town, in which 900 Jewish workers were members. He described the educational and cultural activities that this institution hosted on Fridays and Saturdays and the special literary evenings held there during Passover, with emphasis —reflecting the wishes of the Jewish workers—on study of Jewish history, Polish language, and Yiddish language and literature.[28] By the end of World War I, the Jewish unionization drive in Warsaw alone had organized more than 15,000 Jewish workers in fifteen different unions. By the end of the 1930s, the Jewish unions in Poland, in their various settings and party affiliations, had more than 70,000 members.[29]

In May 1922, the National Council of Jewish Class Trade Unions (JCTU), the largest and most important Jewish workers' organization in Poland, held its second convention in Warsaw. Viktor Alter, secretary-general of this organization and a Bund leader, addressed the convention:

> Our Jewish trade unions have a special nature that sets them apart from Polish trade unions and those of Western Europe. Their activity does not focus only on the occupational affairs of the Jewish worker. . . . One may call them *arbayter haymn*

(workers' homes)—institutions where the worker develops socially and becomes a proletarian with a well-formed worldview. The trade unions also provide the Jewish worker with a social club and a library. He spends his spare time there and becomes a fighting proletarian. The Jewish trade unions are not only offices in which the members organize . . . in matters of strikes and unemployment. They are full-fledged social, educational, and cultural institutions. We must keep our trade unions this way. . . . To protect the special complexion of our movement, the Jewish workers need to consolidate their self-consciousness. They should be fully able to take action on their own.[30]

The great problem of Jewish unionization in Poland in its early years can be fixed between Zygielbojm's estimations and Alter's assertions. Alter adroitly identified the uniqueness of the Jewish workers' situation and understood that they had needs not shared by their Polish counterparts. Therefore, by the early 1920s Alter prescribed a very broad basis for Jewish unionization: Jewish workers should be given job protection along with educational and cultural tools. Alter's approach, which became the basis for most Jewish trade unions in Poland, was part of the effort to implement the Bund's idea of Jewish national and cultural autonomy.

The Jewish and Polish trade unions negotiated an agreement in late 1921 that preserved the major components of the Bund idea of cultural autonomy. Yiddish was recognized as the official language of the Jewish trade unions, and the unions' right to communicate with the Jewish proletariat in this language, in their broadsheets and manifestos, was acknowledged. The agreement created a framework for organizational partnership between Jewish and general trade unions in Poland, but it did not solve all problems.

One of the major preoccupations of the Jewish trade unions after 1925 was defined as the fight for a collective Jewish "right to work." A formal decision was made to launch a public and political struggle for equal occupational rights after the Polish government banished Jewish workers from important fields of employment, such as the tobacco industry and various public works. The decision to embark on an organizational struggle of this kind was, of course, problematic from the standpoint of the Bund and its affiliated trade unions. Bund writers went out of their way to stress that their party had consulted extensively with the PPS trade unions and that the decision to struggle for the Jewish proletariat's "right to work" was taken jointly by the Jewish and the Polish unions.[31] A headquarters established for the right-to-work struggle opened local offices in many Polish cities and responded to assaults and discrimination against Jewish workers. Union activists, in cooperation with PPS delegates to the Sejm (Polish national parliament) and municipal authorities, attempted to modify regulations and decisions that created workplace discrimination against Jews.[32]

Studies of the interwar Jewish economy illuminate a unique ethno-economic reality, different from that of Poles and other nationalities in the Second Republic. Jews exhibited less intergenerational occupational mobility than any other national group—hardly any, in fact. A Jew's occupation and employment were often dictated from birth. Polish statistics defined two-thirds of the Jews as "merchants" or "artisans." Jews also populated a unique economic category called "home workers" (*chalupnicy*). These were subcontractors who brought raw materials home, performed various sewing or bootmaking tasks, and turned over the finished goods to the main contractor, who undertook to sell them. Entire families, including children, were often employed in this fashion. In the occupational nomenclature of the government and, of course, in the eyes of a labor movement, they were self-employed. According to the 1931 census, Poland had no Jewish industrial workers to speak of. There were many reasons for this—some historical, others stemming from the government's discriminatory policies, still others connected with the policies of the Polish labor unions. Be this as it may, 88 percent of Jews were defined as artisans. Only 2 percent were considered industrial workers—members of the proletariat by class criteria.[33]

The activity of the Jewish trade unions in interwar Poland was centered on two kinds of needs of Jewish workers. True, only one-third of the Jewish working class was organized in Jewish unions, but the members found in their unions a supportive setting that dealt with the basic problems of their rights. By the 1920s, the unions had already evolved into complex systems of education, general learning, cultural activity, and social support for the Jewish worker.[34] The unions were not necessarily involved in "class education," that is, enhancing Jewish workers' organizational and class consciousnesses. Jewish unionization efforts had to confront socioeconomic processes unique to the Jewish collectivity. The steady economic decline of the Jewish middle class; the difficulty that educated young Jews encountered in finding jobs in their fields, forcing many to become low-income unskilled workers; the singular problems of Jewish women breadwinners; employer-employee relations in Jewish workshops—all of these elements underscored the distinctness of the Jewish working class within the overall working class in Poland.[35]

In 1927, Maurycy Orzech, a member of the Bund's Central Committee, initiated and established a trade union of artisans: the Socialist Association of Artisans of the Republic of Poland (Sotsiyalistn hentverker farband). This trade organization was anomalous in the landscape of occupational settings that the Bund had been creating since World War I. The party conducted an important and principled debate concerning it. The artisans' union directed its message to the *chalupnicy* and to merchants who would actually be better characterized as peddlers. The Bund needed to justify to itself, and more so to its opponents and to the Jewish Communists, the formation of a trade union composed of these hardscrabble Jewish working people who had little in common with socialism.

The Bund's explanation for establishing this union rested entirely on the correspondence between these artisans' ethnicity and their economic situations. These Jews, stated the party's programmatic journal *Unser tsayt*, belonged to the most impoverished and exploited group of all. The Jewish socialist movement's unique mission was to offer this group its patronage and to attempt to better its circumstances by organizational, cultural, and educational means.

> We are coming into contact with the poorest and least organized [elements] in Jewish society. We are making contact with those who approach us from the *kheder*, from the *shtibl* . . . those who are seeking our organizational frameworks and culture. . . . Especially important is our liaison with the young generation of the artisans and *chalupnicy* . . . With respect to them, we have a historical task to perform. . . .[36]

During the years in which the socialist artisans' union was active, Orzech tried to use it to promote efficiency and modernization in its members' working methods. For example, he tried early in the summer of 1939 to obtain financial support from the American Jewish Joint Distribution Committee for the purchase of modern transport vehicles that would facilitate the labor of some 400 Jewish porters and meat haulers.[37] Above all, however, it seems that this trade association engaged more in cultural and educational functions (by offering general instruction, vocational courses, and cultural events in the evenings) than those of a trade union.

Two years after its formation, the association had built up a membership of 7,200 in thirty-seven locals across Poland. This was not a stunning organizational success. However, though the Bund had aimed to recruit masses of supporters who had not belonged to the traditional pro-Bundist public, the very attempt to organize a Jewish collective that was impoverished, religious, and conservative in its way of life—and that ultimately delivered few members to the party ranks—was quite a departure from the Bund's traditional ideology.

Another example of particularistic social-class organization was the women's association YAF (Yidishe arbeter-froy organizatsye). The Bund made efforts to recruit Jewish women throughout the interwar period. However, because of some party members' opposition to seeing Jewish women's needs as different from those of the proletariat at large, the party's appeals to women emphasized the imperative of enlistment for class and social struggle. Victory in this struggle, it was argued, would solve the basic problems that beset Jewish women: children's education, severe wage discrimination, and inferior working conditions, to name only three.[38]

The role and status of Jewish women and mothers in Poland changed radically in the interwar period. The changes occurred in the education and raising of children, in women's and mothers' attitudes toward the modern cultural influences penetrating their families, and in women's economic activity. Modernization processes and the growing influence of the Polish culture and language were felt more by women than men. The Jewish woman, especially of the urban middle class, was the primary agent in the Polonization and acculturation of the Jewish family and society. In these respects, she had greater influence on her children than their father, who was usually an impediment to the spread of modernization in the lives of his family and children.[39] The Bund was conspicuously aware of these family processes and women's role in them, especially in the early 1930s. A Bund journalist, David Ajnhoren, wrote that this revolution, which was unfolding before their eyes without battles, victims, or violence, was transforming the "orders of creation" in society. Modern women could be found in almost all areas of activity, from university chairs to athletic fields, he noted. They were politically active and involved, and their entire educational orientation bore no resemblance to that of their mothers. They treated their children like friends who should be approached with pleasantness, explanations, and cooperation. The modern woman, attuned to new ideas in psychology and pedagogy, was raising her children in an open educational environment.[40]

Parties on the left accepted separate settings for different collectivities of supporters and sympathizers. When the Bund made the transition from illegal revolutionary activity to licit political activity in the early 1920s, it largely adopted the organizational patterns of the Polish socialists. Moreover, in its efforts during the interwar period to create an alliance with the PPS, the Bund stressed the nature of the PPS as an important force in Polish society that struggled for equal rights for Jews and consistently opposed anti-Semitism. When the Bund described the women's organization of the PPS, it was not as a group devoted chiefly to the needs of working women. Rather, it was as an extension to women of a party that acted on behalf of general workers' solidarity among the various minority groups in Poland and opposed the nationalist hostility toward national minorities that the regime was cultivating.[41]

By establishing its own women's organization, the YAF, the Bund leadership saw itself as adapting the modus operandi of other socialist parties in Poland and Western Europe to the Jewish proletariat. Not all Bundist leaders saw it this way. Michalewicz referred several times to the role of women in the socialist movement. He acknowledged no difference between Jewish women and working women generally and, although he spoke of women's social and economic inferiority relative to men, he made no effort to meet their ongoing needs by forming specific settings for this purpose. His solution for the problem of women in modern society was thoroughgoing social reform, in the course of which the status and situation of women would be transformed as well.[42] Henryk Erlich, leader of the Bund in interwar Poland, stated—on the few occasions that he addressed himself to the issue of Jewish working women—that the party's goal was to encourage them to join and integrate into the organizational array of the Jewish proletariat, with no buffers between them and men. The duty of women, he explained, was to participate in the general and universal struggle of the proletariat against fascism and capitalism and on behalf of social and cultural progress. He saw no point in establishing a Jewish women's organization that would concern itself mainly with the particularistic needs of women.[43]

One of the most important needs of working women was to arrange child care and assistance while away from home. If we bear in mind the growing centrality of Jewish women's labor in family support, we may appreciate the immediate problem they faced in this regard. The YAF therefore became intensely active in creating daycare facilities for the children of working women. From the early 1920s on, daycare centers for the children of Jewish working mothers were established in Warsaw, Lodz, Lublin, Bialystok, Wilno (Vilna), Piotrkow-Tribunalski, and other hubs of Bund activity. These centers, which in Warsaw in the early 1930s met (at some level) the needs of 450 preschool children, were urgently required by Jewish working women because the state offered them no affordable solutions. During summer vacations, the YAF continued to entertain children of working Jewish women by offering half-day summer camps in town. Needless to say, this activity seriously strained the scanty budget set aside for these goals, and more than once Bund women activists had to close a children's house or terminate summer camps because of budget difficulties.[44]

Another need, which over the years became central in the activity of the YAF, was the formal and general education of working Jewish women. This is the most obvious example of the internal development of the organization and its gradual evolution into an important agent of modernization among women supporters and sympathizers of the party. YAF women activists were well aware that the very membership of Jewish women in the working class did not obviate the fact that most of them lived in traditional conditions and, in their families, adhered to a way of life that assigned women the typical responsibilities and powers of traditional Jewish society. As a result, the YAF established an information system that aimed to modify—or shatter—these patterns within the Jewish family. YAF women's clubs hosted lectures, activity groups, and encounters on relations between men and women in modern society, child education and health, family planning, father-son relations, and managing the family budget, as well as other topics. Much of this information effort was devoted to specific aspects of women's lives, such as personal needs, time management of paid labor and housework, annual vacations, fashion, and household management. The groups made a special effort to complete working women's basic educations and teach them literacy. These YAF settings met another important need by providing working women with a social setting after work.[45]

Thus, the typical pragmatism of the Bund was again manifested in the activity of its women's organization. Bund leaders and spokesmen assigned pronouncedly ideological goals to the YAF and considered the organization one of several devices to use in recruiting women supporters and activists for the party. The YAF steadily developed systems of activity that, above all, responded to the daily needs of Jewish working women. This fulfillment of existential needs—education, information, and a social setting—attracted women who did not necessarily share the party's ideology. Even if such a common denominator evolved over time, it was not their main reason for joining the organization and participating in its activities.[46]

It is difficult to estimate exactly how many women took part in YAF activities. Reports in the party press tend to cite figures that indicate an upward trend in order to show party supporters that the effort was succeeding. Keeping this in mind, one may estimate that 500–600 women took part in YAF activities in Warsaw. In Lodz, an important interwar Bund center with a large population of Jewish working women, 800–900 women participated in YAF activities in the late 1930s, when Bund influence reached its peak. In Bialystok, Lublin, and Wilno, their numbers fluctuated between only 100 and 200.[47]

The main party activists and the leaders of the YAF were quite perturbed about the low number of women Bund members. In the mid-1930s, women activists often exhibited a sense of fatigue and failure. After all, despite more than a decade of intensive organizational efforts they had not managed to break out of the small traditional circle of women activists and create a large organization of Jewish working women.[48] Dina Blond, a YAF leader, wrote in 1935: "Let's be honest: The results we have attained are not far-reaching. We have a few organizations, each of which has a few women, as against the large numbers of women who could and should participate."[49]

About six months before the Nazi occupation, the party conducted a penetrating debate about the status of women in the Bund. The polemic was launched by one of the party's leaders and most prominent educators, Hayim-Shlomo Kazdan, the secretary-general of the Yiddish-language school system, CYSHO (Central Yiddish School Organization). The party's influence among Polish Jews had reached its peak during these months. Its electoral victories and attainments in countrywide municipal elections in late 1938 gave it the sense that it had become the strongest and most influential Jewish party in Poland and that, at long last, it had managed to occupy the center of Jewish public life.[50] Precisely because of these accomplishments, Kazdan started a debate on why the proportion of women among card-carrying members of the Bund verged on 10 percent at best. How could it be, he asked, that after so much effort in the trade unions and the party branches, and in view of the rising overall strength of the Bund, the proportion of women members is so low?

The situation in interwar Poland made the absence of women in the labor movement even more conspicuous. At first glance, all the social conditions should have magnified women's involvement. Women's representation in certain occupations equaled or surpassed men's, but this was not reflected in the membership of women in the trade unions and party organizations. Kazdan traced this to modernization patterns among Jewish women in Poland. In his estimation, Jewish women were more involved in non-Jewish society than were men, and their cultural world actually stood on two foundations, Polish and Jewish. Jewish women —including working-class Jewish women—were more inclined than Jewish men to adopt Polish as their language, to speak with their children in Polish, and to integrate them into general society and its culture. Was it any surprise, then, that the activities of the Bund, which stressed Jewish cultural particularity, Yiddish-language education, and the political doctrine of the Jewish labor movement, had weak resonance among women?[51]

Kazdan's assertions evoked many antagonistic responses, and engendered a debate on the status and roles of Jewish women in the movement. Dina Blond disputed Kazdan's thesis and his argument that assimilation among women was the prime culprit in their failure to integrate into the labor movement. In Blond's view, the main factor was the traditional complexion of the Jewish family and the roles it continued to force upon women. Women did not fit into the Bund because of child raising, she stated. Faithful to her party's socialist principles, Blond reaffirmed that only the socialist path would liberate women from the traditional roles that they played. The obstacle to women's participation in the Bund, she maintained, was not assimilation but the social conservatism of the Jewish woman.[52]

Other party members also tended to blame women's avoidance of the Jewish labor movement on the traditional family framework. A member from Lodz argued that the reason actually should be sought in psychological factors: For years, Jewish women had been in a ghetto of sorts that kept them isolated from social involvement, far from positions of leadership, and, in the modern era, excluded from political action. Most women had not yet been liberated from this ghetto feeling, this member argued, and only vigorous action by men who would regard it as a principal mission in family life could bring this liberation about. Quite a few members who expressed their views on these issues made this stipulation of the centrality of men in achieving the full liberation of women.[53]

It does seem that the main reason for the lack of large numbers of women in the Bund and its organizations was rooted, above all, in their inability to break away from their traditional patterns of life and the rules that governed the Jewish family. Even working-class Jewish families usually invoked traditional patterns in apportioning roles between the spouses. Many husbands, even when involved in activities in the trade unions or party branches, did not manage to implement into their families' daily lives the principles of women's equality and the need for women's full integration into labor-movement activity. Without their husbands' support, women found it difficult to accomplish these things on their own.

Any analysis of Bund organizations in interwar Poland must take into account the Jews' peculiar situation as a national minority. The most important criterion in such a review is the extent of these organizations' abilities to meet the real needs of the community to which they appealed and among whom they worked.[54] Members and activists of the Bund understood that Jews in the working class and groups at the bottom of the socioeconomic pyramid had singular needs created by the condition of the Jewish "home workers," artisans, and women. So, too, organized Jewish workers, teenagers and young adults had some needs that set them apart from their peers among other ethnic groups. In multinational prewar Poland, in which government policies restricted the Jews' entitlements and anti-Semitism was resurgent, the Bund organizations, like those of other Jewish parties and movements, filled a distinctly Jewish national need.

SAMUEL D. KASSOW

5

The Left Poalei Tsiyon in Interwar Poland

AT FIRST GLANCE IT IS EASY to dismiss the Left Poalei Tsiyon (henceforth, the LPZ) party in interwar Poland as a group of sectarian fanatics, who—even by the standards of the time—excelled in ideological nit-picking. After all, this was a party that called for a binational, Yiddish-speaking Soviet Palestine! However, further research on one of the LPZ's most devoted members, the historian Emanuel Ringelblum, invites a more careful look at the LPZ. After all, this was a party that managed to attract a solid core of dedicated followers. It carved out a solid base in the Jewish trade union movement in Poland and played a major role in the battle for secular Yiddish culture and education.

Above all, the LPZ gave the Zionist idea, however modified, a solid foothold on the left. The Communists had countered Zionism with the pledge of a new promised land: the Soviet Union. The Bund constantly hammered home its compelling message of *doigkayt* ("here-ness"): commitment to the Jewish masses, to their struggle in the diaspora and to their language, Yiddish. Of all the Zionist parties, it was the LPZ that most recognized the force of these alternate visions and strove to adapt them to Zionism. Its highly complex ideology strained to combine the charisma of the October Revolution with a commitment to a territorial base in Palestine. More than any other Zionist party, the LPZ struggled to synthesize the *do* (here) and the *dortn* (there), the diaspora and Palestine. Furthermore, the party's Yiddishism and strong commitment to unions overcame the psychological and cultural barriers that alienated many workers and working-class youths from other Zionist parties and youth organizations.

Some might argue that, strictly speaking, the LPZ was not really a Zionist party. It was only in 1937–1938 that the LPZ reconsidered and reversed its adamant boycott of the World Zionist Congress. For most of the interwar period, many, if not most of its members, felt as least as loyal to Moscow as to Palestine.[1] But by the eve of the World War II, the internal dynamics of the party, coupled with growing disappointment in the USSR, had pushed the LPZ toward a much stronger Zionist stance. It ended its boycott of the World Zionist Congress and even began to revise its attitude toward the Right Poalei Tsiyon and the Histadrut, the general confederation of labor in Palestine.

Poalei Tsiyon, Left and Right

The split in the Poalei Tsiyon movement at the fifth conference of the World Union of Poalei Tsiyon in Vienna in 1920 reflected fundamental differences over major questions in labor Zionism. Two key issues stood out: the World Zionist Organization and the Comintern. The Left wanted to continue the boycott, decided on in 1909, of the World Zionist Organization and the Zionist Congress; it also wanted to join the Comintern. The Right wanted to rejoin the Congress (which the World Union of Poalei Tsiyon had voted to do in 1919) and remain in the Second (Socialist) International.[2]

Yet another problem was the issue of Great Britain. The Right gave a cautious welcome to the Balfour Declaration, while the Left dismissed it as a cheap trick of the British imperialists. Only the victory of the Soviet Union, the Left argued, could guarantee the long-term interests of the Jewish workers in Palestine.[3]

But these sharp disagreements exposed more deep-seated conflicts. One source of tension was the relationship between the labor movement in Palestine and the Jewish masses in the diaspora. The growing rift within the Poalei Tsiyon came into stark relief during the polemics leading up to the Vienna congress. The "Palestinians" had taken a major step away from the East Europeans when they founded Akhdut Ha-Avodah, a party committed to the construction of a strong labor-dominated economy for the Yishuv, the Jewish population of Palestine. The leaders of the movement in Poland became increasingly embittered at what they felt was the Palestinians' condescension toward the Yiddish-speaking "tailors and shoemakers" who made up the bulk of the East European membership. This perceived arrogance was epitomized by the Palestinians' insistence on Hebrew over Yiddish. In turn, Palestinian leaders David Ben-Gurion and Berl Katznelson betrayed a growing impatience with the ideological dogmatism of the East European parties that seemed irrelevant to the pressing needs of the Yishuv.[4] The rift between the Palestinians and the East Europeans raised once again the complicated problem of the legacy of Poalei Tsiyon's founder, Ber Borochov: should the movement follow determinism and "prognostic Zionism" or should it endorse the pioneering ideal and support an active labor Zionist role in building the Yishuv?

Ber Borochov and the Identity of Poalei Tsiyon

The party's ideology was "Borochovism"—the teachings of Ber Borochov as interpreted by the party leadership.[5] The ideological mentors of the LPZ, especially Jacob Zerubavel and Nathan Buchsbaum, offered the party faithful a version of Ber Borochov that relied heavily on the arguments of "Our Platform" which appeared in 1906.[6] In this essay, Borochov stressed deterministic processes over voluntaristic action in the development of Palestine; Zionism could now dovetail with the most stringent demands of Marxist economic theory. Not yearning for Zion, not nationalist romanticism, but rather objective economic circumstances would push both the Jewish bourgeoisie and the Jewish working class to Palestine. An ever-greater proportion of Jewish immigrants would head to Palestine because a relentless process of elimination caused by growing immigration restrictions in host countries would leave Palestine as the only suitable destination for both Jewish labor and capital.[7]

This "prognostic" Zionism also prescribed the future role of the Poalei Tsiyon party in Palestine. It should limit itself to political struggle against the Jewish bourgeoisie; by the same token it should avoid collaborating with the bourgeois Zionists in building up Palestine. The party should limit itself to propaganda and agitation (called liberating or *bafrayende* functions). It should convince the Jewish workers in Palestine of the primacy of class struggle, urge them to unite with their Arab brothers and reject the nefarious leadership of the Histadrut. One important goal was to recruit the starry-eyed idealists of the He-Halutz (Pioneer) movement, who would inevitably become disappointed with the bitter reality of capitalist Palestine. But the party should avoid following in the footsteps of the Right. It should take no part in "constructive Zionism." Constructive (*shafnde*) functions—building up the economy, creating an infrastructure—were to be left to the capitalists. The Histadrut stood accused of having repudiated Borochov's legacy.

That Borochov himself significantly revised his approach, especially toward

the end of his life, did not especially trouble Jacob Zerubavel and the other leaders of the LPZ. As Zerubavel explained in 1920:

> For us it is totally unimportant what Borochov said on a particular occasion and
> what he did at some other time. Because we're not concerned with Borochov as an
> individual . . . We're concerned with that Borochov who became the flesh and blood
> of the Poalei Tsiyon movement. Holy to us is that Borochov who is the personifica-
> tion of the Poalei Tsiyon idea, Borochovism, the highest expression of our party's
> self image.[8]

Central to Zerubavel's "Poalei Tsiyon" idea was the highly complex interre-
lationship between the *do* and the *dortn*, the diaspora and Palestine. This made
the LPZ unique among Jewish parties in interwar Poland. Some parties, such as
the Bund, focused on the diaspora. Other groups, such as He-Halutz, focused almost exclusively on Palestine. Still others ceded ideological primacy to Palestine
but nonetheless mounted major efforts in Poland. Examples include the General
Zionists and even the Right Poalei Tsiyon. What made the LPZ different was its
determination to combine the *do* and the *dortn* in a complex, mutually reinforc-
ing relationship. The LPZ emphatically rejected any suggestion that the Yishuv
was "better" than the diaspora community, or that the labor movement in Palestine had a right to dictate to the Jewish workers in the diaspora. Indeed, as we
have seen, this was a major reason for the split in 1920. It followed that the LPZ
became a fervently Yiddishist party. To bring Palestine and the diaspora together
required a commitment to Yiddish. After all, why erect a linguistic and cultural
barrier between Palestine and the Jewish workers in the diaspora? Why cripple
the Jewish worker by depriving him of his mother tongue?[9]

The LPZ, Palestine, and the Soviet Union

As "Our Program" had predicted, growing immigration restrictions elsewhere
forced an ever greater proportion of Jewish immigration into Palestine by the
early 1930s; the LPZ saw this as a clear vindication of its prognostic Zionism.[10]
But it is important to stress that most of the LPZ leadership never envisaged a
day when Palestine would house the majority of the Jewish people. Those in the
LPZ believed that even after the development of a strong territorial center in
Palestine (with the help of the world revolution, of course), most Jews would
still live in the diaspora. The Jewish workers in the diaspora and in Palestine

would then help each other. What the Palestinian movement had to realize, said LPZ luminaries, was that it was pointless to rely on the Balfour Declaration or on British promises. Britain would easily betray the Jewish workers; only the victory of the world revolution, led by Moscow, would provide the requisite guarantee of a successful Jewish presence in Palestine.

During the interwar period, the party press continued to hammer away at the Histadrut and mainstream labor Zionist leadership. LPZ bitterly attacked a lynchpin of Histadrut policy in the Yishuv, *avoda ivrit*, reliance on Jewish labor. In almost every issue of the *Arbeter tsaytung*, the party's main organ, articles warned about the dire consequences of boycotting Arab labor. This could only alienate Arab workers, push them into the arms of the feudal effendis and fuel anti-Jewish terrorism. The Jewish workers had to bring the Arabs into the Jewish economy and integrate them into a future revolutionary, binational socialist Palestine.[11]

The LPZ also maintained its unrelenting attack on the Histadrut's role in *binyan ha'aretz*, the building up of the Yishuv. This rejection of constructivist socialism also determined the party's ambivalent stand toward He-Halutz, the umbrella organization for pioneering Zionist youth in Poland.[12] Many articles in the party press stressed that proletarian Jewish youth had no place in He-Halutz. The LPZ attacked the organization for strikebreaking, for undercutting the wages of Jewish workers, and for bourgeois romanticism that had no place in a proletarian movement. On the other hand, the party faced constant pressure from within its ranks, and especially from younger members, for a more sympathetic attitude toward He-Halutz.

In short, throughout most of the interwar period, the LPZ found it much easier to engage in left-wing protest politics in Poland than to develop a coherent plan of action regarding Palestine. To the growing dismay of many party members, Palestine remained an abstract plank, a bloodless goal somewhere on the far horizon. The party devoted most of its activity to Poland and fastened more and more of its hopes on the Soviet Union.

Therefore, the LPZ was a very pro-Soviet party; its support of the Soviet Union caused it constant persecution at the hands of the Polish police.[13] To read the party press on the Soviet Union was to delve into a case study of political schizophrenia. Even after the last vestiges of the Poalei Tsiyon were banned in the USSR in 1928, the *Arbeter tsaytung* sang the praises of the USSR. It took the LPZ a full year to distance itself from the purge trials in Moscow; meanwhile the *Arbeter tsaytung* published labored accounts about how Soviet former leaders

Grigori Zinoviev and Lev Kamenev might well have been Gestapo agents![14] The *Arbeter tsaytung* was full of enthusiasm for the Stakhanovite movement, for the Stalin constitution and for the Five-Year Plans, even as Communist thugs harassed LPZ meetings and rallies. On the other hand, the LPZ condemned Communist support of Arab terror in Palestine, the policies of the Jewish section of the Soviet Communist Party (the Evsektsiia), and the attitudes of the KPP (Polish Communist Party) in Poland toward the Jewish problem.

For the LPZ, the Soviet Union was a vital link in an ideological triangle that consisted of the USSR, the rest of the diaspora (especially Poland, which boasted the largest LPZ organization), and Palestine. Thus, the internal political dynamics of the party were always closely linked to what was happening in the USSR. This ideology was a great source of optimism. Heartened by the double determinism of Marxism and Borochovism, the party faithful could shrug off defeats at the polls, the growing harassment by the Polish police, the jeers and taunts of powerful opponents like the Bund, the Communists, and the Right Poalei Tsiyon.

But this source of strength was also a source of weakness. Ideological reliance on "inevitable processes" raised the obvious question of how to reconcile determinism and political action. As the Yishuv grew and as Palestine became the major destination of Jewish emigration, the LPZ ran the risk of losing members to other parties and groups (like the Right Poalei Tsiyon and He-Halutz) that actively encouraged *aliyah* and could promise some emigration certificates in the bargain. But a more activist stance on Palestine also risked pushing other members into the hands of the Communists. The ideological balance came at a price, but was central to the identity of the movement. Only when the perception of the Soviet Union changed in the late 1930s was the party ready to revise its thinking.

The LPZ and the Bund

The party in Poland overwhelmingly supported the Left; indeed throughout the interwar period the Polish party was the largest LPZ party in the world. The foundation had been laid during the First World War, when the party built a strong base with its network of schools and soup kitchens. In the 1920s, LPZ established a solid presence in the Jewish labor unions.[15] It built a popular sports organization, the Stern, and a dedicated youth movement, Yugnt.[16] Together with the Bund, the LPZ played a major role in the CYSHO (Central Yiddish School Organization) and maintained its own Borochov schools within CYSHO.[17] Although the party's main strength was in mid-sized provincial towns, the LPZ nonetheless garnered strong support in Lodz and Warsaw, especially in the late 1920s.[18]

True to its Borochovist ideology, the LPZ threw itself into the struggle for secular Yiddish culture. In 1926 and again in 1931 it organized proletarian culture congresses that sparked intense discussions about the role of sports, libraries, and theaters in working-class life.[19] Two of its younger intellectuals, Raphael Mahler and Emanuel Ringelblum, helped run the party's major cultural organization, the Gezelshaft ovntkursn far arbeter (Society for Evening Courses for Workers), which the Polish police closed down in 1934. These two young historians also were active in the historical section of the Yiddish Scientific Institute (YIVO), and Ringelblum, especially, defended the YIVO from more radical elements in the party who suspected it of putting pure research ahead of the political needs of the radical Left. There was, of course a direct link between the YIVO tradition and Ringelblum's Oneg Shabes archive in the Warsaw ghetto.[20] In short, what the party lacked in numbers was partly compensated for by the dedication and idealism of its members. Where did this dedication come from? What niche did the LPZ occupy in the spectrum of left-wing politics in Jewish Poland? The LPZ attracted those workers and radical intellectuals who, but for Ber Borochov and Palestine, could have easily have found their way to the KPP. Indeed, in 1920–1923, the LPZ would have readily joined the Comintern had Moscow shown even the slightest hint of flexibility about the Communist Party's Palestine platform.[21] Like the Bund, the LPZ served its members' needs not only politically but also by creating a rich organizational life.

Not surprisingly, the LPZ saw its major opponent throughout the interwar period as the Bund. Hostility was mixed with a certain amount of grudging respect. The two parties worked together in the CYSHO and when important Bundist leaders died, there were eloquent obituaries in the *Arbeter tsaytung*.[22] On occasion, the two parties collaborated politically, as in the elections to the Lodz city council in 1936.[23] But there were also sharp differences. The LPZ saw the Polish Socialist Party (PPS) as chauvinistic, while the Bund cooperated with it. As for the Second International, the LPZ lambasted it as opportunist, while the Bund joined it in 1930.[24] And, of course, the two parties differed over attitudes toward the Soviet Union. In the LPZ press, the Bund was always depicted as a party that had no real ideology, except for an amorphous *doigkayt*. It was a totally opportunistic party, without principles, ready to latch on to any issue that would attract votes.[25] Reading between the lines, however, one senses great frustration over the fact that since the Bund had a much simpler ideology than the LPZ, it could be much more flexible, and appear more focused and better positioned to reach out beyond the working-class vote.[26]

The debate with the Bund was not about tactics alone. The two parties had fundamentally different interpretations of the Jewish problem. For the Bund, the Jewish problem was, in essence, political. Civil rights, socialism, full democracy, and cultural autonomy would suffice. The Jews were part of the country where they lived, and were linked to its economy. There was neither a separate Jewish economy nor was there an international Jewish question.[27] As for emigration, the Bund recognized it as an individual right and indeed maintained an emigration bureau. On the other hand, the Bund rejected making emigration a national goal.[28] The LPZ disagreed. Following Borochov, the LPZ argued, as we have seen, that the Jewish problem was not only political. It was also economic and existential. Without a territory of their own, Jews could not control the nerve centers of the economy. They were pushed away from primary industries and large factories and exiled to the weaker tertiary sector. But tailors and shoemakers had little political power. After all, railroad workers could shut down an economy. Tailors couldn't. Ultimately, the autochthonous population would begin to push Jews out of the tertiary sector as well.

Thus, for those in the LPZ, emigration was a central fact of Jewish life; unlike the Bund, the LPZ saw the Jewish question as an international issue. But in the long run, only emigration to Palestine could offer a long-term solution, not because all Jews would go there, but because only in Palestine could they create a natural, healthy economic structure that would provide a "strategic base" for Jews in the diaspora. The strategic base would help radicalize the Jewish workers in the diaspora. In turn, world revolution, led by the USSR, would expel the British from Palestine and establish a socialist, binational state. Thus, diaspora and Palestine were intertwined.

In the ideology of the LPZ, Palestine was vital for other reasons as well. Only a territorial base could guarantee the effective modernization of Jewish society and the Yiddish language that would transform Jewish life in the diaspora. Nathan Buchsbaum emphasized how the interrelated processes of emigration and developing of a territorial center would power the development of new models of Jewish life. The great Jewish communities in the United States and the new Jewish society that was developing in Palestine were creating new cultural paradigms that were needed to break the hold of tradition and *shtetl* culture on the Jewish masses in Poland. According to the LPZ, the Bund betrayed the inadequacy of its ideology by not understanding this link between emigration, territorialization, and modernization.[29]

Drawing heavily on the cultural writings of Ber Borochov, the young historian Raphael Mahler made a similar argument with regard to language. The Yiddish of the *shtetl* was poor and underdeveloped. The Yiddish of a locomotive driver or of a steelworker would "obviously" be richer and more creative than the Yiddish of a small town shoemaker. Without the prospect of a territorial base, there were limits to the development of the Yiddish language. Mahler's article was written in a manner to suggest that Birobidzhan could indeed serve as an acceptable territorial center and even as a substitute for Palestine.[30]

The Bund fought back with a number of points. Palestine was a pipe dream, economically not viable. Bundist polemicists such as Victor Alter and Jacob Lestchinsky criticized Borochov's fundamental diagnosis of the Jewish question. What was wrong, after all, with being a tailor? A Jewish tailor was no worse than a Polish coal miner. To bemoan the "abnormality" of Jewish occupations betrayed self-hatred.[31] Alter also took aim at a weak point in Borochov's diagnosis: Jewish social mobility in the West. There was nothing wrong with the sons of workers becoming doctors, lawyers, and white-collar workers. There was nothing "unhealthy" about it. Although the Bund admitted the worsening economic plight of Polish Jewry in the 1930s, it took sharp issue with the LPZ diagnosis of the problem. Bundist publications emphasized glimmers of hope. According to Alter, Polish Jews were waging—and slowly winning—a tough war of economic self-defense. They were moving into big cities like Warsaw and Lodz and even into Western Poland; there they were carving out new economic positions. Building on the arguments made by Jacob Lestchinsky in the late 1920s, Alter also stressed that Jews were indeed becoming proletarianized. Traditional prejudices were falling away, and Jews were determined to move into factory work.[32]

Rebutting Alter's arguments, Yitzhak Lev, the LPZ's main polemicist against the Bund in this sphere, emphasized that instead of looking at the city, one had to focus on the *shtetl*. It was in the decline of the Jewish *shtetl* that Borochov's analysis was being borne out. Furthermore, Alter was misinterpreting the significance of Jewish urbanization. The Jewish percentage of the urban population was constantly falling, and the Jewish occupational structure in big cities betrayed growing economic weakness, not strength. There was greater concentration in smaller enterprises in the traditionally Jewish occupations, and a growing Jewish influx into cottage industry.[33] In its polemics with the Bund, the LPZ suffered from an obvious disadvantage. How does one fight for the rights of the Jewish working class in Poland if, at the same time one is talking about long-term processes that marginalize the Jewish workers in the diaspora? The Bund asked how parties like the LPZ could fight revisionist leader Vladimir Jabotinsky's call for evacuation and then talk about the inevitable need for emigration? The LPZ replied by stressing its basic theme—the link between the *do* and the *dortn*. Only tough Marxist struggle would defend the working class, both here in Poland, and there against the opportunistic Mapai (the dominant non-Marxist socialist party of the Yishuv) and the bourgeois Zionists. Not all Jewish workers would end up in Palestine, but a strategic base in Palestine would greatly help the Jewish workers' struggle in the diaspora. Obviously, this was not a simple message to understand.

In its polemics with the Bund, the LPZ relied heavily on the experience of the USSR. Here the chief villain was the Evsektsiia, the Jewish section of the Communist Party. Until its dissolution in 1930, the Evsektsiia, according to numerous articles in the LPZ press, had advocated nothing more than applied Bundism.[34] It, too, had believed that once the Jews achieved equal rights in a socialist society, their economic problems could be easily solved through free migration, retraining, and a voluntary shift to other economic sectors. But the Soviet government had finally recognized the bankruptcy of the Evsektsiia line and offered Birobidzhan, the territory in the Soviet far east. Although it obviously was no substitute for Palestine, Birobidzhan, in the view of the LPZ, constituted a Soviet admission that Borochov had been right all along. While civic equality in a socialist state could solve the Jewish problem on an individual basis, it begged the national issue.[35] Without a territory, the Jews would assimilate. Indeed, the dynamic process of geographic dispersion and economic mobility of Soviet Jewry was dispersing the previously compact communities in the Pale and weakening the base for Jewish culture. So the Bundist slogan of extraterritorial autonomy did little to solve the national question. One could put this in another way: the Bund's failure to address the territorial issue would leave the Jewish working class gravely weakened, even after a socialist victory.[36]

But developments in the Soviet Union, especially the Birobidzhan issue, confronted the LPZ with knotty ideological problems. In the eyes of many party members, the early promise of Birobidzhan, coupled with the rise to power of Hitler, made the Soviet Union seem all the more attractive and important. In 1934, Jacob Zerubavel published a series of theoretical articles in the *Arbeter tsaytung* that set off a sharp debate.[37] The articles were a response to calls coming from within the party—in both Palestine and Poland—for more active involvement in the problems of the Yishuv. The specific catalyst for Zerubavel's articles was a broadside issued by Ze'ev Abramovich, one of the leaders of the Palestinian party. Abramovich had sarcastically noted that the LPZ threw itself into practically every cause except that of Palestine. Palestine was an afterthought, a "dessert" (*lekekhl*) that had little impact on the party's day-to-day life. Abramovich attacked the bedrock of the LPZ's ideology, the *do/dortn* synthesis. It was time to say openly and clearly that the purpose of political struggle in the diaspora was to prepare Jewish workers for emigration to Palestine.[38]

Zerubavel responded with a vengeance. In his articles he reaffirmed the *do/dortn* synthesis and equated "Palestinocentrism" with a betrayal of the movement's principles. Palestine was indeed important to the movement, but no more so than the diaspora. The LPZ should resist Abramovich's heresy. There was no reason to change course, no cause to turn the party into an "emigration bureau" for Palestine and succumb to national romanticism. Jews would go to Palestine because of objective economic developments. The Great Depression, Zerubavel argued, had done more for emigration to Palestine than decades of Zionist propaganda. The job of the party in Palestine was not to participate in illusions of *binyan ha-aretz*, the building up of the land, but to radicalize the Jewish working class and undermine the petit bourgeois fantasies of He-Halutz.

This in itself was nothing new. But Zerubavel then went on to talk about the significance of Birobidzhan. It demonstrated, he emphasized, the far-reaching possibilities for productivization and social transformation (*umshikhtung*) of the Jews that existed in a truly socialist state. Building the territorial center in Palestine and transforming the Jewish people in the diaspora were simultaneous processes. They were also of equal value and significance. Here Zerubavel stressed the principle of "everywhereness" (*umetumikayt*). Transformation was taking place everywhere: Palestine was an important part, but hardly the central part, of a worldwide process. The articles drove home Zerubavel's main point—the fate of the Jewish people was being determined in the Soviet Union. These articles cut to the bone. Without really undertaking a major revision of party ideology, Zerubavel made it clear that the Soviet Union was decisive. But if that was the case, what indeed was the point of Palestine, especially now that the Jews had received a territory in Birobidzhan? Zerubavel did not flinch. If the territorial base could be achieved in Birobidzhan, so be it. Meanwhile, Zerubavel himself packed his bags and left for Palestine in 1935!

Other party veterans were quick to attack Zerubavel, and in 1934 and 1935 an intense and fateful debate took place in the party press. While several party stalwarts took issue with Zerubavel, they did not agree among themselves. Nahum

Nir-Rafalkes in Palestine, and Bezalel Sherman, the leader of the American wing of the Left Poalei Tsiyon, harshly criticized Zerubavel for blurring the line between the LPZ and the Communist Party. If the Jewish question could be solved in the diaspora through Communist territorialism, what was the point of a separate party? To paraphrase Nir-Rafalkes, you go to Palestine, good luck to you, I'll work here. "That attitude threatened the liquidation of the party."[39] Sherman responded to Zerubavel with a sharp reminder that things were not as rosy in the Soviet Union as he seemed to think. Birobidzhan was, when all was said and done, a failure. Soviet Jewry was rapidly dispersing and assimilating.[40] But both Sherman and Nir walked a fine line. While they warned against the "liquidationist" danger lurking in Zerubavel's approach, they also reiterated their opposition to Abramovich's call for Palestinocentrism.

The Polish party now faced a full-fledged crisis. On one hand, there were wholesale defections to the Communist Party, especially from within the LPZ's youth organization. On the other hand, there were growing calls for a more positive stance toward Palestine. The leader of the Palestine "activists" within the Polish party was Yitzhak Lev, a genuinely popular figure who was a fixture on the Warsaw City Council. While Lev did not go as far as Abramovich, he nonetheless attacked the LPZ's leadership for excessive passivity on the Palestine question. It was time to wake up and realize what was happening in Europe. Zerubavel's analysis of the Jewish situation in the diaspora was nonsense. Where Zerubavel saw "productivization" and "social transformation," Lev saw rapid economic and political decline. Lev was even more skeptical than Nir and Sherman about the situation of Soviet Jewry and more insistent on making Palestine into a priority. Soviet Jewry was perpetuating the old Jewish problem of an "abnormal" economic structure by flooding into white-collar jobs and the bureaucracy. This, in turn, exacerbated the ugly problem of anti-Semitism within the USSR. It was time to openly work in favor of *aliyah*. The party had to remember its fundamental purpose. There had been too much ideological rigidity. The negative developments in the USSR, the Depression, and the rise of Hitler made it all the more urgent for the party to snap out of its torpor and begin to stress Palestine as a major focus of political effort.[41] There was yet another point to consider. The lessons of Hitler's rise to power showed that Marxist parties had to put political realism ahead of ideological purity. They had to reach out to the large strata of the lower middle class and petite bourgeoisie. The LPZ was paying a high price for its ideological orthodoxy. By sharpening its focus on Palestine, the LPZ could begin to reach out to the Jewish lower middle classes and especially to the youth who were flocking to He-Halutz.[42]

Lev was alienated enough to split the Polish Party at the end of 1934.[43] Until his group rejoined the party the following year, he put out his own newspaper, *Arbeter vort*. One article in *Arbeter vort*, by Ze'ev Abramovich, featured a pointed commentary on Borochov's famous 1917 speech, in which he seemed to be calling for more voluntarism and a more active role of the workers in the building up of Palestine.[44] The party, Abramovich argued, had to rethink its ideological distinction between "liberating" and "constructive" work in Palestine.

The split plunged the Polish Party into a deep crisis. Membership plummeted, as internecine conflict took its toll. The party's financial position went from bad to worse, and for much of 1936, *Arbeter tsaytung* did not appear. Zerubavel's own decision to settle in Palestine made matters even more desperate. By 1936, the party's fortunes were so low that even Lev's opponents began to call for a re-unification. After the reunification that year, the LPZ began a slow recovery and began to take a new course.[45] The party now began to move toward much greater involvement with Palestine, a process that culminated with the 1937 decision to rejoin the World Zionist Organization.[46] Several external events pushed the party towards a more activist Zionist identity. Probably the most decisive development was growing disappointment in the USSR. The truth about the purge trials finally began to penetrate the party press just as news came that Stalin had liquidated the local leadership in Birobidzhan.[47] Another factor that brought a new influx of members into the party was Stalin's decision to liquidate the KPP in 1938. At the same time that the LPZ was absorbing the impact of the news coming from the USSR, important developments in Palestine were pushing the party toward changing long-held positions. The 1937 Peel Commission report held out, for a short time, the hope of Jewish statehood. The prospects of basic changes in the status of the Yishuv and the need to take a stand on the issue of partitioning Palestine reminded the party leadership that it might be time to end the boycott of the World Zionist Congress. When a delegation of the LPZ arrived in Palestine to take part in the tenth world conference of the movement in December 1937, it received red carpet treatment from the leadership of the Histadrut, including a far-ranging tour of the Yishuv. Even convinced leftists like Shakhne Zagan and Nathan Buchsbaum returned to Poland full of enthusiasm for the achievements of the Yishuv; it seems that an important psychological barrier between the LPZ and the Yishuv had been pierced.[48] Now the party press talked about "Erets Yisroel" rather than "Palestine."

The shelving of the Peel Commission report, the Arab Revolt, and growing fear that Britain would betray the Yishuv brought the LPZ even closer to the mainstream Zionist labor movement. The LPZ stressed that it was not suspending its fight against the Zionist bourgeoisie or the Mapai, but in face of the common danger, it was time to end the old policy of haughty isolation.[49] By the same token, the LPZ began to revise its stance of hostility toward the Histadrut and the Right Poalei Tsiyon. In the fall of 1938, the LPZ joined the Right Poalei Tsiyon in a "Workers Conference for Erets Yisroel." In the opinion of Dr. Garncarska-Kadari, the party was rapidly moving toward a reunion with the Right Poalei Tsiyon on the eve of the war.[50] As the Bund stepped up its attacks on Palestine and began to enjoy major electoral successes, the LPZ became more defiant.[51] In the face of growing adversity, the LPZ press took a much more forceful line in defending the Zionist enterprise. Confronted by great Bundist victories at the polls, the LPZ leaders repeated Borochov's old dictum: "It's hard to be a member of the Poalei Tsiyon" (echoing the well-known Yiddish phrase, *"s'iz shver tsu zayn a Yid,"* or "it's hard to be a Jew"). That is, one could not accuse the LPZ of taking the easy road. It rejoined the World Zionist Organization in the middle of the Arab Revolt, and just when the Bund was winning major victories at the polls![52]

Zerubavel, Buchsbaum, and others took an almost perverse pride in the party's difficulties. After all, they were convinced that Borochov was right, and that eventually the Jewish worker would see the light. This defiance reached new heights after the issuance of the White Paper in 1939, when the party drew even closer to the Zionist mainstream. Whether in the long run the party's new attitude toward the Zionist movement would have brought it more popularity is moot point since the war began in 1939.

One should not judge the LPZ solely on the basis of its performance at the polls. On the eve of the war it was showing signs of rebirth. But more to the point, it was a party that not only gave Zionism a place on the radical left, but also attracted a cadre of loyal and selfless followers whose impact was far greater than their numbers. To cite one example, Emanuel Ringelblum, Adolph Berman, and Shakhne Zagan played major roles in the Warsaw Ghetto's political and cultural life.

As Professor Arcadius Kahan once wrote, in interwar Poland, ideological radicalism often had a positive side: it imparted hope and inspired the energy to fight back against seemingly hopeless odds. This too was an indisputable legacy of the LPZ.

6

Imitation, Rejection, Cooperation

Agudat Yisrael and the Zionist Movement in Interwar Poland

IT IS A COMMONPLACE THAT the Agudat Yisrael movement arose out of the struggle between European Jewish orthodoxy and the Zionist movement.[1] Among the founders of Agudat Yisrael were those who had resigned from the Zionist movement in protest against the decision of the tenth World Zionist Congress (1911) to embark on educational-cultural activity in the diaspora. With the founding of Aguda, a worldwide organization of Orthodox Jews, the struggle with Zionism moved from a stage of sporadic, local manifestations of opposition to a stage of international coordination.[2] Agudat Yisrael rejected entirely the basic concepts of secular Zionism, namely that the Jewish people is a nation like all other nations, and that the Jewish national movement must act out of a neutral stance toward religious matters.[3] Similarly, Aguda rejected the position of religious Zionism that it was possible for religious Jews to work within the framework of the World Zionist Organization to promote religious interests and protect the traditions of the nation.

Alongside this image of Agudat Yisrael as the polar opposite of Zionism, however, we find quite different descriptions of that same movement. Take, for example, the words of Dr. Ignacy (Yitzhak) Shvartzbart, a leader of Polish Zionism in the interwar period who also served as a deputy to the Polish Sejm (parliament):

> [A] few words about the "Aguda"—it began out of struggle with the Zionist "criminals." Then the Agudists, step by step, adopted the organizational forms of

the Zionist movement—instead of "hadarim" [traditional religious elementary schools] they founded schools, instead of fighting against women's participation in public life they founded their own women's organizations, instead of fighting against the international organization of Jewry they founded their own international organization, instead of struggle against Congresses they held conventions, instead of a struggle against secularization they slowly left the walls of the ghetto and ran candidates in the elections for municipal councils and for the Sejm. In short, there was no small amount of secularization in the forms of daily activity.[4]

In Shvartzbart's view, Aguda appeared as an imitation, almost a twin of the Zionist movement. We encounter similar tones from another quarter: from Aguda's rivals on the right within the Orthodox camp, who bitterly criticized Aguda for betraying the very ideals it had entered the political fray to defend.[5]

Spokesmen for Agudat Yisrael, acutely sensitive to these words of "praise" from Zionists and right-wing orthodoxy, made every effort to stress the clear boundaries they had set for themselves when adopting the techniques of ideological rivals:

> [W]ith regard to innovations and changes in Torah and tradition, in any law or custom of our law books, Aguda has drawn a line in all of its activities, that clever saying "hadash [that which is new] is forbidden from the Torah."[6] Regarding external and technical means by which the Torah is protected from this forbidden innovation . . . Aguda takes up all the external, modern means that the various secular parties have taken up in order to fight . . . against the rule of Torah . . . in order to protect itself with their very weapons. Organization, literature, press, public speeches, propaganda, lectures, conventions, order, planning and strategy—for orthodox Jews of the older generation all these are "news" . . . but in a time like this, in the war for the Torah we must arm ourselves with the means that our enemies use against us.[7]

Here we find an explicit admission that Aguda had adopted the tools of its rivals, but for lack of alternatives and out of a perfectly justifiable desire for self-defense. We also note in passing the clear generational difference suggested; the older generation evinces hesitation about the entry into politics and the use of political techniques, while it is assumed that the younger generation would take to politics much more naturally.

From the perspective of nearly ninety years since Aguda's founding, the phenomenon of imitation does not seem surprising at all, for two reasons. Chronologically, the Orthodox were the last sector of the Jewish public to organize politically, and did so, for the most part, as a reaction to initiatives by secular groups. This meant that the forms of organization, the rhetoric of politics, and the ways of influencing Jewish opinion had already been set out. Orthodox Jewry had little choice but to adapt itself to prevailing conditions. In addition, the founders of Agudat Yisrael included people who had broken with the Zionist movement after years of participation. It was inevitable that they would bring with them ways of thinking, perspectives, and ideological frameworks that had developed in the Zionist context, even if now the aim was to combat those tendencies.

Nevertheless, the dimensions and nature of the imitation are worthy of attention, for the adoption of techniques and approaches of the Zionist movement (and, less frequently, those of the socialist Bund) touched almost every aspect of the organizational life of Agudat Yisrael, beginning with the supreme body of the movement, the Kenessia Gedola, as an answer to the Zionist Congress, and ending with the educational system, Aguda youth movements, training (*hakhshara*) farms for immigrants to Palestine, and a party daily newspaper.

The title of this chapter draws its inspiration in part from Ahad Haam's noted essay "Imitation and Assimilation."[8] In his essay, Ahad Haam examines the relationship between Jews and the surrounding gentile society, but it is possible to discern similar processes at work in the relations between various groups within Jewry that struggled for hegemony on the "Jewish street." Within this general framework, relations between Agudat Yisrael and the Zionist movement are of a special nature. The activities of Aguda reflect a delicate balance between imitation and rejection (rather than assimilation). On the one hand, Aguda adopted the modus operandi of its rival, but, on the other, it would immediately append to any imitation some form of rejection of that same rival, thus trying to clarify the difference between the two movements.

There are three discernable modes of imitation (although the differences between them are not sharply defined and there is some overlap). They are imitation with a concerted attempt to show difference, competitive imitation, and preventative imitation.

In the first type of imitation, Agudists admitted that they were adopting the methods of the Zionists, but would immediately add a crucial clarification, according to which the adoption of Zionist methods was partial at best. According to the spokesmen of the movement, the orthodox successfully "filtered" the Zionist methods in order to prevent the incursion, in their view, of destructive values into the Orthodox camp, and thus preserve basic values of Jewish tradition.

For example, the model for the Kenessia Gedola (the world Aguda gatherings, held in 1923, 1929, and 1937 during the interwar period) was without doubt the Zionist Congress, and this was not denied. Instead, Aguda spokesmen drew attention to the different nature of Aguda's conventions and conferences. Who were the figures that graced the dais with their presence? They were noted rabbinical scholars and Hasidic rebbes. Yes, there were political speeches at these conventions, but they were always laced with words of Torah, sayings of the Sages, or Hasidic stories. One observer at the national conference of Agudat Yisrael in Poland noted that the speeches heard there were more like rabbinical sermons than political speeches. Although in the eyes of the outside observer this was a blemish that demonstrated the "outmoded" nature of Aguda, it was for the spokesmen of the movement a badge of honor.[9]

The very organization of Aguda as a political party is another example that shows the adoption of the methods of the Zionists and others. Aguda opened branches, built an organizational framework based on a central office in Warsaw, developed a notion of membership similar to the Zionist *shekel* (the largely symbolic membership dues), and even adopted democratic ideas. Up to this point the two movements are indeed similar, but Agudists would always point out that for them, democracy was not a supreme ideal. Though Aguda would claim at the outset of its political activity that it represented the silent majority of Polish Jewry, when election results belied this claim, party spokesmen retreated to an ideological "fall-back position" that their organization spoke for a qualitative majority—those Jews still steeped in ancestral tradition. In reality, and stemming from ideological principles, Agudat Yisrael was democratic in only a limited sense. It was a "directed democracy," under the supreme authority of the Torah Sages (*gedolei ha'Torah*). Aguda's spokesmen noted with pride that the sages provided Aguda with a "safety net" that secular parties did not possess. Unbridled democracy could lead to people and their leaders being swept up in the emotions of the moment and acting rashly. The advice of the rabbis and their ongoing supervision prevented this in Agudat Yisrael.[10]

The first attempt to found an Orthodox daily newspaper in Poland preceded the founding of Agudat Yisrael by several years. With the inspiration and support of the Gerer Rebbe, head of the largest Hasidic group in interwar Poland, the first orthodox paper was established in 1907 out of a desire to provide the Orthodox public with a "kosher" newspaper. In the interwar period, circles close to Aguda (but not the party itself in an official capacity) published a daily in Warsaw —for the first ten years under the title *Der Yid*, afterward under the title *Dos Yidishe Togblat*.[11] Thus, Aguda behaved like its rivals on the "Jewish street," all of whom regarded a party daily as a necessary tool for spreading the message of the party. But here, too, Aguda took pains to show its uniqueness. Of course Aguda's daily had no gossip or immodest material as in other newspapers, but that was taken for granted. The main difference from other party dailies was not in the content of the paper, although that was important, but in the attitude to the newspaper. The leaders of Aguda, including the rabbis, would urge the party's members and supporters to read the paper and subscribe to it, but in the end, they regarded the paper as an after-the-fact (*be'diavad*) concession to reality, and not an ideal. Reading the party's newspaper could never be regarded as a religious obligation (*mitzvah*), and reading the paper should never be at the expense of Torah study. Aguda members should not read the paper on Sabbaths or holidays.[12]

Agudat Yisrael also absorbed the approach of its secular rivals regarding the issue of Jewish nationalism. Aguda accepted the notion of Jewish nationalism and the concomitant call for national-minority rights (even if its representatives would express this demand in a more moderate manner).[13] This process took place despite the fact that rabbinical figures associated with Aguda often denounced nationalism as the second great "wrong turn" of the Jewish people in the modern era, with the Berlin Haskalah (Enlightenment) being the first.[14] The political activists of Agudat Yisrael, whether they struggled on the international level against the Zionist movement or the Jewish Agency for Palestine or on the national level in Poland against the Zionists and the Bund, used the accepted political terminology and spoke of the Jews as a national group. Alongside these national declarations, however, they would append some caveat, such as, "Our nationality is not a standard nationality, for it is based on the Torah, and the Torah is the basis of our national existence." With all the qualifications, though, it is clear that the secular movements set the rules for the Jewish political game at the beginning of the twentieth century. The representatives of Agudat Yisrael joined the playing field late in the game, and played according to the rules in force, where the national idea was paramount. Once involved, Agudat Yisrael would not retreat, even when conditions were distinctly disadvantageous from its point of view. Among the Jewish political movements, only the Bund would withdraw for some years from communal (*kehilla*) politics for ideological reasons. The Orthodox Agudat Yisrael could not take a similar step, and even under the most adverse circumstances did not follow the example of the separatist Orthodox communities of Frankfurt-am-Main or of Hungary, which refused to participate in a united communal body with Reform Jews.

As Ahad Haam explains competitive imitation in his essay, one imitates one's rival with the expressed intention of struggling with him.[15] It is also possible to see this as inspiration that one's rival can provide. In the case of Agudat Yisrael, we can point to several instances where the Zionist rival provided such inspiration:

The central Zionist principle that an overarching interest of achieving a refuge for Jews in the Land of Israel unites all Jews in the world found an echo or parallel in the major idea of Agudat Yisrael. According to Aguda's view, an "ecumenical" orthodox interest (in Menahem Friedman's terminology[16]) outweighs any particularistic interest of one group or another in the Orthodox world. First and foremost, opposing groups—Hasidim and Misnagdim, Germans and Hungarians, Poles and Rumanians—must see themselves as Orthodox Jews with common interests. Zionist circles had developed the notion that in this time of emergency for the Jewish people, all sectors must cooperate despite the ideological differences between them. Agudat Yisrael and Orthodox circles adopted a similar cry that cooperation, in spite of differences of opinion, was the need of the hour.

In his efforts leading up to the first Zionist Congress, Theodor Herzl, founder of the world Zionist movement, had devoted serious efforts to attract the masses of Eastern European Jewry to his cause. He made gestures to the rabbis of Eastern Europe, hoping to arouse sympathy for the Congress and the movement.[17] The leaders of the separatist orthodoxy of Frankfurt, who were among the founders of Agudat Yisrael, did their utmost to attract those same orthodox masses and those same rabbis of Eastern Europe to their new movement. They sought to combine the organizational skills of Western Jewry with the prestige of the leading rabbis and yeshiva deans of Poland and Russia, thus carrying with them the millions of traditional Jews in Eastern Europe and depriving the secular Zionists of their most important reservoir of potential support.

The phenomenon of Jewish youth movements reached its apogee in interwar Poland. Clearly, neither the concept of teen years as a special stage in the life of young people nor psychological approaches to adolescence were acceptable in Orthodox circles.[18] Despite this, those same Orthodox circles, especially the relatively young rabbis connected to the Tzeirei Agudat Yisrael youth movement, had a sense of mission to work among the youth that came out of a desire to compete with the Zionist and socialist youth movements. Aguda received inspiration from their secular rivals, and adopted their methods, all the better to contend with them. In addition, the Orthodox youth movement helped Agudat Yisrael to show that "we have everything that they have." In a typical example of this approach, one leader of Tzeirei Agudat Yisrael compared the traditional garb of the Orthodox youth to the shirt and neckerchief "uniform" of young people in Ha'Shomer Ha'Tzair.[19] Another spokesman praised the discipline and exemplary organization of the Bund youth movement, recommending that the Tzeirei Aguda adopt similar methods.[20]

The third type of imitation is preventative, and it resembles the second in some respects. The people of Agudat Yisrael adopted methods of the Zionists in order to prevent further erosion of the Orthodox camp, lest Orthodox Jews be attracted to the Zionist movement. Preventative imitation explains many of the Aguda's activities related to the Land of Israel, especially after the Balfour Declaration of 1917. It is true that the Orthodox community exhibited great interest in the Jewish population of Palestine throughout the nineteenth century, and that the Gerer Rebbe (Rabbi Abraham Mordecai Alter), one of the leaders of Agudat Yisrael, had genuine interest in settling the Land. In fact, in the 1920s, he urged his followers to purchase land in Palestine, looking to their eventual settlement there.[21] All this, however, is insufficient to explain the intensity of activity connected to the Land of Israel in the interwar period. Aguda established an *aliyah* (immigration to Palestine) office and the Keren Ha'yishuv (Settlement Fund) as an Orthodox answer to the Jewish National Fund. These and other activities were intended to stave off further erosion of the Orthodox camp in the wake of the burst of enthusiasm that swept Eastern European Jewry after the Balfour Declaration. In a characteristic spirit of the times, the Gerer Rebbe wrote to Rabbi Yosef Yitzhak Schneerson, the Lubavitcher Rebbe, in 1922:

> [W]ho here does not know the war we had with the rabbis of Warsaw who decreed the recitation of "Hallel" [psalms of praise recited on holidays] on the day of the Balfour Declaration—the war was difficult, because the entire community was as if seized by a frenzy, and money was no object for the Zionists, and the camp of the orthodox was reduced daily by thousands and tens of thousands of pure souls who joined them [the Zionists], so then we had to save the faith with all our strength and to proclaim the fund for the Land of Israel, but only for the commandment of settling the Land without any other notion added.[22]

There was an urgent need to act; otherwise, the erosion of the Orthodox camp would continue undisturbed.

For Agudat Yisrael, preventive measures among the youth had particular importance. The leaders of Polish Zionism did not hide their view that Orthodox youth constituted a large potential reservoir for future members of Zionist youth movements of all varieties. The leaders of Tzeirei Agudat Yisrael and of Poalei

Agudat Yisrael (Aguda's workers' movement), the two sister organizations of Aguda aimed at the younger generation, invested most of their efforts to prevent Orthodox youth from defecting to the Zionists.

In regard to the symbols of Jewish tradition, the preventative measure was aimed at stopping imitation by the other side. The Agudists, foremost among them the rabbis and publicists of the movement, tried to prevent, or at least to warn against, what they saw as the "hijacking" of religious and traditional symbols by the Zionists, who made them into solely national symbols.[23] Rabbi Elhanan Wasserman mocked the changes that the Zionists had made in the commandments of the Torah:

> [T]he commandment of settling the Land of Israel is one of the holiest commandments of the Torah. The Evil Inclination foresaw that it could profit from this mitzvah [commandment], so it took it for itself as a monopoly. In order to fulfill the holy commandment, we must establish funds, whose aim is to raise Hellenists in the Land and in the Diaspora. To be worthy of settling in the Land, we must set up "hakhsharot" [training farms]. The function of the hakhsharot is not to make things kosher, ["lehakhshir" is to make kosher] but rather treif [ritually unfit for consumption]. If the halutz [pioneer] is not completely treif, the kibbutz must complete the process of being treif . . . There is a commandment to bring the first fruits. This mitzvah is not observed in the present era. But the national revival demands that we also revive the ceremonies of ancient times. They take some old man who is in place of the high priest, and in place of the priests and Levites they take some cultic prostitutes and they offer up the first fruits. There is a commandment of Torah study, so we must establish an institution of higher education, where they must study—Biblical criticism.[24]

It has often been said that imitation is the sincerest form of flattery. Agudat Yisrael may not have wanted to flatter its Zionist adversary, but the varied types of imitation demonstrate that Orthodox Jews felt a very real threat from the Zionist movement. The threat from the Bund, which may have been more worrying in the circles of Poalei Agudat Yisrael, still seemed secondary. The revolutionary rhetoric of the Bund, and even more its openly antitraditional stance, made it less of a temptation to the circles associated with Agudat Yisrael. The Zionists, on the other hand, who used the vocabulary and symbols of tradition, and who, from the 1930s onward, could offer to searching youth the increasingly attractive option of settlement in Palestine, attempted to reach some of the same constituency that Aguda saw as its own.

The historical picture is, of course, more complex than the patterns of imitation and rejection used by Agudat Yisrael and Zionism. Despite ideological rivalry and oftentimes nasty electoral campaigns, on the everyday level, the two movements engaged in continuous cooperation.[25] This in no way intends to gloss over the extreme enmity exhibited on many occasions during the interwar period. In polemical articles in the Jewish daily press (never noted for a genteel writing style), Zionist leaders denounced in vehement terms what they regarded as the outmoded politics of *shtadlanut* (intercession) of Agudat Yisrael, offering as an alternative the "new, proud politics" of the Zionists and asking the voters to give a "death-blow" to orthodoxy.[26] At the conclusion of the campaign, the dust of the polemic settled and Jewish politics returned to its daily, frustrating reality, a reality, as one historian defined it, in which "the severity of the situation stemmed not from problems of legislation, which involved limitation of rights and discrimination. The root of the evil was in the everyday reality of arbitrariness and faulty administration, against which the individual Jew stood helpless."[27] In attempting to alleviate this situation, Agudat Yisrael and the Zionists were in the same boat. They were members of the same parliamentary faction, represented each other's interests in Sejm committees, and participated in the same delegations to government ministers and provincial governors. Only the socialist Bund stuck to its ideological guns and refused to cooperate with the "bourgeois" Jewish parties. They preferred, literally, to march to their own drummer, even organizing their own marches with Polish socialists to protest Nazi Germany. The ideological "orthodoxy" of the Bund puts in perspective the relative pragmatism of Agudat Yisrael.[28]

The Agudists did not regard their cooperation with Zionists as an ideal. In Polish national politics, the two movements found themselves, for lack of an alternative, part of the lonely and frustrating struggle of Jewish politics in Poland. A basic common commitment to Jewish solidarity overcame the groups' ideological differences. They also had to work together on the intra-Jewish level, in the *kehillot*, due to the long stalemate between the various Jewish parties. No Jewish party achieved hegemony on the "Jewish street" in Poland. Each party had its centers of power (Zionists in the Sejm, Aguda in the *kehillot*, the Bund in the unions), but the internal Jewish debate would never be resolved to the advantage of any side.

In other words, with certain restrictions, Agudat Yisrael would participate in political alliances, in parliamentary factions, and in *kehilla* coalitions with its Zionist adversary. These pragmatic relations proceeded alongside a long-standing struggle on the national and international levels, where each movement staked its claim to the title of spokesman of the Jewish people. Agudat Yisrael would never give up on its demand to serve as an independent Orthodox voice (for example, at the St. James Conference organized by the British government in 1939 to bring Zionists and Arabs together). In the end, Agudat Yisrael and the Zionists in Poland would be ideological rivals, but no less were they reluctant partners.

The title of this chapter could be "acquiescence and denial," in that the national idea did indeed become the defining principle of Polish Jewry, as it did for Polish society as a whole. There may have been arguments, often bitter, about the definition of the nation, over the nature of the reborn Polish state and the exact relationships between the various groups that made up the Second Republic, but the national idea reigned supreme. Orthodox Jews, the supporters of Agudat Yisrael, did not joyfully accept the notion of Jewish nationalism, which carried more than a tinge of the secular rebellion against Jewish tradition. Yet they played along, even as they tried to stake out their own notion of the Jewish nation based on religious concepts.

Nor were the Orthodox Jews alone in this reserved acceptance of Jewish nationalism. The Bund, no less than Agudat Yisrael, trod a long and tortuous path until it adopted a pro-national position.[29] Even after that, for the Bund, class concerns and socialist ideology played roles of equal to, and perhaps of greater importance than, nationalism. The withdrawal of the Bund from *kehilla* politics in Poland for several years reflects this vacillation.

The victory of the national ideal in interwar Poland was ideologically impressive, if not complete. It should not, however, be allowed to dictate the historical narrative dealing with that period to the exclusion of other trends. As with any conclusion we might draw regarding interwar Polish Jewry, there remains a strong element of speculation as to what would have transpired had not the Holocaust wiped out most of Poland's Jews. While assimilationism as a political ideology had been discredited at the polls, processes of acculturation continued apace, and may even have accelerated under the strong influence of Polish public education and the Polish university system. Although Polish Jews—of all political stripes—had a commitment to continued group existence, they saw themselves as loyal citizens and active participants of the Polish Republic. Thus, they continued their attempts to integrate with Polish society, even though that integration was impeded by social and other forms of discrimination. Historians dealing with this period should attempt to follow these trends as well as those that focused on the Land of Israel.

MICHAEL C. STEINLAUF

7

Jewish Politics and Youth Culture in Interwar Poland:

Preliminary Evidence from the YIVO Autobiographies

IN 1932, 1934, AND 1939, the YIVO Institute (Jewish Scientific Institute), then located in Vilna, announced three autobiography contests for Jewish youth.[1] The project was the brainchild of Max Weinreich, who hoped to use the autobiographies to study the psychosocial development of Jewish youth in Poland as a means of alleviating the crisis that beset that youth. Weinreich, like the other YIVO founders, was a diaspora nationalist who sought to strengthen Jewish life and culture in Poland. What better way to accomplish this task than by strengthening Jewish youth? Alongside sections devoted to history, economics, linguistics, and literature, Weinreich founded a *yugnt forshung,* or youth studies, section at YIVO dedicated to research based on the autobiographies as well as on related materials, such as diaries and letters, that YIVO had also begun to collect.[2]

Those submitting autobiographies had to be between sixteen and twenty-two years of age. They were promised anonymity and encouraged to write candidly. The prizes, considering contemporary Jewish poverty, were attractive; first prize, for example, was 150 zlotys or about 30 dollars. Also attractive was the possibility of being honored by YIVO, which for many Polish Jews represented the pinnacle of modern Jewish cultural achievement. The first autobiographies competition, limited in outreach to Vilna and its environs, yielded 34 documents; the second competition yielded 252, and the third, whose winners were to be announced on September 1, 1939, had yielded several hundred autobiographies by the time war broke out.

After the war, a portion of the autobiographies was discovered by the American army in Germany and returned to YIVO in New York. The collection at YIVO currently includes 386 documents, some incomplete and damaged. Several more autobiographies have been discovered among the YIVO materials recently recovered from Vilnius. The majority of the autobiographies are in Yiddish; a significant number, about eighty, are in Polish, and about a dozen are in Hebrew. The average length of the autobiographies is sixty handwritten, notebook-sized pages. About ninety of the autobiographies were written by young women. The great majority of writers came from working-class and lower middle-class backgrounds.[3]

A flyer announcing the contest sketches the following guidelines:

> Each writer has complete liberty in the choice and arrangement of material. We mention, however, several points it would be good to touch upon: You and your family. Relations among family members. The war years. Teachers, schools and what they have given you. Male friends, female friends and your relationships with them. Youth organizations. Life in a political party and what it has given you. How did you decide on a trade or how are you going about deciding on one. What event in your life has made the greatest impression on you.[4]

The young writers fully complied with this agenda; the documents they created offer an ocean of information about every aspect of the inner and outer lives of the last generation of Polish Jews before the Holocaust. This chapter discusses only one element in their lives, but a rather significant one; that, taken in the broadest sense of the word, is their politics. Before turning to the responses to crisis, however, it is necessary to develop some sense of what the crisis itself entailed, what, in other words, caused these young people to be commonly referred to as a youth without a future.

The foundation of the crisis was economic. It was occasioned, first of all, by the very creation of a Polish nation-state. The "reborn Poland" that emerged in the aftermath of World War I was a pastiche of territories that for over a century had belonged to three different empires. Integrating these territories, with varying political, economic, and administrative traditions into one state was difficult enough. The war itself added the vast destruction of life and property. Finally, there was the catastrophic situation of Polish industry, centered in the prewar Russian territories. This industry, primarily textile, developed by German and Jewish entrepreneurs during the second half of the nineteenth century, had once clothed the Russian Empire. Now, with its old markets in Belarus, Ukraine, and further east locked inside revolutionary Russia, Polish textile factories were forced to compete, much to their disadvantage, against their Western European counterparts.

The situation of the Jews was especially grave. The Russian army had targeted the Jewish population of the lands it occupied during the war for particular oppression. With little exaggeration, Sh. An-sky entitled his book about Russian-occupied Galicia, *Khurbn Galitsye* (The destruction of Galicia).[5] In the eastern borderlands in the years following the war, Ukrainian, Polish, and Russian forces were responsible for attacks that resulted in tens of thousands of Jewish casualties and the sacking of entire communities. The new Polish state, ill-disposed toward the third of its population that was not ethnically Polish, made Jewish economic life especially difficult. The tobacco and liquor industries, previously in Jewish hands, were made state monopolies. Jewish shopkeepers and small producers were subjected to additional taxation, while employment in the expanding public sector, both national and local, was closed to Jews. By the 1930s, the situation became even worse, compounded by the effects of the world economic depression and the rising popularity of an aggressive Polish nationalism that called for economic war against the Jews.

This, then, was a world in which Jewish young people found it extraordinarily difficult to find a place. Children of shopkeepers watched the family business fail and their parents forced into the working class or the economic margins. One young woman, whose lineage linked her to the aristocratic Alexander Rebbe,[6] described the following progression in her family: the grandparents were owners of an iron foundry on their own estate; the father owned a haberdashery business but was forced to sell it and seek employment in the stigmatized occupation of *melamed* (teacher of young children).[7] Children of the working class found themselves shunted into seasonal and unskilled labor. A great many were unable to find work at all. Not just poverty, but the experience of severe and protracted hunger figures in a significant portion of the autobiographies. At the same time, this was a world in which traditional modes of explaining one's place had been profoundly undermined. Old and new modes of reasoning coexisted in radical discontinuity. Max Weinreich encapsulated the spirit of the times when he told of two women from the same *shtetl* traveling to Warsaw, one to an abortionist, the other to a *tsaddik* to implore him for a son after the many daughters she had borne.[8]

The Jewish youth movement in Poland was profoundly divided along ideological lines, from clandestine Communist groups and the Bundist Tsukunft on the left to a range of Zionist groups—Hashomer Hatsair, He-Halutz, Yugnt, Gordonia, Frayheyt-Dror, Betar—as well as orthodox groups linked to Agudat Yisrael and so-called nonparty (*umparteyishe*) organizations.[9] Moishe Kligsberg, a YIVO staff member, used the autobiographies—along with other sources such as memorial books and his own memory—to analyze the social context of Polish Jewish youth politics as a whole.[10] Its foundation was reading. The importance of reading for this generation is impossible to overestimate. In the autobiographies it is referred to as a passion and a mania; young people "hurl themselves on books like a hungry wolf."[11] Reading is the salvation of the lonely youth dreaming of "far horizons" amidst an uncomprehending family; reading and discussion of reading is what friends and comrades do with each other and what lovers do as well. What was read? Political writings, it turns out, took second place to what was called *beletristik* (belles lettres), especially world literature: Dostoyevsky, Byron, Shelley, Heine, translated into Yiddish and Polish. The most widely read book was doubtless Romain Rolland's *Jean Christophe*, a vast and vastly popular romantic novel about a tormented, great-spirited musician.[12] Writing paralleled reading: these young people wrote letters, kept diaries, and deluged newspapers and magazines with their unsolicited writings; there was frequent talk in the Jewish press of an epidemic of "graphomania." School, whether it was Jewish or Polish—anything but the traditional *kheyder*—was venerated. In the autobiographies, school is referred to as a second home, as better than home, as something magical, as a palace, as a temple, as the sun.[13]

Regardless of their ideology, the youth movements were rooted in these needs. The first action of a newly formed youth group in a small town was to establish a lending library. A typical *shtetl* might have two or three such libraries, each containing between several hundred and several thousand books. Kligsberg estimates that such public libraries, including some very large ones in the big cities, contained about one million books, and that in an average year the 450,000 Polish Jews aged fourteen to twenty read these books fifteen times over.[14] Adjoining the library was the party headquarters, or *lokal*, where courses, lecture series, seminars, and evening classes of various kinds were held, and where, above all, young people simply hung out. The social function of the *lokal* and its library for youth was entirely comparable to the function of the *besmedresh* (house of religious study) for their fathers.

The youth groups developed a new lifestyle that was shared across all ideologies. It was partially rooted in educational activities that made one more knowledgeable, more aware, in the language of youth—*bavustzinik*.[15] Just as importantly, it was based in practices that reevaluated one's relationship to the physical world, to nature, and to one's own body. Wasn't manual labor, after all, be it that of the proletariat or the *halutsim* (Zionist agricultural workers), destined to transform the world? Hiking great distances was a favored social activity. Pairs or groups of young people walked in town, or preferably on its outskirts, or through the countryside, all the while engaged in furious discussion of books, culture, and politics. In contrast, dancing and similar "frivolous" activities were frowned upon, as was ostentatious dress. Movement members favored simplicity: linen shirts, kerchiefs around the neck, berets, sandals in summer; the colors worn identified the wearer's politics. Betar, the youth movement of the Zionist Revisionists, was the only exception in this respect; its members favored military-style uniforms.[16] Many youth organizations maintained summer camps for their members, and there were associated sports clubs as well. This was one of the profoundest results of half a century of Jewish political activity in Eastern Europe: the construction of a "new kind of Jew whose back is straight," who no longer resembled, in other words, the stereotype of the cringing Jew that the *maskilim* had internalized from the gentile world.[17]

The results transformed all aspects of behavior. This example from the autobiographies touches upon all of the aforementioned themes as well as their unforeseen complications. The writer, a young Łódź worker who had passed in and out of Communist organizations as well as prison, described his first girlfriend:

> I met Reza in the classes of the Borochov School, and later on the boulevard.[18] Her origins and education were petit bourgeois, but she was a worker, and like all the *khalupnikes* [cottage workers], she worked from fourteen to fifteen hours a day. This put muscular creases in her face, as on a working man whose muscles are developed through labor. She was strongly built, a heroic figure among girls, and she was a wellspring of energy. She would always compete with me in reading books and being quick at it. She was always looking for some work or other, for something to do. "My hands are eager for action," she said to me. She was extremely curious, hungry for knowledge. She wanted to know and experience everything.
>
> This was all that appealed to me in a girl. I didn't show how much I liked her. I waited to see how she felt about me. But with a person of that kind there was no room for idle chatter. Every time I saw her there had to be a clear reason for it. If that was the case, it was enough to see each other once a week. My pride led me to prove to her that we could deal with matters just as efficiently if we saw each other every two weeks. So we began to go our separate ways.[19]

Jewish politics was also crucial in reconfiguring the Jewish language system. At the end of the nineteenth century, Jewish assimilationists in Poland still dreamed of the Jewish masses learning Polish and thereby becoming *Polacy wyznania mojżeszowego*, "Poles of the Mosaic faith." But when masses of Jews finally became fluent in Polish in the interwar years, the overwhelming majority hardly thought of themselves as Poles. On one hand, Polish society was increasingly less accepting even of those Jews who wanted to identify as Poles; indeed, even converts found themselves marginalized. On the other hand, Jewish politics and culture increasingly made room for Polish-speaking Jews. Hundreds of Jewish political publications, primarily Zionist, appeared in Polish during the interwar years, and Polish permeated segments of Jewish schools, Jewish daily newspapers, Jewish theater, and Jewish literature. A modern Jewish identity developed that, in practice, expressed itself in two languages, Yiddish and Polish. Polish, in other words, had become Judaized.

The distinction between the use of Yiddish and Polish was now partly a function of geography. In Galicia, for example, there was a relatively high proportion of Jews whose primary language was Polish. But above all, language choice reflected class differences. Within the youth movements whose members were primarily middle class, such as Hashomer Hatsair and Betar, as well as in some of the Communist groups, there were Jews who did not know any Yiddish. On the other hand, even the Bund, a group whose entire identity was bound up with the Yiddish language, issued youth publications in Polish.[20] Most of the Polish-language autobiographies were written by children of the middle class, but a good number were also written by working-class youths. Regardless of class background, most of these writers were involved in Jewish political movements. A young working-class woman from Bialystok, who had worked on and off in Communist groups, had contracted tuberculosis and spent months in various sanatoriums. In her autobiography, she wrote about one of those sanatoriums, located in Galicia: "I didn't care for the atmosphere. It felt very assimilated. All the patients spoke Polish and intended to go to Palestine."[21]

But politics, particularly in this time and place, was ultimately about ideology. What was the function of ideology for these young people? What were its uses? One use, it seems, was to overcome the radical isolation that so many experienced at home. As expected, there were deep silences across the generations. Here is one account:

> We live in a dark room, where the filth makes me cringe, although there's nothing I can do about it. I and [his brother] Perec work at home with our father, sitting at machines sewing baby shoes . . . My father is a wretched, overworked man. . . . [My]

father and I are two separate worlds, and aside from sentimental filial attachments, nothing binds me to him. He doesn't comprehend me and therefore knows nothing about me . . . I can't share my thoughts with him or ask his advice . . . Father has never had a real conversation with me . . . If he weren't my father, there would be nothing binding me to him.[22]

What is more surprising is that isolation also seems to characterize relations between siblings. Most of the writers came from large families, but as a rule they are either silent about their siblings or refer to them unsympathetically. Children of the middle class described characteristically lonely childhoods devoted to books and dreams; more shocking are numerous references to the physical isolation occasioned by poverty. One young woman recalled that her mother "used to go away for days and lock us in the house. I was so hungry that I would eat pieces of coal and raw potatoes." Of a later period, the same writer remembered: "We could not go out all winter because we had no warm clothing. So we lay in bed, nothing but our faces showing, and waited for our mother."[23] The young Łódż worker whose account about his girlfriend appears earlier in this chapter also wrote: "Before I started going to school, my father and sister would get up to work before dawn and lock me in the house from the outside. The world was narrow then. All sorts of plans and fantasies arose in me and also thoughts of suicide."[24] The experience of the street, of course, brought no relief; the economic crisis only reinforced the sense of being trapped. Over and over in the autobiographies, the writers communicate a similar lament: "Why must I choke in narrow confines when everything in me longs for broad horizons?"[25]

Ideology reconnected these young people to the world. Intellectually, it offered them an explanation of the world, of their own place in it, and of their necessary link to other people. In this respect, it replaced one of the functions of religion. All this comes together in the words of a troubled young Orthodox woman, a member of the girl's organization Bnos, which was linked to the Aguda. She related the experience of reading some pamphlets supplied by a new friend, and subsequently converting to socialism:

A new world opened up. It seemed a new world, that is, but in reality it was an old story that lived in me. The newness lay in the fact that I now perceived it. I recognized the naked truth. I raised the backdrop and looked behind the scenes at charity and the philanthropist, benevolence and the benefactor. I looked at people differently. I did not see them as bad or guilty. They were born neither bad nor good. Their motivations depended on the material and social conditions under which they developed. Was then the policeman who had made me lose my job simply fulfilling his duties as dictated from above? Was the director of the [teachers'] seminary [who had refused to admit her] entirely innocent? . . . But the question remains: Is that good? Is it right that one person should suffer and another live happily without even appreciating it? An eternal question. A difficult problem: "Why do the wicked prosper and the righteous suffer?" Can I justify suffering in this world with a reward in the "other world"? I had suffered too much from people, who were after all made "in the image of God," for my beliefs not to have weakened. I was too young to think of my share in the "world to come." Nor was I interested in going there. This world was calling to me. What was one to do? Now that I perceived the truth, I stopped idealizing everything. . . . Moreover, I did not feel alone. The whole world felt closer. The millions of brothers and sisters, proletarians like myself, felt closer. I saw myself among their ranks, among all the sufferers. . . . It was the threads of our common fate that bound us together. . . . I became a silent admirer of socialism. Its truth illuminated my life.[26]

For most of these young people, of course, commitment to an ideology was anything but silent, anything but passive. Commitment meant action; its nature varied, depending on one's ideology, from organizing strikes and demonstrations to raising crops and quarrying stone in *hakhshara* (labor training for emigration to Palestine). Its ultimate goal varied as well, from proletarian revolution to a Jewish homeland. But what all such activity had in common was the linking of present to a future young people were creating together with their comrades. The youth without a future could thereby construct a future itself, but only by abandoning individual struggles for a future and committing to a collective one, be it of the working class or the Jewish people or both. Here was something more than a substitute for religion. But the attempt to break out of their isolation forced these young people into history; their goal, using a Marxist formulation that is quite appropriate here, was no longer to be the objects but the creative subjects of history.

This is the note on which Moishe Kligsberg ends his study. Summarizing the significance of the youth movement as a whole, he spoke of its "enormous dynamism, profound belief in the ideal, optimism in its ability to realize its goals, and proud feeling of historical importance."[27] This conclusion is directly related to how he frames his study, which begins with the Warsaw Ghetto uprising. The uprising, as we know, was entirely the work of members of Jewish youth groups.[28] But Kligsberg makes additional claims for it. "The uprising was . . . the high point in the life of a generation of Jewish youth" and "the [historical witness to] the incomparable idealism and limitless devotion and readiness for sacrifice that characterized the innermost essence of the Polish-Jewish youth movement during its entire existence in independent Poland."[29] Kligsberg's study is explicitly designed to explain how such a movement came about. But this is less history than hagiography. Moreover, it negates one of the most important features of the autobiographies, the fact that they view the prewar Jewish world without Holocaust lenses.[30]

It is from this very prewar perspective that the autobiographies reveal the place of Jewish youth politics. While politics played a significant role in nearly all these young writers' lives, for the most part it did not define their lives. Certainly, there was a core of young people in all the youth movements for whom politics was everything. But attentive reading of the autobiographies tends to contradict the notion of a generation of true believers living under the sign of ideological struggle and political activism. Not only did the writers typically move from group to group, trying on various ideologies, but most of them seem to have moved in and out of political involvement itself. The previously cited Łódź worker spent months as a passionate Communist only to lose his faith in prison, where he discovered that, even there, where "we're all materially on equal terms . . . and the problem of private property has been solved," Communism did not work. He then backed away from all politics, declaring that "deciding and giving orders was dirty business, because even if whoever gives the orders means well, things turn out badly."[31] Others found that looking for work or family responsibilities pulled them away from politics; still others were suddenly overwhelmed by incapacitating bouts of depression. Politics is a key context of their lives but seldom the center.

Politics, rather, along with reading, writing, studying, and endless impassioned discussions, seems to have shaped a culture whose core was aspiration rather than certainty. Regardless of their ideologies, the way in which these primarily secular young people most commonly described their longings, from their hunger for books to their hunger to transform the world, was by using the word *gaystike*, which means "of the spirit." What is implied, it seems, is a movement upwards and outwards, that begins in the constricted present and reaches out toward the far horizon. This movement speaks the language of politics but also of aesthetics and morality; it aspires toward the highest, the best, the most beautiful, the purest. This generation thereby proved themselves true heirs of I. L. Peretz, whose restless, endlessly striving sensibility laid the foundations of the culture they inherited and then shaped.[32] Their motto may well have been the title of one of Peretz's most beloved stories, "Oyb nisht nokh hekher" (If not still higher).[33] This, in turn, takes inquiry one step higher, because for Abraham Joshua Heschel, another of Peretz's heirs, such a sensibility lay at the very heart of Ashkenaz: "Ashkenazic ethics . . . knew no perfection that was definable; its vision aimed at the infinite, never compromising, never satisfied, always striving —'Seek higher than that.'"[34]

Politics and Culture

DAVID E. FISHMAN

8

The Bund and Modern Yiddish Culture

A 1907 ARTICLE MARKING the tenth anniversary of the Bund offered the following glowing evaluation of the movement's role in the rise of modern Yiddish culture: "The Bund created a modern Yiddish culture. . . . It turned the market jargon into a language in which serious scientific matters could be discussed. . . . The Bund taught the Jewish masses how to read. . . . The Bund created a great circle of readers who needed good books and newspapers, and it created a new literature for this circle."[1]

This self-congratulatory, partisan assessment was subsequently adopted and elaborated upon in Bundist historiography, and from there it entered into mainstream scholarly literature and popular consciousness, where the close connection between Bundism and Yiddish culture has become a truism.[2] This assumption may be challenged by reconsidering this relationship critically, focusing on the period from the 1890s until the outburst of World War I, when both the Bund and modern Yiddish culture emerged as major forces in East European Jewish life.

To speak of the rise of modern Yiddish culture between 1890 and 1914 is more than a rhetorical flourish, meant to allude to the artistic achievements of Sholem Aleichem, I. L. Peretz, and other authors. It is an apt characterization of a series of sweeping developments related to the position of Yiddish in Jewish life. For example, these years saw a dramatic increase in the publication of Yiddish books and periodicals. When Sholem Aleichem compiled a list of Yiddish books printed in the Russian Empire in 1888, he recorded seventy-eight titles. Twenty-four years later, in 1912, an analogous list prepared by Moshe Shalit consisted of 407 titles.[3] In 1888, only one Yiddish periodical appeared in all of Russia; in 1912, there were forty.[4]

Moreover, Yiddish readership expanded significantly. In the 1880s, Russia's sole Yiddish newspaper, the weekly *Yudishes folksblat*, reached a peak circulation of 7,000 copies. In early 1905, the only Yiddish daily in the empire, *Der fraynd*, distributed close to 50,000 copies. By 1912, the combined circulation of the two most popular Yiddish dailies (out of seven), *Haynt* and *Moment*, was 175,000.[5]

Yiddish cultural institutions were also emerging. To become a truly modern culture, Yiddish culture needed more than writers and artistic performers. It needed institutional infrastructures to support the creative elite and its audience —schools (elementary, advanced, adult education), publishing houses, libraries, standing theaters, and literary-cultural societies. While there were no such Yiddish institutions in 1890, they were numerous by 1914. To cite just one example, until the 1890s, the publication of Yiddish books was a sideshow for Hebrew printing presses in Odessa, Vilna, Warsaw, and lesser centers. Publishing houses dedicated primarily or exclusively to Yiddish book printing first arose at the turn of the twentieth century, and proliferated after 1905.[6]

The appearance of sophisticated journals such as *Literarishe monatshriftn* (1908), and *Di yidishe velt* (1912–1916) were clear indicators of a Yiddish intelligentsia coming to light.[7] This class of intellectuals and professionals with exposure to Western culture spoke and wrote in Yiddish not only in order to communicate with the less-educated "masses," but also for communication among themselves. Their use of Yiddish for high cultural functions represented a sharp departure from the centuries-old dominance of Hebrew—and the nineteenth-century dominance of Russian—in this area.

A new Yiddishist ideology was on the rise. Adherents saw Yiddish language and culture as Jewish national values to be strengthened and perpetuated, and supported Yiddish as the primary medium for a Jewish national renaissance in the diaspora. The major event marking this ideological trend was the conference for the Yiddish language held in Czernowitz in 1908.[8]

In broad historical perspective, the rise of modern Yiddish culture was an intrinsic part of the rapid modernization of East European Jews in the late nineteenth and early twentieth centuries. During those years, Jews experienced the processes of massive urbanization, industrialization, rapidly increasing literacy, secularization, and political mobilization. At the same time, the Jews' acculturation to Russian and Polish proceeded at a much slower pace than the other trends. According to the 1897 Imperial Russian census, only a quarter of the Jewish population could read and write in Russian, whereas it is safe to assume that the overwhelming majority of Jews was literate in Yiddish.[9]

There were many reasons for the large disparity between the Jews' acculturation and other aspects of their modernization. To note only the most obvious causes: their large population and compact residence (in towns in the Pale of Settlement, Jews were commonly the majority group, and even in major cities such as Warsaw and Łodź, they constituted 30 percent of the population); the quotas limiting Jews' access to Russian higher education; widespread anti-Semitic attitudes among their Polish and Russian neighbors; and the rise of Jewish nationalism, which itself became a force preserving Jewish social and cultural cohesiveness. One consequence of the disparity between the rates of modernization and acculturation was the flourishing of modern literature, politics, and culture in Yiddish.

The question that needs to be addressed is the extent to which the Bund led or simply participated in the Yiddish renaissance at the turn of the twentieth century.[10] By and large, the growth of Yiddish proceeded along analogous lines in radical and nonradical milieus. Indeed, most of the landmark events in the history of modern Yiddish culture were not sponsored by the Bund nor led by Bundists. It is worth recalling them here. The first Yiddish literary "thick journals" (Sholem Aleichem's *Yidishe folksbibliotek*, 1888–1889, Mordechai Spektor's *Hoyzfraynd*, 1888–1896) were edited by bourgeois writers. Moreover, the first daily Yiddish newspaper in Russia (*Der fraynd*, founded in 1903) was published by a group of Zionists, led by Saul Ginzburg. The first standing (as opposed to traveling) Yiddish theater company, the Kaminsky Theater, which established its base in Warsaw in 1905, had no radical or proletarian orientation. Additionally, the bourgeois diaspora nationalist Nathan Birnbaum launched the Czernowitz conference for the Yiddish language, and its leading figures—Chaim Zhitlovsky and I. L. Peretz—were sharply at odds with the Bund.[11]

The Bund's Yiddish-language activity needs to be seen in context and in proportion. It is fair to comment that while Yiddish played a crucial role in the history of the Bund, the Bund did not play as central a role in the history of Yiddish culture as its partisans believed.

Language

There would not have been a Bund were it not for the decision by Jewish social democrats in 1890s Vilna to shift the language of their activities from Russian to

Yiddish. Instead of conducting Russian-language "circles," in which elite Jewish workers were educated in Russian reading and writing, mathematics and natural sciences, and eventually political economy and Marxism, Jewish socialists shifted their emphasis to political and economic "agitation" among workers in Yiddish.[12]

For the founders of the Bund, Yiddish was the *sine qua non* for creating a mass Jewish labor movement; it was the essential linguistic tool by which to disseminate their economic and political ideas. One of the Bund's founders, Shmuel Gozhansky, argued in his pioneering brochure "A Letter to the Agitators" of 1893 that the leadership of the Jewish workers' movement should train its agitators partly in Yiddish in order to assure their effectiveness in speaking to the workers "who know Russian poorly and will need to learn everything in zhargon."[13] The Vilna-based "Group of Jewish Social Democrats" issued its first Yiddish brochures—in manuscript, hectograph, and print—in 1894 and 1895, and the number of brochures increased substantially after the establishment of the General Jewish Workers' Alliance of Russia, Lithuania and Poland, the Bund, in 1897.[14]

But until approximately 1905, the Bund's connection to the language was utilitarian, and not a matter of ideology or principle. Indeed, the top echelon of the Bund's leadership consisted of Russified Jewish intelligentsia, most of whom knew Yiddish quite poorly. One of the Bund's organizers and journalists, A. Litvak (pseudonym of Chaim Helfand), recalled that when he first met Alexander (Arkady) Kremer, the "father of the Bund," in 1895, the latter's Yiddish consisted entirely of a few juicy curses. As late as 1905, the members of the Bund's Central Committee—Isaiah Eisenstadt, Vladimir Kosovsky, Pavel Rosental, and Vladimir Medem—submitted their contributions to the party's daily newspaper *Der veker* in Russian, to be translated, because they could not write them in Yiddish.[15]

The Bund's early Yiddish pamphlets and newspapers were composed by its second-tier leaders, such as Gozhansky, Litvak, and Israel-Mikhl Kaplinsky, who had not studied in Russian gymnasia and universities. Often former yeshiva students who had become "infected" with socialism, these autodidacts, or "half-intellectuals," as they were called, knew their readers' language, milieu, and mentality, and were instrumental in translating the concepts of modern socialism into Yiddish.[16]

There can be no doubt that Bundist propaganda and agitation in Yiddish stimulated greater Yiddish literacy among the Jewish working class. Bundist agitators did teach Jewish workers how to read, in both a literal and metaphorical sense. The Bund's underground pamphlet literature and press also played a major role in creating a modern Yiddish lexicon and "high register" for the discussion of political, social, and economic problems. But the claim that the modernization of the Yiddish language first occurred in Bundist literature and then spread to non-Bundist Yiddish writing is highly questionable.[17]

While Yiddish was the language of the workers' circles and cells, and of the underground pamphlets and newspapers, Russian was the dominant language of party deliberations in the early years. Not a single participant in the founding conference of the Bund in 1897 spoke in Yiddish. It was first afforded equal status with Russian at the party's seventh conference, held in October 1906, at which all speeches were translated from one language to the other. Only at the eighth party conference in 1910 did Yiddish become the official language of the proceedings.[18]

Literature

The Bund's early Yiddish publications were dedicated to political and economic issues, with relatively little space devoted to literature and culture per se. Its underground newspapers, *Di arbeter-shtime* (1897–1905) and *Der yidisher arbeter* (1896–1904) published little poetry and virtually no imaginative prose. Indeed, the absence of belles lettres from the early Bundist press was a feature that distinguished it from legal Yiddish periodicals such as the weekly *Der Yud* (1899–1903), the daily *Der fraynd* (1903–1913), and subsequent newspapers, where short stories and serialized novels were a mainstay. Of the ninety-one pamphlets published by the Bund between 1897 and 1905, eighty-one were dedicated to politics, economics, and the history of socialism, four were anthologies of revolutionary poetry, and six were works of literary prose.[19]

While the formal, organizational connection between the Bund and Yiddish literature was quite weak, both drew considerable inspiration from each other. Major Yiddish writers, such as Peretz and Avrom Reisin, were deeply impressed by their early encounters with organized Jewish workers in the 1890s, and the Bund, in turn, used their works (published legally, under Russian censorship), as tools to educate and agitate among the workers.

In 1895, Jewish socialists formed *zhargonishe komitetn* ("jargon," or Yiddish Committees), which established Yiddish workers' lending libraries in Vilna, Minsk, and Bialystok. Their holdings included the satires of Mendele Mocher Sefarim and I. J. Linetsky, the radical stories and feuilletons of I. L. Peretz's miscellanies (the *Yontev bletlekh* [occasional pieces], 1894–1896), and short stories on proletarian suffering and struggle written by David Pinsky and Avrohom Reisin. After its founding, the Bund conducted literary "readings" (*forleṛungen*) and evenings (*ovntn*) to discuss works of Yiddish literature (as well as Yiddish translations of Russian and Western literature), and thereby cultivated an interest in modern Yiddish literature in the ranks of the labor movement.[20]

Yiddish poetry was central to the life of the Bund. The proletarian and revolutionary poems of Morris Vinchevsky, Dovid Edelshtadt, Morris Rosenfeld, and Avrohom Reisin were extremely popular among organized workers and youth, and secret meetings of Bundist cells and trade unions usually concluded with the recitation or communal singing of their poems. Poems about the workers' struggles were also posted on placards during strikes, and sung at mass demonstrations. Recitation and communal singing at secret meetings and illegal public gatherings added to the emotional power of the poems, and strengthened workers' attachment to Yiddish poetry.[21]

In short, there can be no doubt that a strong Yiddish literary culture grew within the ranks of the Jewish labor movement. But it was a very peculiar and skewed literary subculture. For, as Litvak noted in his memoirs on the *ṛhargonishe komitetn*, labor activists "viewed modern Yiddish literature merely as a tool for agitation; they attributed no intrinsic value to it."[22] For the Bund, poetry and prose were politics pursued by other means, and works of literature were measured according to their suitability for agitation. Pinsky and Reisin were read avidly and endorsed by the movement, while the works of Sholem Aleichem and Sholem Asch—both of whom were enormously popular among Russian Jewish readers at large—were neglected by the Bund's circles, because they were of no use to it.

The Bund's attitude toward Peretz was tempestuous. He was their cultural hero during the mid-1890s, but his popularity among them dropped as his works shifted to national romanticism, neo-Hasidism, and symbolism. Peretz's 1906 essay "Hope and Fear," in which he warned that the revolutionary movement might prove to be as oppressive and intolerant as tsarism, caused grumblings among Bundists. And in 1908, when he concluded his modernist drama *Bay nakht afn altn mark* (At Night in the Old Market Place) with a *badkhn* (jester) calling out "*in shul arayn!*" ("back to the synagogue!"), Bundists were appalled, and attacked him for supporting a return to religion. They became similarly disillusioned and antagonistic toward Sh. An-sky, the author of the Bund's own anthem, *Di shvue*, when An-sky's writings developed in a neo-romantic direction.[23]

Since the Bund valued Yiddish literature first and foremost as a vehicle for agitation among the masses, it had difficulty reconciling itself with the sophisticated and modernist Yiddish writing which arose after 1905. When the journal *Literarishe monatshriftn* appeared in 1908, it was heralded by many as the beginning of a new era in the Yiddish cultural renaissance. The journal was self-consciously devoted to Yiddish art for its own sake, and was explicitly aimed at an intellectual (rather than mass) readership. The composition of its editorial committee, which consisted of a socialist territorialist (Shmuel Niger), a Bundist (A. Weiter), and a Zionist (Shmaryahu Gorelik), signaled that Yiddish art and culture transcended political divisions.[24]

For the Bund, the journal was a troubling development. Mark Liber, then a young member of the party's Central Committee, derided its apolitical posture. Politics and culture were inseparable, he wrote. Modern Yiddish culture was itself the product of class conflict within Jewry and the rise of the proletariat, whether the journal's editors admitted to it or not. Litvak and B. Vladek launched frontal attacks on the *Literarishe monatshriftn*. In their own publications, they argued that the *Literarishe monatshriftn*, championing art for art's sake, and excluding articles on social problems, was a declaration of contempt for politics and political parties. By encouraging intellectuals to think only about themselves and their own edification, it cut the intelligentsia off from the masses. It thereby played into the hands of political reaction.[25]

Yiddish and the Evolution of the Bund's National Program

As Jewish national consciousness grew within the ranks of the Bund, Yiddish figured prominently in the movement's internal deliberations on adopting a Jewish national program. At the party's conferences in 1899 and 1901, the first Bundist leaders to advocate "national equality" for the Jews of Russia explained the term as meaning freedom of speech, press, and assembly in Yiddish; protection against forced Russification; and securing the right to communicate with local and imperial state organs in Yiddish.[26] In these early formulations, Jewish national rights and Yiddish language rights were nearly coterminous.

Shortly thereafter, the nationally oriented wing of the Bund advanced a program of Jewish national-cultural autonomy, based on the nationality theories of Karl Renner, Otto Bauer, and the Austrian Social Democrats. But until 1904, a large part of the Bundist leadership objected to adopting such a program. Their opposition was based on many considerations, including doubts regarding the viability of Yiddish, the attachment of the Jewish proletariat to the Russian language, as well as reservations about the very desirability of perpetuating Yiddish among the Jewish working class. The debate reached a climax at the fifth party conference in June 1903, when Sholem Levin, one of the opponents of national-cultural autonomy, declared:

> The misfortune of the Jews in Russia today is that they are not allowed to assimilate. . . . Some here [at the conference] are connecting their national feelings with Yiddish, just as the Zionists aspire to the Hebrew language. But the masses aspire to the Russian language, and this is not because they are prevented from studying Yiddish. . . . If there were no discriminatory laws against the Jews, they would speak Russian.[27]

The authoritative Bundist statement on the subject came in Vladimir Medem's 1904 essay, "Social Democracy and the National Question," which forged a compromise position. Medem professed neutrality on the long-term question of whether the Jews would maintain their nationality or assimilate. But he affirmed that the Jews were at present a national group, and therefore argued for Jewish national-cultural autonomy in Russia.

Medem associated nationality primarily with language, and utilized a class-based analysis to argue for the need to grant equal rights to all languages, including Yiddish, in Russia. While the Jewish bourgeoisie had the time, financial resources, and inherent desire to become Russified, the Jewish working class knew no language fluently except for its mother tongue. The state relegated the Jewish proletariat to an inferior, disadvantaged existence by forcing Jewish workers to use Russian in their everyday lives, or to send their children to Russian-language schools. Thus, he concluded, securing equal status for Yiddish in the public arena and for Yiddish-language schools served both national and social objectives.

True equality of languages, Medem continued, could be achieved and protected only by removing education and culture, matters which were most contingent upon language, from the hands of the state authorities, and handing them over to the jurisdiction of the nationalities themselves, who would establish public bodies to direct them. This was the true meaning of national-cultural autonomy.[28]

The Bund formally adopted its program of Jewish national-cultural autonomy at its sixth party conference in October 1905. From that point on, the Bund championed the cause of the recognition of Yiddish in the public arena. A resolution on the "struggle for equality of the Yiddish language," adopted unanimously at the eighth party conference in 1910, delineated the Bund's position:

a) The distinction between official languages and tolerated languages is unacceptable; b) State institutions and organs of administration must communicate with the populaces in the local languages . . . d) In advance of the realization of national-cultural autonomy . . . it is essential to attain the right for every national group to establish public schools in its own mother tongue; e) In the struggle for these demands, it is necessary to stress insistently the rights of the Yiddish language, which is more deprived of rights than all others, and is unrecognized even when other non-official languages are afforded partial recognition.[29]

Bundists and Yiddish Cultural Institutions

The revolution of 1905 was a turning point in the development of Yiddish culture in Russia. As part of the state's concessions toward society, the authorities lifted the near-total ban on the Yiddish periodical press and the longstanding prohibition of Yiddish theater. Yiddish newspapers, books, and theaters flooded the public cultural marketplace, causing Hebrew literature to undergo a crisis of readership and confidence. Meanwhile, the democratic and populist fervor that seized the Jewish intelligentsia led to numerous calls for a positive reevaluation of the role of Yiddish in Jewish life.[30]

The Bund was a direct beneficiary of the newly attained freedom of the press in Russia, which enabled it to publish a legal Yiddish daily of its own between late 1905 and 1907. (The Bundist organ changed its name from *Der veker* to *Naye folkstsaytung*, and later to *Di hofenung*, before it was closed down and its editors arrested.) Even after the restoration of political reaction in 1907, Bundist journals and newspapers were permitted intermittently by state censors. But the party press never enjoyed mass appeal. Less than 10,000 copies of *Folkstsaytung* were printed in 1907, compared to the 50,000 press run of the liberal (and pro-Zionist) *Der fraynd*. In an attempt to compete for readers, Bundist newspapers and the party's newly established publishing house began to devote more space and resources to belles lettres. But this was an instance of the Bund following rather than leading.[31]

If their impact on the press and publishing was surprisingly modest, Bundists were the main pioneers in the establishment of modern Yiddish schools. Although they conducted this activity as private individuals rather than at the movement's behest or under its auspices, the schools they founded were an organic extension of the Bundist tradition of workers' education, applied to children and youth.

Bundists were at the helm of the Vilna Jewish evening school, which was licensed to provide a Russian grammar school education to workers above age 16, but which, beginning in 1906, surreptitiously taught all subjects in Yiddish, including an optional course in Yiddish language and literature. The evening school, whose enrollment hovered between three hundred and six hundred in the years prior to World War I, published the first and most influential anthology of Yiddish literature in 1909, the three-volume *Dos yiddishe vort*, edited by the Bundist Moishe Olgin.[32] At roughly the same time, Bundists in Warsaw established a Yiddish division of the Polish "Society to Combat Adult Illiteracy," whose Yiddish-language evening courses were attended by over a thousand students.[33]

Bundists also organized two of the earliest full-day Yiddish elementary schools. In Vilna, 180 students attended the four-grade "Deborah Kupershtein School," which embraced a progressive pedagogical philosophy of holistic education. And in Warsaw, the four-grade "Hinukh Yeladim" attracted a group of teachers (such as M. Birnboim and Yankev Levin) who penned the first generation of Yiddish textbooks for children. Both schools operated in violation of the law, which stipulated that Russian was the only permitted language of school instruction. The Bundist skills of concealment and subterfuge were necessary to ensure their survival.[34]

In the years after the restoration of political reaction, Yiddish education became a focal point of Bundist activity and writing. Bund-sponsored publications devoted considerable attention to the ideological, psychological, political, and pedagogical issues surrounding this newest type of Jewish school. Esther Frumkin was the most prolific author on the subject. Meanwhile, Bundist teachers in the field (mainly in Warsaw and Vilna) experimented with curricula, developed Yiddish terminology for teaching math and science, and applied their democratic ideas to student admissions, parent relations, and school governance.[35] While qualitatively impressive, the scope of modern Yiddish schooling prior to World War I was extremely modest, because much of it was illegal.

The post-1905 years saw the legalization of various Jewish associations, including the St. Petersburg-based Jewish Literary Society (*Evreiskoe literaturnoye obschestvo*), established in 1908. While the Society was officially dedicated to advancing Jewish literature in all three languages (Hebrew, Russian, and Yiddish), its charter permitted it to conduct public lectures and programs in Yiddish, activities that were previously prohibited by law. By mid-1910, the Society had a total of fifty-five branches in the Russian Empire. Its lectures, concerts, and dramatic performances were conducted overwhelmingly in Yiddish.[36]

The St. Petersburg leaders of the Jewish Literary Society were liberals and nationalists, none of whom were Bundists. Indeed, for a number of years, the Bund opposed, and refused to participate in, nonpartisan Jewish cultural associations. At the 1908 Czernowitz conference for the Yiddish language, Esther Frumkin vigorously opposed Peretz's and Zhitlovsky's attempts to establish a permanent umbrella organization for Yiddish culture. She argued that there could be no cultural cooperation between the bourgeoisie and proletariat, since each had distinctly different cultural conceptions and needs. Peretz and Zhitlovsky were forced to settle for a bureau with no authority to initiate programs.[37]

But as the Jewish Literary Society's popularity grew, and local societies for Yiddish literature cropped up throughout Russia, and as the prospects of political organization and action diminished, the Bund was forced to alter its position. In late 1909, it began to encourage its members to become active in Jewish cultural associations, in order to exert an influence on their programs and orientation.[38] In Warsaw, where I. L. Peretz chaired the local branch of the Jewish Literary Society, Bundists joined en masse and effectively took over the organization. Bundist leader Bronislaw Grosser eventually replaced Peretz, and shortly thereafter the Russian authorities forcibly closed the Jewish Literary Society (including its Warsaw branch).[39]

Yiddishism and the Bund

Until 1905, the language issue was not politicized in Russian Jewry. The Bund was not Yiddishist (and anti-Hebrew) and Zionism was not Hebraist (in the sense of being anti-Yiddish). In 1901, at its third conference, the Bund passed a resolution condemning Zionism as a bourgeois, reactionary political movement. Yet the resolution specifically excluded the (mainly Hebrew) cultural work of Zionist groups from its condemnation, noting laconically that "the conference relates to it as it does to any legal activity."[40] Meanwhile, the Zionist Ahiasaf publishing house issued a modern Yiddish weekly, *Der Yud*, from 1899 to 1903, which served not only as a movement organ for Zionist news and views, but also as a forum for the publication of Yiddish literature, including works by Sholem Aleichem, I. L. Peretz, and Sholem Asch.[41]

Although Chaim Zhitlovsky propagated Yiddishist views prior to 1905, his idea of a Jewish national renaissance based on the Yiddish language was too overtly nationalist for the Bund at the time.[42] In the years after 1905, Yiddishism enjoyed broad support across a large part of the Jewish political spectrum. Its leading spokesmen included liberal Jewish nationalists such as Nathan Birnbaum and Israel Zinberg; socialist diaspora nationalists associated with the Jewish Socialist Workers' Party (known as the "Sejmists") such as Zhitlovsky himself and Nokhem Shtiff; socialist territorialists such as Shmuel Niger; and socialist Zionists, led by the father of the Poalei Tsiyon party, Ber Borokhov. Notable Yiddishist voices even existed in the leadership of the general Russian Zionist movement, including those of Joseph Luria, editor of *Der Yud* and of the official Zionist weekly, *Dos Yidishe folk* (published in Vilna in 1906–1907), and the young Yitzhak Grunbaum, who caused a storm in 1909 when he insisted on addressing the fifth conference of Russian Zionists in Yiddish.[43]

The divide between Yiddishists and Hebraists was not between Bundists and Zionists, nor between socialists and non-socialists, but between those movements (or factions within those movements) that affirmed continued Jewish national existence in the diaspora and those who rejected such a prospect. It was no coincidence that Luria and Grunbaum were both champions of the Helsingsfors platform, passed at the 1906 second conference of Russian Zionists, which endorsed Jewish national rights (i.e., autonomy) in the diaspora.[44]

The Bund's contribution was to articulate a version of Yiddishism that, unlike others, was staunchly Marxist, secularist, and anti-Hebrew. Its major advocates were Bundist "young Turks" who rose in the movement's ranks after 1905, such as Moishe Rafes and Esther Frumkin.

The Bund's radical Yiddishism came to the fore at the 1908 Czernowitz conference. On the main issue that dominated the proceedings, the question of the status of Yiddish, Frumkin proposed the most extreme of the five alternate resolutions: "The conference recognizes Yiddish as the only national language of the Jewish people. Hebrew has the significance of a historical monument, whose revival is a utopia." It was rejected in favor of a resolution that Yiddish was a national language, and that the conference took no position on Hebrew.[45]

Also at Czernowitz, Frumkin scoffed at Sholem Asch's proposal that the conference endorse preparation of a new literary translation of the Bible into Yiddish, so as to ensure that the riches of ancient Jewish culture reverberate in the new Yiddish renaissance. In the eyes of the Jewish proletariat, said Frumkin, the Bible was material for historical scholarship; its Yiddish translation was no more important than the translation of other classics of world literature. Writing after the conference, she alluded to the proposal as having been a bit of Zionist propaganda. But once again Frumkin was in the minority; the conference enthusiastically supported Asch's project.[46]

A major forum for Yiddishist-Hebraist debates was the annual conference of the Society for the Dissemination of Enlightenment among the Jews of Russia (in Hebrew, *Khevrat mefitse haskalah*), where the language issue dominated deliberations on the desired curriculum of modern Jewish schools. A Yiddishist "opposition" first arose in the organization in 1905, and argued for reserving a place for Yiddish both as a language of instruction and as a discipline. Its most prominent spokesman was the literary critic and historian Israel Zinberg.[47]

When Bundists joined the Society for Enlightenment in 1910 (after the movement's decision to join Jewish cultural associations), they espoused a much more radical position than the Yiddishists who had preceded them. At the 1911 conference, Moishe Rafes argued that Jewish schools should use Yiddish as their only language of instruction, and should exclude confessional subjects such as the Bible and Hebrew from their curricula. Moreover, echoing Medem's "neutralism," Rafes argued that Jewish schools should not have any specifically national objectives, such as strengthening Jewish identity. Rather, by virtue of their use of Yiddish as the language of instruction, Jewish schools should be natural products of the Jewish environment. Rafes's resolution was resoundingly defeated, but the resolution that passed in its stead was the first Yiddishist victory in the Society for Enlightenment. It stated that "all Jewish schools must teach [the] Bible and Hebrew; in those places where the Jewish masses speak the Yiddish language, the latter must occupy a place as a language of instruction and as a discipline."

Conclusion

Though the early Bund (1897–1905) pretty much ignored cultural matters, it was ineluctably drawn into them. Literature, education, and the arts became increasingly politicized as Bundists and Zionists, among others, staked out their positions. After 1905, the Bund championed a radical version of Yiddishism.

Even within the Yiddish cultural movement, the Bund occupied a politically sectarian position. It was reluctant to participate in Yiddish cultural organizations it could not dominate or control, and it was troubled by the rise of modernist Yiddish literature, which did not serve the ends of popular edification or political struggle.

While the Bund tugged Yiddish culture to the political left, its positions did not dominate the Yiddish literary and cultural scene between 1890 and the First World War.

RUTH R. WISSE

9

The Political Vision of I. L. Peretz

In 1908 I. L. Peretz recorded the following vision:

In a number of years from now, it is possible that Grzybowska numbers 6 and 28
will lie in ruins, not a single stone in place; little demons will frolic in the sand,
blowing it loose across the seven seas, to the very ends of the earth. And on Tisha
B'Av, a Jewish woman will sit there, dressed all in black; she will sit on a mound of
sand, with a *Tsene rene* in her hand, weeping and mourning. . . .

Betar was destroyed over a wagon wheel, Tur Malka for the sake of a rooster and
hen, Jerusalem because of Kamtza bar Kamtza—and the largest Jewish community in
Europe will be destroyed over a trifle—the negligible foreskin of a small dead child.
And nearby will stand a palace . . . It will have a huge chimney, like a giant factory.
Fiery flames will come shooting out of the windows, as if from a lime-kiln, and a
thick fat smoke of human flesh and bones, marrow and blood, will curl over the chimney as over a sacrificial altar—a crematorium where the dead will be incinerated . . . [1]

Given that Grzybowska 6 and 28 were buildings of the Warsaw Jewish Community Council, Peretz's crematorium vision seems an uncanny prophecy of the
slaughter that would overtake Polish Jewry thirty-five years later. In a 1960 "Essay
on Cassandra," the Polish writer Jerzy Stempowski wrote about a number of
Jewish and non-Jewish intellectuals he knew in the period between the two world
wars who had accurately predicted certain features of the looming catastrophe.
One of them was Szymon Askenazy, the son of a rabbinic family of Vilna who

had been professor of modern history at the University of Lwow (Lemberg) before World War I, and spent the final years of his life in Warsaw. In 1932, while watching the groundwork being laid for the new National Museum, he said, "I wonder why people waste money and energy erecting expensive buildings in a city doomed to destruction? Just now, when we are sitting here on this bench, I almost see German planes dropping bombs on the city." When Stempowski said he was skeptical about such prophecies, Askenazy reacted emotionally; "How can you not see it? Just think for a moment. Can it be otherwise?"[2] Was Peretz an even earlier forecaster of that rare kind? Is this passage a visionary warning of the dangers facing the Jews in Poland?[3]

The immediate context of Peretz's prophecy was an open letter that he wrote over a debate then raging within the Jewish press. It concerned the burial of a ten-month-old Jewish boy whose atheist father had refused to circumcise, and whom the rabbis required to undergo ritual circumcision before he could be interred in the Jewish cemetery. Freethinkers who attacked circumcision as a barbaric rite took up the father's case. Yet when the secularists tried to get the Polish authorities to force the rabbinate to bury the uncircumcised child, they offended the sensibilities of ordinary Jews. A number of Jewish writers were provoked into coming out in defense of circumcision. Peretz put forth his own views in this brochure "On the Circumcision Scandal," in which he tried to adjudicate among all the vying parties. His cryptic, allusive style makes it hard to trace the line of argument—this being one of the most common criticisms leveled against Peretz from the beginning to the end of his literary career—but it is worth trying to follow Peretz to see just how the crematorium vision arises and what it signifies.

Peretz opens with a brief historical analysis. A few years ago, he posits, the circumcision scandal would not have created so much bad blood. There were more serious and important issues waiting for solutions, and the public was more radical, more freethinking. By "a few years ago," Peretz is referring to the revolutionary fervor that climaxed in 1905, and that had since given way to disillusionment with politics. He attributes the heat of the present quarrel to the disappointment of that failed uprising. Collapse of the "red flag" had destroyed the public's confidence in progressivism. The Left was frustrated and demoralized by its political setback, and some of its members had unwisely seized on this symbolic protest against the rabbinate to show that there was still some life in the radical sector. The Right had come to the defense of tradition, joined by the "gray man in the middle" who was in a reactionary mood. Peretz calls the ensuing crisis a tragicomedy: a father who knows he has to consign his dead child to the ground, yet threatens to call in the police if it is deprived of a piece of skin; a hypocritical rabbinate that will uphold the sacred law—unless, of course, it is threatened by the police; the masses, assimilationists, intellectuals, each with their contorted calculations of how to exploit the scandal, and the Jewish people, for whom the circumcision of a dead child becomes a matter of life and death, threatening the destruction of an entire community: "un tragikomish is a folk, bay velkhn di frage fun mal zayn a toyt kind vert a lebns-frage un es ken kumen tsu a khurbn fun a kehile . . ." [Tragic is a people for whom the issue of circumcising a dead child becomes a vital question and it can lead to the destruction of a community.] It is in this context of this tragicomedy that Peretz brings the images of the lime-kiln, the burning bodies in the crematorium, the gigantic altar of the Holocaust. He foresees that on the site of the *khurbn* (destruction) a memorial will someday be dedicated to the father, the son, and the secular cause.

Peretz's use of the term tragicomic reflects his mixed perspectives on the problem. Speaking as a European intellectual, he discovers in the *milah* (circumcision) scandal all the properties of a mock epic, something like Alexander Pope's "The Rape of the Lock." The circumcision of a dead child lends itself to satiric treatment as the *reductio ad absurdum* of organized religion. As in Pope, the deflation of the subject is achieved by the inflation of the image that is used to describe it. Peretz mocks the puny scandal by casting it in terms of Lamentations. But his crematorium vision signals the threat of destruction coming from outside, not inside, the fractured community. The Jewish writer feels the growing menace of Poles seeking their independence from Russia and Russians who want to dominate the Poles. Not the satirist, but the politics of anti-Semitism have inflated the danger to the Jews, so that the mock epic style actually reduces the danger Peretz thinks he is exaggerating.

The displaced anxieties enter the picture by way of historical memory. The three cited rabbinic references—to Kamtza and Bar Kamtza, the broken shaft in the litter of the royal princess that brought about the destruction of Betar, and the theft of the cock and hen by the Roman soldiers at Tur Malka—all attribute the destruction of the Second Temple and the defeat of the Jewish uprising to apparently insignificant provocations. Each rabbinic example underscores exactly the same discrepancy between a trivial cause and an apocalyptic consequence that Peretz senses in the crisis over the dead boy. His allusions evoke a parallel between the catastrophe that overtook the Jews under Rome and the danger they face in the aftermath of the failed revolution of 1905. His crematorium prophecy is based on the legends that were imprinted on his mind as a child.

Peretz offers these disparate views of the Jewish condition using different levels of analysis and within different categories of discourse. Speaking as an intellectual, he uses the vocabulary of social science. Thus, in the latter part of the essay, he tries to demystify circumcision in anthropological terms. The primitive Orthodox Jews still serve a God of sacrifice through the attenuated sacrificial ritual of circumcision—and they don't always bother to take proper sanitary precautions for the newborn child. They do not understand that the prophets released the ethical content from the legalism of the bible, and that modern Judaism should be liberating itself from all such outworn rites.

Peretz does not go so far as to argue for the abolition of circumcision because he acknowledges that all peoples need their rituals. He berates his fellow moderns for having turned on their people over such a trifle as circumcision at a time of national crisis. Yet while freethinkers ought to accept Jewish national discipline, so the Orthodox and the rest of the people should respect the views of individual Jews. Don't raise your hands against the dissident father and artist! This is the essay's final word. When all is said and done, intellectual freedom must prevail.

By contrast, when Peretz uses images from Jewish memory and myth, his intuition grasps what his analysis obscures; the homey midrashic language lets him leave unexamined the implications of what he perceives. His image of Jewish Warsaw going up in flames, rendered in the language of Judaea falling to the Romans, suggests that Jews habitually displace the greater cause by the smaller, sublimating through fraternal arguments the blame they dare not direct at their oppressors. The examples from Roman times imply that minor quarrels are dangerous only because a much stronger force is intent on exploiting them. But Peretz then succumbs to exactly the same displacement by devoting all his analysis to the internal argument without any corresponding analysis of the real and present danger. He asks for change in Jewish religious behavior, but he does not conceive of change in Jewish political behavior. To be sure, when Peretz uses religious imagery, he speaks as a poet, not as a religious prophet, and he uses Jewish images suggestively, without believing in their metaphysical power. But he does not study the Jewish situation as a political problem, in political terms, any more than the religious Jew. Like a believer who looks to God as the protection against the powers-that-be, the poet finds in the language of the religious Jew a deliverance from political urgency.

The term "tragicomedy" was, of course, more commonly associated with the work of Peretz's chief rival, Sholem Aleichem, in which its application is altogether different. Sholem Aleichem's tragicomedy derives from the discrepancy between the tragic circumstance and his characters' perception of it.[4] The two vicious competitors who haggle for customers and turn out to be husband and wife; the father who considers himself the luckiest man in town because he has managed to get the doctor to visit his dying child; the Jewish prisoner who is smuggled to freedom by a bribe from the community, and who then blackmails the community for having bribed his guards; the two Jews in a railroad compartment who try to keep a whole seat for themselves by going to sleep under an anti-Semitic newspaper—Sholem Aleichem draws attention to and away from the dangers that beset his characters by showing what inappropriate adjustments they make to the threatening realities.[5] He proposes no solution to the problem of their existence beyond admitting the human paradoxes. Our laughter explodes the gap between what we know and what the characters perceive. But when Peretz calls his vision tragicomic, we note the discrepancy between tragic circumstance and the author's perception of it. It is he, not the characters, who obscures the tragic potential of his account.

This problem of political perspective first surfaced in Peretz's 1891 statement of literary purpose, when he launched his first Yiddish publication, *Di yidishe bibliotek*, with a proposed program of Bildung, Jewish national education. A far more optimistic European than Ahad Ha'am, Peretz expected the model of a multiethnic Austro-Hungarian Empire to be taken up by the rest of Europe, and he believed that on a demilitarized continent with free trade, the Jews could more than hold their own. As he explained to his readers, an evolutionary process was transforming the continent from a barbaric past to a pacific future. Although modern nationalisms were on the rise, armies and wars were growing weaker and were about to become a thing of the past. Nations would soon learn to compete with each other culturally rather than militarily, across unguarded frontiers. True, nationalism still fomented wars and Jews, who were the "weakest people on earth," still suffered terrible indignities and hardship. Peretz speaks of the Jews as a folk—a people—as one of the many other *felker*, or peoples, in the world, and since he lived in Poland, he had no trouble imagining the Jewish polity along similar lines, militarily weak but culturally viable. Poland had never enjoyed political sovereignty during his lifetime, yet the Poles were clearly a people with a language and culture of their own. The Jews would likewise pursue their national aims through the development of their national languages and culture.

But because the Jews were still stuck on the road to progress at a stage far below their potential, they would have to work much harder if they wanted to keep up with the other nations of Europe, let alone reclaim their place of preeminence. The task of Jewish intellectuals was to get out and educate the Jews so that they might once again become a light to the world.

The intellectual's posture, as Peretz defines it here is identical with the author's in the open letter on circumcision: he stands between two sets of reactionaries, those on the outside and those on the inside:

> Our enemies speak of all Jews as parasites, criminals, rascals. Our detractors say that the Jewish brain is a rotten weed, the Jewish heart is made of flint, the Jewish skin is in a state of decay, and all our limbs are crooked and lame.
>
> Our chauvinists, on the other hand, maintain that Israel is God's only beloved child, that his cradle is faith, his pillow is trust, his swaddling clothes are parchments from Solomon's Temple.
>
> We simply say: Jews are human beings just like all others.[6]

The fight for modern Jewish culture was to be conducted through modern education on two simultaneous fronts: Jews were to resist assimilation by immersing themselves in their own languages and culture, and to resist Jewish clericalism by studying science and other languages. Peretz imagined modern Jewish culture as the golden mean between two equal and opposite forces, each of which demands a choice that the Jew should be unwilling to make.

The proposed content of this modern Jewish culture also anticipates the essay of 1908. Peretz locates the distinguishing feature of Jewish life in *golus*, exile, which refined the ethical values found in the Torah. Peretz praises exile for having pioneered the renunciation of power:

> In the millennial struggle for existence . . . when all other nations marshaled their powers to murder, pillage, and oppress, we gathered our energies and used it to be patient, to endure, to overcome the bad times. **Every other** force will only grow until it meets a greater counterforce and bursts, like a bubble; **our** power will never meet up against any stronger [emphasis in original].
>
> The habits of exile, of having to sit forever at another's table, have freed Jews of egotism and developed in its stead the purest love of humanity [*mentshn-libe*].
>
> Since we are in exile we have on our conscience, on our "Yahadut," no single drop of alien blood; national fanaticism has splattered our flag with mud [*blote*]; we have cleansed it with our blood.
>
> It is to protect this Jewish ethicism that assimilationists should abjure conversion to the majority and that the rabbis should give up their sectarian quarrels.

What Peretz has done in this ostensible polarization of anti-Semitism on one side and clericalism on the other is to create a rhetorical symmetry out of opposite spheres. He adopts the language of physics to articulate a principle of politics, but then alters one of the meanings of power so that the physical force of one side is contrasted with the spiritual force of the other; the two kinds of power are no longer parallel despite the parallel construction of the sentence. Thus, the spiritual nobility of the Jews is irrelevant to a material proposition just as the armies of the gentiles are irrelevant to spiritual competition. And if Jewish power will never face spiritual competition from the gentiles, then it is at least equally true that gentile power will never face physical competition from the Jews, and that virtually guarantees the *khurbn*, the cleansing bloodbath that Peretz foresees at the end of each cycle of exile. This is not symbolic or metaphoric language that invites reading on more than one level of perception at once. Rather, Peretz applies different levels of meaning to the Jewish and gentile spheres, obviating the possibility of true comparison between them. The result of this rhetorical incongruity is attribution of positive value to the political imbalance between gentiles and Jews. It is what came to be known as the "double standard" when it was articulated by a gentile rather than a Jew.

Peretz himself was well aware of the degree to which his imagination was fired by the clash of opposites. A lawyer by profession, he said that he found contrast the most effective way of associating ideas: "If ever reality, the thesis, comes to a standstill, it can be reactivated by its antithesis," like a seesaw or a scale.[7] In the battlefield of modern Jewish politics prior to World War II, it was common to divide Peretz into the realist and the romantic according to the presumed conflict between socialism and nationalism in his work. In this view, the realist furthered the socialist cause by drawing attention to suffering and injustice, while the romantic drew on legends and tales to inspire a renewed sense of national cohesion. But this critical attempt to divide him in terms of political inclinations seems destined to miss the very fusion of cultural politics that he was trying to create. One need only look at the *Yontev bletlekh*, the series of periodicals that Peretz edited between 1894 and 1896, cited by Marxists as the purest fruits of his radicalism, to see the difficulty of separating what was so organically joined. These little magazines certainly did try to elude tsarist censorship by hiding behind religious symbols, and they did subvert religious language for political ends. But they also reinforced and renewed the spirit of each holiday they celebrated. An issue like *Di treyst*, published for *shabes nakhamu*, the Sabbath following Tisha B'Av, forges a connection with the Jewish past that is at least as powerful as the critique of that past. In one of his most often cited essays, "Our Solace and Hope," Perez writes: "The old hell with its demons is gone, once and for all! We will no longer be devoured, enslaved, burned and tortured, driven away. The stronger is also a human being, and as human beings grow more refined, the battles milder, the weapons more humane, the life of the weak is also becoming easier, less bitter."[8]

Peretz offers a vision of comfort to what he calls the "weakest people on earth" that is no less messianic than the words of any preacher on that Sabbath of comfort. T. E. Hulme's description of Romanticism as "spilt religion" comes dynamically to life. Peretz's political optimism has its source in the prophets rather than in Marxism, which is why he so quickly withdraws from radicalism once he sees it hardening into a political movement.

It is true that the Marxist critique, leveled against Peretz with increasing ingenuity under the screws of Stalinist Leninism in the 1930s, damns the writer for just such "crimes" as are described here. In his hunt for ideological purity, the Soviet critic A. Rosenzweig accused Peretz's naive folk socialism of draining the revolutionary impulse because it failed to appreciate the political roots of the social problem. According to Rosenzweig, Peretz may have wanted to distance himself from Sholem Aleichem's conservative-nationalistic realism, but the bourgeois in him pushed him in the direction of "intellectual-individualistic egocentricity" and "idealistic romanticism."[9] The lock-step rigor of this analysis does not obscure, however, some of the critic's finer insights, nor can it be allowed to inhibit continuing inquiry into some of the same issues that Rosenzweig probes. Like so many intellectual writers of his day, Peretz thought that artistic freedom allowed for deeper insight into the condition of his society than could be offered by politicians or political theorists, and he might have offered up his *khurbn* image as evidence of that contention. Political visions, however, are also subject to political analysis, precisely because they do have the kind of "deeper" influence that Peretz claimed.

Since Peretz was an artist, an intuitive rather than a systematic thinker, the blending of spheres is most pronounced in his literary works, where it produces some of his richest effects. Irving Howe described how "[from] Hasidism, Peretz tried to extract its life-strength, without finally crediting its source."[10] Peretz made special use of the supernatural in his modern folktales. Through the introduction of a heavenly court, Peretz animates the Jewish conscience, that highly refined product of centuries of self-discipline, and maintains the rights to the vocabulary of judgment despite the erosion of its basis in religion. The most famous of such stories, "Bontshe shvayg" (1894), opens with a spare, ironic summary of a pauper's life, then moves its venue to the perfectly just court in heaven. Although Bontshe has satisfied the standards of suffering sainthood, this version of ultimate justice condemns the metaphysical system for producing an image like Bontshe's, for discouraging the realism that might have made Jewish life more meaningful on earth. "Baym goyses tsukopns" (At a Deathbed) similarly contrasts the natural and supernatural spheres to the advantage of the first: The angel of goodness is about to claim Leyb Konskivoler after a lifetime of ritual piety when the angel of evil turns up a bag of ill-gotten money that lands the swindler in hell. The good angel is next about to claim Nahmanke of Zbarasz despite his few oversights in religious observance. But when Nahmanke discovers the inanity of heaven, he chooses to go hell to be among the forgotten and the damned. Both these stories expose the Jewish system of belief for subordinating the welfare of human beings to useless or repressive traditions.

But as the idea of progress fell into disrepute, Peretz weighted this same mixture to the other side. In many of the *Folkstimlekhe geshikhtn*, the neo-folktales Peretz began publishing in 1904, the ideal of goodness triumphs in the afterlife, with the irony falling against pragmatic considerations of cause and effect, economic necessity, political probability. The poor families in such stories as "Zibn gute yor" (Seven Good Years), "Der kishefmakher" (The Magician), "Nisim afn yam" (Miracles on the Sea), and "Der oytser" (The Treasure) receive magical rewards for their ethical behavior; an array of *shtume neshomes*, mute souls, are recognized and rewarded by the heavens for acts of private loving-kindness. Peretz's most intelligent admirer, the critic Shmuel Niger, appreciated how the sophisticated author adapted kabbalistic motifs: "Faith is a divine power. It creates a *yesh meayin*, aught from naught: when we hear something that others believe in, it comes alive for us, although we don't share that belief."[11] In a famous statement, Chaim Nachman Bialik, the Hebrew poet, said that *halacha*, *aggadah*, and *Kabbalah* were represented in the modern literary family by Ahad Ha'am, Mendele Mocher Sefarim, and Peretz, thus emphasizing the function of yearning rather than realism in Peretz's work.[12] Self-styled secularists who wished to remain Jews considered Peretz's neo-folktales the foundation of a modern Jewish culture and of a school system that would support that culture.

But Peretz's folktales are more ambiguous than their champions realized. "Shma Yisroel, oder der bas" (Shma Yisroel, or the Bass) is set in the small Polish town of Tomaszow, about midway between Krakow and Lublin. One day a stranger arrives, a man who seems better attuned to another world than to the one around him. His responses to inquiries could as well be those of a "son of God" as of a pious Jew, since he has no mother, no father beyond the One in Heaven, no knowledge save the Shma Yisroel an old man once taught him in the forest, no talent save music. When the bass player of the local wedding band is killed on the road, the stranger Avreml—for that is his sole name—is conscripted to fill his place. Avreml is precipitously married off to the dead man's widow so that she can feed her five children on his salary. But when this "replacement" plays with the group, "he seemed to be accompanying another band of musicians that was playing in some far faraway place, and that he alone could hear."[13] Hence his fellow musicians sometimes amuse themselves and the wedding guests by letting him drone on after they have stopped.

One day Tomaszow hosts a wedding that joins two prominent families—that of the president of the Jewish community of Lublin to that of the Rabbi of Krakow. At the height of the festivities, after the three bands from Lublin, Krakow, and Tomaszow have exhausted their repertoires, Avreml the bass player drones on, as is his wont. But since the Rabbi of Krakow does not laugh, no one else indulges in the usual merriment. The wedding mood grows strained. Suddenly, an old man enters at the head of a mob of paupers to announce that Avreml is playing *khtsos*—in commemoration of the destruction of the Temple in Jerusalem—and that events have been arranged with the very purpose of having the rabbi present to hear this music. The roof of the building opens as he plays, and the celestial choir is revealed singing its accompaniment. As Avreml finishes playing his prayer, the heavens close and the musician falls dead. "'Rabbi of Krakow'—announces the stranger—'you have come not for a wedding, but for a funeral. Avreml has been called to the *pamalye shel malah*, to the celestial ensemble, where they were missing a bass.'" Peretz situates an otherworldly character within a geographically familiar setting, indeed, in the region the author knew best around his native city, Zamosc. The musician is a familiar stand-in for the artist who points the human community toward its unrealized ideals. The title, "Shma Yisroel, oder der bas," draws attention to its mediation between religion and culture, as if announcing its intention of transposing the one into the other.

Down-to-earth Tomaszow can hardly appreciate the spiritual potential that comes to reside in its midst. Since the town thinks only of its material needs, it conscripts Avreml on a utilitarian basis, mocking whatever else he performs as superfluous. Avreml *vert nisgale* (is revealed) in the same way Hasidic leaders were revealed as instruments of the Sublime. But somehow, Peretz manages to be most realistic at the moment that he resorts to transcendence. The wedding has to turn into a funeral before Avreml's sanctity is revealed. It is the music of mourning that manifests Avreml's holiness. The transposition of Jewish religion into culture is an appeal to a heaven without powers of enforcement, to an ideal of goodness without protection. Death is the only realm where such a vision can receive its reward. Avreml expires playing a dirge for his community that still believed it was celebrating a wedding on earth.

Peretz splits the heavens to let the glory of Jewish ideals penetrate his modern story, but the Jewish ideals of goodness have created the political imbalance that has the death of the Jews—the *khurbn*—as its inevitable end. We are back in the "tragicomic" construct where those caught in a dire situation do not recognize its political source. Peretz tried to balance the realistic and romantic in an attempt to forge a modern politics of culture. But since his idea of Jewish culture is the culture of exile, its transposition into politics creates a culture of death. He could only have cut the Gordian knot by thinking in terms of political power that would have meant, as he saw it, betraying the values of *golus*, of exile. Instead, he adopted a mythic language stripped of its metaphysical power. This meant that he would either have to minimize the real threats that were everywhere increasing against the Jews (his tendency in the 1890s) or anticipate the destruction of the exilic community (as he did increasingly after 1903). The great myths of exile had supposed that a divine force would ultimately vindicate the Jews, and reaffirm their sovereignty in universal terms. Peretz's mixture of rhetorical categories put Jews in the service of God without hope of His protection.

Dissolution of boundaries is one of the hallmarks of modernism. In today's postmodernist discourse, to point out real distinctions between religion and politics, between transcendence and realism, might seem like arguing for the existence of a flat earth. But the obscuring of language has antirational consequences, and may itself lead to ideas just as distorted. When the Jews developed a politics of accommodation in exile, they staked more on God than did their Christian neighbors, because they postponed their ultimate political triumph for such time as God would return them to power. Hence they were left far more defenseless than the Christians by the decline of God. Consider the ignominy of Jewish existence that lacks real political power and forfeits all hope of messianic redemption. Jewish survival might then signify some stupid derangement rather than the proud evidence of an ethical force. Peretz was unwilling to face the implications of remaining a nation under such debased conditions, and as part of that unwillingness to let go of the glory of the Jewish redemptive mission, he transmuted the vocabulary of religion into secular cultural literature. "Peretz would have freed the life-energy of the Jews from service to the religious ideal (*derlebn*—that we may live to see the Promise fulfilled) and encouraged it to find direct, creative satisfaction in intrinsic goods."[14]

There is a huge moral and political price to be paid for such distortion. For many years now, the argument has raged over the relation between Nietzsche's Zarathustra, his dramatization of the will to power, and the subsequent history of Europe. In a thoughtful overview of this debate, Steven Ascheim argues that the Nietzschian framework of thinking provided a "crucial conceptual precondition" for the implementation of genocide and mass murder and that "his radical sensibility [provided] a partial trigger for its implementation."[15] There has been no corresponding argument in modern Jewish thought over the relation between what we might call Peretz's will to powerlessness and the political history of the Jews in Europe, or over the legacy of Jewish secularism forged in its prism. The will to powerlessness may be defined as the promotion of the moral ideals of exile as an end in themselves, without either true faith in the ultimate restorative justice of a just God or a political plan for national self-protection. Peretz was one of the most influential promoters of this diaspora politics of culture. The more endangered the culture of exile became, the more Peretz protected it— thinking that he was thereby protecting the Jews whose culture it was. In this he could not have been more mistaken.

Yet Peretz also warned against what he promoted: over and over again, as in the eerie prophecy of the *khurbn* with which this chapter begins. In this and other writings by Peretz, the subtext admitted the catastrophic implications that the plots and arguments struggled to deny. From his earliest *Impressions of a Journey through the Tomaszow Region* and its related stories, "The Pond" and "The Dead Town," to the modernist drama *Night in the Old Marketplace* that he was still reworking when he died, Peretz was haunted by the image of death-in-life, by intimations of doom. Death stalks his *Neo-Hasidic Tales* and *Tales in the Folk Manner* to a degree that the critical literature has yet to recognize. While Peretz remained prominent among the *doistn* (those who affirmed the diaspora), and his commitment to Jewish life within Poland and Warsaw was strengthened as he contributed more and more to its cultural development, great writers reveal more than they intend. The ruin of Peretz's politics of exile is powerfully registered in his own art.

DAVID ABERBACH

10

Hebrew Literature and Jewish Nationalism in the Tsarist Empire, 1881–1917

THE RENASCENCE OF THE Hebrew language and literature in tsarist Russia between the outbreak of the pogroms in 1881 and the 1917 revolution is arguably the most important development in Hebrew since the Bible. Hebrew literature was the main cultural spur to the rise of modern Jewish nationalism. As in previous periods of outstandingly original creativity in Hebrew, 1881–1917 was a time of severe imperial crisis.[1] Prior to 1881, the Russian Jewish population had been moving toward increased acculturation within the tsarist empire and hoped for emancipation and civil rights. They were deeply wounded, psychologically as well as economically, by Russian government policies legislated in a futile reactionary struggle to adapt to major changes in socioeconomic conditions and the international balance of power.

Hebrew literature might be treated as a gauge of sociological phenomena, a record through Jewish eyes of imperial upheaval, social and cultural metamorphosis and wanton violence. The very fact of writing Hebrew itself often expressed, or implied, a strong current of religious-nationalist feeling. The literature of 1881–1917 continued the pattern of earlier periods. The main difference between Hebrew literature in the tsarist empire and its antecedents is its predominantly secular character.[2]

This literature, like its contemporary Russian literature, might be interpreted ipso facto as an act of subversion. It represents, on one level, a rejection of tsarist authority, an assertion of Jewish national feeling, and a declaration of independence from the empire. In this vein, it engaged in a dynamic relationship with the dominant literary culture, adapting and assimilating many of its features while aiming at a distinctively Jewish mode of expression. Hebrew literature grew both as an ethnic branch of Russian literature and as a counterculture.[3]

Historians generally agree that the Jewish problem in tsarist Russia was inseparable from the general weaknesses of the empire. In a psychological sense, furthermore, the image of the Jew in Russian society and culture betrayed Russia's distorted self-image under the pressure of the need for rapid change. For to see the pogroms as isolated anti-Semitic outbursts is historically incorrect. They were, in fact, only a small fraction of the general unrest in Russia during the period, a symptom of the breakdown of tsarist authority.[4] Challenged by the intelligentsia and the working masses alike, the government created the first modern police state, with extensive use of spying, repression, and terror. In 1903, when the second wave of pogroms began, about one-third of Russia's infantry and two-thirds of its cavalry were used against its own citizens.[5]

Nevertheless, the Jews suffered under tsarist rule more than most other ethnic groups. Even prior to 1881 the Russian Jews were burdened with countless laws and restrictions. Most prominent was their confinement within the so-called Pale of Settlement on the western frontier of the empire. The pogroms brought on an "ideological metamorphosis" for the Jews, away from adaptation and merging with Russia and in favor of mass emigration: "spontaneously in almost every town of any size societies were founded for the colonization of Palestine."[6] The May Laws, passed in May 1882, which officially blamed the Jews for bringing the pogroms on their own heads, further accentuated their exclusion from Russian society. From then on, they were subjected to escalating waves of anti-Semitic violence and official discrimination. They left the territory of the empire in exceptionally large numbers. The majority—about two million in all—went to America, but two waves of these emigrants, totaling about 65,000, comprised the first *aliyot* (migrations to Palestine). The number of Jews who left Russia during this time comprised two-thirds of the total rate of emigration, though the Jews were less than 5 percent of the empire's population.

For these reasons, 1881 is often regarded as the crucial date in modern Jewish history. Most significantly for the purposes of this essay, 1881 roughly marks a point of artistic departure in modern Hebrew literature.[7] The structural innovation in Russian Jewish politics after 1881—its autonomy not only in relation to the state but also to the established Jewish leadership, which it now opposed—was reflected in Hebrew literature.[8] Prior to 1881, Russian Hebrew writers did not, for the most part, create works of enduring aesthetic value; after 1881 they did.

From the time of the freeing of the serfs in 1861 until 1917, the Russian Jews produced three different generations of writers and bodies of literature (though there was some overlap), each representing a different mode of Jewish adaptation to the crumbling tsarist empire. The first, in Yiddish, was led by Mendele Mocher Sefarim (1835?–1917)[9] and by his younger contemporaries Sholem Aleichem (1859–1916)[10] and I. L. Peretz (1852–1915). Yiddish literature became to a large extent—although unsuccessfully, as it turned out—a vehicle for the survival of the Russian Jews as an ethnic minority within a clearly defined territory. A second, younger group consisted of assimilated Russian Jews such as Isaac Babel, Osip Mandelstam, Boris Pasternak, and Ilya Ehrenburg. These writers were born in the last years of the Pale of Settlement, which was abolished by the 1917 revolution. They rejected Yiddish and Hebrew in favor of Russian. They eventually came to prominence as major Russian writers under Soviet rule.

The third group—the subject of this chapter—had the most far-reaching influence. It created a literary culture that acted as midwife to the birth of Zionism and the State of Israel. Hebrew literature of 1881–1917 was inseparable from the rise of political Zionism. Yet, the nationalism of this literature was Herderian in its primary concern with Jewish culture rather than with politics. The literary movement is perhaps best characterized by the attitudes of its most celebrated writers. Mendele, the movement's outstanding artist in fictional prose, was contemptuous of political Zionism. Chaim Nachman Bialik (1873–1934), though hailed as the poet laureate of the Jewish national renaissance, persisted in writing deeply personal lyrics while neglecting national themes. Ahad Ha'am (1856–1927), the exceptional theoretician, was locked in fierce debate with political Zionists in the years after 1897, when Theodor Herzl (1860–1904) founded the World Zionist Organization.[11] Other important Hebrew writers of the period, including David Frischmann (1859–1922), Gershom Shoffman (1880–1970), and, above all, Uri Nissan Gnessin (1879–1913), were primarily interested in the creation of art rather than in having educational or political influence. This literature, in contrast with much pre-1881 Hebrew literature, attached great importance to childhood and to Jewish legend (*aggadah*) and myth, to the exploration of the inner life of the individual, and to the creation of a distinct Jewish aesthetic as part of the developing national consciousness.[12] Bialik and M. Y. Berdichevsky (1865–1921), who in many ways were ideological opponents, agreed about their high valuation of *aggadah.* Each writer produced anthologies of *aggadah*; Bialik's, edited jointly with J. H. Ravnitzky (1908–1911), has become a modern Hebrew classic while Berdichevsky's work has been undeservedly forgotten. Though socioeconomic distress played a part, as in other modern nationalisms, the crucial spur in the Jewish national awakening was cultural. In this regard, it resembles other cultural nationalisms, such as those of the Slovaks within the Habsburg Empire, the Greeks within the Ottoman Empire, and the Irish within the British Empire.[13]

Historical and Literary Background

During the nineteenth century, the Jewish population of Russia rose to nearly five million. It made up the largest, most homogeneous and dynamic, and most persecuted Jewish community of the time. The failure of the Polish revolt of 1863 and the Russian–Turkish war of 1877–1878 set off waves of Russian nationalism which, in turn, led to violent anti-Semitism. It may be that the use of Jew-hatred was not sanctioned officially as a diversion from revolutionary unrest within the empire, yet there is little doubt that the pogroms had this effect up to a point.[14] By the end of the Reform Era in 1881, Russian Judaeophobia came "to incorporate literally all of the fears and obsessions of a society in the midst of traumatic social change."[15] There were two major waves of pogroms in the Pale of Settlement, from 1881–1884 and from 1903–1906. From the outbreak of pogroms in 1881 until the 1917 Revolution, these circumstances stirred up a new Jewish national self-consciousness, with profound cultural and political consequences.

Hebrew literature prior to 1881 was a vital part of the background to the cultural nationalism of post-1881 Hebrew literature. The Odessa pogrom of 1871 was a significant turning point.[16] After this, Jewish intellectuals such as Mendele and Peretz Smolenskin (1842?–1884) began to question Haskalah (Enlightenment) ideals, and elements of Jewish nationalism entered Hebrew literature. Elie Kedourie has noted that the leading Hebrew poet of the Haskalah, Judah Leib Gordon (1830–1892), communicates the alienation and the violent revolt against authority and oppression that are characteristic of national movements.[17] The lexicographer Eliezer Ben-Yehuda tells in his autobiography that under the impact of the Russian nationalism stirred up by the Russian–Turkish war of 1877–1878, he conceived of Hebrew as a vehicle for Jewish nationalism in Palestine. Nevertheless, prior to 1881, Hebrew literature was, for the most part, non-nationalistic, heavily didactic, artistically clumsy, and linguistically shallow. The rise of Jewish nationalism after 1881 was a critical force galvanizing both the language and the literature. Within two generations, it brought Jewish literature into the front ranks of Western literature. (Samuel Joseph Agnon, the leading Hebrew novelist after Mendele's death in 1917, went on to win the Nobel Prize for Literature in 1966). Before 1881, Hebrew in the tsarist Empire had been used mainly as a catalyst for educational reform and the assimilation (or "Russification") of Jews into Russian society. The eighteenth-century Age of Enlightenment and the liberal ideals promulgated by the French Revolution and spread by the Napoleonic wars had their Hebrew offshoot in the Haskalah movement. As in Germany and Galicia in the late eighteenth and early nineteenth centuries, Hebrew was adopted in Russia as the language by which the largely uneducated Jews could be introduced to the arts and sciences, particularly the latter. As long as Hebrew writers believed that emancipation and civil rights—above all, the abolition of the Pale—were possible under tsarist rule, they used Hebrew to promote secular education.

The Russian Haskalah, lasting from the 1820s to 1881, was the springboard for post-1881 Hebrew literature. It inspired many translations of educational works as well as experiments in poetry, drama, and autobiography. It stimulated the creation of the first Hebrew novels, starting with Abraham Mapu's *Ahavat Tsiyon* (The Love of Zion, 1853) and including influential works by Gordon, Smolenskin, Mendele, Reuben Asher Braudes, and others.[18] Though this work has scant artistic merit, its historical importance is vast. Its relationship with post-1881 Hebrew literature brings to mind a fable by Russia's leading satirist of the late nineteenth century, Mikhail Evgrafovich Saltykov-Shchedrin. In his story, a ram is troubled by a word that it cannot clearly remember—freedom. In the same way, the Jews were dimly aware of a viable national identity beyond Russia's borders: the pogroms were the main trauma bringing it to consciousness.

The Pogroms and Hebrew Literature

The pogroms which broke out after the assassination of Tsar Alexander II in 1881 were the deathblow to Haskalah ideology and the hope of Jewish emancipation under tsarist rule. After 1881, Hebrew literature was inseparably part of a critical mass of national feeling, of will and creativity liberated by trauma and the new realism that followed. Hebrew writers no longer used Hebrew literature primarily to teach the ideology of assimilation and Russian patriotism. They aimed instead to depict Jewish life as they saw it, for its own sake and with empathy. Apart from the aforementioned fiction of Mendele, poems of Bialik, and essays of Ahad Ha'am, the high points of their achievement include: four short novels by Gnessin; a group of semifictional autobiographies by Mendele, Bialik, M. Z. Feierberg (1875–1899), J. H. Brenner (1881–1921), and Berdichevsky; poems by Saul Tchernichowsky (1875–1943); the Hebrew translations of Sholem Aleichem's stories by I. D. Berkowitz (1885–1973); and the Hebrew translations (by Peretz and others) of Peretz's stories. The chief literary characters in Hebrew at the turn of the century, Mendele the Bookpeddler and Sholem Aleichem's Tevye the Dairyman—both tragicomic creations—are without precedent or parallel in Jewish or any other literature. Interestingly, these characters are based on Yiddish originals, but they became an inseparable part of Hebrew literature. The bulk of this work, comprising a dozen or so volumes in all, was published in the fifteen years between 1896 and 1911. Rarely has a literature undergone such massive changes as Hebrew literature did in this short time.

This body of work has a unique sociolinguistic character. Its writers were all native Yiddish speakers. Their leader was Mendele, who had a seminal role as the "grandfather" of both modern Yiddish fiction and modern Hebrew fiction. His novels, most of which were written twice, first in Yiddish and then in Hebrew, were the principal achievement in Hebrew prose fiction prior to 1939. Two of these Yiddish works, *Die kliatsche* (The Mare) and *Masos Binyomin ha-shlishi* (The Travels of Benjamin the Third), predate 1881; the latter, published in Hebrew in 1896, became the first classic in modern Hebrew. Mendele was the first to recognize Yiddish as a catalyst for the creation of lasting art in Hebrew. Mendele's novels are mostly set during the reign of Nicholas I, and the Hebrew drafts sometimes postdate the Yiddish ones by as much as thirty years and more; yet the basic conditions of the Russian Jews in the time of Nicholas II, when all of the Hebrew drafts were written, were little better than they had been a half-century previously. Consequently, they retained their social relevance after 1881.

Unlike post-1948 Hebrew writers, Hebrew writers of 1881–1917 were self-taught intellectuals, most without even a high school diploma. Although they had generally lapsed from their religious backgrounds, most had been outstanding scholars at rabbinical seminaries (*yeshivot*). The richness of their style, at its best, reflects years of individual study. They brought a fervor and reverence for the Hebrew language, adapting its classical idioms to modern secular art. Perhaps the closest literary analogue to this aspect of their achievement is James Joyce's *Ulysses*. These writers denied through mock heroic satire the sacred authority of the sources but implicitly accepted their imperishable value and their power to inspire.[19]

Hebrew and Jewish Liberation

The metamorphosis of Hebrew after the pogroms of 1881–1882 helped to bring about political change. Russian Jews soon became the largest and most influential group in the Zionist organization. Zionism promoted Hebrew as the national language of all Jews and the growth of creative literature in Hebrew as an integral part of the national renaissance. The sudden, steep rise in the status and artistic value of Hebrew literature would have been highly unlikely had the Russian empire been stronger and less gripped by Jew-hatred. Jewish literature became a vehicle for a form of emigration into a private national domain, the full dimensions of which would soon be mapped out.

While there was and could be no open call for revolution, a number of new features of Hebrew literature were revolutionary: Bialik revived the biblical prophetic style: bitter, angry, critical of the status quo, striking in imagery and rhythmic power, and strong in demands for truth and justice. Berdichevsky called for the Nietzschean release of the instinctual power of the individual. Tchernichovsky idealized the heroes and mythology of ancient Greece, whose healthy, democratic nature implicitly contrasted with the repression of tsarist rule and the stifling narrowness of Russian Jewish life. Feierberg, Brenner, Berdichevsky, and others introduced the heretic as a sympathetic character. The defiant spirit of the age is best captured, perhaps, in Bialik's poems, such as "En zot ki rabot tzerartunu" (Nothing but Your Fierce Hounding), written in 1899:

> Nothing but your fierce hounding
> Has turned us into beasts of prey!
> With cruel fury
> We'll drink your blood.
> We'll have no pity
> When the whole nation rises, cries—
> "Revenge!"

Not least of the revolutionary elements was the elevation of the common Jew as a subject of serious Hebrew literary art, rather than as a catalyst for an educational message. This transformation began in 1886, when Mendele first introduced Mendele the Bookpeddler into a Hebrew story after over two decades of depicting this character exclusively in Yiddish fiction. This act implicitly rejected the idea of inborn superiority, for even an ordinary Yiddish-speaking Jew—a bookseller, a bathhouse attendant, or beggar—could be presented artistically and with human significance. This literature counteracted the dehumanization of the Jews resulting from anti-Semitic violence, poverty, and discrimination.

The disdain that Russian Jewish intellectuals previously felt for the ignorant, superstitious Jewish masses now largely disappeared. It was replaced by warm and curious, though not uncritical, sympathy. The populist movement in Russia in the late 1870s, with its idealization of the Russian peasant, also left its mark on Jewish literary self-perceptions. Even the Hasidim, who throughout the nineteenth century had served as the chief satiric targets in Hebrew literature, were now described far more seriously as repositories of profound folk wisdom.[20]

The waves of pogroms during 1881–1884 and 1903–1906 liberated the Hebrew language and literature in specific practical ways. Emigration to Palestine triggered by the pogroms brought about the creation of hundreds of Hebrew-speaking groups in Russia. Suddenly, it became clear to the young, Russian Jewish men and women who were thinking of emigrating that the emerging Jewish community in Palestine was the most heterogeneous in the world. Only one language united its varied groups—Hebrew.

The pogroms were the catalyst for a historic encounter between the Russian Jewish lower middle class and the Hebrew intelligentsia. This led to a phenomenal increase in Hebrew journalism and in Hebrew readers, who, in the 1880s, already numbered almost 100,000.[21] For the first time, Hebrew writers could, in theory, make a living from their writings, and publishers could make substantial profits. In the 1890 short story "Bi-Yme ha-Ra'ash" (In Stormy Days), Mendele gives a brilliant satirical picture of the time: a bedraggled *melamed* attempting to escape the pogroms travels to Palestine via Odessa and is converted, literally overnight, into a private tutor of modern Hebrew. The upsurge of interest in the study and creation of modern Hebrew and journalism naturally increased the market for Hebrew literature. As a result, the artistic standard of this literature rose impressively after 1881. Hebrew readers of important writers such as Mendele, Bialik, Brenner, and Gnessin during this period rarely exceeded a few thousand, but this was far more than during the pre-1881 period. These readers constituted a widely read and discerning elite, mostly self-taught, but familiar with European and Russian literature. Hebrew literature, previously imitative, now became competitive. It aimed, largely successfully, to become an important part of European literature. The optimism and didacticism of Haskalah literature were turned around. Much post-1881 Hebrew literature is pessimistic and anxiety-ridden, foreshadowing the tone of post-World War I European literature. Yet, this literature also includes two outstanding humorists—Mendele and Sholem Aleichem (again, in Berkowitz's translation)—who convey a Yiddish comic sensibility, which, in retrospect, appears to have been virtually a condition of survival in the Pale. As mentioned previously, Mendele's comic novella *The Travels of Benjamin the Third* was recast from a Yiddish original of 1878. However, it is highly significant in the consideration of 1881 as a psychological divide in Jewish history and literature. Whereas in the Yiddish draft of *The Travels* the quixotic Benjamin does not reach Palestine, in the Hebrew draft of 1896 he does. In the Hebrew version, Benjamin emerges as a courageous visionary rather than an unbalanced figure of fun.

Following the 1903 pogrom in Kishinev, Bialik developed a program of *kinnus*, the "ingathering" of fragments of Jewish culture in an effort to give new force and direction to the growing Jewish national consciousness. *Kinnus* found practical expression in Bialik's work as a publisher and editor. He coedited important versions of the legends and folklore of the Talmud and Midrash, as well as of the medieval Hebrew poetry of Solomon ibn Gabirol and Moses ibn Ezra. But Bialik's own poems, particularly the prophetic "poems of wrath," are themselves a major contribution to *kinnus*, a harmonious amalgam of Hebrew strata parallel to Mendele's achievement in prose.

Maxim Gorky, who read the "poems of wrath" in Russian translation, called Bialik a modern Isaiah. Most of these poems were written during and in response to the pogroms of 1903–1906. They express the outrage and impotence felt by the Russian Jews as well as the aggressiveness that led to increased militancy, especially among the young. It is estimated that by 1903, about half of those arrested for revolutionary activities in Russia were Jews. The official tendency to identify revolutionaries with "the Jews"—though the vast majority of Russian Jews were not revolutionaries—is exemplified in a letter of Tsar Nicholas II to his mother on October 27, 1905: "nine-tenths of the revolutionaries are Yids."[22] Bialik's "poems of wrath" are the outstanding literary expression of the growing radicalization of the post-1881 generation. They mark a turning point in modern Jewish history, the beginning of a far-reaching change in Jewish consciousness, and the emergence from powerlessness:

As our voices entreating lift into the darkness—
Whose ear will turn?
As our raw blasphemy streams to heaven—
Over whose crown will it trickle?
Grinding tooth, knuckling ire-veined fists—
On whose scalp will the fury drift?
All will fall windily
Down the throat of chaos;
No comfort remains, no helping hand, no way out—
And heaven is dumb;
Murdering us with dispassionate eyes,
Bearing its blame in blood-torn silence. [23]

The art that Russian Jewish writers created from 1881 until the revolution is built upon the conviction of holding the moral high ground. Their alienation from Russia, painful though it was, forced them to break from the ideology of assimilation and to seek inner sources of strength and freedom. The following lines from Feierberg's 1899 novella *Le'an?* (Whither?), though put into the mouth of a madman, sum up the metamorphosis which turned many disillusioned young Russian Jews back to their Semitic roots and to Palestine:

The greatest enemy that Judaism has ever had has been . . . the West, which is why I believe it to be unnatural that we Hebrews, we Easterners, should throw in our lot with the West as we set out for the East . . . I believe that this great people, without whose books and spiritual genius the world could not possibly have achieved what it has, will again give a new civilization to the human race, but this civilization will be Eastern.[24]

Hebrew and Russian Literature

As pointed out earlier, nineteenth-century Hebrew literature was closely linked with contemporary Russian literature. In some respects, including its counter-cultural qualities, it might be regarded almost as a branch of Russian literature. The Russian and Hebrew writers came from radically different social and religious backgrounds. The first group was largely aristocratic and wealthy; the second, mostly from impoverished homes. Yet they lived in the same empire at the same time, describe the same general world, and confront similar problems. Revulsion at the poverty, backwardness, and injustice of life in tsarist Russia is common to

Russian, Hebrew, and Yiddish literature. Each of these literatures explores social and psychological malaises that contributed to the breakup of the tsarist empire. The humane depiction of the ordinary Jew in late nineteenth-century Hebrew fiction—a phenomenon that began before 1881, though initially without lasting artistry—was as revolutionary as that of the Russian peasants in Ivan Turgenev's 1852 *Notes of a Huntsman*.

The quarter-century rule of Alexander II (1855–1881) produced an unrivalled body of Russian prose fiction, including *Fathers and Sons* (1861), *Crime and Punishment* (1865–1866), *War and Peace* (1865–1868), *Anna Karenina* (1874–1876), and *The Brothers Karamazov* (1880). The subtlety and depth of Russian literature, its moral power, the astonishing variety of its great characters, its heady blend of realism, idealism, and universalism, its potential subversiveness—and its anti-Semitism—all left their mark on Hebrew literature. No Hebrew writer equaled Leo Tolstoy or Fyodor Dostoyevsky at his best. Anton Chekhov, a major influence on the generation of Hebrew writers born around the 1881 watershed (Gnessin, Shoffman, Brenner), is far and away their superior as an artist as they themselves would have admitted, notwithstanding their crucial importance in the development of modern Hebrew fiction. For inasmuch as these writers set Russian literature as their chief model for the depiction of modern life, it became an ideal to which they inevitably could not measure up. Hebrew at the time was still too wooden and undeveloped. Some Hebrew writers, notably Mendele and Bialik, tried to develop the language to match the goals they had for it. They adopted Western literary standards and created a new style of Hebrew based on the full richness of the Hebrew literary tradition. (Often they did this after writing a first draft in Yiddish.) These writers had far greater artistic success, and their work more effectively became part of the fabric of Russian literature. Mendele's dual achievement in Yiddish and Hebrew is comparable with that of Gogol or Turgenev, and certainly with that of Saltykov-Shchedrin. Characters such as Mendele's Benjamin the Third or Aleichem's Tevye the Dairyman, both recast from Yiddish originals, are indigenous to Russia though they are manifestly Jewish; Russia (or, to be more specific, Ukraine) is their native soil. Bialik's best poetry matches up with the poems of Lermontov or the young Pushkin. Also, as a charismatic literary figure in the Jewish national movement, Bialik had an influence on Russian Jewish society that was in some ways even greater than that of Tolstoy on Russian society.[25]

Perhaps at no other time was a secular literature valued so highly among its readers—even as a compass of moral direction and social and political change—

as in Russia in the second half of the nineteenth century. For the Russian Jewish intelligentsia, this view of literature came easily; it traced a long tradition back to the Bible and Talmud. Hebrew writers largely adopted the Russian perception of literature as a means of changing society, though by the 1890s, the "art for art's sake" movement affected both literatures.

The two often-overlapping streams of Hebrew literature, one drawing from native Jewish culture and the other from Western influences, are closely paralleled in the two main directions of Russian literature, the Slavophile and the Western. The treatment of the village in Russian literature, notably the fiction of Ivan Bunin, was echoed in the use of the *shtetl*, as a stock setting of Hebrew literature, often treated with contempt, or in a sentimental or semisatirical style. Gogol describes the "quixotic" element in the Russian character in his 1842 *Dead Souls*. This element is duplicated among the Russian Jews: Mendele's *Travels of Benjamin the Third*, as indicated earlier, tells of a Jewish Quixote who sets off with his Sancho Panza for the Holy Land. Mendele's satiric juxtapositions of biblical and talmudic characters and allusions with contemporary realities bring to mind similarly absurd juxtapositions in Russian literature, for example, in Nikolai Leskov's "Lady Macbeth of Mtsensk" or Turgenev's "A Hamlet of the Shchigry District." The Russian character of the "superfluous man" and the Hebrew *talush* ("uprooted") are in fact the same man: the man with gifts which have no outlet, alienated and trapped in conditions over which he has little control.

Russian and Jewish literatures of the late tsarist period are united in their critical attitude to the role of education in a society in which the dominant problem was getting enough to eat from day to day. The purpose of education, both secular and religious, is called into question. The most striking poetic expression in Hebrew of being at an educational crossroads is Bialik's 1910 poem "Lifne aron ha-sefarim" (In Front of the Bookcase). The poet stands in front of a bookcase whose sacred books no longer meet present-day needs. Although Bialik's scene lacks Chekhov's tragicomic irony, it is nevertheless reminiscent of the scene in *The Cherry Orchard* (1904), when Gayev addresses the family bookcase. Gayev and his family are about to lose their estate through bankruptcy. The bookcase is a symbol of loss, not only of the property but of noble ideals identical with those of the Haskalah:

Dear bookcase! Most esteemed bookcase! I salute your existence, which for more than a hundred years now has been directed toward the shining ideals of goodness and truth. For a hundred years your unspoken summons to fruitful labor has never faltered, upholding [in tears] through all the generations of our family, wisdom and faith in a better future, and fostering within us ideals of goodness and of social consciousness.

The radical critique of orthodox religion is another feature that binds Russian and Hebrew literature together in an age of imperial decline. This critique was especially vehement prior to 1881, when Haskalah ideology emerged in opposition to what was often seen as a stifling puritan tradition based on outmoded rabbinic authority. In some cases, the attacks on the rabbis may have been unnaturally severe because the Jewish clergy, like the Russian Orthodox priests, represented the status quo and therefore became symbolic of oppressive authority. The rabbis, like some of the priests in Russian literature, were acceptable targets for social criticism and satire, unlike the totalitarian government that had subjected the Jews to hundreds of restrictive laws. The anticlericalism of Hebrew literature remained after 1881 but in a toned-down fashion as the Jews were galvanized into unprecedented unity by Christian hatred.

Censorship deeply affected both Hebrew and Russian literature. It made open criticism of the government impossible and encouraged self-blame and self-hate. Jewish writers, intentionally or not, resorted to displacements or, following the lead of Saltykov-Shchedrin, used an "Aesopic" language of fables to hint at their intentions. In the greatest of these allegories, Mendele's *The Mare*, the battered mare is a symbol of the Jewish people whose miserable state is caused by prejudice and discrimination. However, when it comes to the question of blame, the Jews are themselves held responsible for the mare's pathetic state. In much the same way, Gogol was forced by the censors to alter his "Tale of Captain Kopeikin" in the 1842 work *Dead Souls*, because the original contained attacks on the uncaring tsarist bureaucracy that denied a proper pension to a soldier mutilated in war. In the revision, Gogol puts the blame for Kopeikin's misfortune on Kopeikin, not on the authorities.

In Hebrew, as in Russian literature, censorship taxed the ingenuity of the writer to convey a desired meaning subtly and allusively. In this way, Hebrew writers such as Bialik discovered that the resources of Jewish history and literature gave cover to thoughts and emotions that would otherwise have been banned. The poem quoted above, "Nothing but your fierce hounding" got past the censor because it was originally called "Bar-Kochba," which set it safely in the second century C.E.

In a social system where there was scarcely room for individualism, literature became a vital individual outlet and indirect act of rebellion. The idea expressed by Ivan Karamazov in Dostoyevsky's *The Brothers Karamazov* (1870–1880) that "If God is dead, all things are possible" is implicit in Hebrew literature. Bialik's poem "Al ha-shehitah" (On the Slaughter), written after the Kishinev pogrom in 1903, questions the existence of God, apparently for the first time in Hebrew:

> Heaven, beg mercy for me—
> If you have a God and he can be found—
> Pray for me!

In Feierberg's *Whither?* the hero's break from the authority of family and religion, as well as his incipient Zionism, is signaled by the momentous act of blowing out a candle in synagogue on Yom Kippur. If such sacrilege is possible, then anything is possible—even the overthrow of the tsar, the restoration of the Jews to their ancestral homeland, and the revival of Hebrew language and literature.

Hebrew Literary Stereotypes

Perhaps the most striking and important similarity in Hebrew and Russian literature is the low opinion—often coupled with great affection—the writers of each language appear to have of their own people. This aspect of Russian literature may be taken to presage the need for revolution; in Hebrew literature it is part of Jewish self-criticism accompanying the national revival. Almost every Jewish literary stereotype crops up in Mendele's writings. Though vile and expressive at times of Jewish self-hate, these stereotypes are exploded through empathy and the passion for social change. They are seen as a symptom, not a cause, of poverty and backwardness whose elimination would allow a new type of Jew—free, strong, and confident—to emerge. For this reason, though not a political Zionist, Mendele was adopted by the Zionist camp, and his writings, with their ambivalence toward and satire of diaspora Jews, were interpreted as a justification of Zionism.[26]

Mendele's ambivalence toward his own people is often expressed through the lens of the impartial entomological observer. Like a natural scientist (in the 1860s and 1870s he had produced the first Natural History in Hebrew), the narrator of his stories constantly likens the Jews to ants or fleas. For example, in Mendele's 1894 fictional autobiography *Ba-Yamim ha-Hem* (Of Bygone Days), mostly recast from a Yiddish original of the same period, the narrator complains: "We are a congregation—no, a heap—of ants. In a book on natural history you find a chapter on ants, not on any one ant."[27] In *Ha-Nisrafim* (The Fire Victims) of 1897, an indigent Jew complains to Mendele the Bookpeddler that the house of study where he slept has burned down in a fire that destroyed the whole town (this often happened in Russia). Mendele cruelly remarks to himself, "Fleas, if they could talk, would argue so after losing their lodgings in houses and beds."[28] Blatant anti-Semitic stereotyping occurs frequently in Mendele's description of typical Jewish noses, the Jews' uncleanliness and unhygienic manners, their ridiculous appearance, and love of money.

Russian literature prior to the 1880s was full of similar anti-Semitic stereotyping, though without the empathy and reforming zeal which mark Mendele's fiction. Lermontov's play *The Spaniards*, Turgenev's story "The Jew," Gogol's novels *Taras Bulba* and *Dead Souls*, Dostoyevsky's fictional memoir *The House of the Dead*, the satires of Saltykov-Shchedrin, and Tolstoy's *Anna Karenina*, among others, betray prejudice and hatred nourished by the church and kept alive in the popular imagination. Whatever their personal views of the Jewish people, pre-1881 Russian writers fell short of their liberal, humanistic ideals when they wrote of Jews. The literary stereotype built largely on church-driven anti-Semitism poisoned the image of living Jews. In *The House of the Dead*, Dostoyevsky tells of the Jew whom he met while imprisoned in Siberia:

> He was the only Jew in our barrack, and even now I cannot recall him without laughing. Every time I looked at him I would think of the Jew Yankel in Gogol's *Taras Bulba* who, when he undressed in order to climb, together with his Jewess, into some sort of cupboard, looked uncommonly like a chicken.[29]

The anti-Semitism here, as elsewhere in Dostoyevsky's major writings, is muted in comparison with the virulent hatred spewed out in his publicistic works.[30] Perhaps the most disturbing side to this literary stereotype was the fact that while most Russian Jews lived in conditions of unspeakable poverty and degradation, Russian literature persisted in depicting "the Jew" as being wealthy and in the habit of using his wealth to oppress Russians. Russian writers prior to 1881 seem to have been largely unable to contemplate a Jew without medieval associations of moneylending, miserliness, trickery, and extortion. In *Dead Souls*, for example, Chichikov tries to persuade Nozdryov to sell his dead souls and Nozdryov, sensing a trick, keeps urging him to buy something of value; "what Jewish instincts you have," thinks Chichikov.[31] The Jewish revolutionary Liamshin in Dostoyevsky's *The Devils* is singled out as a traitor to Russia, a "new Judas," though Jewish involvement in the Russian revolutionary movement at this time was minimal.[32]

Even in *Anna Karenina* the only Jewish character is presented stereotypically. Prince Oblonsky covets a lucrative post on the railway board and to his annoyance is kept waiting by Bulgarinov, a Jew whose support he needs.[33] Although these Russian works are counted among the classics in world literature and are peopled with a wide range of characters, the negative image of the Jew is the only one that appears in them. There are no realistic or even sympathetic portraits of Jews to balance the negative portrayals, as, for example, Riah in Dickens's *Our Mutual Friend* is a corrective to Fagin in *Oliver Twist*. Jewish nationalism and the accompanying creation of a vibrant Hebrew literature became a means of fighting this racist stereotype by means of more balanced self-portrayals.

Russian Literary Stereotypes

The distorted perception of the Jews corresponds, in most respects, to the generally low view of the Russian people in Russian literature. This sense of inferiority made the Russians especially vulnerable (as were the Germans in the 1920s and 1930s) to the projective identification of anti-Semitism. The self-hatred expressed by the characters in Russian literature (who in some cases are authorial mouthpieces) might be seen as foreshadowings of the collapse of the Romanov empire inasmuch as it implicitly calls for radical change. A similar self-image is reflected in Hebrew literature of 1881–1917. Bazarov puts it succinctly in Turgenev's *Fathers and Sons*: "The only good thing about a Russian is the poor opinion he has of himself."[34] Gogol's particular genius was to delineate with sharp, precise strokes of satire this allegedly inferior side of the Russian character— similar, in an almost uncanny way, to Mendele's satires of the Jews. Numerous examples of Gogol's jibes at the Russians appear in *Dead Souls*: (1) "no Russian likes to admit before others that he is to blame"; (2) "You know perfectly well what a Russian peasant is like: settle him on new land and set him to till it, with nothing prepared for him, neither cottage nor farmstead, and, well, he'll run away, as sure as twice two makes four"; (3) "In general, we somehow don't seem to be made for representative assemblies"; (4) "a Russian is wise after the event"; (5) "a Russian likes spicy words; he needs them as much as a glass of vodka for his digestion"; (6) "A Russian, to judge by myself, cannot carry on without a taskmaster: otherwise he will only drowse off and go to seed."[35] The contempt Jewish writers often felt for the Yiddish language had its parallel in the disdain the Russian intelligentsia had for Russian. As the narrator sarcastically remarks in *Dead Souls*, "To ennoble the Russian tongue even more, almost half its words were banished from their conversation, and because of that they had very often to have recourse to French."[36]

Russia's weaknesses were betrayed in her perception and treatment of the Jews and in the Jews' vulnerability. It is a lesson of history that a nation's Jewish policy is a gauge of its self-image. The psychologist Erik Erikson has described how individuals belonging to a hated minority might in any case come to hate their own people: "The individual belonging to an oppressed and exploited minority which is aware of the dominant cultural ideals but prevented from emulating them, is apt to fuse the negative images held up to him by the dominant majority with the negative identity cultivated in his own group."[37] The "negative images" are likely to be more vicious if the dominant majority has a strongly negative self-image. Indeed, it is striking how the main criticisms of Russia voiced in Russian literature are echoed in pre-1881 Hebrew depictions of the Jews, especially in Mendele's work. For example, both literatures charge their peoples with lack of dignity, parasitism, backwardness, and demonic corruption. In *Dead Souls*, Gogol implicitly levels the charge of parasitism against the privileged classes—the landowners and the bureaucracy—who treat human beings like property. Identical charges against the Jewish upper class appear in Mendele's novel *Dos kleyne mentschele* (The Parasite). In the 1840s, the Russian critic Nikolai Chernyshevsky attacked the total lack of originality in Russian intellectual life: "What have the Russians given to learning? Alas, nothing. What has learning contributed to Russian life? Again, nothing."[38] Turgenev went so far in his novel *Smoke* as to suggest that if Russia were destroyed it would be no great loss to civilization. These assessments are echoed in Hebrew writers' critique in Haskalah literature.

The low national self-image depicted in Russian literature, though not unmixed with pride and empathy, came largely out of the awareness that most of the empire's population were desperately poor and ignorant. The disgust and condescension often felt by educated Russians toward the peasants is well expressed in Dostoyevsky's *Crime and Punishment*, set shortly after the liberation of the serfs in 1861. The examining magistrate Porphiry jokes sardonically with Raskolnikov that no educated murderer would take refuge in the Russian countryside. "Our modern educated Russian would sooner be in jail than live among such foreigners as our peasants."[39] In *The House of the Dead*, Dostoyevsky expresses amazement at the number of literate prisoners among whom he was incarcerated for four years in Omsk, Siberia, in the early 1850s: "In what other place where ordinary Russians are gathered together in large numbers would you be able to find a group of two hundred and fifty men, half of whom could read and write?"[40]

Russian literature even includes images of the Russian people possessed by the devil, a representation more commonly turned against Jews in traditional stereotypes (and illustrated in Mendele's *The Mare*). At the end of Dostoyevsky's *The Possessed*, the dying progressive scholar Stepan Verhovensky retells the New Testament story of the devils entering the swine as a parable of contemporary Russia: "That's exactly like our Russia, those devils that come out of the sick man and enter into the swine. They are the sores, all the foul contagions, all the impurities, all the devils great and small that have multiplied in that great invalid, our beloved Russia, in the course of ages and ages."[41] This roughly corresponded with Dostoyevsky's own view of Russia.[42]

Not surprisingly, then, Russia's leading satirist of the late nineteenth century, Saltykov-Shchedrin, who influenced Mendele in his satiric portrayal of towns such as Glupsk and in beast fables such as *The Mare*—he used the battered mare as a symbol of the exploited Russian peasant—took a deeply negative view of Russian society and institutions, which he characterized as being ruled by "arbitrariness, hypocrisy, lying, rapacity, and vacuity."[43]

A further sign that Russian Jewish writers often took their cue from Russian writers may be seen in the way the portrayal of Jews began to change. When Russian writers, in part because they were shocked by the pogroms of 1881–1882, began to depict Jews favorably—for example, in works by Leskov, Chekhov, Vladimir Korolenko, and Gorky—the image of the Jew in work by Mendele and other Jewish writers became markedly less satirical and more realistic and positive.

The negative image in Hebrew literature, as in Russian, might represent on one level a breaking away from this image, a declaration of "not us," a function not unlike that of anti-Semitic literary stereotypes in Russian and other literatures. This splitting away from diaspora Jewry, which was perhaps inevitable in the creation of a new national identity, has resulted to this day in a deeply ambivalent Israeli view of the diaspora.

Conclusion

Hebrew literature of 1881–1917 in some ways marks a revolutionary point of departure both from previous Hebrew literature (and, indeed, from Judaism and the predominantly sacred Hebrew literature of the past) and also, in its assertion of Jewish distinctiveness, from Russian and European literature. At the same time, the social and political causes that forged Hebrew into an artistic instrument for Jewish cultural nationalism also gave Russian literature its revolutionary impetus.

The extraordinary artistic quality of Hebrew literature of this period must be ascribed to the convergence of cultural influences in which each major stratum of Hebrew literature in the past and much of the most important nineteenth-century world literature played their part. Imitation came to serve the cause of Jewish national assertion. The growth of European nationalism and anti-Semitism in the latter part of the nineteenth century drove many of the Russian Jews to rediscover their religious-cultural roots while rejecting traditional clerical authority. In doing so, they redefined their national identity by asserting a new aggressive creativity, mainly through massive development of literary and spoken Hebrew. This revival of an ancient language has no parallel in cultural history. Following its meteoric ascent, in 1881–1917, Hebrew was exiled by the Soviet empire, driven back to its birthplace and only homeland. In the Land of Israel, Hebrew has continued as a critical mouthpiece for Jewish national identity. It has grown with confidence and creative vigor lacking since the time of the Bible.

SETH L. WOLITZ

11

Vitebsk versus Bezalel

A Jewish Kulturkampf *in the Plastic Arts*

MARC CHAGALL (1887–1985) is immediately recognized today as a Jewish artist; furthermore, if there is a Jewish art, he is its most famous representative.[1] One hundred years ago, the very concept of a Jewish artist was embryonic, and Jewish art was barely a conception. Chagall's existence hypostatizes both. I maintain that there is a Jewish art, and that there was and is a continuous battle over its definition and parameters and, ultimately, who deserves to own and practice it. Vitebsk (or the descendants of Yehuda Pen's Art School and its socialist / folkist inheritance) and the Zionist-oriented Bezalel School of Jerusalem represent the antipodes of this theorizing and defining of a Jewish artistic praxis. But before there was a positing of a Jewish plastic vision of the Jew, the ownership of the Jewish image belonged mainly to the gentile artist.[2]

In the nineteenth century, gentile artists in the West depicted the Jew according to the interests and prejudices of the national culture. In Polish territories with a large Jewish population, gentile artists tended to paint Jews more frequently than most other Western nations.[3] The range of interpretation was generally limited: the Jew usually appeared in the margins of the painting, reflecting his place in gentile society. He often looked exotic and was placed in a picturesque role, as in *Tashlikh Scene* (1890) by Alexander Gierymski (1850–1901). A full portrait generally showed the Jew empathetically as representative of his craft, as in Waclaw Koniuszko's (1854–1900) *Jew Repairing a Rug*; or negatively, as in *Jews Filing Down Gold Ducats* by Jan Moraczynski; or worse, *A Ritual Murder* (eighteenth century, anonymous). The gentile artist created the Jew of his imaginary world, a construct built on an outsider's vision, appreciation, and prejudices. For the most part, the Jew appears in nineteenth-century art as a projection of European orientalism—the outsider, exotic, and a curiosity.

The artist of Jewish origin emerged in the latter part of the nineteenth century as part of the general accommodation to Western civilization and, in Eastern Europe, due to the Haskalah's esteem for the aesthetic role in civilization.[4] The first artists of Jewish origin sought to participate in the general, current European pictoral conventions. A Jewish image or motif was introduced gingerly, often in imitation of Rembrandtian style and Biblical subject. As Ezra Mendelsohn has shown, Maurycy Gottlieb (1856–1879) is an integrationist in his famous painting of *Christ Preaching in Capernaum* (1879) and the Semitic *Ahasuerus* (1876), which is his masked self-portrait in the Esther story.[5] Artists such as Mark Antokolsky (1843–1902) and Samuel Hirszenberg (1865–1908) represent the first stirrings of Eastern European artists of Jewish origin aware of the possibility of becoming Jewish artists, i.e., giving visual representation to the Jewish presence and self-consciousness.[6]

The concept of being a Jewish artist implies, minimally, a national identification and a self-consciousness that registers this awareness in the production of visual artifacts. These artifacts are to be aesthetic objects in their own right and recognizable as such within the aesthetic conventions of the West. The Jewish artist therefore eschews isolation for participation in Western art by proffering a new cultural *frisson*. Chagall's 1914 portrait of a *Jewish Rabbi* has become the icon and marker of this expression of the Jewish artist and even of Jewish art.

The Jewish artist uses the canvas as a conquest of Jewish aesthetic territoriality. This imaginary space is no less real than any material topography, for a small people needs recognition on a cultural map. From the perspective of the West, any national absence from a cultural map implies a lack of civilization. (Jewish self-removal from visual representation, whether sanctioned by the Ten Commandments or affected by sociopolitical and cultural forces, provided no relief for accusatory attacks on Jewish artistic inferiority.) The Jewish artist, therefore, stakes out both a personal and a national presence. The gentile gaze may predominate but it must encounter the Jewish imaginary that can become contestatory.

The gaze, as Foucault interpreted it in *Discipline and Punish*, is a source of power, definition, and control.[7] Thus, he who paints and projects his gaze or interpretation of the world imposes both an aesthetic vision and an ideological shaping of the world upon the viewer. Jews who were entering Western cultural practices in the latter part of the nineteenth century quickly became aware that the aesthetic realm was more than a space for either personal, grand humanistic dramas or presentations of human aporias. It was the battleground of nationalities staking out claims to cultural hegemony. The cartography of culture was fought over as intensely as the world map being carved up by the contending European powers. A people without a recognized cultural production could not receive any assent as either civilized or worthy of any attention, or possible autonomy, cultural or political. Wagner's accusation that Jews were not truly creative (in *Das Judenthum in der Musik*, 1850) reflected not only his anti-Semitism but a general European hegemonic perspective against any accused declared lacking a high cultural production.[8] A "nation" (meaning *ethnos*) which had no *Hochkultur* was either not a legitimate grouping or it was still barbarous.[9] Jewish sensibility was still smarting even fifty years after Wagner's withering accusations as defenders of Jewish authenticity and nationhood sought to refute or explain away the aesthetic failures or aesthetic nonproductivity of the Tents of Jacob.[10] The Jewish artist therefore inevitably became, consciously or unconsciously, a participant in the ideological and aesthetic nationalist battles raging throughout Europe.

The Jewish artist provides the visual representation of the Jewish intellectual and cultural *zeitgeist*. The canvas becomes the potent space of historical recuperation, creating wholeness out of the depressed and fragmentary, and even of accusation.[11] The contemporary Beaux Arts tradition of historical painting permitted Jewish artists, in imitation of the Polish historical scenes of the most famous Polish artist, Jan Matejko, to restore a glorious past to the Jews and imply a possible glorious future. This explains the Gottlieb setting, among others, of biblical and post-biblical paintings.

At the beginning of the twentieth century a *Kulturkampf* took place on both external and internal levels. The external encounter took place when the Jewish artist sought to construct a distinct personal and corporate aesthetic expression and differentiate himself from the Other within definable parameters. The internal conflict, on the other hand, was a *Kulturkampf* between two Jewish ideologies that had come to the surface with the establishment of the Zionist movement and of the Bund in 1897. Few, if any, plastic artists wrote tracts in favor of one or the other ideological persuasion, and few were even art theoreticians.[12] Their art provides our best means to ascertain their personal convictions. And their loyalties were not according to party lines so much as to aesthetic and often eclectic principles that, by induction, imply a fused political-cultural ideology. Nevertheless, it is possible to align certain artists with the Zionist perspective and others with positions embraced by the various Jewish socialists and folkists. Individual artists passed back and forth, and, in reality, the lines were not rigid. Still, the appellations, "Vitebsk" and "Bezalel," permit ideal terms to distinguish socialist / folkist aesthetic principles and their adherents from those of the Zionists.

Between 1900 and 1920, the Jews, as a minority people with an emergent secular culture, faced a cultural imperative: to establish and legitimate its existence both to itself and to the dominant Others. As Yiddish literature was framing its distinguishing identity by erecting the triumvirate of Mendele Mocher Sefarim, I. L. Peretz, and Sholem Aleichem, the Zionist Jewish art world sought to project and legitimate its cultural ideological vision in the chosen artists whose works fill the publication of *Juedische Kuenstler* as the models for the new Jewish art renaissance.[13] Martin Buber was the major Zionist cultural ideologue in the plastic arts and used his discourse before the Fifth Zionist Congress in 1901 to establish the importance of a Jewish art, the purpose of which was to fashion a "national Soul."[14] Buber carefully distinguished between the achievements of the Jews in the arts where a Jewish self-consciousness exists and the reality of a Jewish art. In his essay on artist Lesser Ury, whose Jewish consciousness he admired, Buber nevertheless argued that a Jewish art was not possible in Europe: "A national art has need of a native soil from which to sprout and a sky toward which it blooms. We Jews of today lack both of them."[15] This position veers too closely to Wagnerian sensibilities about Jewish creative paucity and displays a cultural subordination before the admired German *Hochkultur* that served as a model. Mark Gelber identifies this type of thinking as "a central component of *voelkisch*-racialist brand of cultural Zionist ideology" that predominates in the writings, thinking, and publishing of Buber, Berthold Feiwel, Ephraim Lilien, David Trietsch, and Alfred Nossig.[16] In 1902, they founded together the Juedischer Verlag that published reproductions of Jewish artists. In 1903, Buber persuaded Jewish artists Josef Israels, Lesser Ury, and Max Lieberman, among others, to accept the distinct honor of being included in *Juedische Kuenstler*, published by Juedischer Verlag. These artists were not Jewish activists, nor do their particular works go beyond conventional depictions of bourgeois Jews, except for using Rembrandtian chiaroscuro portraying Talmudists and scribes. Yet the Zionist Jewish art world sought to project and legitimate its cultural ideological vision in the chosen artists whose works fill the publication of *Juedische Kuenstler* as the models for the new Jewish art renaissance.[17]

The men who created the Juedischer Verlag were nationalists imbued with a "*Blut und Geist*" (blood and spirit) ideology (as well as "*Blut und Boden*"—

blood and soil—since they were seeking a homeland), which insisted that there was a unified Jewish aesthetic waiting to be enunciated with its clarion call from Jerusalem. If their thinking partook of the "*Wir sind ein Volk*" (we are a people) vision of Theodor Herzl, it also shared with writer Ahad Ha'am the central idea of building a cultural inheritance, and Friedrich von Schiller's perspective of the importance of an aesthetic education. Ephraim Moses Lilien (1874–1925), the only plastic artist to identify openly with the Zionist political and ideological perspective, organized the first major exhibit of Jewish artists for the Fifth Zionist Congress of 1901. It included Jehuda Epstein, Alfred Nossig, Herman Struck, Lesser Ury, and, centrally, himself.[18] This was the first time Jewish artists were shown in a Jewish national context in Europe.

Martin Buber's real contribution to Jewish plastic art, in hindsight, was to impose a Jewish gaze that mapped the future based on an integrated political and cultural ideology called Zionism. He dared to theorize a cultural politics for Jewish art that placed it in a Jewish homeland, where it would reflect the ideals of the Jewish people as it progressed. Jewish artists had before them a program: the depiction of Biblical heroism, the return and the restoration of the Land of Israel, the beauty of the new / old national landscape as fatherland, and the rich variety of Jewry constituting the scattered folk yearning for reintegration.[19] Buber provided a theme and a figure. He didactically wove an aesthetic belief within an agitation and propaganda effort that would evolve into a new synthetic Jewish art. Buber sought for a Jewish art a definition of its role as *kulturtraeger*, imbricating the historical past with the Jewish future. This late nineteenth-century national cultural thinking galvanized the delegates and readers of his press, for it articulated what seemed an impossibility—Jewish art—and challenged the imagination of both delegates and readers alike.

Lilien's art provides the best contemporary example of the Buberian integration of Zionist ideology and plastic narrative. By espousing the *Jugendstil* (the German Art Noveau movement), Lilien embraced the driving force in Buber's *Jungjuedische Bewegung* by infusing *lebenfreude* and nationalist endeavors into art.[20] Josef Israel and Lesser Ury worked in academic and neo-Romantic realism. Lilien, instead, embraced Art Nouveau with its organicist perspective. What could be better suited to express the new Zionism in art than the call to the telluric, the wild new efflorescence of nature? Lilien brought the Zionist *kulturisten* deal forward: contemporary Western form adapted to Jewish content.

Lilien's celebrated *Postcard from the Fifth Zionist Congress* (fig. 1) defines his narrative voice in clear, symbolic, plastic terms. The picture divides along two axes: the horizontal separates the dark plane of the present from the upper lighted plane of the Zionist future, and the vertical divide sets the left side, burdened religious ideals in an exilic condition, against the right side with its laboring youth and redemption. The angel, (an ironic reappropriation of a classic Christian image) mostly likely the archangel Michael, is established as Jewish by his *Mogen Dovid*. He dominates the scene and conjoins the parts with his wide wings of inclusion, an Egyptian motif that alludes to the Passover theme of being led out of Egypt. He is the unifying theophanic figure, placed inside the scene as a framing device and an indicator of the future. He points the despairing, old, religious Jew entrapped by the crown of thorns bush away from the *galut* to the promised redemption in Zion.[21] The presence of the supernatural, the supernal angel, provides an iconic vision of a God-directed universe. The Zionist ideal functions inside the sacral. Against the *byt*, or routine of static daily life of the old man seated in despairing, exilic reverie, the daily life in Zion of the seemingly banal plowing of the field becomes a singular act of fulfilled living: *zhizn'*, an act of holiness tying Jewish man to Jewish transcendence.[22] Returning to the soil, to nature, and to land is a blessed ideal. Opposite the (unproductive and wild) thorns is the (creative, useful) wheat with the biblical allusion to Psalm 126: "as you sow in tears, you will reap in joy."

The iconic perspective, tilting upward from the eye level of the seated Jew, implies an *aliyah*, both religious and secular—a going up into the old / new land. The eye movement requires a shift from the lower left to the upper right with the implication: Rise! Go east, young man, Go east! That is the future![23] The visual structure demands the movement of the observing eye to share in the directive munificence of the angel: passing from stagnant exile to meaningful homebuilding. The postcard's icon serves as a mediating force creating wholeness from the necessary fragmentary position of the viewer, expunging present time by drawing the golden past into the golden future, and fusing space at Zion's horizon from its fragmentation in exile. The drawing plays the sacramental role of an Orthodox Christian icon, initiating the viewer via the visual mode into the ineffable bliss of Zionist theurgy. The viewer becomes initiate, witness, and can provide testimony.

In short, the iconography blatantly appealed to the contemporary Jewish cultural consciousness by exploiting traditional thoughts redirected to Zionist goals.[24] The framing device, two Mogen Dovids, integrates the Jews into the renascence of nature and Israel. The Hebrew quote from the *Amidah* prayer, "Let our eyes witness Your loving return to Zion," utilizes Hebrew script both as decoration

Figure 1: Ephraim Lilien, *Postcard from the Fifth Zionist Congress* (1901)

and an emotional pull to reinforce the visual message. The Zionist movement, then, is more than a secular activity; rather, it integrates itself within the deepest longings of the Jewish religious tradition. The top frame discretely alludes to the Fifth Zionist Congress in Basle, using Hebrew dating to further integrate the renewing effort of Zionism as a purely Hebraic return and restoration.

Lilien furthered Zionist ideology by seeking to root Jewish art in a homeland. He visited the homeland three times and recorded the landscape and the variety of Jewish faces, particularly Sephardic features which reveal an orientalist influence. *Jerusalem* and its stones particularly draw him and the *Tower of David* with its Zionist flag (1908) expressed clearly the political goal.[25] The *Wailing Wall* with the old women appealed to the continuity of Jews in the homeland and the traditional concept of the *eshes khayil*, the woman of valor. Lilien imagined biblical patriarchs in the Sephardic faces he encountered, and he sought the picturesque in the Yemenite and Bukharan Jews. All these images served to express Zionist ideals of return to the land and the historical unity of the Jewish people.

These subjects continued to appear in Israeli plastic efforts through the 1950s.[26] Zionist art functioned like its political ideology, linking a glorious past to a glorious future while denigrating the diaspora and eclipsing the ever-fragmentary present.[27]

If Zion served as the teleological point of the Zionist movement, the establishment of the Bezalel School in 1906 by Boris Schatz (1867–1932) in Jerusalem represents its allegory and early fulfillment in art.[28] A Jewish art school in the right place, functioning with Zionist ideals, consummated and validated the will of the Zionist Congress and its ideology.[29] Schatz's Beaux Arts sculptural academicism, evidenced in such works as *Matityahu the Hashmonean* (1894) and *Blessing of the Rabbi* (1903), look backwards toward Mark Antokolsky rather than to any new Buberian Zionist art doctrine. Still, Schatz's school did introduce local elements, such as olive trees and camels, drawn from Jewish history and the landscape. The craftwork, particularly, introduced Arab motifs in the attempt to create a new Jewish art style.[30] The Bezalel School succeeded, however, in turning the Jewish religious object into a national secular symbol; the wine cup became a national grail, the candelabra was the projection of Jewish national spirit. The name, Bezalel, alluded to the mythical Biblical craftsman of the Ark of the Covenant (Exodus 36:2), and symbolized for Zionists and non-Zionists alike the reality of a Jewish art renaissance in the making. The school's location, function, and legitimation concretized the emergence of national Jewish creativity.

In 1897, the same year that the Zionists gathered in Basle for the first Zionist conference, Bundists met secretly in Vilna and organized their socialist party, which developed a strong educational and cultural program in the interests of the Jewish proletariat.[31] Although plastic arts were considered part of the cultural activities, the Bund did not attach a theoretical position to art's subject matter and style. It appears fortuitous that in November 1897, Yehuda Pen opened the first Jewish-owned art school in Vitebsk, in present-day Belarus. The school's cultural attitudes were congruous with socialist and folkist thinking about art as an opening to a richer secular cultural existence.[32] The Jewish socialist parties embraced a Dubnovian autonomist political and cultural position opposed to the Zionist nationalist utopian ideal. For the autonomists, Ashkenaz, or Eastern Europe with its distinct Yiddish culture, was the homeland. In art, this concept of *doyiker* (here) took visual shape in the portrayal of the present—of the folk, working families, artisans—and insisted on the rootedness of their Jewish Eastern European milieu. The *Yiddishlikh* presence permeates scenes of the house, the street, the town, the city, and the landscape, underscoring an enracinated Eastern European Jew alive in artwork that celebrates this unique culture. Refusing to enter into a fantasized, synthetic, Zionist integrative vision of *ein volk* consciousness with the three-thousand-year inheritance that Zionist art and culture were determined to revive, the Bundist / socialist culture (particularly the folkist) stressed class consciousness and the rich particularity of the present Yiddish life. This distinction marks the art of Vitebsk painters, so many of whom were graduates of Yehuda Pen's Art School. The term includes, for our thesis, all Jewish artists who adhered to this perspective, whether they were affected by realism, Mir iskusstva, neo-primitivism, expressionism, or cubism. The Eastern European Jewish *volksgeist* dominates their canvas in all its tangible materiality and dreams. Zionist-stylized orientalisms are banished and only the Slavic earth—Judaised—remains. In these artworks, gentiles are rarely seen. The Vitebsk plastic art presents a living culturally unified matrix—in flux, no doubt—but intact: a self-conscious aesthetic expression defending the authenticity, uniqueness, and legitimacy of Eastern European Jewry in itself.

Thus, two major visions of Jewish life confront each other in a *Kulturkampf* on the aesthetic field of plastic art: the socialist / folkist *doyiker* vision of Vitebsk versus the Zionist Bezalel vision. These two distinct artistic expressions extended the dramatic ideological battle lines among contemporary Jews concerning the future direction of the Jewish people. With whom did the future lie? Putting aside religious traditionalism, assimilation, emigration to America, or even accommodationist Russification, seemingly the only creative Jewish options were the Zionist one or the socialist / folkist one. Would Jews express themselves in Hebrew or Yiddish; would Jewish music be based on cantorials and *maqams* or Jewish Eastern European folk melodies; would plastic arts be a synthetic construct of a Zionist ingathering in Palestine or an expression of encounters between Eastern European Jews and Slavs? These were the cultural fault lines that divided and affected every medium of artistic expression and drew their perspectives from ideological, political, and cultural loyalties. Zionism applauded Jewish universality; the Jewish socialists / folkists esteemed the particularity of the Jewish Eastern European masses. The latter drew on the cultural autonomist thinking of Simon Dubnov, the former on Ahad Ha'am's.[33]

Two art books containing putative "Jewish patterns" effectively contrast these two aesthetic positions. In 1905, V. V. Stassov and Baron David Guenzburg published *L'Ornement Hébreu* (fig. 2), a massive book in rich color of old, mainly medieval, calligraphic and ornamental illustrations drawn from Middle Eastern, North African, and Sephardic manuscripts (fig. 3).[34] Stassov (1824–1906), the leading Russian national cultural theorist, encouraged Jews to discover their national art and paint the *byt*, or daily genuine truth of their popular everyday life.[35] He hoped to see a national cultural expression spring forth from the Jews in Russia parallel to that occurring in Russian art, in artists' colonies such as Abramtsevo and Taleshkhino, where artists reworked Russian motifs, and in the genre paintings of groups known as the *Peredvizhniki* or the Wanderers. *L'Ornement Hébreu* sought to provide the roots and routings for developing a renewed Jewish style. It unconsciously leaned toward and expressed Jewish universalist aesthetic principles compatible with the emerging Zionist vision. Guenzburg (1857–1910) was not only a rich Maecenas but a learned figure and much taken with "Jewish Antiquities." *L'Ornement Hébreu* expressed pride in his past and suggested that the full absorption of Jewish historical experience become the basis of a new art. Chagall may have consulted the book's illuminations and ornaments, among others, for the calligraphic play on the banners of his 1922 work *Shtrom* (fig. 4), which shows the influence of the Sephardic calligraphy in *L'Ornement Hébreu*.[36] El Lissitzky (1890–1941) used alphabetic play in *Khad gadya* (1918–1919), which implies that he may have studied the old calligraphy as well. This influential volume expressed the angle of vision and aesthetic ideology proffered by Stassov and Guenzburg. It is an ideology reflected in the book's very title—one that relied on tradition, scholarly antiques, and centrally, the Hebrew language.

Solomon Yudovin (1892–1954) published *Yidisher Folks-Ornament* (fig. 5) in 1920. It consists of twenty-eight Jewish ornaments, mainly tombstone motifs of deer, birds, lions, shofars, and calligraphic play collected during the An-sky Ethnographic Expeditions (1912–1915) to the Pale of Settlement. (figs. 6, 7). These linoleum blockprints represent what is believed to be the authentic visual expression of the Eastern European Jewish folk artist. (The very consciously chosen title of this work, "Jewish Folk's Ornaments," was meant to be in sharp contrast to the rabbinic, Sephardic, Hebraic medieval style in the "Hebrew Ornament.") These motifs and images serve as the basis for many of those reworked in the Jewish art that developed just before and after World War I in Eastern Europe. The Vitebsk aesthetic fused Jewish folk motifs garnered from the anthropological expeditions and contemporary genre settings in a new kind of art.[37] Yudovin's small publication was a last frail voice of the folkist inheritance. The text underscores the folkist / socialist orientation of the editor and is very far removed from the antiquarian, Hebraicist world of Saint Petersburg. Its title is as informative as that of its Bezalel antipode. By locating Yiddish at the heart of the work, and by emphasizing the ornament of the common man, rather than the antiques of the scholar, Yudovin's book reveals itself as the *examplae* of Vitebsk.

Figure 2: V. V. Stassof and Baron David Guenzburg, *L'Ornement Hébreu*, cover (1905)

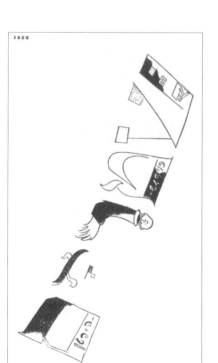

Figure 3: Illustration from *L'Ornement Hébreu*

Figure 4: Marc Chagall, banner of *Shtrom* (1922); © 2002 Artists Rights Society (ARS), New York / ADAGP, Paris

Figure 5: Solomon Yudovin, *Yidisher Folks-Ornament*, cover, linoleum block (1920)

Figure 6: Tombstone ornament from *Yidisher Folks-Ornament*, linoleum
block (1920)

Figure 7: Ornament from *Yidisher Folks-Ornament*, linoleum block (1920)

The Vitebsk school and its socialist / Bundist position challenged the normative traditional authority of Hebrew and rabbinic culture and subverted it as desuet, inoperative, and unacceptable—for it ruled out the Jewish masses, the *am ha-arets*, who now claimed authority as the basis of the new Jewish creative life. The status of the rabbinic intellectual cultural tradition and its functioning, which, from the Buberian Zionist perspective, provided a treasure trove for secular aesthetic elaboration, became diminished in the Bundist / socialist aesthetic, where folkic creations are foregrounded. The contemporary clock maker or barber replaced biblical figures as subjects of Jewish art and as embodiments of the Jewish modern condition. In these figures perhaps lurked the nobility of King David or Samson, but their own authenticity and legitimation came first. This new Jewish Eastern European art, as Dovid Bergelson articulated it, reflected *undzer eygns*: our very own, the organic unity of Ashkenazic Yiddish culture. This did not mean that all biblical or rabbinic elements were removed, as in the Stalinist period, but it implies that the Jewish folk experience presupposed the learned inheritance and not vice versa. Zionist art employed imagery and portrays scenes drawn from the biblical and the synthetic future of the Ingathering of the Exiles, from the heroic figure of the past or coming future, from the restored homeland. Bundist / folkist art insisted instead on the organic present. Zionist art was an engaged art, whereas the art of Vitebsk was celebratory. Both sides wanted the best for the Jewish people and revealed how the aesthetic obsession, *Schoenheitskultur*, as Buber put it, had penetrated and formed modern Jewish life in all camps.[38]

Unlike the Bezalel Academy, which was subsidized by the Zionist Congress, Yehuda Pen's School of Drawing and Painting had no underwriter. Yet the number of significant artists who passed through it, such as Marc Chagall, El Lissitzky, Solomon Yudovin, and Ossip Zadkine (1890–1967), mark its importance as a center of Jewish artists and Jewish art creation. What distinguishes the Vitebsk Jewish artists from the German and Austrian-Hungarian Jewish artists of Zionist persuasion, or from fellow countrymen who went off to Palestine (such as Abel Pann and Yitshok Likhtenshteyn), is their conscious time- and space-boundedness. They grappled with the present and took the present as the given upon which to expand, not flee. The world of the Vitebsk school inherited, but vastly altered, Yehuda Pen's strict adherence to the tradition of the Wanderers. Pen's art captures the popular Jewish life, portraits and landscape of the *shtetl* culture in Vitebsk.[39] Genre scenes include: a winter street scene entitled *Balagole* [drayman] *in the Snow*; a spring scene, *Bathing the Horse;* an interior of a rabbinic court called *Divorce* (1907) (fig. 8); *Shabbos*, a depiction of Jewish observance;

portraits of artisans such as *Old Dress Maker* (1910), and *Clockmaker* (1914) (fig. 9), both allegories of time and the world in disrepair. In the latter the newspaper refers to World War I: *groyse shlakhtn an karpatn* (great battles in the Carpathian Mountains).[40] Pen's art reflects the *byt* of an intact culture, not a projected one. The painterly perspective places one in direct eye contact as an equal. The artist is at one with his community.

Yudovin, An-sky's nephew, exemplifies the folkist / Bundist aesthetic, the Vitebsk school *par excellence*, for his mastery of the woodcut reflects the craft element always conscious in the Jewish socialist / folkist aesthetic. His woodcuts, based mainly on the folk art he recorded on An-sky's ethnographic expeditions, attempt to stylize, via cubist and expressionist elements, an Ashkenazic form with the Ashkenazic content of the *shtetl* world. *Street Scene* (fig. 10), *Bath House*, and *Wooden Synagogue* (fig. 11) emphasize a specific cultural milieu, while the victim in *Pogrom* depicts the negative realities of this culture. Yudovin's *shtetl* world, unlike Pen's, is disintegrating. The foregrounded graves seen in *Vitebsk* are not accidentally marked.[41] Yudovin's art reveals the aesthetic drive of Russian Jewry to create a Jewish style that is iterative as a Chinese painting across the ages.

Joseph Tchaikov (1888–1986) clearly voices the position of post–World War I avant-garde leftist Jewish artists. He is the most thorough example of the "evolved" Jewish artist; he began with the *Jugendstil* and its Zionist / biblical imperative in 1911, passed into folk-national / socialism with cubo-futurist stylization in Kiev in 1918–1920, and became a thorough modernist by 1921 before a later conformity to Bolshevik tasks. For Tchaikov, the new true Jewish art should emerge through form, not content: "pure plastic form is deeply national."[42] Therefore he rejected the folkist / Bundist use of the "*folks-primitiv*" as the basis of the new Jewish art. Tchaikov's position, "stylization is aestheticism," leads nowhere. In the catalog of the Kultur-lige Kiev Exhibition (February–March 1920), this statement appeared: "Modern Jewish art seeks to recreate our artistic inheritance in national forms."[43] But these national forms, though seductive, were elusive. The Vitebsk position had reached an impasse.

Boris Aronson (1898–1980), the designer of *Fiddler on the Roof* (1964), recognized the limits of the two major Jewish perspectives, Bezalel and Vitebsk. He lambasted art built on "Zionist slogans . . . for these artists [Lilien, Steinhardt, etc.] could not liberate themselves from tendentious literary lines of thought . . . [and] tendentious motifs such as palm trees, Stars of David . . ."[44] Aronson had little belief by 1923 that Jewish stylized art—the Vitebsk artists like Yudovin and El Lissitzky—was leading to a national style either. "A Jewish style has not yet

Figure 8: Yehuda Pen, *Divorce* (1907)

Figure 9: Yehuda Pen, *The Clockmaker* (1914)

Figure 10: Solomon Yudovin, *Street Scene* (1926)

Figure 11: Solomon Yudovin, *Wooden Synagogue*, woodcut (1920)

been created."[45] As Aronson and Issachar Rybak—and most Jewish artists of the period agreed—if a Jewish artist, and possibly a Jewish art, existed, then Chagall approached that ideal most.[46] But this was not the way to a distinct Jewish style, a distinct national form, or a distinct national art. The Vitebsk school of *byt* and *folks-primitiv* stylizations was grinding to a halt by 1923 as the best artists moved on to abstraction. The Jewish esthetic *Kulturkampf* was over, seemingly with either two losers or a stasis.

As the Jewish aesthetic *Kulturkampf* played itself out before art history, Jewish artists, whether prone to Jerusalem or to Vitebsk, knew that both, indeed the entire tsarist empire, were too provincial for their aesthetic needs. Paris inescapably figured as the center of modern artistic creativity and Jews followed all the others there to learn, create and discover esthetic and intellectual freedom. The artists' colony called La Ruche (the beehive) in Paris served as the temporary ingathering of Jewish artists, and became the site of a showdown between the Vitebsk and Bezalel schools in 1912.[47] Putting aside the neutrals, Modigliani and Soutine, who were also present, Chagall would represent the proto-Vitebsk school and face Yitshok Likhtenshteyn, Ossip Zadkin, Joseph Chaikov, Leo Kenig, Marek Shvarts, and other prodigies of the Bezalel cultural Zionist perspective, still heavily influenced by the *Jugendstil* and Lilien. These young Zionists, determined to create the new Jewish art, published an art journal called *Makhmadim* (The Precious Ones) (fig. 12). Each issue was dedicated to a Jewish holiday and filled with biblical scenes; for example *Adam and Eve* (fig. 13) by Marek Shvarts appeared in 1912, in an issue devoted to the Shavuot holiday.[48] Chagall riposted in the same year with his own, modernist version of *Adam and Eve* (fig. 14), a fine piece of cubism and not even draped! By choosing the biblical Adam and Eve as subject matter, Chagall not only invaded the Zionists' chosen territory—up to that point, he had stayed within the "Vitebsk present"—but exploded their antiquarianism and rearguard approach to Jewish matter and the creation of Jewish art.[49] Their *Jugendstil* was not only hopelessly passé in 1912 Paris, but its intention of using Jewish iconography as decorative elements to serve as a basis for Jewish art was futile and vapid (as Aronson noted belatedly ten years later). Chagall pours lust into his canvas with the vibrant nudity and Garden of Eden freshness, before the Fall, represented by the apple tree. He forces the viewer to see the scene in its contemporary moment and not as a latter-day iconic moment drained of libido. The very use of the cubist design, with its simultaneity of perspectives, projects temptation; the subjects' bodies flow as a wondrous dance of desire, emphasizing the dynamic role of Adam and Eve as the procreators of humanity. They are lusty humans conjugating: contemporary in their time and made contemporary in our time by the shared human performance; far from the flat, static, flaccid designs of the *Jugendstil* so awkwardly drawn by Marek Shvarts. Jewish art would need the dynamism and complexity of contemporary Western artistic perspectives and techniques. Chagall debunks the Zionist synthetic art project that simplemindedly invokes Biblical imagery, and believes it has resuscitated the glorious past and forced a glorious new existence.

The *Adam and Eve* painting underscores for us how advanced Chagall was both in painterly treatment and modern secular interpretation. He had already absorbed the Mir iskusstva colors of Bakst and the Fauves, the neo-primitivism of the Russians, Larionov and Goncharovna, the Orphism of Robert and Sonia Delaunay, as well as analytic cubism. As he wrote, "I gaily laughed at the futile ideas of my neighbors on the fate of Jewish art. Fine, you talk, I'll work."[50] Chagall's *Adam and Eve* subverts the Bezalel school on its own grounds and for its naïve essentialism, backward-looking attitudes, artificiality, and inability to express contemporary Jewish sensibility in contemporary form or style. He dared to argue in the *Adam and Eve* painting that one is most Jewish when one is most human! And Jewish art would be most valid when it went beyond a Jewish parochialism. When the specific is revealed to incorporate the universal, a valid modern Jewish art can emerge.

This perspective has its roots in the Vitebsk School of Drawing and Painting, where Pen validated the use of contemporary Jewish urban folk life. Going way beyond his Vitebsk teacher, Chagall cracked open the Jewish Vitebsk world to reveal its hidden *seelenlandschaft*, where its humanity joins the universal. From an outside street scene of *The Violinist* (1911), the interpreter of the soul, to an inside intimate genre, the *Spoonful of Milk* (1912)—a Philemon and Baucis rehearsal of the universal image of loyal old conjugal love—to *Birth* (1912), a complex multi-perspectival scene in full folkic existence, the artist displays not only the fusion of Western technique with contemporary Jewish Eastern European existence, but the common humanity of the Jews. What appears at first foreign and exotic melts into a shared human condition. The contemporary *shtetl* Jew becomes a symbol—as much as the traditional biblical figure—of what is the human universal.

Nor was Chagall afraid to reappropriate Christological imagery for national Jewish interests. The *Golgotha / Calvary* of 1912 may have shocked his *Makhmadim* comrades, but this dark work, according to Amishai-Maisels, is also a comment on the persecution of the Jews at this period of the Beilis Trial.[51] If Beilis,

Figure 12: Makhmadim,
cover, hectograph (1912)

Figure 13: Marek Shvarts, *Adam and
Eve*, hectograph (1912)

Figure 14: Marc Chagall, *Adam and Eve* (1912); © 2002 Artists Rights Society (ARS), New York / ADAGP, Paris

and by extension the Jews of Russia, is the Christ victim in the painting, we see that Chagall absorbed the Russian icons he had seen in his Vitebsk youth and subverted them for Jewish accusation: through the Jewish gaze, the Jewish artist voices the Jewish response of victimization and outrage, using the reappropriated Christological imagery for shock value. Here we see what the "Vitebsk present" permitted and the Bezalel / Zionist vision could not perform.

The publishers of *Makhmadim* ceased the journal's publication shortly after Chagall's *Adam and Eve*. Were they affected by this painting? Marek Shvarts stated thirteen years later that Jewish artists at that time were unaware of their past and when they did look inward, they only "wanted to orientalize" in the style of the Bezalel school.[52] Chagall had proved the limits of the Bezalel approach. In his memoirs, Yitshok Likhtenshteyn, who had studied in the Bezalel Academy, does not even mention *Makhmadim*, of which he was one of the founders, but describes the *nakhes* (pride) felt by the Jewish artists at La Ruche when they saw Chagall's "provincial motifs [read Vitebsk] on the walls of a cosmopolitan city's salons [read: Paris!]."[53] In terms of art history, this moment was a victory for Chagall and the Vitebsk school in the *Kulturkampf* with Bezalel. Of the *Makhmadim* artists, Yosef Tchaikov would become a cubo-futurist, Marek Shvarts, an expressionist, and Ossip Zadkine, a member of the *École de Paris*. Leo Kenig became a shrewd art critic and wryly chided himself for his *Makhmadim* days.[54] The La Ruche encounter was a victory for Yiddish modernism and the Vitebsk perspective personified by Marc Chagall.

Chagall did not create a Jewish form or an iterative Jewish style, but succeeded in creating what can be called a Jewish point of view, a perspective that distinguishes a Jewish work from a non-Jewish artwork; a Jewish expression which depends on *double entendre*. Ziva Amishai-Maisels calls it an "in-joke," but I consider it something far more serious.[55] I call it a Marranism (from the Spanish, *marrano*)—the condition in which Jews have existed for centuries in the diaspora: living on two levels, that of the general populace and that of the specifically Jewish. Chagall lived this reality in his art and also in the various worlds in which he moved—worlds that were not fused, but imbricated. Having learned from cubism the power of simultaneity, he adapted its system in art to that of a Marrano living and functioning in two different existences at the same time. His art sends one message to the general public and another to Jews who spoke his language.[56] This dyadic condition could be accomplished by visual puns or carefully placed images on the canvas, sending different cognitive and emotional meanings.[57] It obviates the question of creating a new "style" but renews and exploits an old Aesopian tradition that was simultaneously universal and particular. This permits full participation in the Western tradition but allows a hidden space for a Jewish presence and commentary when a direct Jewish gaze was not always admissible.[58]

In 1911–1912, for example, Chagall painted *Half Past Three in the Morning— Poet* (fig. 15).[59] This work first confounded viewers, but later received the approbation of the surrealists, who saw it as an example of their dynamic vision.[60] For one who knows Yiddish, the work called forth the idiom *fardreyter kop*, literally, "his head is turned upside down!" or a little crazy.[61] This has been common knowledge among Yiddish-speaking viewers for a long time but it was it recorded only in the 1960s. Chagall himself never admitted to these *double entendres* that permitted non-Yiddish speakers to see surrealist expressions and personal fantasies at work. This Aesopian visual language, Marranism, harbors a secret and meaningful Jewish gaze where Jewish art really exists: a distinct *eygns* (one's own) hidden under a Western universal order. This same system of the Jewish Marranic gaze can be detected even in a Jewish leftist universalist artist such as Louis Lozowick (1892–1973) in his 1964 lithograph, *Arch of Titus* (*Titus Harasha*), (fig. 16).[62] This work seems to be an innocent depiction of a Roman antiquity, in the *veduta* (view) tradition of Giovanni Battista Piranesi. The angle of the lithograph focuses upon a candelabra carried in a triumphant march by captives. An educated Westerner would recognize the candelabra as the temple *menorah* on the shoulders of Jewish captives, paraded for the glory of Titus' conquest of Judea. But the lithography fills the tunnel inside the Arch of Triumph with passing figures, one of which, in the same *grisaille*, turns upward toward the *menorah* and has a short beard. The allusion is clear here: beard equals Jew. But that is not the whole message. In the background, through the archway, appears the ruined Colosseum. In reality this is an impossibility, but in art, all is possible—and for a reason. The reading suddenly becomes more evident: The Romans destroyed Israel the state, but the Jews as a people are still here. The Jew looks up to the *menorah*, whereas the triumphant Romans, like their ruined Colosseum, are gone. The whole *veduta* could be based on the Hebrew Zionist phrase: *Am Yisrael khai*, the people of Israel live! This work, then, produces two meanings, a scene of Roman antiquity and the Jewish gaze in a Marranic posture commenting on Jewish continuity. This, too, is Chagall's real contribution to the continuous creation of a Jewish art.

Chagall understood early on that a "pure" Jewish art as a distinct style for a "peoplehood," as in Egyptian or Greek art, was impossible; those cultures functioned in a self-contained world, whereas the Jews were living among other people. Modern Jewish art could function only as a hybrid. In the give and take of artistic creativity, the Jewish artist combines the elements of the "culturally

Figure 15: Marc Chagall, *Half Past Three in the Morning—Poet* (1912); © 2002 Artists Rights Society (ARS), New York / ADAGP, Paris

Figure 16: Louis Lozowick, *Arch of Titus*, lithograph (1964). Courtesy Mary Ryan Gallery

definable" popular elements of the old "home" culture with the discoveries and breakthroughs in painterly techniques and vision of the surrounding cultures and the reality of contemporary multicultural hybridity. Chagall's art eschews the essentialist views of the *Makhmadim* artists who were still addressing a *Blut/Geist/Boden* vision of Jewish artistic identity, determined to identify or construct a unique Jewish style. In 1917, Lissitzky's remarkable *Sikhes khulin* still employed the *Jugendstil* framing style, tied to the frontispieces of talmudic volumes. For Chagall, the *Jugendstil* of the *Makhmadim* in Paris 1912 was a desuet hybrid style. Like the later Tchaikov, who would argue that a Jewish art should emerge from temperament and tradition via personal form, Chagall in prewar Paris considered Jewish props as outer trappings and not Jewish art.[63] Hybridity was the essence of Jewish modern art; it allowed Jewish expression to go beyond the limited iconic possibilities in the traditional culture. The resources of neo-primitivism, cubism, futurism, and expressionism as stylistic approaches that transcended any definable national culture proffered to the young Jewish artist a means to fuse his "Jewish" experience into a contemporary visual image and language which were at once personal, communal, and European. This latter perspective contains the cultural ideological position prevalent in the Vitebsk vision of Jewish artistic manifestation. The Vitebsk school refused an essentialist vision of Jews but adopted a progressive one rooted in the Eastern European Jewish culture.

Chagall and the many Jewish artists who followed him, such as Altman, Tchaikov, and El Lissitzky, had no difficulty absorbing "Russian" elements, for they accepted the Bundist/folkist autonomist position that saw itself as part of the all-Russian cultural life. Indeed, the stabilization of this Eastern European Jewish art accepted its unique Jewish rooting as part of the "*Ruslendishe*" cultures (the various cultures inside the Russian realm) as opposed to subordinate to Russian culture. Such a position radically differs from the Buberian Zionist cultural perspective in which the Palestinian landscape and varieties of Jews serve as a source with the *muskeljudentum*, in Max Nordan's word, of the new Jewish art. But by World War I even the Zionist artists abandoned *Jugendstil* and the trappings of Lilien's Hebraic motifs for the newer European artistic styles, while also probing Hebraic sources and Sephardic traditions, as opposed to the popular Eastern European Jewish traditions of the Vitebsk school.

The Vitebsk school as heir to Dubnovian folkist and An-skian aesthetics produced greater artists than the Zionists. The Zionist expression through the Bezalel school served as a ground for the elaboration of contemporary Israeli art and its minor accomplishments. But by basing their Jewish art on the contemporary and folkic sources, the Vitebsk school tapped into a living inheritance that paralleled the Russian artistic experience.[64] It later found institutional support through the *Kultur-lige* in Kiev 1918. By 1920, the Vitebsk perspective of Jewish art had passed into abstraction and world fame.

Jewish art, like any other art, does not exist just because it is prescribed by a political cultural ideology. It emerges from internal cultural combat. The Jewish *Kulturkampf* in the plastic arts at the beginning of the twentieth century permits us to see today the width, array, and energy of Jewish aesthetic thinking and creativity represented by the various warring factions. Their cultural productions are now artifacts hanging on the walls of the world's finest art museums. Between 1897 and 1920, they accomplished a small miracle: the creation of a Jewish presence in the plastic arts. The emergence of a Jewish gaze is indisputable, and that gaze is now indelible.

East European Jewish
Politics in Emigration

JONATHAN FRANKEL

12

The Bundists in America and the "Zionist Problem"

WITHIN A FEW YEARS OF ITS FOUNDATION in 1897, the Bund emerged, if only for a brief moment, as the most prominent political force in the Russian Jewish world. It took the lead and set the tone during the revolutionary year of 1905. With tens of thousands of members, the Bund served as a model which other Jewish parties of the Left (autonomist, Zionist, territorialist) sought, with varying degrees of success, to imitate.[1] In 1917, the Bund was cut off from much of its constituency by the German conquest of Poland and Lithuania. Nonetheless, it again played a significant role in both the stormy politics of Russia at large and in internal Jewish affairs. Most specifically, it took the lead in the attempt to call together a democratically elected Jewish national assembly.[2] Bundists— Mark Lieber (the "defensist") and Rafael Abramovich (the "internationalist"), for example—were among the most influential figures in the Petrograd Soviet between February and October 1917. Outlawed in Communist Russia in 1921, the Bund was able, despite profound inner conflicts, to reconstitute itself in independent Poland and in 1936–1939 once again, as in 1905, won for itself a leading, even dominant, position in the arena of Jewish party politics.[3]

It may seem surprising that a party that prided itself on its allegiance to orthodox Marxism and the doctrine of class war was able (if only periodically) to gain such support from a people still largely traditionalist in its way of life and habits of thought. Perhaps this can best be explained as resulting from a complex combination of factors. First, the Bundist ideology, for all its sectarian and schismatic characteristics, still fused the utopian and quasi-messianic appeal of revolutionary socialism with a nationalism grounded in the urgent need to win Jewish self-determination not far away in space or time but, rather, in the here and now. This dual message could hardly fail to have a ready appeal, albeit at only certain moments, to a population made up largely of workers, artisans, and casual laborers suffering from impoverishment and overcrowding, low wages, excessively long hours, and chronic economic insecurity.[4] The fact that the Jews of the Polish-Russian borderlands (Lithuania, Belorussia, Galicia, Ukraine) were one of a number of linguistically differentiated peoples living in a multinational environment also served to increase the attraction of Bundism. Cultural-national autonomy was seen as a logical enough demand in a still predominantly Yiddish-speaking context. To these objective factors one must add the remarkable ability of the Bund to create for its members and supporters something of an all-encompassing subculture that combined political activism with support for party-oriented trade unions, schools, publishing houses, newspapers and journals, youth groups, and social services. At its best, the Bund was considered something of an extended family. Finally, there was the fact that the Bund was perceived as particularly well constituted to defend Jewish interests in times of immediate challenge or threat. Its underground experience equipped it to organize armed self-defense against pogroms, and its ties to fraternal socialist parties (the Russian Social Democratic Labor Party in 1905 and 1917; the PPS in interwar Poland) promised an escape route from Jewish isolation in moments of crisis.

In the wake of the mass immigration of Jews from the Russian Empire before the First World War, it was only natural that an organization inspired by, and largely modeled on, the Bund should have been established in the United States. The Jewish Socialist Federation was set up in 1912 by veterans of the Bundist movement and, like the Bund, was constituted as a subunit within a broader multiethnic framework, the Socialist Party of America. Also like the Bund, it sought to combine its socialist message with an emphasis on Jewish pride, meaning the cultivation of Yiddish language and culture.[5] For all its vicissitudes (and a name change in the 1920s), this organization would play a significant role in the American Jewish labor movement, and hence in American Jewish life as a whole, until after the Second World War.

In retrospect, however, it is obvious that there was no realistic chance for the Federation to reproduce the measure of relative success achieved by the Bund in the tsarist empire and later in independent Poland. The immigration law of 1924 would eventually cut off the flow of reinforcements, leaving the movement exposed to inexorable erosion by deep-running socioeconomic forces. These included the upward socioeconomic mobility that constantly depleted the ranks of the Jewish proletariat and the residential mobility that attenuated group cohesion.[6]

The truth is that from the very start the Federation faced almost insurmountable hurdles. Clearly, the idea of Jewish cultural-national autonomy underwritten by the state had no place in America and was never proposed by the Federation. Even the call for the reinforcement of Yiddish could have only limited appeal in an immigrant community that was determined to see at least the younger generation rapidly acquire a complete mastery of English. For all the talk in the Progressive era of "cultural pluralism," the melting pot remained the norm of everyday life. And, of course, there was no room in the United States for an armed vanguard of Jewish people either to counter pogroms or to prepare for violent revolution. In the practical and everyday terms that were of overriding concern to the immigrants who arrived penniless in America, the Federation had almost nothing to offer. The Socialist Party, as a third force in a two-party system, could not compete with the big city political machines of the Tammany Hall variety, either in the distribution of carrots (contracts, jobs) or in the wielding of sticks (the withdrawal of permits, the imposition of fines). Moreover, within the Jewish labor movement, the Bundists had arrived too late. It was the generation of socialists, anarchists, and populists who had reached America in the 1880s that had set in place the institutions that would meet the basic needs of the post-1905 immigration. Those trade unions in which Jewish workers predominated were grouped under or around the United Hebrew Trades, an umbrella organization founded in 1888; insurance could be obtained via the Workmen's Circle (the Arbeter Ring) set up in 1892; and for news there was the socialist Yiddish daily, *Forverts*, established in 1897.[7]

It was thus only logical that the Bundist immigration to the United States made its most dramatic impact not so much in organizational terms, through the Jewish Social Federation, but rather through its individual graduates who, facing the challenge of the New World, struck out in various, often radically opposed, directions. From among the thousands of Bundists who arrived in America (their exact number cannot be known) many became publicly prominent, winning real fame in some cases and no small measure of notoriety in others. Nothing else was to have been expected. They were, after all, mainly members of the 1905 generation, their formative years indelibly stamped by the revolutionary experience in the Russian Empire. Strikes, demonstrations, sudden mobilization of mass support, the burgeoning of political activity and party rivalry, a clandestine and semilegal press, pogroms and self-defense units, gunrunning, street clashes with Cossacks, highly attended political funerals, arrests, imprisonments and the years of exile in Siberia—all this could not but produce a crop of young people with political experience and skills totally unprecedented in modern Jewish history. The heady mix of revolutionary utopianism so central to Russian socialism with the "redemptionism" inherent in the Jewish expectations of emancipation —whether socialist or national or both—proved to be an inexhaustible source of political energy.[8]

Thus, the Bundists in America have to be seen as an integral part of a generation of Jews who, recruited into the world of radical politics, would attain positions of influence and power—in Palestine, changing the course of Jewish history; in Russia, even perhaps that of world history. For obvious reasons, that generation tended to be very closely clustered in age. To illustrate this fact, it is perhaps worth mentioning some dozen of the better-known Jewish veterans of 1905, those who were contemporaries of the American Bundists, but stayed in Eastern Europe or went to Palestine. Of the Russian revolutionary leaders, Abram Rafailovich Gotz was born in 1882, Lev Kamenev in 1883, Lev (Leon) Trotsky in 1879, Grigori Zinoviev in 1883; of the Bundists, Borekh (Virgily) Cohen in 1883, Henryk Erlich in 1882, Mark Lieber in 1880, Vladimir Medem in 1879; and of the Second Aliyah activists, Ben-Gurion in 1886, Berl Katznelson in 1887, Manya Shokhat (Vilbushevich) in 1880, and Yitzhak Tabenkin in 1887.

Arriving very young in America, the Bundists still had their lives before them. Their enormous energy and varying degrees of ideological fervor were bound in most, though not all, cases to seek broader fields of action than those offered by the Jewish Socialist Federation. Some made a name for themselves as mainstream American politicians, most notably perhaps Baruch Vladeck. Born near Minsk in 1886, he ended up as the majority leader of the New York City Council, representing the American Labor Party in the days of Mayor Fiorello LaGuardia and District Attorney Thomas Dewey. (Vladeck's brothers were Shmuel Niger and David Charney, both very prominent in the world of Yiddish letters.) Others, such as Moishe Olgin, born in Odessa in 1878, and Alexander Bittelman, born near Kiev in 1890, moved in the opposite direction, serving as top leaders of the American Communist Party in the interwar period and even beyond. Many of the best-known names in the left-wing Yiddish press were graduates of the Bund, among them Ben-Zion Hoffman (Zivion), born in Courland in 1874, and Gavriel Krechmer (Liliput), born in Riga in 1883, both associated primarily with *Forverts*. Pesach (Paul) Novick, born in 1891, was from the first a central figure on the editorial board of the Communist newspaper *Frayheyt*. Fishl Gelibter, born in Zamosc in 1884, served as the executive secretary of the Workmen's Circle from 1915–1926, and Joseph Baskin, born near Minsk in 1880, was its general secretary from 1917–1952.[9]

Between the wars, graduates of the Bund stood at the head of the two most powerful unions in the needle trades. Sidney Hillman (born in Lithuania in 1887) was president of the Amalgamated Clothing Workers of America, and David Dubinsky (born in 1892 in Brest-Litovsk) was president of the International Ladies Garment Workers Union (the ILGWU). Between them, the two unions claimed a membership in the 1940s of some three-quarters of a million. Both men became closely associated with the politics of Roosevelt's New Deal, and during the Second World War Hillman was appointed director of the labor division of the War Production Board.[10] Legend has it that he had the last and decisive voice in Roosevelt's selection of Harry S. Truman as his vice-presidential running mate, with the president reputedly telling his associates at the crucial moment on July 14, 1944, to "clear it with Sidney."[11]

Many Bundists who had settled in the United States joined the stream of émigré socialists who returned to Russia following the February Revolution of 1917. Some, such as A. Litvak and Pesach Novick, eventually found their way back to New York. But others threw in their lot with the Soviet regime during the Civil War. Max Goldfarb (Lipets) (born in Berdichev in 1883) had served in America as a leader of the Jewish Socialist Federation, but back in Russia he rapidly rose to high rank in the Red Army and, as General Petrovskii, was appointed to a key post in the Moscow military academy; in the late 1930s he fell victim to the purges.[12] Shakhne Epstein, another prominent member of the Federation until returning to Russia, had a still more bizarre career, serving as an editor of Communist papers in Yiddish both in America (he was back in New York in the 1920s) and in the Soviet Union. He was also reputedly a spy who even organized (so it is said) the liquidation of a renegade comrade in the United States. Finally, he served as a central figure in the wartime Jewish Anti-Fascist Committee.[13]

Of course, not all the well-known veterans of the Bund who ended up in the United States arrived between 1906 and 1914. Vladimir Medem, for example, reached New York in 1921, causing a constant stir with his demands that the Jewish socialist movement have no truck with either Soviet Communism or Zionism. Rafael Abramovich (born 1880), David Einhorn, the poet (born 1886), Grigorii Aronson (born 1887), and Shloyme Mendelson (born 1896)—together with the founding fathers of Bundism, Noakh Portnoi and Vladimir Kossovskii—were all plucked out of Europe, with the help of the Jewish Labor Committee, at the very last moment in 1940–1941.[14]

What can be seen as obvious, even inevitable, in retrospect, was by no means so readily apparent to those involved at the time. During the first five years of its existence, the Jewish Socialist Federation appeared, at least to the more optimistic of its members, to be headed in an extremely positive direction and indeed on its way to becoming an American version of the Bund. The Socialist Party of America, under the leadership of Eugene Victor Debs, was growing by leaps and bounds; its membership, a mere 25,000 in 1905, had grown to 118,000 by 1912. In 1914 Meyer London was elected from the Lower East Side as the first socialist representative to the US Congress. On every side, the Jewish labor movement —the unions, the fraternal orders, the press—was expanding at an extraordinary rate, fed as it was by the huge influx of new immigrants in 1906–1914.[15]

But it was the First World War that promised to transform the Federation from a peripheral into a central or even, as some hoped, a hegemonic factor in the movement. The World War presented the Jewish socialists in America with a triple challenge. First, news began arriving in the winter of 1914–1915, that the tsarist army was engaged in the massive expulsion of Jews from the war zone. This clearly called for some kind of major protest from the labor movement. For the immigrant population what happened in Eastern Europe, in the *heym*, was in many ways more meaningful than anything occurring in America. After all, parents, siblings, or other very close relatives had often been left behind. Second, no sooner had the war started than mounting attention began to be focused on the issues of the postwar peace settlement. All around, the various immigrant communities—Czechs, Poles, Finns—were organizing in support of their respective national claims; vociferous demands were being made to have the American Jews do likewise on behalf of those Jewish populations in Europe which had hitherto been denied equal rights, most obviously in Russia and Romania.[16] Finally, these two problems were inextricably linked to a third, internal, issue. The Zionist camp, under the new leadership of Louis Dembitz Brandeis and able to count on a suddenly invigorated Poalei Tsiyon, had been the first to respond to the crisis of the war with its demand for a democratically elected congress to give a single, united, powerful voice to American Jewry.[17]

There were some in the upper echelons of the Jewish labor movement— Avrom Lesin, for example—who were prepared to accept the call for unity at its face value and as a logical response to the crisis facing the Jews in Eastern Europe. But the dominant view was that the socialist camp had to guard its separate identity and resist the Zionist bid for hegemony in the American Jewish community. The labor movement should agitate in its own name in defense of Jewish interests abroad. In line with this reasoning, the National Workmen's Committee on Jewish Rights in the Belligerent Lands was established in April 1915.[18] Here, then, was a development, as it seemed to many, that had finally provided the Jewish Socialist Federation with a key function to play, for it was only logical that the campaign in defense of the East European Jews should be directed by the graduates of the Bund. It was the Bund, after all, which had inscribed the fight for Jewish rights in Russia and Poland, including national rights, at the center of its banner. The National Workmen's Committee had been constituted by the joint action of the unions (the United Hebrew Trades), the Arbeter Ring (the Workmen's Circle), *Forverts,* and the Jewish Socialist Federation. But it was to the leadership of the latter organization—Jacob Salutsky, Max Goldfarb, Moishe Olgin, and Shakhne Epstein (Bundists all)—that the direction of the new body naturally fell.

For close to two years, the strategy pursued by the National Workmen's Committee was marked by a very considerable degree of success (serving, *inter alia*, to raise the membership of the Jewish Socialist Federation from a mere two thousand in 1914 to some eight thousand in 1916).[19] The ad hoc alliance that it established together with the American Jewish Committee proved powerful enough to halt what had been becoming a Zionist juggernaut in its tracks. It was eventually agreed that the American Jewish Congress, even though democratically elected, would have a strictly limited and predetermined agenda—the call for "full rights" for the Jews everywhere, including "group rights" in Eastern Europe and "Jewish rights" in Palestine— and thus block any chance of a Zionist takeover.[20]

The decision to ally the labor movement (officially dedicated to the causes of class-war and democratization) with the American Jewish Committee (popularly identified with such plutocrats as Jacob Schiff)—an alliance often referred to as linking the *genossen* to the *yahudim*—caused some derisive comment.[21] Nonetheless, the strategy had justified itself and 1916 undoubtedly constituted the high watermark in the history of the Jewish Socialist Federation. Its subsequent decline was caused, as already suggested, primarily by objective factors beyond its control, but the initial blow was strictly self-inflicted. The setting where the Federation fatefully overplayed its hand was the second National Workmen's Convention that was held in February 1917 and could lay good claim to represent the entire mainstream labor movement. It was attended by 453 delegates representing 190 organizations, with Poalei Tsiyon, of course, excluded. The leadership of the Federation introduced a resolution calling for the National Workmen's Committee to be converted from a temporary body established in response to the crisis in Europe into "a permanent, organic union of all those Jewish organizations that stand for the class struggle in all its forms."[22]

This proposal was generally seen as nothing less than a bid to transform the Jewish labor movement in America from a loose and informal conglomeration of independent organizations into a formal, albeit federal, union. It was an attempt to apply a model close to that represented by the Bund in tsarist Russia to American conditions. But although no longer newcomers, the graduates of the Bund had failed to take into account the fact that they were challenging a structure that had become deeply entrenched before they had even begun arriving in the United States. The founding fathers of the 1880s and 1890s were not about to divide their institutional power with the post-1905 generation, for all its revolutionary credentials. To prove the point, the most prominent trade unionist present, Max Pine—the head of the United Hebrew Trades—led a dramatic walkout from the Convention, thus rendering the idea of organizational unity meaningless.[23]

The subsequent polemics on the pages of the Yiddish press revealed the profound gap that had now opened up between the Bundists and the veterans in the Federation, that is, the unions, the Arbeter Ring, and *Forverts*. There are "two trends," wrote Shakhne Epstein, "one the obsolete trend that is afraid of every new wind, of every new reform because they could, heaven forbid, tear the rudder of power from its hands; and the other, the trend that seeks ever new ways. . . . Those who do not reckon with the 'spirit' of the times must leave the stage; that is the law of life."[24] For his part, Avrom Lesin responded no less angrily in defense of the veterans "who with twenty-five years of work have formed the movement and its very great newspapers for these same 'youngsters' just off the boat and have given them every opportunity to feel so much at ease in America."[25]

This angry division within the mainstream Jewish labor movement could not have come at a worse moment for the Federation. Within less than a year, it found itself faced by a series of challenges of immense and unprecedented complexity: the February Revolution in Russia; the American entry into World War I; and then—all at once in the first week of November—both the Bolshevik Revolution and the Balfour Declaration. Alienated from the powerful Jewish labor establishment, the Federation found itself further weakened by this series of events. Many of its leaders returned to Russia to join the Revolution. The Socialist Party (and with it, the Federation) lost much of its support because of its antiwar stand.[26] Using the February Revolution as an excuse, the Bundists decided to initiate a last-minute boycott of the elections to the American Jewish Congress in July. Confused by the October Revolution, the Federation was first opposed to Bolshevism, but soon showed signs of second thoughts. And, finally, much to its consternation, it found that in the wake of the Balfour Declaration, it had lost the power to hold the labor movement as a whole to an anti-Zionist line. Such prominent old-time unionists as Max Pine and Joseph Schlossberg, and even the convention of the ILGWU, began to express open sympathy for the idea of a Jewish national home in Palestine.[27]

The long-term consequence of this constant erosion of the Federation was an open schism in 1921. The majority, including nearly all the most prominent Bundists (Zivion, Olgin, Salutsky, Liliput, for example) voted to leave the Socialist Party, and they soon allied themselves with the Communists within the newly formed Workers Party. The minority, which remained loyal to the principles of democratic socialism and stayed in the Socialist Party, now formed the Jewish Socialist Farband.[28] There was much that was paradoxical in all this. The Farband claimed to be heir to the Bundist tradition and maintained fraternal (although often tense) relations with the Bund in Poland. Its general secretary, Nokhem Chanin, was a veteran of the Russian Bund; and when the famous Bundist, A. Litvak, settled in America in 1925, he naturally joined the leadership of the Farband. It organized the lecture and fundraising tours for Polish Bundist leaders such as Henryk Erlich and Noakh Portnoi who spent many months at a time in the United States.[29]

On the other hand, it is not surprising that many observers, especially in the early 1920s, believed that the Jewish section of the Workers Party more truly represented the Bundist spirit. It too was led by Bundists such as Olgin and Bittelman, and until 1925 even continued to carry its original title, the Jewish Socialist Federation. Founding its own paper, *Frayheyt*, to raise the banner of revolt against *Forverts*, it could claim to be speaking for the genuine traditions of militant socialism against the old guard which had sold out to capitalist America.[30] Did not *Forverts* indulge in yellow journalism (with its "Bintl Brif" and beauty competitions, for example)? And did not *Frayheyt* defend the Yiddish school movement, while *Forverts*, under Abe Cahan's leadership, was well known for its support of "Anglicization"?[31] And was not the Farband tied hand and foot to *Forverts*, even dependent on the paper for its financial survival?[32]

All this, of course, ran parallel to the similar but not identical situation in Eastern Europe, where the Jewish Section of the Communist Party in the Soviet Union, manned by ex-Bundists and by veterans of other Jewish socialist parties, was widely credited with implementing programs of Jewish nation-building in the spirit of the Bund, and of Jewish colonization in the spirit of the territorialists. The Bund itself, as already noted, together with virtually all other non-Communist parties, had been outlawed by the Soviet regime in 1921.[33]

With the passage of time, many of the Bundists and other non-Communists who had joined the Workers Party resigned or were expelled, in some cases returning sheepishly to write for *Forverts*.[34] The highly centralized and manipulative traditions of Leninism as well as the subservience to Moscow—the Workers Party joined the Comintern in 1925—proved particularly hard to accept in the freewheeling atmosphere of American public life.

It was against this background that the Farband, with its journal *Der veker*, emerged as the most militantly anti-Communist voice in the Jewish labor movement. According to the political logic of the times, the Farband might have been expected to proportionately reduce its hostility to Zionism both because the Zionist cause had gained broad popular sympathy and because the Communists were overtly anti-Zionist. Those leaders of the Jewish labor movement, including Bundist veterans such as David Dubinsky, who had to fight for their lives in the mid-1920s to prevent a full-scale Communist takeover of the unions and the Arbeter Ring, clearly tended to move in this direction, in large part lending their support to the fundraising (*geverkshaftn*) campaigns on behalf of the Histadrut in Palestine.[35] But the Farband was inhibited from following this path by its loyalty to long-standing and deeply entrenched Bundist doctrines which defined Zionism as an inherently dangerous diversion, weakening the will of the Jewish people to defend its vital interests in the real, not fantasy, world.

The strange and complex ways in which the Zionist issue was handled within the Jewish labor movement can be illustrated by a brief examination of two of the most dramatic chapters in the history of what was always a tangled and frequently a surprising set of relationships—the Arab uprising in Palestine of 1929 and the American Jewish Conference of 1943.

The news of sporadic Arab attacks on Jews in Palestine began to be reported in America in mid-August, 1929, and at first there was little to distinguish the headlines in *Forverts* from those in *Frayheyt*. A front-page headline in the August 19 *Frayheyt*, for example, reads: "Arabs Perpetrate New Pogroms Against the Jews in Various Sections of Jerusalem." An editorial of a few days later declared that "England, which believes strongly in religious toleration, allows Jews praying at the Western Wall to be beaten up; allows Torah scrolls and *talesim* to be torn to shreds just as was done by the Petliuras and Balakhoviches during the Civil War in Russia." The primary blame was thus assigned to the British who were trying to appease the Arab "effendis (*pritzim*), mullahs and bourgeois intelligentsia."[36] The Zionists had only secondary responsibility: the excessive uproar they had created at the recent (Sixteenth) Zionist Congress about the newly established Jewish Agency had stirred up Arab unrest. However, an abrupt change in Zionist thinking evidenced itself starting on August 27, when these two typical headlines appeared: "An Arab Mass-Revolt Against England Spreads Over All Palestine"; and, again: "The English Army and Jewish Legionnaires Perpetrate Blood-Soaked Massacres Against Arabs."[37]

In contrast, *Forverts* gave ever more space to the pogrom theme, as on its front-page of August 28: "Arabs Set Fire to Still More Jewish Colonies; Jews the Victims of Pogroms Over All of Palestine; The Pogrom in Hebron One of the Worst Massacres in Jewish History." *Forverts* gave prominent coverage to the Zionist protest march held on August 26 and attended, according to the paper, by some 20,000 people.[38] *Frayheyt*, though, described the event as a "demonstration groveling [*mayofes*] before Yankee imperialism."[39] For its part, the Jewish Section of the Communist Party organized its own mass meeting that, as *Frayheyt* put it, served to "open the eyes of the Jewish workers."[40] Among the speakers was Moishe Olgin who was quoted as saying that "the Bund demonstrated years ago that Zionism means a fight against the Arab masses; they are to be deprived of their land, and the Arab working masses enslaved." As for the accusation that his party was encouraging pogroms, it was "we who fought them when the Jewish bourgeoisie was cowering in cellars afraid to show their noses above ground. . . . We Communists fought against pogroms and we shall continue to do so."[41]

Forverts argued that there were no objective causes—meaning, as it put it, a "clash of economic interests"—to explain the Arab violence. The simple cause was incitement coming from various quarters: economic competitors (both Arab and British); "fanatical Christians"; anti-Semites; and the "Communists, in the interests of world revolution." As for the response in America, declared *Forverts*, "real anti-Semites have never permitted themselves at the time of a pogrom, when the blood of the Jewish victims has still not dried, to come out with such abuse of the Jews under attack as does the Communist press here."[42]

Caught between these two positions, the Jewish Socialist Farband naturally inclined more toward the position of *Forverts*, and *Der veker* called on its readers to contribute money to the campaign launched in aid of the Jewish victims in

Palestine. When it is an issue, declared the journal, of "the Jews having to defend themselves, of standing up for their lives, their property and their honor—there is only one commandment: take up arms! The greatest opponent of Zionism, if he had found himself in Hebron or Jerusalem, would have fought back against the Arabs."[43]

Der veker, too, took the golden opportunity to settle accounts with the Communists, noting that their sudden change of line reflected their customary "barracks-discipline"[44] and had resulted in the defection from *Frayheyt* of such an important figure as Avrom Raisin, the Yiddish poet. "They are creating a Jewish cemetery in Birobidzhan," declared one correspondent, "and support *pogromshchiki* in Palestine."[45]

But *Der veker* was not prepared to explain the violence merely in terms of incitement. It marked itself off from what it termed "the black chauvinist hysteria" against the Arabs that, it declared, had engulfed all the Yiddish press (excluding, of course, *Frayheyt* with its "young hooligan" editors but including, if only by implication, *Forverts*). In the long run, there was no choice but to seek firm ground on which to base "peace . . . between two peoples who live on the same land."[46] In terms far more critical of Zionism, Rafael Abramovich pointed out that the Jewish population, even with immigration, was hardly keeping up with the increase in Arab numbers. With 150,000 Jews facing 650,000 Arabs "there is no hope that Jews will ever be a majority in the country." The most that the Zionists could hope to achieve in Palestine was a colony "smaller than a Warsaw suburb."[47]

In sum, it can be stated that *Frayheyt* suffered great damage in the Jewish world as the result of the line imposed on it by Stalin's leadership in Moscow. It lost support not just from Raisin but from other prominent writers such as H. Leivik and Menachem Boreisha, as well, of course, as from within the left-wing Jewish public at large.[48] But even the middle-of-the-road position adopted by the Farband could not have been popular. As Zivion put it at the time: "In America, Zionism has reached a high point . . . and has won the sympathy of nearly all the Jews with the exception of a few opponents and non-believers among whom I have the honor to count myself."[49]

To move forward to 1943 is, of course, to enter a totally different era in Jewish history, one in which the Jewish people in Europe were murdered systematically. The many historiographical issues involved continue to attract enormous attention, to raise issues of great human and moral import, and stir profound discomfort and anguish among Jews and others. All that is to be attempted here, though, is to sketch in the briefest possible terms the position occupied by the Jewish Socialist Farband in relation to the American Jewish Conference which took place in New York between August 29 and September 2, 1943.

At the level of what can loosely be termed party politics, developments in relation to the American Jewish Congress in 1943 closely paralleled those that had taken place during the First World War. To some extent, indeed, the repetition resulted from a conscious belief that the lessons learned then did not have to be relearned now. As in 1914–1918, so in 1943, the call for the American Jews to elect a representative body to defend the interests of European Jewry had a very broad popular appeal. But the idea was regarded with suspicion by those who saw it as an attempt by the Zionists to exploit a crisis in order to gain unassailable leadership over the American Jewish community. The result, in the Second World War as in the First, was that the Jewish labor movement, now represented not by the long-defunct National Workmen's Committee but by the Jewish Labor Committee, found itself in the same camp as the American Jewish Committee, although this time there was no formal alliance. In 1943 as in 1917, these two otherwise very disparate organizations decided to boycott the elections. In 1917, some 300,000 people went to the polls; in 1943 the number taking part in the indirect elections was put at 1,171,000.[50] However, on both occasions, the Jewish Labor Committee and the American Jewish Committee decided in the end to participate in the actual assembly, using the seats set aside for organizational representation. (The labor movement was allotted twenty such places in 1918; sixteen in 1943.)[51]

The Jewish Socialist Farband was far weaker in 1943 than the Federation had been during the First World War. Rooted almost exclusively in the immigrant community, it had a rapidly aging, and hence declining, membership; and it had split apart for a second time in 1935 (again, as in 1921, over the issue of cooperation with the Communists).[52] But it enjoyed an influence far greater than its numbers suggested. It was, after all, a constituent member of the Jewish Labor Committee, established in 1934 under the chairmanship of Baruch Vladeck to seek appropriate ways to respond to the Nazi threat against the Jews. Like the National Workmen's Committee in its time, the Jewish Labor Committee was an umbrella organization representing the major constituents of the labor movement (and again excluding the Poalei Tsiyon).[53]

Within this framework the Farband, which still had its own journal, *Der veker*, was well situated to advance its dual ideological position: militant anti-Communism on one hand, and opposition to Zionist hegemony on the other.

The decision of the Jewish Labor Committee to take part in the American Jewish Conference was made on two conditions: first, that Jewish Communist organizations be excluded and, second, that the delegation would vote as a single bloc —in other words, that all its members would abstain—from voting on controversial Zionist resolutions.

The American Jewish Congress had hammered out a compromise in 1916 that eventually permitted a united delegation, headed by Louis Marshall of the American Jewish Committee and including representatives of the labor movement, to play a major role at the Paris peace conference in defense of minority rights in Eastern Europe and of a "national home" in Palestine.[54] No such degree of consensus was achieved in 1943. The Revisionist Zionists and Agudat Yisrael complained of underrepresentation and did not attend. The Communist organizations, anxious to participate, were excluded. Zionists, under the impassioned lead of Abba Hillel Silver, pushed through a resolution calling for the establishment of a Jewish Commonwealth in Palestine, thereby endorsing the controversial Biltmore program of 1942. The Jewish Labor Committee and the American Jewish Committee had called for a more cautious resolution condemning the British White Paper of 1939 and demanding the removal of restrictions on Jewish immigration to, and land purchase in, Palestine. Although they did not stage a walkout in protest at the time, the two Committees both subsequently broke away from the framework of the American Jewish Conference.[55]

The knowledge that the Jews of Europe were being systematically annihilated, that perhaps as many as four million had already been killed[56]—in no way brought with it a general decision to achieve compromise or lower the tone of dispute. The contrary was possibly the case. The Farband found itself faced on the right by a huge wave of support for Zionism, and on the left by a Jewish Communist movement that had totally reversed the positions it had held in 1929. In its effort to mobilize American support for the war effort and the Second Front, so taking pressure off the Soviet Union, the Communist movement now provided maximal support not only to the American Jewish Conference, but to the Zionist cause in general. A typical Communist appeal called on the American Jewish Conference to provide "maximal aid to the Yishuv in Palestine, which is involved in the fight, and to guarantee the national rights of the Jews in Palestine."[57] Or, as Pesach Novick put it: "The Palestinian Jews have made a great contribution to the war effort . . . and if [they] end up gaining by it, that is not to be faulted—quite the contrary."[58] Attacking the Jewish Labor Committee, *Forverts*, and the Bundists

—particularly the committee established in New York to represent the Bundist underground in Nazi-occupied Poland[59]—as insufficiently enthusiastic about Jewish unity and Zionism, *Frayheyt* (now the *Morgen-frayheyt*) did not hesitate to use such terms as "traitors within the Jewish people, the Jewish Lavals and Quislings."[60]

In response to this extreme pressure on two different fronts, the Farband and its Bundist peripheries did not adopt a single tone. Some spoke more in sorrow than in anger, other with extreme bitterness. Writing for *Der veker* on the eve of the American Jewish Conference, Nokhem Chanin complained in carefully measured tones that far too little had been done to further a strategy for the rescue of Jews still alive under Nazi control. "That we are not helping is not only their tragedy; it is also our shame—I am referring to criminal indifference." Much of the blame lay with the Zionists in whose hands "all demands made on Washington are narrowed to one demand, a Jewish homeland in Erets Yisroel." But even the Joint Distribution Committee, for all its genuine efforts, had "unfortunately demonstrated too much caution, too much fear."[61]

The Conference did devote much of its time to the issue of rescue, and carried the appropriate resolutions.[62] But Chanin insisted that priorities had still been distorted. It was a "source of great sorrow . . . that a Jewish conference called together in such a terrible period of Jewish history should have occupied itself for three days with the Jewish Commonwealth in Palestine . . . and one . . . with adopting dull resolutions about the present Jewish tragedy." But the failure, he insisted, was implicit in the Zionist viewpoint that anti-Semitism stemmed inevitably from the minority status of the Jews in the diaspora: "This is the way that it has been [they say], that it is, and that it will be. With such a philosophy one has to forego even the great and important need to cry out against the torturers." At least, he added, the conference had had the good sense to keep out the Communists even though they were now ready "to make the Hatikvah their second party anthem."[63] Others were far less restrained. In another postconference article in *Der veker*, David Einhorn could write: "That the true, hard, Zionists . . . are not particularly unhappy about the slaughter and bloody destruction of the Jewish communities in Europe is something we have long known. . . . Don't dance around the *khurbn* [destruction] of the Jewish *golus* [exile, diaspora]."[64]

The graduates of the Bund in America were frequently able as individuals to achieve important positions of influence and leadership within the preexisting labor movement. On the other hand, their attempts to recreate some approximate reincarnation of the Bund never achieved more than marginal success. Finally, a nucleus of loyalists did succeed over a number of decades in upholding with an honorable consistency what can be considered the core of Bundist ideology: opposition to the Bolshevik theory and practice of dictatorship, on the one hand, and to the Zionist critique of the diaspora, on the other.

MAUD MANDEL

13

Genocide and Nationalism

The Changing Nature of Jewish Politics in Post–World War II France

EAST EUROPEAN JEWISH POLITICS "spilled over" to the Americas, Israel, and Western Europe as a result of migration and international communication. Thus, these places experienced an interplay of imported political traditions and national circumstances. In twentieth-century France, Jewish politics has been shaped by three dramatic events: the arrival of approximately two hundred thousand Eastern European immigrant Jews (and somewhat fewer North Africans) during the first third of the century, the Holocaust, and the birth of the State of Israel. The changes brought about by the first of these three are, by now, a well-known story. As part of a larger immigration wave, Eastern European Jewish immigrants more than doubled the native Jewish population of France. Their impact was more than demographic; the new arrivals were poorer, more traditional, more politically active, and more distinctively "Jewish"—in dress, language, and customs—than the native population. The immigrants introduced their own religious and cultural institutions as well as their militantly leftist political activities, challenging the homogenous, upper middle class, and generally republican French Jewish population, and bringing into question a century-long consensus on the nature of Jewish identity in France. Although the interactions between the native and immigrant populations were dominated by conflict, some individuals, particularly from among the intellectual elite and the youth population, began tentatively to explore new understandings of their ethnoreligious heritage. Thus, the arrival of the immigrant population expanded notions of

Jewishness in France and began transforming the makeup and self-conceptions of that population.[1]

We know a great deal about the impact of the encounter between Eastern European Jews and native French Jews during the interwar years, but far less about the ramifications of this encounter on post–World War II French Jewry. Nor do we know much about how Jewish political allegiances shifted, if at all, in light of the other major events in Jewish life, the Holocaust and the birth of the State of Israel. To the extent this question has been considered, it has generally been dismissed. Most scholarship on modern French Jewish history has treated the Holocaust as the dramatic conclusion to a period born with the civil emancipation of the Jews in 1789.[2] Paula Hyman, whose fine study of interwar French Jewish history has defined the field for future scholars, nevertheless concludes her book by arguing that the great social, political, and ideological changes which enlivened French Jewry in the 1920s and 1930s were "cut short by the Holocaust," and that they "withered" after being "denied the test of time."[3] Similarly, scholars of postwar French Jewry have assumed that it took the arrival of three hundred thousand North African Jews in the late 1950s to reinvigorate a community decimated by the Holocaust.[4]

Such assessments overemphasize the impact of the Holocaust on French Jewish life. Certainly, like their brethren throughout Europe, Jews in France suffered severely during the Vichy years. As has been well documented, a wide range of anti-Jewish legislation restricted Jewish movements, property ownership, and civil liberties. Furthermore, the Vichy government collaborated in the internment and deportation of approximately seventy-five thousand Jews, one-third of the prewar population. Of these, only a tiny minority returned to France after the war. Communal life was also severely damaged, as synagogues, schools, and cultural organizations were systematically closed and dismantled.[5] Foreign-born Jews who immigrated to France during the interwar years were hit the hardest. While anti-Semitic policies were directed at all Jews, French xenophobia ensured that those policies were most fiercely enforced against recent arrivals.[6] As a result, immigrant Jews lost property, places of worship, and communal centers, and were deported in larger numbers than native French Jews (over two-thirds of those deported were foreign born).[7]

But the Holocaust was part of their history, not its end. Despite the high deportation numbers, many Jews survived, particularly those from the native Jewish population. Even many East European-born Jews survived the war and remained in France in its aftermath. Their numbers were bolstered by the arrival of approximately thirty-seven thousand Holocaust survivors who migrated to France after the war.[8] Institutional life also rapidly regained its footing, and, as early as 1946, Paris housed nearly two hundred different Jewish organizations representing every religious, ideological, and political strand that had been present before the war.[9]

In light of a certain demographic and institutional continuity, it seems appropriate to ask to what extent the changes occurring in the 1920s and 1930s continued to manifest themselves in the postwar years. How did the Holocaust influence native and immigrant Jews' understandings of their position in their society and their relationship to one another? Did political allegiances shift as a result of the Vichy and German persecutions? How did debates over Jewish nationalism, so heated in the years prior to the war, shift in light of the Holocaust and the birth of the State of Israel?

In the interwar period, interactions with pro-Zionist immigrants as well as an ever worsening Jewish refugee problem in Central and Eastern Europe had forced some native French Jews to reconsider their negative view of Jewish nationalism.[10] World War II strengthened this reappraisal. The Jewish press in France followed the struggle for Israeli independence, as well as the war that followed, with great interest. In addition, cautious support for the fledgling state was widespread among those active in communal life. Aware that the displaced persons camps in Germany were filled with Jewish refugees, communal leaders encouraged the French government to support the new state. Jewish philanthropic organizations contributed a significant portion of their funds to Israel.

However, despite the new and dramatic interest in a Jewish nationalistic agenda, between 1948 and 1985 only 23,227 French-born Jews decided to immigrate to Israel (and some ultimately returned to France). Of those, most went to Israel after the 1967 Six-Day War, more than twenty years after World War II had come to an end.[11] Such low emigration numbers suggest that neither the Holocaust nor the birth of the State of Israel had induced most Jews to question the validity of their French citizenship. While understandings of that citizenship were continuing to broaden in light of the great upheavals of the twentieth century, material and political support for the new state did not translate into an abandonment of the "diaspora condition." Indeed, if contemporary eyes view the Holocaust as a fundamental challenge to the feasibility of living in the diaspora, it did not appear this way to the survivors themselves.

Nevertheless, the Holocaust had made its mark. "The devastation caused by the war and the extermination of six million Jews," wrote Guy de Rothschild of his family's transforming views toward Zionism, "radically changed all our former attitudes. The idea of a Jewish homeland acquired an intense emotional appeal; I myself became an ardent Zionist, without, however, envisaging a change of direction in my personal life or that of my family."[12] Like Rothschild, few expected "a change of direction" in their personal lives because of a newfound Jewish nationalism; nevertheless, a growing interest was evident, one which encouraged native Jews to join their East European brethren in articulating a new, more politically defined Jewish presence in France. Indeed, while it is generally accepted that North African Jews arriving in the 1950s and 1960s gave new life to French Judaism, it is also true that several years earlier, new understandings of ethnic identification and political solidarity had taken root throughout the population.

From the birth of political Zionism at the end of the nineteenth century, French Jews exhibited little enthusiasm for establishing a Jewish state. Philanthropists such as Baron Edmond de Rothschild had sponsored Jewish agricultural settlement in Palestine, but most French Jews, committed to preserving their position in their own land, were at best indifferent to, and at worst, threatened by, an ideology that affirmed a Jewish identity transcending national boundaries. Such fears intensified as anti-Semitic attitudes spread throughout Europe and took firm root in France. As ever larger numbers of Jewish immigrants took advantage of France's open-door policies, the native French Jewish leadership became increasingly worried that the newcomers' "foreignness" would undermine their own position in French society. As a result, they began actively encouraging the newcomers to acculturate. Prevailing upon them to adopt French customs and shed their "Jewish" traits, the native Jews argued that in exchange for such transformations, the centralized government would provide immigrants with citizenship and defend their equality.

The newcomers, having originated from countries where state-sanctioned anti-Semitism was the norm, did not have the same confidence in the state, nor did they share the goals and desires of their native-born coreligionists. Few trusted that any national government would act benevolently. According to one scholar, the Eastern European Jewish immigrants "remained unimpressed by native arguments about the differences between an 'enlightened' French government and 'backward' eastern European regimes."[13] Rather than adopting the native Jewish population's priorities, then, the newcomers immediately sought to establish their own communal structures, avoiding the bourgeois and acculturated native institutions in favor of their own *landsmanshaftn* (immigrant associations), schools, charitable organizations, welfare institutions, newspapers, *shuls*, and political parties. Between 1918 and 1939, no fewer than 133 Yiddish periodicals were established. Within these publications and elsewhere, Zionists, Bundists, and Communists fought each other. They established their own schools, cultural organizations, and clubs. Even those middle-class immigrant Jews disinclined to participate in leftist politics turned to the Fédération des sociétés juives de France, a pro-Zionist umbrella organization uniting numerous *landsmanshaftn*, rather than participating in native French Jewish establishments.[14]

Largely due to the arrival of these newcomers, Zionism became a significant force in France.[15] Of course, not all members of the immigrant Jewish population were Zionists. Indeed, the Jewish labor movement, also an Eastern European import, remained actively hostile to Zionism, viewing it as a backward nationalist movement that threatened class consciousness. Nevertheless, the Zionist movement in France began as an immigrant-based movement and, from there, slowly entered French Jewish self-conceptions, at least among certain sectors of the population. This change was not rapid, since native Jews initially dismissed all ideological movements linked to the immigrant population. By the 1930s, however, as the position of Central and East European Jewry became increasingly precarious, native Jews began reevaluating their understanding of Jewish nationalism. While never entirely embracing Zionist ideology per se, some sectors of French Jewish society, particularly the youth movements, were influenced by its promotion of Jewish pride, legitimation of an ethnic Jewish identity, support for the development of Jewish and Hebrew cultural creativity, and pioneering spirit. Even French Jewish notables—rabbis and some of the consistorial leadership —were more willing to support Zionist goals, even if only as a means to help refugees from the East. Nevertheless, by 1939, the vast majority of French Jews did not define themselves as "card-carrying" Zionists, nor did they create a pro-Zionist institutional base in France.[16]

During the German occupation, however, the movement found a new legitimacy, especially among immigrant Jews. What had once been a divided, institutionally weak movement among the immigrants became more unified as various factions began working together to bring relief to families in distress. During the interwar years, the Zionist movement in Paris had been highly sectarian, as secular nationalists, socialists, religious traditionalists, and philanthropists debated, in ideological and oftentimes utopian terms, the nature of a future Jewish state and how best to achieve it.[17] The German occupation, however, transformed the movement into a unified relief effort. After the occupation of Paris, most Zionist leaders fled to the southern zone where they became actively involved in welfare, relief, and resistance activities. Moreover, the emergence of a common enemy and a common goal—overthrowing the German occupants and the Vichy government —allowed Communist, Bundist, and Zionist groups to work together.

Native French Jews were slower to join the Zionist relief efforts. On the whole, French-born Jews were sincere patriots, who maintained a strong conviction that the state would protect them as an integral part of its populace. When, in October 1940, the Vichy government enacted the Statut des juifs, officially relegating Jews to a position as second-class citizens, the immigrant Jews were, in some ways, more psychologically prepared, since they already doubted the ability or willingness of their host society to protect them. Native Jews, however, no matter how aware of anti-Semitism in their midst, were taken by surprise when Vichy imposed its anti-Jewish legislation.[18] As Richard Cohen has written, native Jews responded to the legislation with "pain and anguish," while immigrant Jews re-acted with "nothing like the emotional soul-searching that characterized native Jewry's response."[19]

To our contemporary understanding, the shock and dismay of the native Jew-ish leadership may seem incomprehensible given the increasing anti-Semitism of the 1930s. But this perception mistakes the relationship of French Jews to the state in which they lived. Although Vichy was born out of the dismantling of the Third Republic, it was, nevertheless, its legal successor. For native-born French Jews, the anti-Jewish statutes were not an inevitable outcome of Vichy, but an aberration from the republican tradition it had inherited. As the war continued, however, it became increasingly difficult for French Jewish citizens to defend their *patrie*; Vichy's anti-Jewish policies, which at first affected immigrant Jews more than the native born, soon caught up with even the most devoted French Jewish patriots.[20] As the "Final Solution" progressed, even the native Jewish leadership, formerly the staunchest supporters of the emancipatory doctrine, were no longer secure in the knowledge that their government would protect them. When many found that the war's end did not bring immediate comfort, as it seemed to do for their gentile compatriots, they began stressing their loyalty to other Jews over their de-votion to France. Guy de Rothschild, for example, wrote to the American Jewish Joint Distribution Committee in 1945 that the "tragedy is too great to be fully grasped but it dwarfs in the eyes of France the wonderful, victorious war news."[21] During the same month, the *Bulletin d'information* (a journal devoted to gathering and republishing national and international Jewish news), reported: "If French and foreign Jews hail [the victory] with immense joy, the same as all their compatriots, they have been too branded in their flesh and spirits by the defeat of June '40 and by the ignominious Hitlerian persecution to be able to detach themselves for even a moment from the memory of their dead and their martyrs."[22]

Yet, if for some, France's victory was shrouded with memories of the preceding years, for others, the end of the war meant principally the immediate abrogation of Vichy's discriminatory statutes. Whatever conclusions had been reached during the war now had to be reassessed in light of the restoration of full equality. On one hand, the previous four years had proven that Jewish emancipation was reversible and hence insecure, bolstering the immigrant Jewish perspective. Yet, on the other hand, the restoration of full equality also suggested that Vichy rule had been only an aberration (as many native Jews had hoped all along). The active attempts to defeat the Germans, the flowering of a native French resistance movement, and the postwar prosecution of Vichy officials strengthened this latter theory and validated the prewar position of the native Jewish leadership. For nearly 150 years republican government had protected Jewish rights, and it would continue to do so as long as fascist dictators were contained.

Not surprisingly, in the postwar years both "camps" again found willing advocates, as survivors reconsidered, or in some cases reconfirmed, their understandings of Jewish national identity in light of their wartime experiences. Samuel René Kapel, a native-born rabbi and a member of the Orthodox Zionist organization Mizrachi, repeatedly stressed that if there was one lesson to be learned from the "bloody events," it was that emancipation had failed to ensure Jewish integration. "It is in our interests and in that of our children to reject assimilation once and for all," he declared. "We will no longer allow ourselves to be deluded by vain promises; the awakening was cruel and our deception profound." Kapel believed that anti-Semitism had so infected French society that it would take years for it to be purged; his own solution was a Jewish nationalism that would allow Jewish voices to be heard and Jewish culture and traditions to flourish. Indeed, in 1954, after working for ten years to encourage the spread of Zionism throughout the local youth population, he settled permanently in Israel. For Kapel, therefore, the Holocaust had proved the need for a Jewish homeland. Assimilation was a profoundly dangerous choice, not only became it undermined Jewish life, but because its adherents had misjudged its success, believing themselves safe in a country that, in fact, showed itself ready to turn against them without provocation. Equally important, however, was the obligation of French Jews to take a public, political, and unified stance in favor of all Jews who had been hurt during

204 / *Maud Mandel*

the previous four years. That the new French government's restitution policies did not fully account for French Jewish losses proved to Kapel the need for a strong communal response: "We would prove unworthy of the deported Jews who still suffer in camps in Germany if we should accept this policy of silence. What will they say when they know that we occupied ourselves above all with our own interests while thousands of informers, administrators, and purchasers of Jewish goods circulate freely without any justice intervening to make them provide restitution and to punish them."[23] The Holocaust demonstrated clearly that French Jews, whether fighting for a Jewish state or protecting their rights at home, must take an active political stance in their own defense.

Not all of Kapel's coreligionists, however, shared his strong response. For others, recent events reconfirmed that assimilation was, in fact, the correct response to resolving the Jewish Question; Jews should adopt no unified political action and eventually the problem would disappear. Jean-Jacques Bernard, for example, a well-known native French Jewish writer (and son of the even better-known French dramatist Tristan Bernard) who had been interned in Compiègne from December 1941 to February 1942, became a public proponent of radical assimilation. In the mid-1930s, Bernard was already insisting that integration was the only plausible response to the Jewish Question. Profoundly uncomfortable with his own heritage (although he would have never admitted any discomfort), he believed that "a union of all people could come about," but only if "Israel will not hesitate to throw itself into the path, as the Jews of France have demonstrated, and integrate into the great mass of humanity." Responding to increasing anti-Semitism in Central Europe, Bernard suggested that no parallel problem existed for Jews in France. At the heart of his analysis was a critique of Jews themselves; while those in France had pursued a path of integration, those elsewhere had chosen "to colonize" and, as such, had helped bring the problem on themselves. Only when Jews had "offered themselves in sacrifice" (it is disconcerting, given subsequent events, that Bernard chose the term "holocaust" to denote a sacrificial burnt offering), would the Jewish problem disappear.[24]

Bernard was interned as part of a sweep of French intellectuals, not Jews; his father was arrested in a roundup of Jews. Despite these experiences, and the increasing anti-Jewish hostility in his society, Bernard's faith in France never wavered. Rather, the events of World War II reconfirmed his belief that assimilation was the answer to any residual anti-Jewish sentiment in French society. As if proving that one's religion could be changed as easily as an old suit, Bernard converted from Judaism to Catholicism soon after the war.[25] In his memoir, as well as in several controversial articles, he argued that he, like most native French Jews, went into and came out of the war with their understanding of citizenship, loyalty to the nation, and love for their country intact.[26] In other words, for French Jews, France was their nation and Judaism their religion. "We cannot hold two nations in our hearts," he wrote, and French Jews could and should only be loyal to France.[27] Even in the concentration camp, Bernard claimed, he had no national link to non-French Jews, only a "complete solidarity with our brothers of persecution, without distinguishing between origins."

Bernard adamantly refused all Jewish national aspirations: "If anyone claimed or still claims to impose a purely Jewish solidarity upon us, we resisted, and we will still resist any claim that continues exactly in the same direction as Hitlerian racism." He urged assimilation upon foreign Jews. To those who wanted to become good French citizens, Bernard offered, "we are ready to help them." For those whose only true desire was "to annex us, to demonstrate to us that land that is ours is not really our own, to chain us in their vagabond fate," Bernard declared, "we will oppose them with the same stubborn 'no' with which we opposed Hitler."[28]

The publication of Bernard's book and articles unleashed a storm of controversy. Some accused Bernard of providing fodder for anti-Semites in his criticisms of fellow Jews.[29] Others insisted that the war years had proved that whatever ideological, religious, and political divisions separated Jews from one another, they all shared a common fate. Immigrants and natives had both been persecuted and must henceforth stand together. Indeed, being French and Jewish were not mutually exclusive; one could be proud of and participate in both heritages equally.[30] Marc Jarblum, the president of the Fédération des sociétés juives de France, took such a stance. In a review of Bernard's *Le camp de la morte lente*, published in the Zionist paper *La Terre retrouvée*, Marc Jarblum criticized Bernard for placing his French citizenship ahead of his Jewish heritage. "The facts are in: the Germans arrested many Frenchmen, but because they were socialists, communists, Catholic resistors, and not because they were French. On the other hand, they arrested Jews independent of their opinions or their nationality—in France as well as in Belgium, Holland, and other occupied countries." Nevertheless, Jarblum did not urge his readers to revoke their citizenship, nor did he criticize France for its role in persecuting Jews. Rather he, like Bernard, placed the burden of guilt upon the Germans and maintained that Jews who fought in the resistance and at the front offered those efforts in their "double capacity" as French citizens and as Jews.[31]

Intrigued by the controversy and by the "strange silence" surrounding the Jewish persecution and losses in postwar France, Emanuel Mournier, editor of the journal *Esprit*, devoted the September 1, 1945, issue to the Jewish Question. In the journal, Jean-Jacques Bernard's assimilationist views were pitted against those of Henri Hertz, a poet, novelist, and critic who rejected all such notions.[32] Like Bernard, Hertz was a native-born French Jew who had distinguished himself in journalism and literature. Unlike Bernard, however, even before World War II he had been drawn to the nascent Zionist movement, writing much on Jewish problems in the French press, and in 1925, becoming the general secretary of France-Palestine, an early Zionist organization.[33] For Hertz, who survived the war while fighting in the resistance, the Holocaust reinforced his belief in a Jewish national identity.[34] In his article, he advocated a double patriotism, claiming that if there was no identifiable Jewish "race" there was certainly a Jewish people. For him, like Kapel, the war provided a clear indication that emancipation had not worked; rather, Jews must be given the "city, metropole, political center that they have lost." However Hertz, like Jarblum, did not propose that French Jews should abandon their birthland for a new national homeland. Instead, he suggested that such a state would provide them with "a clear and distinct reference of their lineage and of their legitimacy."[35] Thus, even among those most willing to criticize Bernard's stance, there was a clear preference to emphasize dual loyalties. The Vichy legacy did not mean that Jews had to reject their French patriotism; rather, they had to supplement their loyalty to France with a stronger commitment to Jewish nationalism.

What is most striking to the contemporary reader, however, is the degree to which neither Bernard's call for total assimilation nor Hertz's notion of double patriotism resonated for those in positions of communal authority, despite the upheaval that their community had recently experienced. Certainly Bernard's assimilationist stance, and particularly his conversion to Catholicism, proved unacceptable to those striving to rebuild Jewish life after the war. Georges Wormser, president of the Consistoire de Paris, called Bernard's views "repugnant."[36] Even prior to World War II, the Consistoire was willing to condemn all forms of radical assimilation. This was particularly notable because the Consistoire—which had originally been a state-sponsored organization—had historically stood at the center of native French Jewry's assimilationist core. Still, Consistoire officials had not entirely abandoned previous understandings of the place of Jews in the polity. While deploring Bernard's pro-conversionist stance, they proved unwilling to respond publicly to his positions on the assimilation of immigrant Jews and on French Jewish national affiliation. During a meeting following the appearance of Bernard's article in *Le Figaro*, Consistoire representatives agreed that "the moment did not seem propitious for engaging in politics" and, therefore, refrained from publishing a response.[37] Clearly, for them, the "strange silence" surrounding the Jewish Question was preferable to a public debate on the place of Jews in French society. In this way, the Consistoire leadership, always cautious to avoid emphasizing any political nature to Jewish identity, remained committed to their pre-Vichy policies.

Others, such as the editors of the *Bulletin du Centre israélite d'information*, reflected the measured response of the Consistoire leadership and adopted an actively "centrist" position on the controversy. "It is fitting to note that 'double patriotism' is Mr. Henri Hertz's personal conception . . . [which] corresponds to the tendencies of only a limited faction of Zionists, while on the other hand, Jean-Jacques Bernard, author of *Camp de la morte lente*—which presents the assimilationist view—recently converted to Catholicism, which was naturally his right, but which does not indicate the position of those Jews in favor of assimilation."[38]

The controversy surrounding Bernard's publication provides a window into postwar Jewish responses to the Vichy years. It is clear that for most, the losses and upheavals associated with these years substantiated much of what they had already assumed prior to the war's outbreak. For Bernard, confinement in a concentration camp provided strong evidence that his allegiances lay not with other Jews but with fellow French prisoners. His postwar conversion and publications served as public pronouncements of that loyalty, but the ideas themselves took root in the years preceding World War II. Similarly, Hertz, Kapel, and Jarblum were politically active in the 1930s, stressing even then the need for a Jewish national homeland. Jarblum had been one of the founders of Poalei Tsiyon in Poland, and has come to Paris in 1907 as a law student. He continued his active engagement in the movement, filling important positions in international Zionist organizations and editing two Zionist papers in France, *Unzer vort* and *Di naye tsayt*. Active in the resistance throughout World War II, even after moving to Switzerland in 1943, he returned to France after hostilities ended. Then, in the 1950s, he, like Kapel, immigrated to Israel.[39] For Jarblum, then, the Holocaust provided ample evidence that his views on the need for a Jewish state had been correct and that all those calling for assimilation had been, and continued to be, wrong. And for those representing native French Jewish institutions, such as the

Consistoire leaders and the editors of the *Bulletin du Centre israélite d'informa-tion*, Vichy was a cause neither for radical assimilation nor for a repudiation of French citizenship.

In all these cases, the Holocaust did not cause a complete break with past ways of thinking. This is even clearer when we consider the responses of those not in positions of communal authority. While difficult to document, most evidence suggests that the years of Vichy persecution had not visibly shaken most native Jews' faith in the French state. While Bernard's views may have resonated with very few—mass conversions did not occur in the postwar years despite the fears of some communal leaders—it is also clear that for the majority, France still re-mained a country of liberty and justice. In other countries that had been under Nazi rule, such as Poland, returning Jews encountered persecution in the postwar period, making resettlement an intimidating prospect and causing many returnees to flee again. In contrast, returning Jews in France displayed little inclination to leave their native land. While occasionally complaining that the government was not attending to their needs rapidly enough, few French Jews voiced ambivalence, publicly at least, about their country or its leaders. Indeed, the opposite seems to be true; most seemed secure in the belief that republican law in general, and the provisional government in particular, would right Vichy's wrongs.

A profound example of Jewish citizens' faith in the new French regime is their attempts to reclaim property after the war's end. Confident that the state would return what was rightfully theirs, thousands applied to government-established restitution offices for compensation. Their requests indicate that most had not lost faith in France's will or power to protect its citizens, Jews and non-Jews alike. Moreover, their letters illustrate that they understood their citizenship as their his-torical right. Many claimants indignantly reminded officials of their sacrifices for *la patrie* and of their roots in France dating back to the Revolution. One claimant, Maurice P. wrote, for example, that he belonged to a family of old French stock (*de vieille souche française*) and that his father had been a veteran of the Franco-Prussian war.[40] Another demanded the arrest of one of his French persecutors in the name of the restored republic: "In the name of French humanity and for the future and security of the Republic, re-conquered at such a high price, this man must be punished for his criminal acts." The petitioner strengthened his own rights by citing his participation in both world wars and his son's service in the resis-tance.[41] Still others traced their family's roots in France back to the Revolution.[42] These Jewish citizens did not hide from the public spotlight nor did they assume that the persecution they had suffered would have negative repercussions on their postwar status in French society. Rather, they insisted on their legal rights to defense and financial reparations on the grounds that their citizenship offered such protection. Moreover, the overwhelming majority categorically refused to accept any racial label that delegitimized their "Frenchness." Thus, one association formed to protect Jewish claims after the war limited its work to French Jewish citizens. "We have limited our action to the defense of French Israélites," insisted organizational literature, "because we . . . energetically reject the racial thesis that the Germans forced the French to adopt labeling us simply as Jews in all countries."[43]

True, not every returning Jew proved quite so willing to overlook persecution at the hands of their French neighbors. As one quipped when demanding that his provisional administrator be prosecuted, "It was bad enough that we had to suffer through the continual persecution of the enemy without also having to suffer through that of the French."[44] Despite an awareness of having suffered at French hands, however, some Jews were quick to excuse the majority of French citizens from any connection with the persecution. Even Robert Gamzon, the head of the Eclaireurs Israélites de France and a leading member of the Jewish resistance, stressed that "with the exception of very few, the French people helped us a great deal. I can say, without exaggeration, that every living Jew in France was saved at one time or another by a non-Jew."[45]

In their willingness to "forget," if not forgive, governmental and individual participation in four years of discrimination and persecution, Jews, like other French citizens, upheld the public myth that Vichy had been an anomaly; that the persecutions they had endured had been part and parcel of the German occupation; and that the French sins belonged to a handful of collaborators. By placing the blame on Germany in this way, Jews, like other French citizens, were able to exonerate their own society from its role in their persecution.[46]

Even much of the international Zionist leadership proved reluctant to criticize France's role during the war. Certain Jewish militants compared British actions in Palestine with Hitler's during World War II and complained bitterly that the return of racism in France was preventing authorities from intervening on behalf of world Jewry. But in general, few Zionist organizers voiced any anti-French sentiment.[47] Indeed, most took the opposite stance and praised France for its liberal traditions, which they hoped would ensure its support of a Jewish homeland in Palestine. At one rally, on July 4, 1946, Ben-Gurion paid homage to

France as "the country of liberty, the country of the Revolution of 1789 and of General de Gaulle, symbol of the Resistance." Unwilling to make waves in his host country, Ben-Gurion simply requested that France join the international community in calling Great Britain to task for its actions in Palestine.[48] Even the Irgun's propaganda in France did not adopt the militant tone for which it was famous in Palestine. In one flyer, the Irgun asked the French government to allow Jewish immigrants and arms to pass through French land without interference. While denouncing British policies as a new form of Hitlerian persecution, the Irgun invoked France's tradition of siding with the oppressed as a means to encourage French support.[49]

Given the Zionist leadership's desire to build international allegiances in the postwar years, such rhetoric can be dismissed as the most politically expedient choice. Optimistic that the French government might support them in their fight against Britain, the Zionist leadership had no desire to antagonize the French government by dwelling on its recent past. Nevertheless, the pro-French tone contributed to an atmosphere in which the local Jewish population could join their non-Jewish compatriots in putting the war rapidly behind them.

Indeed, with the restoration of republican government, native Jews fully expected to regain their former civil status; the four years of disruption did not lead most to reevaluation of their position in the French social order. As the president of the Consistoire de Paris remarked in 1955, "The Jewish community in France enjoys a position of complete equality in national life. . . . [T]o be a Jew is merely one of the many ways of life for a citizen in a country where diversity is an essential feature."[50] Such a comment, coming only ten years after the end of the war, suggests that belief in France's liberal tradition remained strong, and that the massive disruptions of the war years had few long-term effects on how Jewish citizens understood their place in their surrounding society.

For Eastern European Jewish immigrants, however, particularly those who had actively participated in the Zionist movement, World War II proved that the status quo was untenable. As one Zionist paper chastised in its first postliberation edition:

[N]umerous are those among us who believe that the pure and simple return to the pre-war status quo will suffice to end [the war] and to make us forget the nightmare through which we have lived; according to them we must simply cross our arms and wait until the complete abrogation of all anti-Jewish measures redresses the wrongs that were done. . . . However, there are those of us who believe that a return to the past, however marvelous [it] can seem amidst the infernal distress in which we currently reside, is not enough, and that it is necessary, on the contrary, to uncover in this past all the germs which could breed the illnesses from which we suffer today in order to eliminate them.[51]

Clearly, such sentiments, expressed mostly by Zionist militants, were not shared by the representatives of native French Jewry. And, yet the French Jewish leadership became increasingly willing to speak out on issues they saw as politically important to France's Jewish minority. If the Holocaust did not provide a complete break with past ways of thinking and understanding oneself and one's place in the nation, there is evidence of some shifting attitudes regarding Jewish ethnic and political mobilization. While unwilling to "give up" on France, some Jewish organizations nevertheless began more active and sustained campaigns to guarantee Jewish rights within the polity. Indeed, as the war came to a close, the head of the Consistoire Central, Leon Meiss, entered into negotiations with immigrant Jewish leaders to form a new umbrella organization, the Conseil Réprésentif Israélite de France (CRIF). It was to study political questions, particularly those of postwar restitution programs, and provide a unified front to the government on issues affecting Jewish lives in France.[52] Such an organization was unheard of in pre-occupation years when immigrant and native Jews were unable to agree upon a common agenda and the majority of native Jews remained wary of any political mobilizations that focused on their Jewishness.[53] Now this council represented all political, religious, and social tendencies and took an active and vocal stance defending Jewish rights in the postwar political culture.

Despite its lofty goals, CRIF's ability to effect change was "practically non-existent."[54] While in certain circumstances it voiced a united public voice against further anti-Semitism or lobbied the government on behalf of French Jewry, its influence was minor and its impact on Jewish life limited.[55] The rivalry between Communists and non-Communists prevented the organization from achieving a position of absolute unity with regard to political questions, weakening it in the eyes of its constituents. Nevertheless, the attempt to organize a unified front in this way suggests that the native Jewish leadership was becoming increasingly willing to adopt a politically vocal stance in defense of French Jewry. Moreover, such cooperation between natives and immigrants is evidence that the latter's views were moving further into the mainstream. Certainly with regard to Zionism, CRIF took an unequivocal stand, arguing for the elimination of the White Paper, open immigration of refugees to Palestine, and an official political resolution to the problems in Palestine. This one organization, uniting all components of French Jewry around a single charter, gave Zionism the legitimacy it had previously lacked.[56]

This new institutional recognition provided room for those who were previously ambivalent about Zionism to become more active in Jewish nationalistic activities. In the spring of 1945, the Chief Rabbi of France, Isaïe Schwartz, reported to the ministry of foreign affairs that French Jews, having felt abandoned by government authorities during the war, were adopting attitudes toward Zionism that were less reserved than they had been in the 1920s and 1930s: "[N]ow they have a real and active attraction to this movement." Schwartz's support of Jewish national interests and the agenda of CRIF signaled a new willingness on the part of communal leaders to take a public and political interest in Zionism.[57]

The belief that Zionism had captured the hearts and minds of French Jews was shared by immigrant Jewish leaders, as well. As early as October 1944, Joseph Fisher, director of the French chapter of Keren Kayemet Leyisrael (the international fundraising arm of the Zionist movement) prior to the war, founder of the Zionist paper *La Terre retrouvée*, and member of the managing board of the FSJF (Zionist Federation), reported to the Zionist Executive that "The Zionist movement in France has never been as strong as it is now."[58] Certainly this statement was correct as it applied to an organized movement. The surviving immigrant community, already pro-Zionist prior to the war, continued to produce militant Jewish nationalists who held vocal rallies denouncing all assimilatory projects and calling for the immediate creation of a Jewish state. There were only two solutions to the Jewish problem, proclaimed one Revisionist Zionist at a rally in June 1946: "A Jewish state . . . or the crematoriums."[59] As we have seen, most of the war's anti-Semitic persecution had been aggressively directed at those not born in France. Immigrant Jews were uprooted and deported in higher percentages than native Jews, and their survival rates were considerably lower. Already skeptical that any state was willing or able to provide a safe and neutral haven for them prior to 1940, immigrant Jews became all the more so when peace was finally restored. As two pro-Zionist writers asked: "Did the so-called civilized countries, belligerents and neutrals, do everything in their power to save our hundreds of thousands from deportation and extermination?"[60]

In addition, the immigrant Jewish population, while decimated by the war, soon saw its numbers increase as waves of new refugees, freed from the concentration camps, sought shelter in France. Many of these newcomers held pro-Zionist views as a result of their wartime experiences. Throughout the mid-1940s,

Zionist rallies held in Yiddish attracted these newcomers, as participants protested British actions in Palestine and anti-Semitism in Eastern Europe, and called for the immediate transfer of all Jewish refugees from the DP camps to Palestine.[61] Such rallies gave Zionism visibility in Paris and elsewhere. Though often numerically small, they attracted many important figures from French public life. On July 4, 1946, for example, 2,500 people gathered to hear several former cabinet members, Léon Blum, and David Ben-Gurion.[62] The participation of such well-known figures gave the postwar Zionist movement a legitimacy it had lacked in the prewar years.

Thus, although cooperation among different Zionist groups that had taken shape during the war did not extend into the postwar years—political differences still divided revisionists, general Zionists, and others—from the end of the war until the declaration of the State of Israel, the Zionist movement acquired a new visibility in French public life.[63] This new visibility did not necessarily spread enthusiasm for the Zionist agenda to all members of the French Jewish population. Most rallies attracted no more than several thousand people. Indeed, one Zionist organizer complained, "In the aftermath of the liberation of our territory, the Jews have concerned themselves principally with recuperating their stolen belongings rather than with the Zionist movement."[64]

Those hoping for more visible and actively involved pro-Zionist responses from French Jewry suggested that fear of an anti-Semitic resurgence prevented the population from acting. In August 1945, for example, David Ben-Gurion explained, "In France, people are not interested in Zionism; they are afraid that anti-Semitism will grow and deepen."[65] Far more likely, however, was that most Jews no longer felt threatened once the war had come to an end. As suggested above, the rapid restoration of republican norms eased fears of recurring persecution. Once again assured of their position in society, French Jews felt no driving need to become Zionist activists. That said, far more people had been touched by the new Zionistic atmosphere than the more militant activists conceded. "[E]ven in the circles most removed from Zionism," noted one government report, "people generally approve of the energetic attitude of Zionists of all tendencies and of Jewish patriots who call for the creation of an independent Jewish state in Palestine."[66]

Attitudes among native Jews toward Zionism had shifted. If few were marching in the streets to support the Zionist effort, a passive support had begun to spread throughout much of the population. This is particularly evident in an examination of the Consistoire. This organization, historically opposed to any conception of Jewish nationalism that might throw the position of Jews in France into question, began shifting its views following World War II. Nevertheless, its approach remained cautious, suggesting that even in the aftermath of Vichy persecution, native French Jewish institutions remained committed to their long-held conceptions of the place of Jews in French society.

Founded in 1806 by Napoleon, the Consistoire was created to act as the administrative body of French Jewry, overseeing all religious activities, supervising the work of the rabbis, and officially representing French Jews to the state.[67] Before 1906, when church and state were separated, Consistoire representatives were directly responsible to the government, and, as such strove to protect Jewish rights and to prove that Jews' primary loyalty was to the French nation.[68] After 1906, the Consistoire retained its organizational position in communal affairs on a voluntary basis, directing religious life for affiliated Jews throughout France. In this role, it continued to stress a strictly religious definition of French Jewry and to insist on "the ultimate goodness of France and its bond with the Jewish religion." As Richard Cohen has argued, Vichy's anti-Semitic persecutions did not force the Consistoire leadership to reconsider such notions. Indeed, throughout the war, the Consistoire rejected all racial distinctions, maintaining that Jewish communal affiliation remained a voluntary religious affiliation with no bearing on national or racial makeup. Even by the end of the war, when Consistoire officials had comprehended the severity of the crisis and begun to adjust accordingly, they did not reject their faith in the republican tradition.[69]

Such faith in France remained firmly in place after liberation. In 1946, at his first official appearance as president of the Consistoire de Paris, Georges Wormser outlined the organization's main tasks: to guarantee the regular and dignified practice of Judaism, to maintain a well-managed Parisian Jewish community, and to demonstrate that Jews deserved their citizenship because of their loyalty and devotion to their *patrie*.[70] In addition, the Consistoire leadership, like the French government, was uninterested in overemphasizing the distinct nature of Jewish suffering during World War II. As Annette Wieviorka has shown, the initial commemorations built for Jewish war victims focused first and foremost on those "martyrs" who had fought in the French army or in the resistance, thus deemphasizing the "Jewishness" of their suffering.[71] Even though the Consistoire Centrale immediately began gathering names for a memorial to French Jewish losses, their interest was in distinguished and wounded soldiers, prisoners, and resistance fighters.[72] The great majority of Jews who had died in deportation were not included in this list.

Similarly, to families who hoped to rebury their war dead in Jewish cemeteries, the Consistoire gave only an ambivalent nod. Concluding that individual families must decide the fate of their own kin, Consistoire officials nevertheless strongly recommended Jewish soldiers remain interred with others who fought for France:

> The interest and honor of Judaism requires that the Israélites who were condemned to death and shot stay mingled with the other victims of the capitulation, occupation, collaboration, and treason. If Jewish martyrs are kept shut away in our own cemeteries, the public would forget what contribution we made to the Resistance and to the Liberation.[73]

Clearly, the Consistorial leadership felt no inclination to call attention to Jewish wartime losses, preferring instead to unite their own experiences with those of their non-Jewish compatriots. In this respect, the Consistoire's stance mirrored its prewar positions, which had placed national identity and religious affiliation in different spheres; Jews had fought as French citizens, not as Jews.

If certain Consistoire attitudes mirrored those of previous decades, new ideological stances were also reflected in the discussions and policies of those directing religious life. Support for Zionism, for example, increased notably, particularly after the founding of the State of Israel. Nevertheless, this support was tempered by past fears that support for Jewish nationalism would evoke accusations of disloyalty. Members of the Consistoire sent a telegram congratulating the Chief Rabbi of Palestine after the United Nations declared its support for the creation of an autonomous Jewish state, but the telegram noted that the new refuge was specifically for "our brothers still in distress," implying that it would in no way impinge on the status of Jews already well established elsewhere.[74]

The varying opinions among the Consistoire leadership concerning the organization's relationship to Zionism were brought into sharp focus by Israel's creation. Some leaders stressed religious links to Israel above all else, others encouraged a cautious stance toward the new state, while still others insisted that the Consistoire link its own interests directly with those of the new state. Hence, in May 1948, immediately after Israel's declaration of independence, one Consistoire official requested that all synagogues include a special prayer on behalf of Israel in addition to the traditional prayer for the French republic. Similarly, he proposed adding prayers for the Haganah (Israeli army) and for dead Israeli soldiers.[75] Others went further and requested that a formal ceremony be held in one of the Parisian synagogues honoring the birth of the new state. The administrative council for the Montmartre synagogue, for example, "convinced that the life and honor of worldwide Judaism [was] implicated in the struggle in Palestine" strongly urged the Consistoire de Paris to "demonstrate its sympathy as well as its moral and material support for Israel."[76]

Georges Wormser, president of the Consistoire de Paris, expressed an opposing view. He still feared that if French Jews linked their aspirations with the new state too rapidly, their loyalties would come into question. Professionally, Wormser had long been involved in French national politics. A graduate of the École Normale and an *agrégé* in letters, he had worked closely with Georges Clemenceau, first as his civil staff director in 1919 and then, in 1934, as the head of the ministry staff of the postal system. In later years he worked in the department of the interior. During this period, Wormser was not entirely hostile to Zionism, and while serving as a member of Clemenceau's cabinet in 1917 and early 1918, played a significant part in France's recognition of a Jewish settlement in Palestine.[77] Nevertheless, in a speech to the directors of the Consistoire de Paris in June 1948, Wormser pleaded that they respond cautiously to Israel's arrival on the international stage. For him, the new state posed a real dilemma. While he believed it important for Jewish refugees uprooted by World War II to have their own nation, he felt compelled to remind the Consistoire leadership that French Jews were French first. "Jews and gentiles alike [must] know that we, who enjoy all the rights of Frenchmen and in so doing accept all its obligations, are determined to remain French above all else." It was essential to him that the Consistoire refrain from recognizing Israel until France had done so. In this way, their loyalties to their own country would remain unquestioned.[78]

Interestingly, on this issue, Wormser's views did not correspond with those held by most of the Consistoire leadership. In response to the heated debate which followed Wormser's speech—Wormser temporarily resigned when his colleagues would not accept his position—Consistoire officials ultimately compromised, agreeing to hold a religious ceremony which recognized Israel's struggles without pledging political support to the new state.[79] Even this small step, however, marked a change from the Consistoire's prewar position on Jewish nationalism. Wormser's more traditional appeals for caution were rejected on the grounds that it would not be prudent for the Consistoire to ignore the birth of the new state, and that a show of strength and solidarity was the only wise position. As one official remarked: "In light of the current struggle, we cannot be cowardly and [we must] associate with those who fight for Palestine." Another member noted: "An attitude that is too cautious will put the Consistoire in a poor position vis-à-vis our enemies and our friends."[80] Indeed, even those who did not believe the Consistoire should hold an official celebration of Israeli independence believed that, at the very least, they should organize a religious service commemorating those dying in the War of Independence and praying for future peace.

While not all members agreed on the extent to which they should support the new state, it is clear that many, if not most, Consistoire officials accepted that a relationship between French Jews and Israel must now be articulated. For most, ignoring Jewish nationalism was impossible in a world that included a Jewish state. Moreover, most Consistoire officials believed that public sentiment stood in favor of the new state and feared alienating their Jewish constituency.

The Consistoire, then, if not ready to depart entirely from previous articulations of French Jewish identity, nevertheless moved closer to that of their immigrant coreligionists, both in joining with them to form CRIF and in adopting a positive, if measured, attitude toward Israel. Likewise, it is evident from Consistoire observations and from those of other communal observers that the native French Jewish public was exhibiting an unprecedented interest in Jewish nationalism. In 1948, for example, the American Jewish Joint Distribution Committee's representative in Paris, Harry Rosen, called the concern for Palestine among French Jews "the strongest single cohesive force" in communal life.[81] While such assessments of Zionism's strength may have been exaggerated, there is no question that throughout the late 1940s and beyond, interest in Zionism—evidenced, in part, by fundraising efforts—was significant. By June 1948, a variety of pro-Zionist organizations had raised two hundred million francs on behalf of the Haganah and other organizations, and fundraising for Israel continued to attract sizable contributions throughout the 1950s.[82]

Even more noteworthy than the steady financial support for Israel among French Jews was the fact that following World War II no clearly organized opposition to the Zionist movement was articulated in France. This absence stands in sharp contrast to the years before the Holocaust, when native French Jews maintained a deep skepticism about any project which might call their own loyalties into question, and when organizations proved cautious toward, and often hostile to, the immigrant Jews' Zionist activism.

Postwar support for the new Jewish state was also aided by the fact that although the French government did not officially recognize Israel until more than a year after its creation, public sentiment lay strongly in Israel's favor. Well-publicized events, such as that of the plight of the Jewish refugees on board the ship *Exodus*, bolstered French public opinion in favor of a Jewish state. In this famous incident, the British Navy attacked and captured a boatload of refugees (killing three) after the ship had attempted to enter Palestine clandestinely in the summer of 1947. Although the boat had sailed from French ports, the French government would not permit the British to defuse the issue by returning the refugees to Marseilles. In frustration, the British government forced the boat to return to Germany, where the passengers were compelled to disembark and then placed under military guard. The plight of these refugees was well publicized in France, creating sympathy for the Zionist cause. Both during the *Exodus* incident and after the declaration of the State of Israel, newspaper articles and government officials declared support for a Jewish nationalist agenda. In this atmosphere of popular support, those who had feared that a Jewish state would place their own national allegiances in doubt now had evidence that Jewish and French national interests were not at odds. French Jews could thus take an active interest without compromising their loyalties to their country of birth.

Despite this new, publicly articulated identification with Israel, some native Jews continued to bristle when their national allegiances came into question. "A French Jew is above all else French," wrote a Parisian Jewish lawyer and member of the Consistoire more than a decade after Israel's birth:

> [F]or a French Jew is French and feels French like a French Catholic, Protestant, Muslim or free thinker. French Jews love France as much as any other French citizen, feeling equally the joys of their homeland and commiserating with its misfortunes. They know how to live and die for it. . . . And if against all odds, war should break out between France and Israel, the duty of French Jews, no matter what it would cost them, would be to fire against the Israelis. . . . For if we feel the greatest admiration and love for Israel, we—French Jews—would put France, our country, above all others. And if there is a Jew who declares: 'I am Jewish before French,' he should leave.[83]

If such sentiments remained part of native French Jewish circles, it was also true that Zionism's hold on the population had shifted markedly since the 1930s. Low *aliyah* numbers indicate that neither the Holocaust nor the birth of the State of Israel had induced most native French Jews to question the validity of their own citizenship. These low figures as well as the Consistoire's declarations concerning the continuing loyalty of French Jews to their country show that few French Jews responded to the arrival of the new state by completely abandoning previous understandings of their national identity. Yet those understandings were shifting from a religious to an ethnic identification, as they had begun to do in the interwar years. While Jewish leaders in nineteenth-century France stressed the religious character of Jewish identity, the immigrant Jews of the early twentieth century brought with them broader definitions of Jewish life. The plurality of their religious, political, and ethnic expressions brought options to the largely homogenous French Jewish population.[84] World War II served to solidify these changes. In its aftermath, as immigrant Jews became more integrated into the population, and with the legacy of the war behind them, French Jews began to explore new modes of expressing their Jewish identities. Their increasing interest in Zionism was one part of their expanding self-definition.

RONALD GRIGOR SUNY

Postscript

East European Jewish Politics
in Comparative Perspective

THIS VOLUME, AND THE CONFERENCE at the Frankel Center for Judaic Studies, University of Michigan, that begat it, were a fascinating excursion into a number of historiographies that I know far too poorly. The first impression I came away with was that in order to do my own work on nations and nationalisms, I needed to know more about the Jews in Eastern Europe and Russia. The second impression was that valuable contributions to scholarship come from comparison and theorization of particular experiences of small nations. For several decades I have been dealing with problems of Soviet nationalities, more specifically the peoples of Transcaucasia, even more specifically the Armenians. As I worked in the field of Armenian studies, I was struck by the unnecessary isolation of the field and its almost deliberative separation from comparative studies—a ghetto-ization of the subject that limited its theoretical reach and its relevance to non-Armenians. Moreover, the study of Armenians by Armenians was marked by a deep essentialism, the idea of an unbroken consistency and continuity to the Armenian people and their history, as if this history of over two millennia were in fact of a single piece, and that piece would be the self-realization of a nation. Concentration on Armenians was so focused that there was little space to consider the experiences of the peoples with whom they lived. Over the years, I became quite critical of this essentially ahistorical reading, which imposed a wholeness and homogeneity to a complex, fractured story that combines several narratives. Yet, even to question that wholeness and unbroken narration of the past was seen by many, both in the Armenian community and among its scholars, to be a form of treachery at a moment when that small nation was in mortal danger.

How then does one do scholarship that can both refuse to flinch before the evidence and the questions it raises and satisfy the national needs of the people most fervently committed to a certain reading of that history? The chapters by Ben Nathans and Samuel Kassow provide a window to an answer. They are both well-grounded studies in politics that were alternatives to the two main movements with which this volume is principally concerned—the Bund and the mainstream Zionists. They open the way to other readings of what looks like an overly determined teleology to the story of the Jews—a nation in all times yearning for statehood in a national homeland, the end of the disaster of diaspora in the new gathering in an ancient refuge.

Ben Nathans offers a new appreciation of the Russian Jewish liberals who have too often been neglected by scholars in favor of the apparently more exciting socialists and Zionists. Instead of liberalism being a modernized version of a premodern politics of intercession by men of power with the gentile world, he argues that Russian Jewish liberalism was a modern Jewish politics that promoted the rule of law and was a serious movement of "small deeds" that effectively protected Jews in a time of growing anti-Semitism. Jewish politics in the diaspora was inevitably involved in the non-Jewish power structures, and Russian liberal lawyers used the newly reformed judicial system, and later the elected Duma to create a space for a new modern politics. Nathans does not write off the diaspora as others do; he does not equate it with hopelessness or failure. Diaspora, after all, is the postmodern "other" of the nation-state and has acquired its own enthusiasts and scholars.

This particular psychology of the Russian Jewish liberal should be further explored. In a community in which intense discussions went on about the dangers of assimilation, the perilous choice between revolutionary politics and working within the system, and (particularly after 1881) emigration or some other form of abandonment of former hopes in Russia, liberals did not reject Russia, but autocracy. Educated in Russian universities and steeped in Russian literary and philosophical culture, the liberals were never as alienated as the Zionists or revolutionary socialists. Oskar Gruzenberg, for example, maintained a residue of faith in legal means and a conviction of the basic good in the Russian people. His enemy was the willfulness and arbitrariness of the tsarist system, of the bureaucracy, which disregarded the most elemental notions of justice. He managed somehow to regain hope in "the conscience of a Russia which would never condone the destruction of an innocent person." Interestingly enough, his victories, as often as they came from his extraordinary knowledge of the minutiae of Russian law and juridical precedence, were also aided by his close personal contacts with influential officials (including the minister of justice)—a bit of premodernity within modern politics.

Nathans hints at a questioning of the standard narrative of Russian Jewry, which sees 1881 as a major watershed in the relations of Jews to the Russian state. Maybe this needs some rethinking. Certainly the pogroms affected key figures who moved on to lay the groundwork for both the Zionist and Bundist movements and to encourage emigration from Russia, but, Nathans seems to suggest, there was another tendency—the continuation of the liberal political engagement with tsarism. That engagement, as Nathans mentions, was about a much more complex identity than just being Jewish in Russia; it created a hybrid Russian Jewish identity that made it difficult to tear oneself out of the fabric of Russian life. Intellectually, this identity might be seen as a civic Russian self coexisting with an ethnic Jewish self, but in fact the Russian part was also about culture, the culture of the *russkii intelligent* if not the *muzhik*. As several scholars have noted, civic and ethnic senses of nation are closely related.

Samuel Kassow's chapter is a fascinating treatment of the Left Poalei Tsiyon, the Polish Jewish party that linked secular Yiddish culture with a dedication to the proletariat. They dreamed of a binational, Yiddish-speaking Soviet Palestine. This party tried to combine loyalty to the diaspora and to Palestine. The party was quite pro-Soviet, though not uncritically, and Kassow is to be applauded for bringing the Soviet Union back into the discussion. For besides Zionism and Bundism, a third major player in modern Jewish politics in Eastern Europe was Communism, and certainly the Soviet Union loomed large in the imagination and political horizons of all of these movements.

These chapters and others in the volume make important contributions to our knowledge and understanding of the cases they deal with. Work in Armenian and Jewish studies suggests to me that the study of small nations requires broader engagement with theory and comparison and this volume both provides invaluable raw material for such further work and begins to raise questions about more modernist and constructivist approaches to the nation that have deeply influenced scholarship in the last several decades. In my own view, future scholarship should address issues of continuity and change in the "nation," and the usefulness of the term.

History itself is a human creation and does not "exist" in a real sense as do objects that we see and touch. Historical "facts" are those selected by historians, and from them they create narratives with some purpose, often moral or political, sometimes more neutral and scientific. History is a fabrication, then, something made, but not necessarily false. When historians do their job well, as they have in this volume—tell coherent and persuasive stories, rely on evidence that can be found and checked—those histories come as close as we humans can make them to critical, objective, neutral accounts of the past. But when histories are molded to the purpose of the nation, to inspire or mobilize people, to discipline them in what is authentic and genuine national behavior and thinking, then the more objective aims of historians are often compromised. History and nations have since the late eighteenth century at least been coconspirators. Historical reconstruction of fragmented pasts were instrumental in providing the intellectual and emotional base for nations, while at the same time the new salience of the nation gave historians powerful positions in the new national intelligentsias. History was largely written about the nation and in the national framework well into the twentieth century, but its very literariness was not acknowledged.

The word "nation" is notoriously elusive. Its meanings seem deceptively transparent but have come to refer to many different things. Most usefully, we might think of the nation as a group of people who imagines itself to be a political community distinct from the rest of mankind and deserving self-determination. That self-determination usually entails self-rule, control of territory (the "homeland"), and perhaps a state. Within the discourse of the nation that became hegemonic in the nineteenth century lies a powerful political claim that groups defined largely by culture (language, religion, a myth of common origin) ought to rule themselves. This discourse acted as a time bomb under the feet of diverse, multinational empires led by foreign rulers. Rather than military conquest or divine right conferring legitimacy on governments, nations proclaimed that they themselves possessed sovereignty and the right to political representation. It was within this universe of meanings that ethnoreligious communities, like the Armenians and the Jews, could aspire to the kind of national statehood that had earlier arisen in Western Europe. Historians played an important role in turning their complex pasts and multiple experiences into coherent narratives toward nation and statehood. As historians of the early twenty-first century, in the age of postmodernism and globalization, we are positioned to reexamine those national narratives and recover the paths not taken.

I should note that two different ideas of nation-making must be distinguished. In the first, the nation exists even when people argue about what it is; in time they will get it right. In the second, the nation is precisely that cultural and political space where people create and recreate their sense of who they are. Like culture, it is an arena of contestation, an argument about membership, boundaries, and authenticity. Certainly Jews were constantly thinking, talking, arguing about how to define the people or the nation, who is included, what language it ought to speak, even where it lies, in the diaspora or in a "homeland." As a diaspora Armenian, I can tell you that the discussion over membership and boundaries in the Armenian world is especially intense and periodically leads to transgressors being told "*Haiches*" (You are no Armenian!) or labeled *davejan* (traitor).

It would be fascinating to know more about the different forms of imagined communities—to borrow Benedict Anderson's redolent phrase—that Jews went through in different places and times, before they borrowed the language and concepts of the Enlightenment and the French Revolution and imagined themselves in the sense of the modern discourse of the nation, with ideas of popular sovereignty, the nation sanctioning rulership, and claims to a particular piece of the world's real estate. While Jews are a nation like any other nation and therefore subjects for comparison, comparative politics, and comparative history, most Jewish scholars would insist, and I agree, that they are also distinct. The grand narrative of the nation that has come down to us—and that is embedded in the modern discourse of the nation—is deeply indebted to the Old Testament. Ancient Israel was, to some extent, the model of political community for the European world, just as modern dispersed Jews became the antithesis of the rooted, bounded nation-state in the nineteenth century. The ways in which biblical polities, with their stories of divine sanction, antiquity, and genealogy became models for the paradigms of legitimation of modern nations have yet to be explored. Here, too, there is a lost story, for arguably the first modern nation-states —the United States in the decades after 1776 and France in 1789—as well as some postcolonial nations in Latin America and Africa did not refer back to a primordial past to justify their right to exist, but rather praised newness and creativity. Regrettably, this trope did not survive into the universal discourse of the nation, and over time, primordial and ethnic sources of nationness won out over civil and self-consciously constructed ones.

However ancient Jewish tradition is, and however much people in different times imagined themselves to be part of a continuous narrative, those things should not be conflated with the modern notion of nationhood. Whereas in the past, appeals to God, heredity, conquest, or notions of superiority justified ruler-ship and the existence of a state, other systems of legitimation make the modern nation a different kind of polity. For the nation-state justifies its existence as the representative of a people, conceived in some culture (ethnic or civic), which has the right to rule itself. Popular sovereignty of a people over a specific territory is the norm of modern national politics, and the presumption is that people of the same culture—that is, of the same nation—will desire to be ruled by a single state. How different this is from ancient and medieval polities, in which Greeks or Armenians or Jews lived, and were loyal to, different political leaders or dynasties and fought with their "fellow countrymen" or coreligionists! Older traditions and practices fed into our modern national understandings, but metamorphosed into something different and uniquely modern. We students of peoples of long tradi-tions should keep in mind both the power of those traditions and the ways they changed over time.

Armenians and Jews share many things in common—their survival as a named group from ancient to modern times; their loss of their original homeland and the years living in dispersion; their position in foreign societies as "bourgeois" middlemen, the quintessential outsiders; their experience of genocide and near-annihilation; and the "restoration" of a national state. Nationalists have played down or disparaged the experience of diaspora, yet the centuries of statelessness definitely marked Armenians and Jews. Ironically, just as globalization and Euro-pean integration seems to presage the end of exclusive national states, Armenians and Jews, at least in their independent states, cling to notions of ethnonational-ism with disastrous results. How paradoxical that peoples who suffered the worst forms of ethnic repression, deportation, and systematic murder at the hands of chauvinist states, should themselves try to build a future on homogeneity. In a world of constant movement and change, the idea that each nation should have its own exclusive state, and that each state should have but one nation, is truly utopian. Matching the boundaries of culture and politics in a world of perpetual mixing requires permanent vigilance and readiness to resort to violence. The more relevant experience from the Armenian and Jewish pasts for their futures may be precisely the transnational experience of living with others. In many ways, dias-pora and multiculturalism may be the only ways to guarantee survival in the fu-ture. Here, historians recovering the multiple experiences of the past make an essential contribution.

NOTES

Chapter 1

1. Nahman Syrkin combined Zionism with socialism by advocating a Jewish state based on social justice and welfare. Ber Borochov called for a synthesis of Marxism and Zionism. Later, Vladimir (Ze'ev) Zhabotinsky founded a "revisionist" Zionist movement that demanded the Jewish state be established on both sides of the Jordan River, as originally envisioned by the British. Religious Zionists argued that Zionism was inherent in Judaism and a Jewish state would enhance religious observance. See Arthur Herzberg, *The Zionist Idea* (Cleveland: Meridian Books, 1960).

2. See Sammy Smooha, "Minority Status in an Ethnic Democracy: The Status of the Arab Minority in Israel," *Ethnic and Racial Studies* 13, no. 3 (July 1990); Yoav Peled, "Ethnic Democracy and the Legal Construction of Citizenship: Arab Citizens of the Jewish State," *American Political Science Review* 86, no. 2 (June 1992); Oren Yiftachel, "The Concept of 'Ethnic Democracy' and Its Applicability to the Case of Israel," *Ethnic and Racial Studies* 15, no. 1 (January 1992); Boaz Evron, *Jewish State or Israeli Nation* (Bloomington, Ind.: Indiana University Press, 1995).

3. Victor Shulman, ed., *Henrik Erlikh un Viktor Alter* (New York: Unzer Tsayt, 1951), 39; Bernard K. Johnpoll, *The Politics of Futility: The General Jewish Workers' Bund of Poland, 1917–1943* (Ithaca, N.Y.: Cornell University Press, 1967), 224. See also Abraham Brumberg, "The Bund and the Polish Socialist Party in the Late 1930s," in *The Jews of Poland Between Two World Wars*, ed. Yisrael Gutman, Ezra Mendelsohn, Jehuda Reinharz, and Chone Shmeruk (Hanover, N.H.: University Press of New England, 1989). A brief sketch of the Bund in the early years of independent Poland is found in Rudolf Korsch, *Zydowskie Ugrupownia Wywrotowe w Polsce* (Warsaw: n.p., 1925).

4. Joseph Marcus, *Social and Political History of the Jews in Poland, 1919–1939* (New York: Mouton Publishers, 1983), quoted in Daniel Blatman, "The Bund in Poland, 1935–1939," *POLIN* 9 (1996): 79.

5. Four exceptions are Yoav Peled, *Class and Ethnicity in the Pale* (New York: St. Martin's, 1989); Arye Gelbard, *Sofo shelo kitkhilato: kitzo shel ha'Bund' harusi* (Tel Aviv: Tel Aviv University, 1995); Henri Minczeles, *Histoire generale du Bund—un mouvement revolutionnaire juif* (Paris: Editions Austral, 1995); and, most recently, Jack Jacobs, ed., *Jewish Politics in Eastern Europe: The Bund at 100* (New York: New York University Press, 2001).

6. An interesting comparison in this regard is made in Jan Blommaert, "Language and Nationalism: Comparing Flanders and Tanzania," *Nations and Nationalism* 2, no. 2 (July

1996). See also William Safran, "Language, Ideology, and State-Building: A Comparison of Policies in France, Israel, and the Soviet Union," *International Journal of Political Science* 13, no. 4 (1992).

7. R. A. Schermerhorn, *Comparative Ethnic Relations* (New York: Random House, 1970), 12. See also Anthony D. Smith, *The Ethnic Revival in the Modern World* (Cambridge: Cambridge University Press, 1981), 64.

8. Professor Antony Polonsky pointed out to me that Jews' preference for English in Quebec may be due to the fact that most Jews sent their children to Protestant schools, where the language of instruction was English, rather than to (French) Catholic schools, not because of the difference in languages but because the Catholic hierarchy and French-Canadians were perceived as more hostile to the Jews. Professor Maurice Friedberg noted, however, that Ukrainian immigrants—many of whom were Uniate and thus closer to Catholicism—also adopted English, not French, in Quebec.

9. See Emanuel Goldsmith, *Architects of Yiddishism at the Beginning of the Twentieth Century: A Study in Jewish Cultural History* (Rutherford, N.J.: Fairleigh Dickinson University Press, 1976).

10. Chaim Jitlovsky (Zhitlovsky), "What Is Jewish Secular Culture?" in *The Way We Think*, ed. Joseph Leftwich (South Brunswick, N.J.: Thomas Yoseloff, 1969), 1:92, 93, 95.

11. Israel Cohen, *Vilna* (Philadelphia: Jewish Publication Society, 1943), 117.

12. Ibid., 118.

13. See, for example, O. Margulis, *Yidishe folksmasn in kamf kegn ẓeyere undterdriker* (Moscow: Der emes, 1940); O. Margulis, *Geshikhte fun Yidn in Rusland* (Moscow-Kharkov-Minsk: Tsentraler felker farlag fun FSSR, 1930); T. Haylikman, *Geshikhte fun der geẓelshaftlicher bavegung fun di Yidn in Poiln un Rusland* (Moscow: Tsentraler farlag far di felker fun F.S.S.R., 1926).

14. Scholars debate if the Bund had a national program from its beginnings, if it shifted to a more national program as a result of the pressure by the rank-and-file, or if it underwent this change as a result of intra-intelligentsia struggles over power, ideology, and money. On the first position, see Moshe Mishkinsky, *Reshit tenu'at ha-po'alim ha Yehudit be-Rusyah* (Tel Aviv: Hakibutz Hamechad, 1981); on the second position, see Henry J. Tobias, *The Jewish Bund in Russia from Its Origins to 1905* (Stanford: Stanford University Press, 1972) and Ezra Mendelsohn, *Class Struggle in the Pale* (New York: Cambridge University Press, 1970); on the third position, see Jonathan Frankel, *Prophecy and Politics* (New York: Cambridge University Press, 1981). Peled, in *Class and Ethnicity*, concludes that "what the leadership was doing . . . was attempting to broaden the base of the movement by addressing what they believed were the particular concerns of the masses of Jewish workers at any given point" (110). This is my own impression and I read this as a form of political responsiveness. For a different explanation of the Bund leadership's behavior, see Henry Tobias and Charles Woodhouse, "Primordial Ties and Political Process in Pre-Revolutionary Russia: The Case of the Jewish Bund," *Comparative Studies in Society and History* 8, no. 3 (April 1966).

15. T. M. Kopelson, "Evreiskoe rabochee dvizhenie kontsa 80-kh i nachala 90-kh godov," quoted in Henry Tobias, "The Bund and Lenin until 1903," *The Russian Review* 39, no. 4 (October 1961): 344–45.

16. Robert Brym, *The Jewish Intelligentsia and Russian Marxism* (London: Macmillan, 1978), 95.

17. Larry Diamond, Juan Linz, and Seymour Martin Lipset, eds., *Politics in Developing Countries: Comparing Experiences with Democracy* (Boulder, Colo.: Lynne Rienner, 1988), 6–7.

18. See, for example, Arthur Hertzberg, ed., *The Zionist Idea* (New York: Meridian, 1960); Shlomo Avineri, *The Making of Modern Zionism* (New York: Basic Books, 1981); Yisrael Kloizner, *Mikatovitz ad Basel*, 2 vols. (Jerusalem: Hasifriya hatsionit, 1965); David Vital, *The Origins of Zionism* (Oxford: Clarendon, 1975); Vital, *Zionism: The Formative Years* (Oxford: Clarendon, 1982); David Vital, *Zionism: The Crucial Phase* (Oxford: Clarendon, 1987); Jehuda Reinharz and Anita Shapira, eds., *Essential Papers on Zionism* (New York: NYU Press, 1996); Frankel, *Prophecy and Politics*.

On Zionism in Russia, see Yitzhak Maor, *Hatenua hatsionit beRusiya* (Jerusalem: Hasifriya hatsionit, 1973); *Katsir: kovetz l'korot hatenua hatsionit beRusiya*, 2 vols. (Tel Aviv: Masada, 1964 and Tel Aviv: Tarbut vekhinuch, 1972); Aryeh Tsentsiper (Refaeli), *Paamay hageulah* (Tel Aviv: Tversky, 1951); Tsentsiper, (Refaeli) *Bamaavak ligeulah* (Tel Aviv: Davar, 1956).

19. Yosef Gorny, "Hashinuyim bamivneh hakhevrati vehapoliti shel 'haaliyah hashniyah' bashanim 1904–1940," *Hatsionut* 1 (Tel Aviv: Hakibbutz hameuhad, 1970), 219.

20. On the Zionist-Socialists, see Yehuda Erez, ed., *Sefer Ts"S* (Tel Aviv: Am Oved, 1963).

21. Yosef Goldshtain, *Ben Tsiyonut medinit le-Tsiyonut ma'asit* (Jerusalem: Magnes Press, 1991), 162–63. I would like to thank Professor Steven Zipperstein for this reference.

22. Ibid., 170–71.

23. Shlomo Zalman Landa and Yosef Rabinovich, comps., *Sefer or layesharim* (Warsaw: 1900), quoted in Eli Lederhendler, *The Road to Modern Jewish Politics: Political Tradition and Political Reconstruction in the Jewish Community of Tsarist Russia* (New York: Oxford University Press, 1989), 156.

24. The photographs are in Tsentsiper (Refaeli), *Paamay hageulah*, 81–84, 116–17, 125–26, 130, 132.

25. Henry Jack Tobias, *The Jewish Bund in Russia* (Stanford: Stanford University Press, 1972), 44.

26. Data compiled from J. S. Hertz, ed., *Di geshikhte fun Bund*, vols. 1–3 (New York: Unzer Tsayt, 1960–66). On Esther Frumkin's career, see Zvi Gitelman, *Jewish Nationality and Soviet Politics* (Princeton: Princeton University Press, 1972).

27. Anna Rozental, "Froien geshtaltn in 'Bund,'" *Naye folkstsaytung* (Warsaw), November 19, 1937, quoted in *Unser tsayt* 3–4 (November–December 1947): 60–61; reprinted again in *Unser tsayt* (October–December 1972): 10–12.

28. Tobias, *The Jewish Bund in Russia*, 245.

29. Frankel, *Prophecy and Politics*, 181.

Chapter 2

I would like to thank Eli Nathans and Derek Penslar as well as the participants in the conference "A Century of Modern Jewish Politics" held at the Frankel Center for Judaic Studies,

University of Michigan, for their comments on earlier versions of this essay. Generous financial support during the period when the essay was written came from the National Council for Soviet and East European Research and the Social Science Research Council, both under authority of a Title VIII Grant from the U.S. Department of State. Additional support was provided by the Memorial Foundation for Jewish Culture.

1. The most detailed study of the Society remains I. M. Cherikover, *Istoriia Obshchestva dlia rasprostraneniia prosveshcheniia mezhdu evreiami v Rossii, 1863–1913* (Petersburg: n.p., 1913), the first volume of which was published in commemoration of the Society's fiftieth anniversary. The planned second volume never appeared. See also Y. L. Rosenthal, *Toldot hevrat marbei haskalah be-erets rusiyah,* 2 vols. (Petersburg: n.p.,: 1885–90), which consists mostly of primary sources relating to the Society's history, translated into Hebrew. For a more recent view, see John D. Klier, *Imperial Russia's Jewish Question, 1855–1881* (Cambridge: Cambridge University Press, 1995), 245–62.

2. Jonathan Frankel, *Prophecy and Politics: Socialism, Nationalism, and the Russian Jews, 1862–1917* (Cambridge: Cambridge University Press, 1981), 2.

3. Frankel includes a judicious review of several such works in his essay, "Assimilation and the Jews in Nineteenth-Century Europe: Towards a New Historiography?" in Jonathan Frankel and Steven Zipperstein, eds., *Assimilation and Community: The Jews in Nineteenth-Century Europe* (Cambridge: Cambridge University Press, 1992), 1–37. See also Michael Stanislawski, *For Whom Do I Toil? Judah Leib Gordon and the Crisis of Russian Jewry* (New York: Columbia University Press, 1988), 146–47; Eli Lederhendler, *The Road to Modern Jewish Politics: Political Tradition and Political Reconstruction in the Jewish Community of Tsarist Russia* (New York: Oxford University Press, 1989).

4. Dan Miron, "The Image of the Shtetl in Yiddish Literature," *Jewish Social Studies* 3 (1995): 35–69. For a similar perspective, see Barbara Kirshenblatt-Gimblett, introduction to *Life Is with People: The Culture of the Shtetl,* rev. ed., ed. Elizabeth Herzog and Mark Zborowski (New York: Schocken: 1995), xxxi–xxxiv.

5. Lederhendler, *Road to Modern Jewish Politics.*

6. See the biographical data (pertaining to the years 1908–16) on founders of the dozens of branches of the Society for the Spread of Enlightenment in *Tsentral'nyi gosudarstvennyi istoricheskii arkhiv goroda Sankt-Peterburga* (TsGIA-SPb), f. 287, op. 1, d. 85, ll. 56–236. For the educational profile of the leadership of the Union for the Attainment of Equal Rights, see Stanislav Kel'ner, "Soiuz dlia dostizheniia polnopraviia evreiskogo naroda v Rossii i ego lidery," *Iz glubiny vremen* 7 (1996): 3–14.

7. *Rossiiskii gosudarstvennyi istoricheskii arkhiv* (RGIA) f. 733, op. 226, d. 27, ll. 8–148 contains scattered data on Jewish enrollment by faculty at Moscow, Petersburg, Kiev, and Novorossiiskii universities in the 1870s. See also *Spisok studentov i postoronnikh slushatelei imperatorskogo Novorossiiskogo universiteta za 1865–66 akademicheskii god* (n.p., n.d.) and *Spisok studentov i postoronnikh slushatelei imperatorskogo Novorossiiskogo universiteta za 1880–81 akademicheskii god* (n.p., n.d.).

8. *Evreiskaia entsiklopediia. Svod znanii o evreistve i ego kul'ture v proshlom i nastoiashchem* (Petersburg: Obshchestvo dlia nauchnykh evreiiskikh izdanii i Izdatel'stvo Brokhaus-Efron, 1906–13), 13:50.

9. The official police report on the three days of rioting set the total damages at ten million rubles, including hundreds of vandalized and looted shops and damaged homes. See John Klier, "The Pogrom Paradigm in Russian History," in John Klier and Shlomo Lambroza, eds., *Pogroms: Anti-Jewish Violence in Modern Russian History* (Cambridge: Cambridge University Press, 1992), 2.

10. For accounts of the lawyers' efforts, see M. G. Morgulis, "Bezporiadki 1871 goda v Odesse (po dokumentam i lichnym vospominaniiam)," in "Teoreticheskie i prakticheskie voprosy evreiskoi zhizni. Prilozhenie k zhurnaly," *Evreiskii Mir* (Petersburg, 1911), 42–44; *Evreiskaia nedelia* 3 (April 29, 1910): 8–14.

11. I. G. Orshanskii, *Russkoe ʐakonodatel'stvo o evreiakh* (Petersburg: A. E. Landau Printers, 1877), 336.

12. See, for example, RGIA, f. 821, op. 9, d. 87, l. 2. For further instances, see Benjamin Nathans, *Beyond the Pale: The Jewish Encounter With Late Imperial Russia* (Berkeley: University of California Press, 2002).

13. TsGIA-SPb, f. 422, op. 2, d. 1, ll. 18–24. It is important to note that despite their fierce disagreement on the proper response to the pogroms—chiefly, whether to promote Jewish emigration—delegates to the conference were nearly unanimous in the view that discriminatory legislation was the root cause of the violence. Other, secondary factors mentioned were the deliberate incitement of anti-Semitism by certain Russian newspapers, and the government's failure to censor such incitement, thereby giving the appearance of official approval. See also *Nedel'naia khronika voskhoda* nos. 30, 33, 34, and 36 (1882), especially no. 34: 926–27. For Russian attitudes, see John Klier, "The Russian Press and the Anti-Jewish Pogroms of 1881," *Canadian-American Slavic Studies* 17, no. 1 (1983): 199–221.

14. Zalkind Minor, *Posle pogromov, ili tri glavy o evreiskom voprose* (Moscow: n.p., 1882), 4.

15. S. Gol'dshtein, "Emmanuil Borisovich Levin (1820–1913). Po avtobiograficheskim zametkam," *Evreiskaia Starina* 8, no. 3 (1915): 253; *Evreiskaia entsiklopediia*, 10:114.

16. G. B. Sliozberg, *Dela minuvshikh dnei. Zapiski russkogo evreia*, 2 vols. (Paris: Committee for the Seventieth Birthday of G. B. Sliozberg, 1933–34), 1:156, 301.

17. Ibid., 1:302.

18. Ibid., 1:216–18; 2:7–15. Also see V. Fridshtein and I. V. Gessen, eds., *Sbornik ʐakonov o evreiakh s ras"iasneniiami po opredeleniiam Pravitel'stvuiushchago Senata i tsirkuliaram Ministerstv* (Petersburg: Izd. Iurid. Kn. Magazina N. K. Martynova, Izdanie Neoffitsial'noe, 1904), vii, for this statement: "Appeals concerning 'Jewish' issues constituted a very considerable percentage of the total number of cases in the First Department [of the Senate]."

19. Sliozberg, *Dela minuvshikh dnei*, 1:303; 2:15.

20. Shaul M. Ginzburg, *Amolike peterburg. Forshungn un ʐikhroynes vegn yidishn lebn in der reʐidents-shtot fun tsarishn rusland* (New York: CYSHO, 1944), 88–100. In his preface to Sliozberg's memoirs, Ze'ev Zhabotinsky goes so far as to claim that Sliozberg's fame among the Jewish masses outshone that of his patron, Baron Gintsburg. This seems exaggerated. See Ze'ev Zhabotinsky, preface to Sliozberg, *Dela minuvshikh dnei*, 1:x.

21. M. L. Gol'dshtein, *Advokatskie portrety* (Paris: n.p., 1932), 27.

22. On the Defense Bureau, see Christoph Gassenschmidt, *Jewish Liberal Politics in Tsarist Russia, 1900–1914* (New York: Macmillan: 1995), 8–10.

23. Ibid., 34.

24. See Ezra Mendelsohn's otherwise superb interpretive essay, *On Modern Jewish Politics* (New York: Oxford University Press, 1993), 60.

25. Gassenschmidt, *Jewish Liberal Politics*, 88–89.

26. Leonard Schapiro, *Russian Studies,* ed. Ellen Dahrendorf (New York: Penguin: 1986), 51.

27. RGIA, f. 1565, op. 1, dd. 26–76.

28. Gassenschmidt, *Jewish Liberal Politics*, 72–135.

29. See the list of branch openings and members in TsGIA-SPb, f. 287, op. 1, d. 85, ll. 56–236.

30. On the Society's membership and budget in these years, see Gassenschmidt, *Jewish Liberal Politics*, 99, 128.

31. Sliozberg, *Dela minuvshikh dnei*, 2:301.

32. Ibid., 2:301–2.

33. Jacob Katz, *Out of the Ghetto: The Social Background of Jewish Emancipation, 1770–1870* (Cambridge, Mass.: Harvard University Press, 1978), 42–56.

34. Sliozberg, *Dela minuvshikh dnei*, 1:4.

35. Ibid., 1:91–92, 2:301.

36. See M. L. Gol'dshtein, *Reichi i stat'i* (Paris: 1929), 49.

37. Sliozberg, *Dela minuvshikh dnei*, 1:91–92.

38. Solomon Pozner, "Bor'ba za ravnopravie," in *Maksim Moiseevich Vinaver i russkaia obshchestvennost' nachala XX veka. Sbornik statei* (Paris: 1937), 168.

39. See Pozner's recollection of Vinaver in "Bor'ba za ravnopravie," 167.

40. Ferdinand Tönnies, *Community and Society*, trans. and ed. by Charles P. Loomis (East Lansing: Michigan State University Press, 1957).

41. The distinction between civic and ethnic bases of citizenship plays a central role in an important school of thought on modern nationalism, beginning with Hans Kohn, *The Idea of Nationalism: A Study in Its Origins and Background* (New York: Macmillan, 1944) and recently continued by Liah Greenfeld, *Nationalism: Five Roads to Modernity* (Cambridge, Mass.: Harvard University Press, 1993). It is worth recalling that the attempt to legally secure both individual civil and political rights and collective cultural rights of stateless ethnic groups did not gain significant momentum until the Paris Peace Conference in 1919. In the interwar period, formal treaties guaranteeing minority rights were signed by the League of Nations and most of the newly created states of Central and Eastern Europe, though not by the Soviet Union, where the Bolsheviks pursued a radically different approach to nationalities policy. See Oscar Janowsky, *The Jews and Minority Rights (1898–1919)* (New York: Columbia University Press, 1933).

42. Oskar Gruzenberg, *Ocherki i rechi* (New York: Grenich Printing Company 1944), 159. A similar assessment of Sliozberg's career was offered by the lawyer M. L. Gol'dshtein, in *Advokatskie portrety*: "The Jewish people, like other peoples, in addition to its vital problems, has thousands of small needs, concerns and fears, it has so to say not only its great festivals but also its weekdays. With other peoples these concerns are handled by thousands of bu-

reaucrats, hundreds of chancelleries, departments and bureaus. With the Jewish people in Russia this entire titanic job . . . was performed by one person—Sliozberg" (29).

43. Zhabotinsky, preface to Sliozberg, *Dela minuvshikh dnei*, 1:x.

Chapter 3

1. Bernard K. Johnpoll, *The Politics of Futility: The General Jewish Workers Bund of Poland, 1917–1943* (Ithaca, N.Y.: Cornell University Press, 1967), 195.

2. Majer Bogdanski, *Jewish Chronicle* (London), October 31, 1986.

3. Joseph Marcus, *Social and Political History of the Jews in Poland, 1919–1939* (New York: Mouton Publishers, 1983), 468–69.

4. Antony Polonsky, 'The Bund in Polish Political Life 1935–1939," in *Jewish History: Essays in Honour of Chimen Abramsky*, ed. Ada Rapoport-Albert and Steven Zipperstein (London: Halban, 1998), 571–75.

5. Barbara Wachowska, "Lódz Remained Red: Elections to the City Council of September 27, 1936," *POLIN* 9 (1996): 83–106.

6. Jerzy Tomaszewski, "Niepodlegla Rzeczpospolita," in *Najnowsze Dzieje Zydów w Polsce*, ed. Jerzy Tomaszewski (Warsaw: PWN, 1993), 215.

7. Shimon Dubnow, open letter to *Naye folkstsaytung*, July 29, 1938.

8. Henryk Erlich, editorial in *Naye folkstsaytung*, July 31, 1938

9. Israel Zangwill, "Samo-oborona," in *Ghetto Comedies* (New York: Macmillan, 1907), 429–87. I am indebted to Ezra Mendelsohn's *On Modern Jewish Politics* (New York: Oxford University Press, 1993) for this reference.

10. Simon Dubnow, "What Should One Do in Haman's Times? (A Letter to the Editors of *Oyfn sheydveg*, 1939)," in *Nationalism and History: Essays on Old and New Judaism*, ed. Koppel Pinson (Philadelphia: Jewish Publication Society, 1958), 354–60.

11. Ignacy Matuszewski, "Przemyśl i powięci," *Tygodnik Ilustrowany*, no. 48 (1899).

12. Magdalena Opalski, "Trends in the Literary Perception of Jews in Modern Polish Fiction," in *From 'Shtetl' to Socialism: Essays from POLIN*, ed. Antony Polonsky (Oxford: Littman Library of Jewish Civilization, 1993), 162.

13. Roman Dmowski, *Mysli nowoczesnego Polaka* (1903; reprint, London: Nakladem Kola Mlodych Stronnictwa Narodowego, 1953), 87.

14. Leila P. Everett, "The Rise of Jewish National Politics in Galicia," in *Nationbuilding and the Politics of Nationalism: Essays on Austrian Galicia*, ed. Andrei S. Markovits and Frank E. Sysyn (Cambridge, Mass.: Harvard University Press, 1982), 149–77.

15. Alexander Swietochowski, "O Zydach," *Kultura Polski*, no. 12 (1912).

16. Alexander Swietochowski, *Wspomnienia* (Warsaw: Zaklad Narodowy Ossolinskich, 1966), 86.

17. Tim Snyder, *Nationalism, Marxism, and Modern Central Europe: A Biography of Kazimierz Kelles-Krauz (1872–1905)* (Cambridge, Mass.: Harvard University Press, 1997).

18. "Proceedings of the Second Congress on the Jewish Communities and the Jewish National Assembly. Stenographic Reports," *Yidishe shtime* (Kaunas), February 1922, quoted in

Samuel Gringauz, "Jewish National Autonomy in Lithuania (1918–1925)," *Jewish Social Studies* 14, no. 3 (July 1952): 225–46. See also Sarunas Liekis, "Jewish Autonomy in Lithuania" (Ph.D. diss., Brandeis University, 1997).

19. Samuel Gringauz, "Jewish National Autonomy in Lithuania," 234.

20. Ibid., 237.

21. On Agudat Yisrael, see Ezra Mendelsohn, "The Politics of Agudas Israel in Inter-War Poland," *Soviet Jewish Affairs* 2 (1972): 47–60; Gershon Bacon, *The Politics of Tradition: Agudat Yisrael in Poland, 1916–1939* (Jerusalem: Magnes Press, 1996).

22. The issue of *shekhita* has given rise to a vast literature which is well reviewed by Emanuel Meltzer in his *Maavak medini be-malkodet; Yehudey Polin 1935–39* (Tel Aviv: Diaspora Research Institute, 1982), 97–110. [English translation: *No Way Out. The Politics of Polish Jewry 1935–1939* (Cincinnati: Hebrew Union College Press, 1997).]

23. Celia Heller, *On the Edge of Destruction* (New York: Columbia University Press, 1977).

Chapter 4

1. Jerzy Tomaszewski, *Rzeczpospolita wielu Narodow* (Warsaw: Czytelnik, 1985), 18–19.

2. Stanislaw Ciesielski, Zbigniew Fras, Krzysztof Kawalec, Teresa Kulak, "Narod i narodowosc polska lat 1795–1945 w badaniach historycznych," in *Polska—Polacy—mniejszosci narodowe,* ed. Wojciech Wrzesinski (Wroclaw: Ossolineum, 1992), 10, 22.

3. Ezra Mendelsohn, *Zionism in Poland—The Formative Years, 1915–1926* (New Haven: Yale University Press, 1981), 4.

4. Tomaszewski, *Rzeczpospolita,* 42–46.

5. Andrzej Chojnowski, *Koncepcje polityki narodowosciowej rządow polskich w latach 1921–1939* (Wroclaw: Ossolineum, 1979), 135–39.

6. Bernard K. Johnpoll, *The Politics of Futility: The General Jewish Workers Bund of Poland 1917–1943* (Ithaca, N.Y.: Cornell University Press, 1967), 41–42; Moshe Mishkinski, "Ben 'ha-Bund ha-yashan' la-'Bund ha-polani'" (Between the 'Old Bund' and the 'Polish Bund'), *Gal-Ed, On the History of the Jews in Poland* 12 (1993): 122.

7. J. S. Hertz, "Der Bund in poyln (in di yorn fun der ershter velt-milkhome)," in *Di geshikhte fun Bund,* ed. J. S. Hertz, vol. 3 (New York: Unzer Tsayt, 1966), 287–88.

8. Arye Gelbard, *Bi-se'arat ha-yamim, ha-Bund ha-rusi be-'itot mahapekha* (Stirring times—the Russian Bund in revolutionary days) (Tel Aviv: Tel Aviv University, 1987), 115–16.

9. Vladimir Medem, "Di kehilla. Tsi art si unds?" *Lebens-fragn* 44 (December 1916).

10. Hertz, "Der Bund in poyln," 3:290–91.

11. This had been a crucial issue in the political doctrine of the Bund since its inception in Vilna in the late nineteenth century. Research points in several directions concerning the development of the Bund's national ideology in its early years. See Jonathan Frankel, *Prophecy and Politics, Socialism, Nationalism and the Russian Jews, 1862–1917* (Cambridge: Cambridge University Press, 1981), 185–227; Yoav Peled, *Class and Ethnicity in the Pale: The Political Economy of the Jewish Workers' Nationalism in the Late Imperial Russia* (New York: St. Mar-

tin's Press, 1989); Gregor Aronson, "Di natsyonale un organizatsyonale frage," in *Di geshikhte fun Bund*, ed. J. S. Hertz, vol. 2 (New York: Unzer Tsayt, 1962), 529–36.

12. Roman Wapinski, "Mit dawnej Rzeczypospolitej w epoce porozbiorowej," in *Polskie mity polityczne XIX I XX wieku*, ed. Wojciech Wrzesinski (Wroclaw: Wydawnictwo Uniwersytetu Wroclawskiego, 1994), 87.

13. Eugeniusz Koko, "PPS wobec kwestii ukrainskiej w latach 1918–1939 (ze szczegolnym uwzglednieniem okres ksztalowania sie zaszadniczych koncepcji do 1925r.)," in *Polska— Polacy—mniejszosci narodowe*, ed. Ewa Grzeskowiak-Luczyk (Wroclaw: Zaklad Narodowy im. Ossoli'nskich, 1992), 345–47; Michal Sliwa, "The Jewish Problem in Polish Socialist Thought," *POLIN* 9 (1996): 26–28; Abraham Brumberg, "The Bund and the Polish Socialist Party in the Late 1930s," in *The Jews of Poland Between Two World Wars*, ed. Yisrael Gutman, Ezra Mendelsohn, Jehuda Reinharz, and Chone Shmeruk (Hanover, N.H.: University Press of New England, 1989), 76.

14. Johnpoll, *The Politics of Futility*, 73.

15. Mishkinski, "Ben 'ha-Bund ha-yashan' la-'Bund ha-polani'," 130; *Doyres Bundistn*, ed. J. S. Hertz, vol. 1, (New York: Unzer Tsayt, 1956), 332–33; Gelbard, *Bi-se'arat ha-yamim*, 108.

16. Yisrael Gutman, "Polish Antisemitism Between the Wars: An Overview," in *The Jews of Poland Between Two World Wars*, 99–100; Johnpoll, *The Politics of Futility*, 74–75; Azriel Shohat, "Parashat ha-pogrom be-Pinsk" (The Pogrom in Pinsk, April 5, 1919), *Gal-Ed, On the History of the Jews in Poland* 1 (1973), 135–73.

17. J. S. Hertz, "Der Bund in umophengikn Poyln 1918–1925," in *Di geshikhte fun Bund*, ed. J. S. Hertz, vol. 4 (New York: Unzer Tsayt, 1972), 22.

18. *Glos Bundu* (Warsaw), June 3, 1919; Hertz, "Der Bund in umophengikn Poyln," 44–46.

19. Hertz, "Der Bund in umophengikn Poyln," 4:62–65, 94–108; Johnpoll, *The Politics of Futility*, 91–128.

20. Johnpoll, *The Politics of Futility*, 91–96.

21. Vladimir Medem, *Fun mayn notits-bukh* (Warsaw: Di Welt, 1929), 58–59, 70–71.

22. Hertz, "Der Bund in umophengikn Poyln," 4:26.

23. Bernard Goldstein, *20 yor in varshever "Bund" 1919–1939* (New York: Unzer Tsayt, 1960), 35–40; Hertz, "Der Bund in umophengikn Poyln," 4:109–18.

24. Beinish Michalewicz, "Unser natsyonale program in licht fun praktik," parts 1 and 2, *Unser tsayt* 2 (November 1927): 14–15; 4 (December 1927): 7.

25. Beinish Michalewicz, "Unser natsyonale program in licht fun praktik," part 3, *Unser tsayt* no. 1 (January 1928): 15–16.

26. J. Zef, "Unsere profesyonale faraynen," *Lebens-fragn* 5 (March 1916).

27. Szmuel Zygelboim [*sic*], "Di yidishe profesyonale bavegung in poyln," in *Zygelboim bukh*, ed. J. S. Hertz (New York: Unzer Tsayt, 1947), 91–92.

28. A. Chaver, "Di arbatyer-haym in Lublin," *Lebens-fragn* 17 (May 1916).

29. Zygelboim [*sic*], "Di yidishe profesyonale," 89, 102; Joseph Marcus, *Social and Political History of the Jews in Poland 1919–1939* (New York: Mouton Publishers, 1983), 125–28.

30. J. S. Hertz, "Di profesyonale faraynen fun di yidishe arbeter," in *Di geshikhte fun Bund*, ed. J. S. Hertz, vol. 4 (New York: Unzer Tsayt, 1972), 229–30.

31. Emanuel Nowogrodski, "Kamf far recht oyf arbet," in *Di geshikhte fun Bund*, ed. J. S. Hertz, vol. 5 (New York: Unzer Tsayt, 1981), 147–50.

32. Zygelboim (*sic*), "Di yidishe profesyonale," 99.

33. Mendelsohn, *Zionism in Poland*, 7–8; Marcus, *Social and Political History of the Jews in Poland*, 35, 55–56.

34. *Naye folkstsaytung* (henceforth: *NF*), January 28, 1935; *Sprawy Narodowosciowe* 11, no. 1–2 (1937): 131–32; Report of the *Kultur-lige* in Poland with details on the cultural activities of the Jewish trade unions, September 7, 1937, *Bund Archives—YIVO*, NG-1/157.

35. Bina Garncarska-Kadari, "Some Aspects of the Life of the Jewish Proletariat in Poland during the Interwar Period," *POLIN* 8 (1994): 238–54.

36. E. Mus, "Di sotsyalistishe bavegung bay di hentverker," parts 1 and 2, *Unser tsayt*, no. 8–9 (September–October 1928): 49–50.

37. Isaac Giterman (Warsaw) to JDC (Paris), 27 1939, JDC Archives, file no. 818.

38. "Yidishe arbeterin, froy un muter!" *NF*, January 31, 1928.

39. Celia S. Heller, *On the Edge of Destruction, Jews of Poland Between the Two World Wars* (New York: Columbia University Press, 1977), 241–44.

40. David Ajnhoren, "Gedanken iber der moderner froy," parts 1 and 2, *NF*, February 28, 1930 and March 7, 1930.

41. *NF*, June 6, 1934.

42. Beinish Michalewicz, "Arbeter froyn zayt bagrist," *NF*, March 19, 1926, and "Di arbeter-froy vil oyfhern tsu zayn a mashin oyf tsu kindln," *NF*, August 31, 1928.

43. Henryk Erlich, "Unter der fon fun sotsyalizm," *NF*, April 4, 1930, and "Der froyntog," *NF*, March 27, 1931.

44. *NF*, July 13, 1926; July 30, 1928; March 29, 1929; July 3, 1929; May 25, 1930; August 3, 1931; April 1, 1932; April 5, 1935.

45. "Foters, muters und kinder," *NF*, March 23, 1928; *NF*, December 25, 1928; Dina [Blond], "Ven di babe redt fun unds aroys. . . ," *NF*, May 17, 1936, and "A vort tsu undsere leserins," *NF*, October 17, 1937, and "Urlob far der arbeter-froy," *NF*, June 9, 1939.

46. "Di chaverte Rochl vert a mitglid in 'Bund,'" *NF*, January 3, 1936. The article tells the story of a working woman in Slonim who discovered the YAF's activities by reading a Bund newspaper that her husband had brought home. She visited a YAF club in her town to hear a lecture and quickly began to participate in its programs. The story was typical of many cases in which women visited YAF clubs without any party or ideological background, found a warm and supportive environment there, and became local activists in the YAF and, through it, in the Bund.

47. *NF*, September 12, 1926; February 13, 1938; September 9, 1938.

48. *NF*, December 12, 1937.

49. Dina [Blond], "Tsvishn velkhe froyn," *NF*, May 10, 1935.

50. Emanuel Melzer, *Ma'avak medini be-malkodet: yehudey polin 1935–1939* (Political strife in a blind alley, the Jews in Poland 1935–1939) (Tel Aviv: Diaspora Research Institute, 1982), 280–88; Daniel Blatman, "The Bund in Poland 1935–1939," *POLIN* 9 (1996): 78–81.

51. Hayim S. Kazdan, "Froy un man in undser bavegung," *NF*, February 10, 1939.

52. Dina [Blond], "Vu zenen di froyn?" *NF*, February 17, 1939.

53. *NF*, March 3, 1939; March 10, 1939; April 4, 1939.

54. Ezra Mendelsohn, "Jewish Politics in Interwar Poland: An Overview," in *The Jews of Poland Between Two World Wars*, ed. Gutman, et. al, 16–17.

Chapter 5

This chapter has benefited greatly from the research of Dr. Bina Garncarska-Kadari, who has written a definitive and excellent monograph on the LPZ in interwar Poland. See Bina Garncarska-Kadari, *Bikhipusei derekh: Poalei Tsiyon Smol b'Polin ad milkhemet ha'olam ha'shniya* (In search of their way: Poalei Zion left in Poland up to World War II) (Tel Aviv: Israel Universities Press, 1995).

1. In the party press, at least until the late 1930s, Palestine was used much more often than "*Erets Yisroel*"(Land of Israel).

2. In point of fact the Right also left the Second International, joined the Viennese International, and then returned to the Second International in 1923.

3. Garncarska-Kadari, *Bikhipusei derekh*, 87–88; Nahum Nir-Rafalkes, *Vanderungen* (Tel Aviv: Y. L. Perets Farlag, 1966), 193–201.

4. See, for example, Shabtai Teveth, *Ben Gurion: The Burning Ground* (Boston: Houghton Mifflin, 1987),164–69.

5. A standard version of the "sanitized" Borochov was Yakov Zerubavel's biography, *Ber Borochov: Zayn lebn un shafn* (Warsaw: 1926).

6. The standard work is Matityahu Mintz, *Ber Borochov: Ha-ma'agal ha-rishon* (Tel Aviv: Tel Aviv University, 1978). Also, Jonathan Frankel, *Prophecy and Politics* (Cambridge: Cambridge University Press, 1981), 329–65.

7. As Moshe Erem wrote in the *Arbeter tsaytung* in 1930, "The heavenly Israel (*Erets Yisroel shel maleh*) was replaced by the earthly Israel (*Erets Yisroel shel mateh*) when it was confronted by the stychic processes of Jewish emigration."

8. Yakov Zerubavel, "Tzum dritn yortzayt," *Unʒer lebn* (Warsaw), 1920, p. 4, quoted in Matityahu Mintz, *Naye tʒaytn, Naye lider*, 490.

9. This is one of the major themes of the party press. For examples of the party's Yiddishism, see Yakov Zerubavel, "Poalei Tsiyonizm kontra Palestinatsentrizm," *Arbeter tsaytung* 28 (1934). Also, Nathan Buchsbaum, "Tsum YIVO tsuzamenfor," *Arbeter tsaytung* 35 (1935); Nathan Buchsbaum, "A shtrof vos muz kumen," *Arbeter tsaytung* 46 (1935).

10. For example, see Yitzhak Lev, "Der krizis fun der yidisher emigratsie in Poyln," *Arbeter tsaytung* 39 (1932), and "Di rol fun der emigratsie in yidishn lebn," *Arbeter tsaytung* 19 (1936).

11. A typical exposition of this position is "Tsum 10tn yoyvl fun Histadrut," *Arbeter tsaytung* 1 (1936).

12. The standard treatment of the attitude of the LPZ toward He-Halutz can be found in two articles by Israel Oppenheim: "Yahas Poalei Tsiyon Smol b'Polin l'ra'ayon He-halutz: Ha-reka ha'ra'ayoni," *Gal-ed* 6 (1982): 81-96, and "Yahas Poalei Tsiyon Smol b'Polin l'He-halutz u'lemifal hahalutsi—hahebet ha'ma'asi," *Gal-ed*, No. 7, 1986, 107–34.

13. On persecution by the Polish police, see Yakov Kenner, *Kvershnit* (New York: Tsentral Komitet fun Linke Poele-Tsiyon in di Fareynikte Shtatn un Kanada, 1947), 171–72.

14. One example is "Der Moskver protses," *Arbeter tsaytung* 6 (1937).

15. Pockets of LPZ strength in the Jewish labor movement in Warsaw included the wood-workers, chemical workers, waiters, store clerks, and coal porters. In Łodż, the LPZ controlled or had important influence in the unions for needle workers, chemical workers, waiters, and several other smaller unions. See Kenner, *Kvershnit*, 157. According to Kenner, the LPZ dominated the labor unions in Brest Litovsk, Chelm, and Nowy Sadz. Kenner states that on the eve of the war, there were about 20,000 workers either in LPZ-dominated unions or in LPZ factions within unions led by parties such as the Bund. In the *Landrat fun di yidishe profesionele fareynen*, the major organization of Jewish unions, the Bund played the dominant role.

16. The Stern was one of the most important and popular of the LPZ-affiliated organizations. According to Kenner it had 146 local branches with over 16,000 members. On the Yugnt, see Kenner, *Kvershnit*, 200–217; Garncarska-Kadari, *Bikhipusei derekh*, 250–58. The best primary source is the journal *Fraye yugnt*, issues from 1924 through 1932.

17. "Poyle Tsiyen in der shul un kultur arbet," *Arbeter tsaytung* 7 (1939).

18. The LPZ reached its peak strength in the late 1920s. In the municipal elections of 1927 and 1928, according to the calculations of Yakov Kenner, the party received about 50,000 votes and elected 140 delegates to various city councils. In Warsaw and in Łodż, the Bund far outpolled the LPZ in city council elections, although the LPZ boasted genuinely popular city council members such as Aryeh Holenderski in Łodż and Yitzhak Lev in Warsaw. By the middle and late 1930s, the gap between the LPZ and the Bund widened enormously. As Garncarska-Kadari points out, there were many cities, such as Vilna, Bialystok, Czestochowa, and Krakow, where the party was practically invisible. On the other hand, the LPZ was a dominant party in Brest (Brzesc), Chelm, Bendin, and Kalisz. In Brest the LPZ got more votes than either the Bund or the PPS. See *Bikhipusei derekh*, 232.

19. There is an enormous amount of material on the LPZ's cultural activities in the party press. For an illuminating series of discussion articles prepared for the party's culture congress in 1931 see Yakov Zerubavel, "Tsiln un oyfgabn fun unzer kultur arbet," *Arbeter kultur* (1931); Raphael Mahler, "Oyfgabn fun zelbstbildung krayzn un zeyer organizatsie," *Arbeter kultur* (1931). See also E. R. (Emanuel Ringelblum), "YIVO un di yidishe arbetershaft," *Arbeter tsaytung* 32 (1931); "Di oyfgabn fun bibliotek tzentern," *Arbeter tsaytung* 36 (1931); and "Poyle Tsiyen in der shul un kultur arbet," *Arbeter tsaytung* 7 (1939). See also the memoir of Adolph Berman, *Vos der goyrl hot mir bashert* (Haifa, 1980), 28–43.

20. Ringelblum's Oneg Shabes was the group that documented what was happening in the ghetto. Most of its documentations was found in the ruins of Warsaw after the war and was published in several languages as the "Ringelblum Diaries."

21. A key source on the discussions between the LPZ and the Comintern, to be used with some caution, is Nir-Rafalkes, *Vanderungen*, 212–64.

22. For example, see the obituary for Yosef Lestschinsky (Chmurner) in *Arbeter tsaytung* 31 (1935).

23. Garncarska-Kadari, *Bikhipusei derekh*, 401.

24. *Arbeter tsaytung* 14 (1930).

25. A good example of this approach is Yitzhak Lev, *Arbeter tsaytung* 42 (1930).

26. See, for example, this quote from "In gedenktog fun Ber Borochov," *Arbeter tsaytung* 50 (1935). "The simplicity (*pashtes*) of Bundism has been much easier for the Jewish working masses to understand than the complicated ideology of Marxist Poalei Tsiyonizm. But just because something is simple does not mean that it is true and what is true is not necessarily simple."

27. The best exposition of these views is in Viktor Alter, *Tsu der yidnfrage in Poyln* (Warsaw: 1937).

28. There is a good discussion of this in J. S. Hertz, in *Di geshikhte fun Bund*, ed. J. S. Hertz, vol. 5 (New York: Unzer Tsayt, 1981), 101–7.

29. Nathan Buchsbaum "A PPSesher broshur gegn Bund un Bundizm," *Arbeter tsaytung* 14 (1938).

30. Uriel (Raphael Mahler), "Di kultur badaytung far di yidishe masn in dem kamf farn territorialn arbeter tsenter," *Arbeter tsaytung* 50 (1935).

31. Alter, *Tsu der yidnfrage in Poyln*; Jacob Lestschinsky, *Der bankrot fun tsienizm* (Warsaw: 1927).

32. Viktor Alter, *Antysemityzm gospodarczy w swietle cyfr* (Warsaw: Mysli socjalisticznej, 1937), 26–34.

33. Yitzhak Lev, "Tsionizm un antisemitizm," *Arbeter tsaytung* 13 (1937), and "Bundishe statistik," *Arbeter tsaytung* 33 (1937).

34. For examples see Yitzhak Lev, "Ratnfarbandishe virklekhkayt un yevsekishe umbaholfnkayt," *Arbeter tsaytung* 34 (1930), and "Gezerd: Der even negef fun der yevsektsie," *Arbeter tsaytung* 1 (1931).

35. Adolph Berman, "Nokh eyn shrit faroys," *Arbeter tsaytung* 51 (1935).

36. Buchsbaum, "A PPSesher broshur."

37. Jacob Zerubavel, "Tzu di problemen fun Poyle Tzionizm," *Arbeter tsaytung* 27, 28 (1934).

38. Ze'ev Abramovich, "Der Palestinizm in unzer program," *Tsu di problemen fun Poyle Tsienizm* (Warsaw: 1934), 3–25; quoted in Garncarska-Kadari, *Bikhipusei derekh*, 366–68.

39. Nahum Nir-Rafalkes, "Eretz yisroeldige un khutzle'aretzdike likvidatsie in unzer bavegung," in *Tsu di shtraytfragn inm Poyle Tsiyenizm* (Jerusalem: 1934).

40. Betsalel Sherman, "Poyle-Tsienizm kontra linkistishe umetumigkayt," in *Tsu di shtraytfragn*. Sherman's attack on Zerubavel prompted Nathan Buchsbaum to rush to his defense. See Buchsbaum's sharp rejoinder to Sherman in "Forzikhtiger kh' Sherman," *Arbeter tsaytung* 43 (1934). Commenting on Sherman's warnings that Soviet Jewry was rapidly assimilating, Buchsbaum ironically retorted, "Comrade Sherman has set before us a new task—to rescue the Jewish spirit!" (*tsu rateven dos pintele yid fun untergang!*).

41. See Yitzhak Lev's major article, "Problemen fun der yidisher virklekhkayt in der ibergangstkufe," *Arbeter tsaytung* 48 (1934). This was the last article that Lev was to publish in *Arbeter tsaytung* for a year and a half.

42. Garncarska-Kadari, *Bikhipusei derekh*, 384–85.

43. There is a good discussion of the split in Garncarska-Kadari, *Bikhipusei derekh*, 385–94. The immediate cause of the split was Lev's dissatisfaction with the proceedings of the ninth world conference of the movement, which took place in Palestine in September 1934. It is im-

portant to note that after Lev started his own group, Nir-Rafalkes and Sherman attacked him, notwithstanding many apparent similarities in their political views. For Nir-Rafalkes and Sherman, Lev's sin was to violate the sacrosanct norms of party discipline.

44. Ze'ev Abramovich, "Poyletsiyenizm in der ibergangstkufe," *Arbeter vort* 2 (1930).

45. Garncarska-Kadari, *Bikhipusei derekh*, 396–400.

46. This was not an easy decision to accept. There was a great deal of opposition within the party before it was accepted at the seventh conference of the LPZ in Poland in 1938. See "Di tzente velt kongres fun di Poyle Tsiyen," editorial, *Arbeter tsaytung* 3 (1938); "Der 7er partei tzuzamenfor fun Poyle Tsiyen in Poyln," *Arbeter tsaytung* 20, 21 (1938); Garncarska-Kadari, *Bikhipusei derekh*, 412–16.

47. One example of the party's new attitude toward the trials is Nathan Buchsbaum's "Nokhn Moskver protses," *Arbeter tsaytung* 6 (1938). On the leaders of Birobidzhan, see Yitzhak Lev, "A troyeriker sakhakl," *Arbeter tsaytung* 23 (1938).

48. Garncarska-Kadari, *Bikhipusei derekh*, 413–14.

49. "Mobilizirt di koykhes," editorial, *Arbeter tsaytung* 24 (1938).

50. Garncarska-Kadari, *Bikhipusei derekh*, 418.

51. "Der farrat un durkhfal fun Bund," editorial, *Arbeter tsaytung* 18 (1939).

52. Jacob Zerubavel, "In tseykhn fun akhrayesdige oyfgabn," *Arbeter tsaytung* 20 (1939).

Chapter 6

1. Agudat Yisrael (in Yiddish, Agudas Yisroel, also referred to simply as "the Aguda" or "Aguda") is the world organization of orthodox Jewry, founded at the 1912 Kattowitz (Katowice) conference. The Polish branch of the movement was established in 1916 under the name Agudat Ha'Ortodoksim (The Orthodox League). The name of the movement, which means the League (or Union) of Israel, is derived from a phrase in 2 Samuel 2:25. It appears amidst the liturgy for the High Holidays in prayers for the day when all mankind will form "one league" (*aguda ahat*) to do God's will.

2. On the local stage, see Yosef Salmon, "Ha'hevra ha'haredit be'Russia-Polin ve'ha'tziyy-onut ba'shanim 1898–1900," in *Dat ve'Tziyyonut* (Jerusalem: Ha-Sifriyah ha-Tsiyonit 'al-yad ha-Histadrut ha-Tsiyonit ha-'Olamit, 1990), 50–51.

3. Alexander Zyshe Frydman, *Ketavim Nivharim* (Jerusalem: Moreshet sofrim, 1960), 79.

4. Yitzhak Shvartzbart, *Tsvishn beide velt-milkhomes* (Buenos Aires: Tsentral Farband fun Poylishe Yidn in Argentine, 1958), 165.

5. On this phenomenon, see Gershon Bacon, "Rabbis and Politics, Rabbis in Politics: Different Models within Interwar Polish Jewry," *YIVO Annual* 20 (1991): 53–54.

6. This slogan was coined by Rabbi Moshe Sofer (1762–1839) based on a Talmudic dictum forbidding the use of newly harvested grain (*hadash* in Hebrew) until after the second day of Passover that year. Sofer played on the word *hadash*, which means "new," and used the phrase in a wider and much different context, taking it to mean that any innovation, even though from the point of Jewish law it may be found permissible, is strictly forbidden simply because it is an innovation.

7. Frydman, *Ketavim Nivharim*, 37–38.

8. Ahad Haam, "Imitation and Assimilation," in *Kol Kitvei Ahad Haam* (Tel Aviv: n.p., 1947), 86–89. The essay first appeared in 1893.

9. *Der moment*, February 14, 1922, p. 3.

10. This discussion does not question whether this rabbinical supervision did in fact exist; but focuses on the ideological level alone. For further discussion of the organizational structure of Agudat Yisrael in Poland and the place of rabbinical leadership in the movement, see Gershon Bacon, *The Politics of Tradition: Agudat Yisrael in Poland, 1916–1939* (Jerusalem: Magnes Press, 1996), 54–56, 82–83, 85–91.

11. Moshe Prager, "When Hasidim of Ger Became Newsmen," in *The Golden Tradition: Jewish Life and Thought in Eastern Europe*, ed. Lucy Dawidowicz (Northvale, N.J.: J. Aronson,1989), 210–13.

12. Abraham Mordecai Alter, *Osef Mikhtavim* (Jerusalem: Pinhas Yaakov ha-Kohen Levin ve-Yehudah Leib haKohen Levin, 1967), letters 72, 75–78, 95, 97–99.

13. Bacon, *The Politics of Tradition*, 44–45.

14. Elhanan Wasserman, "Ikveta de'Meshiha," in *Yalkut Maamarim u'Mikhtavim* (Brooklyn: 1987), 36.

15. Haam, "Imitation and Assimilation," 89.

16. Menahem Friedman, *Ha'Hevra Ha'Haredit: Mekorot, Megamot, ve'Tahalikhim* (Jerusalem: Mekhon Yerushalayim leheker Yisrael, 1991), 29.

17. Theodor Herzl, *Iggerot- Mi'reshit ha'peula ha'Tziyyonit ad ha'Kongress ha'Rishon (May 1895–August 1897)* (Jerusalem: 1961), 184; David Vital, *Ha'Mahapekha Ha'Tziyyonit; Kerekh Aleph: Reshit Ha'Tenua* (Tel Aviv: 1978), 263.

18. See for example, Max Weinreich, *Der veg tzu undzer yugnt—yesodes, metoden, problemen fun Yidisher yugnt-forshung* (Vilna: n.p., 1935).

19. On the symbolism of uniforms in the youth movements, see Moshe Kligsberg, "Di Yiddishe Yugnt-Bavegung in Poiln tsvishn beide Velt-Milkhomes," in *Shtudies vegn Yidn in Poiln 1919–1939*, ed. Joshua Fishman (New York: YIVO Institute, 1974), 178–79.

20. *Ortodoksishe yugnt bleter* 7, no. 63 (March 1935): 2.

21. Mendel Piekarz, *Hasidut Polin bein shtei ha'Milhamot u'be'gezeirot 5700–5705 (ha'Shoa)* (Jerusalem: Mosad Bialik, 1990), 255.

22. Yitzhak Alfasi, *Ha'Hasidut ve'Shivat Tziyyon* (Tel Aviv: Sifriyat Maariv, 1986), 145.

23. This claim was raised already at the beginning of the twentieth century. See, for example, Shlomo Zalman Landau and Yosef Rabinovitch, eds., *Or La'Yesharim* (Warsaw: 1900), 32.

24. Elhanan Wasserman, *Yalkut Maamarim u'Mikhtavim*, 122. First published in *Dos yidishe togblat*, July 27, 1934, p. 5.

25. On this complex reality, see Gershon Bacon, "Reluctant Partners, Ideological Opponents: Reflections on the Relations Between Agudat Yisrael and the Zionist and Religious Zionist Movements in Interwar Poland," *Gal-Ed* 14 (1995): 67–90.

26. See, for example, *Haynt*, March 4, 1928, p. 3; Yitzhak Grunbaum, *Milhamot Yehudei Polania* (Jerusalem-Tel Aviv: Haverim, 1941), 289.

27. Moshe Landau, *Mi'ut Leumi Lohem: Ma'avak Yehudei Polin ba'shanim 1918–1929* (Jerusalem: Merkaz Zalman Shazar, 1986), 22.

28. Bernard K. Johnpoll, *The Politics of Futility: The General Jewish Workers Bund of Poland 1917–1943* (Ithaca, N.Y.: Cornell University Press, 1967), 180–81; Robert Shapiro, *The Polish Kehile Elections of 1936: A Revolution Re-examined*, Working Papers in Holocaust Studies (New York: Holocaust Studies Program, Yeshiva University, 1988).

29. This process has been traced in detail by, among others, Jonathan Frankel, Ezra Mendelsohn, Yoav Peled, Henry Tobias, Bernard Johnpoll, and Daniel Blatman in their studies on the Bund in Russia and Poland.

Chapter 7

From 1996 to 1998 I was engaged in preparing for publication a selection of autobiographies written by Jewish youth in Poland in the 1930s. This is my first attempt to organize the ideas that resulted from months of intimate contact with a portion of these documents; what I present are observations and hypotheses, by no means conclusions. Fortunately, I am not the first to arrive on the scene. I have an important predecessor, Moishe Kligsberg, a YIVO staff member. His article on Jewish youth politics, largely based on the autobiographies, was reprinted some twenty years ago: "Di yidishe yugnt-bavegung in Poyln tsvishn beyde velt-milkhomes: a sotsyologishe shtudye" (The youth movement in Poland between the two world wars: A sociological study), in *Shtudyes vegn yidn in Poyln, 1919–1939*, ed. Joshua Fishman (New York: YIVO, 1974), 137–228. See also Kligsberg's pamphlet, *Child and Adolescent Behavior Under Stress: An Analytical Topical Guide to a Collection of Autobiographies of Jewish Young Men and Women in Poland (1932–1939)* in the possession of the YIVO Institute for Jewish Research (New York: YIVO, 1965), as well as his prewar study of Jewish youth in Poland, *Yugnt-psikhologye un sotsyalistishe dertsiung* (Warsaw: Kultur-Lige, 1938). Celia Heller in her book *On the Edge of Destruction: Jews of Poland Between the Two World Wars* (New York: Columbia University Press, 1977) also makes considerable use of the autobiographies.

1. The YIVO Institute for Jewish Research was founded in 1925 in Vilna (Wilno, today Vilnius), which was then in Poland. Its goal was to serve as the academy of the Jewish nation in Eastern Europe; all aspects of the history and culture of East European Jews were to be studied using the Yiddish language. YIVO is an acronym for *Yidisher Visnshaftlekher Institut* (Jewish Scientific Institute). In 1940, the YIVO Institute was reestablished in New York. Dr. Alina Cala of the Jewish Historical Institute in Warsaw is editing a selection of the Polish-language autobiographies collected by YIVO.

2. Max Weinreich (1894–1969) published a theoretical study based on the autobiographies: *Der veg tsu undzer yugnt: yesoydes, metodn, problemen fun yidisher yugnt-forshung* (Vilna: YIVO, 1935); see also his *Studjum o mlodzieży żydowskiej Program i metoda* (Poznan, 1935), 8, first published in *Przeglad socjologiczny* 3 (1935). Weinreich's magnum opus is *Geshikhte fun der yidisher shprakh*, 4 vols. (New York: YIVO, 1973). [English translation: *History of the Yiddish Language*, 2 vols. (Chicago: University of Chicago Press, 1980).]

3. YIVO's populist and Yiddishist orientation distanced it on the whole from the concerns of the Jewish bourgeoisie.

4. Autobiographies of Jewish Youth in Poland, YIVO Archives Collection RG 4, no. 3887.

5. Sh. An-sky, *Khurbn Galitsye: Der yidisher khurbn fun Poyln, Galitsye un Bukovine, fun togbukh 1914–1917*, in "Shloyme-Zanvl Rapoport," *Geʒamlte shriftn*, vols. 4–6 (Vilna: Ferlag Anski, 1924–25). For excerpts in English see Sh. An-sky, *The Dybbuk and Other Writings*, ed. David G. Roskies (New York: Schocken, 1992), 171–208.

6. The Alexander Rebbe was one of scores of hereditary leaders/healers of the Hasidic movement known as *tsadikkim* or *rebbes*, named after the town in which their dynasty was first established, in this case Aleksandrów Łodzki in central Poland.

7. Autobiographies, YIVO Archives Collection RG 4, no. 3559.

8. *Studjum o mlodzieʒy ʒydowskiej*, 8.

9. The best introduction to Jewish politics in interwar Poland is Ezra Mendelsohn, *The Jews of East Central Europe Between the World Wars* (Bloomington, Ind.: Indiana University Press, 1983), 11–83. On the Zionist youth groups, see his *Zionism in Poland: The Formative Years, 1915–1926* (New Haven: Yale University Press, 1981). See also Israel Oppenheim, *The Struggle of Jewish Youth for Productivizatian: The Zionist Youth Movement in Poland* (Boulder, Colo.: Columbia University Press, 1989).

10. Moishe Kligsberg, "Di yugnt-bavegung." Hundreds of memorial books (*yiʒker bikher*) devoted to specific Jewish communities in Eastern Europe and written by their survivors have been published over the past fifty years; see Jack Kugelmass and Jonathan Boyarin, eds., *From A Ruined Garden: The Memorial Books of Polish Jewry* (New York: Schocken, 1983).

11. *YIVO* Archives Collection RG 4, nos. 3585, 3590, 3650, cited in Kligsberg, "Yidishe yugnt-bavegung," 162.

12. There were numerous Yiddish versions of this ten-volume work. It was first translated by L. M. Benyamin under the direction of K. Farnberg (New York: Literarisher Farlag, 1918–21), then retranslated by Aharon Mark and published in several editions (Warsaw: Kooperativ Bikher, 1927; reprinted 1929, Vilna: B. Kletzkin.). There was also a Soviet edition with no translator given (Moscow: Farlag Emes, 1936). Volumes 3 and 4 of the novel were translated into Polish as early as 1911 by Jadwiga Sienkiewiczowna (Henryk Sienkiewicz collaborated on one of the volumes). The first complete Polish edition was translated by Leopold Staff (Wydawnictwo Polskie, 1925–26). I am indebted to Jerzy Halbersztadt for information about the Polish editions.

13. *YIVO* Archives Collection RG 4, nos. 3539, 3559; Kligsberg, "Yidishe yugnt-bavegung," 154; *YIVO* Archives Collection RG 4, no. 3593, cited in Kligsberg, "Yidishe yugnt-bavegung," 157.

14. Kligsberg, "Yidishe yugnt-bavegung," 167–69.

15. Ibid.

16. The Zionist Revisionists, followers of Vladimir Zhabotinsky, sought to establish by force of arms a Jewish state on both sides of the Jordan River.

17. The *maskilim* were Jewish reformers of the nineteenth century who first sang the praises of secular European culture.

18. The Borochov School was named after Ber Borochov (1881–1918), founder of the Marxist Zionist party Poalei Tsiyon (Workers of Zion).

19. *YIVO* Archives Collection RG 4, no. 3701.

20. Paul Glikson, *Preliminary Inventory of the Jewish Daily and Periodical Press Published in the Polish Language, 1823–1982* (Jerusalem: Institute of Jewish Studies/Center for Research on Polish Jewry, 1983).

21. *YIVO* Archives Collection RG 4, no. 3539.

22. Ibid., no. 3598.

23. Ibid., no. 3610.

24. Ibid., no. 3701.

25. Ibid., no. 3559.

26. Ibid.

27. Kligsberg, "Yidishe yugnt-bavegung," 228.

28. See, for example, Yisrael Gutman, *The Jews of Warsaw, 1939–1943: Ghetto, Underground, Revolt* (Bloomington, Ind.: Indiana University Press, 1982).

29. Kligsberg, "Yidishe yugnt-bavegung," 138.

30. Kligsberg has another agenda as well, to show that unlike in the United States of the 1960s and 1970s, oppressed minorities need not turn their frustrations into aggressive behavior.

31. *YIVO* Archives Collection RG 4, no. 3701.

32. The best English introduction to Peretz (1852–1915) is Ruth R. Wisse, *I. L. Peretz and the Making of Modern Jewish Culture* (Seattle: University of Washington Press, 1991).

33. I. L. Peretz, *Ale verk* (New York: CYCO, 1947), 4:98–102. [English translation in *The I. L. Peretz Reader*, ed. Ruth R. Wisse (New York: Schocken, 1990), 178–81.]

34. *The Earth Is the Lord's: The Inner World of the Jew in Eastern Europe* (New York: Farrar, Strauss, Giroux, 1978), 34. Heschel (1907–72), the pre-eminent teacher and theologian of Ashkenazic Judaism, grew up in prewar Poland and came to the United States in 1940.

Chapter 8

1. Vladimir Medem, quoted in Samuel Portnoy, trans. and ed., *The Life and Soul of a Legendary Jewish Socialist: The Memoirs of Vladimir Medem* (New York: Ktav, 1979), 475–76. [In Yiddish: Kh. Sh. Kazhdan, *Fun kheyder un shkoles biz tsisho* (Mexico City, 1956), 269.]

2. For Bundist perspectives, see Max Weinreich's 1917 article "Der Bund un di yidishe shprakh," reprinted in *Finf-un-tsvantsik yor* (Warsaw: 1922), 55–57, A. Litvak, "Afn feld fun kultur," in *Vos geven* (Vilna, 1925), 148–65; J. S. Hertz, "Di umlegale prese un literatur fun Bund" in *Pinkes far der forshung fun der yidisher literatur un prese*, ed. Chaim Bez [Bass] (New York: Congress for Jewish Culture, 1972), 2:294–366. This perspective resonates in Emanuel S. Goldsmith, *Modern Yiddish Culture* (New York: Shapolsky, 1987), 83–84, and Benjamin Harshav, *Language in a Time of Revolution* (Berkeley: University of California Press, 1993).

3. Anonymous, "A reester iber ale zhargonishe vos zenen opgedrukt gevorn inem yor 5648," in *Di yudishe folksbibliotek* (Kiev, 1888), 469–73; Moshe Shalit, "A reshime fun ale yidishe verk vos zenen gedrukt in rusland in yor 1912" and "Statistik fun yidishn bikher-mark in yor 1912," in *Der Pinkes*, ed. Sh. Niger (Vilna: B. Kletskin, 1913), 277–306. Shalit's figures were based on official bibliographic records.

4. A[vrohom] Kirzhnits, *Di yidishe prese in der gevezener ruslendisher imperye* (Moscow, 1930), 10, 44–48.

5. *Yudishes folksblat* figures are according to its editor, Alexander Zederbaum, from S. L. Tsitron, *Geshikhte fun der yidisher prese*, (Vilna, 1923), 132; 1905 figure for *Fraynd* is according to one of its editors, from H. D. Hurwitz, "Undzer ershte teglikhe tsaytung" in *Der Pinkes*, ed. Sh. Niger (Vilna: B. Kletskin, 1913), 246; *Haynt* and *Moment* circulation for 1912, estimated by a student of the Yiddish press, from Zalmen Reijzin, *Leksikon fun der yidisher literatur un prese* (Warsaw: 1914), 679, 711.

6. On publishing, see Khone Shmeruk, "Shtrikhn tsu der geshikhte fun dem yidishn literarishn tsenter in varshe," in *Prokim fun der yidisher literatur-geshikhte* (Tel Aviv: I. L. Peretz 1988), 294–96.

7. On these periodicals, see Elias Schulman, "A halber yorhundert nokh di *literarishe monatshriftn*," in *Portretn un etyudn* (New York: 1980), 406–420, and "Di tsaytshrift *Di yudishe velt*," in *Pinkes far der forshung fun der yidisher literature un presse* (New York: Alveltlekhen Yidishn Kultur-Kongres, 1965), 1:122–70.

8. On Czernowitz, see Emanuel Goldsmith, *Modern Yiddish Culture;* Joshua A. Fishman, *Yiddish: Turning to Life* (Amsterdam and Philadelphia: John Benjamins, 1991), 233–90.

9. Cf. Michael Stanislawski, "Russian Jewry, the Russian State, and the Dynamics of Jewish Emancipation," in *Paths of Emancipation: Jews, the State, and Citizenship*, ed. Ira Katznelson and Pierre Birnbaum (Princeton, N.J.: Princeton University Press, 1995), 275.

10. This entails comparing the growth of Yiddish literature, journalism, and cultural activity inside Bundist circles and non-radical Jewish society, and assessing the influence of the former on the latter. While an exhaustive analysis is beyond the scope of this chapter, I believe the evidence would support the statements that follow.

11. For a discussion of these events, see Goldsmith, *Modern Yiddish Culture* and Fishman, *Yiddish*; also Dan Miron, *A Traveler Disguised* (New York: Schocken Books, 1973), 30–33, and Joshua Fishman, "The Politics of Yiddish in Tsarist Russia," in *From Ancient Israel to Modern Judaism: Essays in Honor of Marvin Fox*, ed. Jacob Neusner, Ernest Frerichs, and Nahum M. Sarna (Atlanta: Scholars Press, 1989), 4:155–71.

12. Henry Tobias, *The Jewish Bund in Russia from Its Origins to 1905* (Stanford: Stanford University Press, 1972), chapters 3 and 4, esp. 31–34; Ezra Mendelsohn, *Class Struggle in the Pale* (Cambridge: Cambridge University Press, 1970), 45–62.

13. Gozhansky's brochure, which circulated in manuscript, was published in Yiddish translation as "A briv tsu di agitatorn" in *YIVO, Historishe Shriftn* 3 (Vilna-Paris, 1939), 626–48. "Zhargon" was the most common appellation in Russian for "Yiddish" until 1905.

14. Elias Tcherikower, "Di onheybn fun der umlegaler literatur in yidish" *YIVO, Historishe shriftn* 3: 579–94; Hertz, "Di umlegale prese," 331–41.

15. On Kremer's knowledge of Yiddish, see A. Litvak, "Di zhargonishe komitetn," in *Vos geven* (Vilna: B. Kletskin, 1925), 98; on Medem, see Portnoy, ed., *Legendary Jewish Socialist*, 177–78, 412; on the others, see Tsivyon (Ber Hoffman), *Far fuftsik yor* (New York: A. Lobe, 1948), 144.

16. On Kaplinsky, whose role as editor of the Bund's first underground newspaper has

been suppressed in official Bundist historiography, see A. N., "Vozniknovenie 'arbeiter-stimme,'" *Perezhitoe* 1 (1908): 264–78. The cultural gap between the Russified upper echelon and the Yiddish-speaking second tier of the Bund led to tensions between them. The Yiddish poet Avrohom Liessin, himself a 'half-intellectual' active in the movement before he emigrated to America, complained to Arkady Kremer in 1906 that talented individuals such as Litvak and B. Charney-Vladek were not being advanced to the top ranks of the Bund "because they were orators only in Yiddish, who had come over from the world of the yeshiva, and had never worn the brass buttons of a Russian gymnasium student." Avrohom Liessin, *Zikhroynes un bilder* (New York: Tsiko Bikher Farlag, 1954), 296.

17. I would venture that a comparative stylistic analysis of the Bundist *Arbeter-shtime* (Vilna, 1897–1905), and the Zionist weekly *Der yud* (Odessa / Krakow, 1899–1903) would detect no noticeable difference between their languages. Cf. the Bundist perspectives in Weinreich, "Der Bund un di yidishe," Litvak, "Afn feld fun kultur," and Hertz, "Di umlegale prese" with the more balanced assessment by Max Weinreich in his *Geshikhte fun der yidisher shprakh* (New York: YIVO, 1973), 1:295–97 [English translation: *History of the Yiddish Language* (Chicago: University of Chicago Press, 1980), 291–92.] Weinrich, Litvak, and Hertz cited the claim that "the modernization of the Yiddish language first occurred in Bundist literature."

18. J. S. Hertz, ed. *Di geshikhte fun Bund*, vol. 2 (New York: Unzer Tsayt, 1962), 363, 576.

19. Hertz, "Di umlegale prese," 294–366.

20. See Mendelsohn, *Class Struggle in The Pale*, 116–25. On the *zhargonishe komitetn*, see Litvak, *Vos geven*, 69–115, but note the cautionary remarks by Tcherikower, "Di onheybn fun der umlegaler," 596–97.

21. See A. Litvak's unique essay, "Dos yidishe arbeter lid" in *Vos geven*, 226–43.

22. Litvak, *Vos geven*, 98

23. See A. Litvak, "Di zhargonishe komitetn," 80–85; Chone Shmeruk, "Yiddish Literature in the USSR," in *The Jews in Soviet Russia Since 1917*, ed. Lionel Kochan (Oxford: Oxford University Press, 1978), 245, and in his book, *Peretz's yiesh vizye* (New York: YIVO, 1971), 200–205.

24. See the editorial introduction to *Literarishe monatshriftn* 1 (1908); Schulman, "A halber yorhundert," and "Di tsaytshrift."

25. M. L-R, *Di naye tsayt* 3 (1908): 92–96; Litvak, *Vos Geven*, 256–58; Brokhes [Charney-Vladek], "Vegn undzer kultur-problem," *Di naye tsayt* 4 (1909).

26. See *Materialy k istorii evreiskogo rabochego dvizhenni* (St. Petersburg: Tribuna, 1906), 74–75, 112.

27. Sholem Levin, "Di diskusye vegn der natsionaler frage afn 5tn tsuzamenfor fun Bund, Yuni 1903, Zurich," *Unser tsayt* 2 (1927): 90, 95.

28. Vladimir Medem, *Sotsialdemokratiia i natsionalnii vopros* (St. Petersburg, 1906), 50–57. [In Yiddish: *Vladimir Medem tsum tsvantsikstn yortsayt* (New York: Amerikaner reprezentants fun Algemeynem Yidishn Arbeter-bund in Polyn, 1943), 212–19.]

29. Moshe Rafes, *Ocherki po istorii Bunda* (Moscow: Moskovskii rabochii, 1923), 394–95. For an elaborate program of implementation, see Esther Frumkin, "Glaykhbarekhtikung fun shprakhn," *Tsayt-fragen*, 3–5 (1910).

30. David Fishman, "The Politics of Yiddish in Tsarist Russia," 4:155–71, and "Language and Revolution: The 1905 Upheaval in the 'hevrat mefitse haskalah'," in *Dimensions of Yiddish Culture* (Syracuse University Press, forthcoming).

31. On the Bundist press, see Hertz, "Di umlegale prese." The circulation figure for the *folkstsaytung* is based on Litvak, *Vos geven*, 274.

32. G. Pludermakher, "Di ovntshul afn nomen fun Y. L. Peretz," in *Shul-pinkes* (Vilna, 1924), 223–38, and Kazhdan, *Fun kheyder un shkoles*, 173–76. *Dos yiddishe vort* published its fifth edition in 1919; its compiler, Olgin, went on to become the editor-in-chief of the Communist daily *Morgn frayhayt* in New York and a leader in the American Communist Party.

33. Hertz, *Di geshikhte fun Bund*, 2:433–36.

34. Pludermakher, "Folks-shul afn nomen devoire kupershteyn," in *Shul-pinkes*, 167–76; Kazhdan, *Fun kheyder un shkoleso*, 191–93. A third Yiddish elementary school, in Kiev, was run by socialist-territorialists and Sejmists; Kazhdan, ibid., 187–91.

35. See the articles by Levinson and Esther Frumkin on "national education" in *Tsaytfragen* 1, 2, 5 (1909–10). The early history of Yiddish education is surveyed in Kazhdan, *Fun kheyder un shkoles*.

36. On the Jewish Literary Society, see "Evreiskoe literaturnoe obshchestvo" in *Evreiskaia entsiklopediia* (St. Petersburg: Brokhaus-Efron, 1913), 7:450; and the report on the Society's activities in *Lebn un visnshaft* 1–4 (1911): 122–42.

37. *Di ershte yidishe shprakh konferents* (Vilna: YIVO, 1931), 89–91, 118–20.

38. The growth of Yiddish literary societies can be followed on the pages of *Lebn un visnshaft*, no. 2 (June 1909), 180–85; no. 3 (July 1909), 155–59; no. 4 (August, 1909), 148–51; no. 5 (September 1909), 147–52. On the change in the Bund's position, see the editorial. "Di shtime fun Bund," cited in Hertz, *Di geshikhte fun Bund*, 2:554–55, and Rafes, *Ocherki po istorii bunda*, 392.

39. See Hertz, *Di geshikhte fun bund*, 2:554–58; Dovid Mayer, "Yidishe literarishe gezelshaft in varshe," *Unser tsayt* 11–12 (1957): 104–5; on the liquidation of the Society, see *Der fraynd* 21 (January 21 / February 6, 1912) and 70 (March 25 / April 4, 1912).

40. *Materialy k istorii evreiskogo rabochego dvizhenii* (St. Petersburg, 1906), 127.

41. See Ruth Wisse, "Not the 'Pintele Yid' But the Full-Fledged Jew," *Prooftexts* 15, no. 1 (1995): 63–88.

42. On Zhitlovsky, see Goldsmith, *Modern Yiddish Culture*.

43. See the biographies of these individuals in Zalman Reijzin's *Leksikon fun der yidisher literatur, presse, un filologye*, 4 vols. (Vilna: B. Kletskin, 1926–29). On the Grunbaum affair, see Arye Tsentsiper, "Ve'idot artsiyot shel tsiyonei rusiya," *Katsir* 2: 254–55.

44. On Helsingsfors, see David Vital, *Zionism: The Formative Years* (Oxford: Clarendon Press, 1988).

45. *Di ershte yidishe shprakh-konferents* (Vilna, 1931), 106.

46. Ibid., 84, 90.

47. David Fishman, "Language and Revolution: mefitse haskalah in 1905," in *From Ancient Israel to Modern Judaism: Essays in Honor of Marvin Fox*, eds. Jacob Neusner, Ernest Frerichs, and Nahum M. Sarna (Atlanta: Scholars Press, 1989), 48. See Kazhdan, *Fun kheyder*

un shkoles, 383–86; A[vrohom] Kirzhnitz, ed., *Der yidisher arbeter* (Moscow: Yidisher arbeter, 1927), 3:54–57.

Chapter 9

1. Isaac Leib Peretz, *Vegn mile-skandal* (About the circumcision scandal) (Warsaw: Edelshteyn printers, 1909), 3. Reprinted in I. L. Peretz, *Ale verk*, vol. 3 (New York: CYCO, 1947). Subsequent references are to this reprint edition.

2. Jerzy Stempowski, "Essay for Cassandra," trans. Jaroslaw Anders, in Jan Kott, ed., *Four Decades of Polish Essays* (Evanston, Ill.: Northwestern University Press, 1990), 28.

3. I have returned to this subject repeatedly, like a dog worrying a bone. See, among other things, Ruth Wisse, "The Jews Talking: a View of Modern Yiddish Literature," *Prooftexts* 4 (1984): 35–48; idem., "A Monument to Messianism," *Commentary* (March 1991): 37–42; and idem., conclusion to *I. L. Peretz and the Making of Modern Jewish Culture* (Seattle: University of Washington Press, 1991).

4. For the most recent interpretation of Sholem Aleichem's tragicomedy as a humor of consolation, see Peter L. Berger, *Redeeming Laughter* (New York: Walter de Gruyter, 1997), 115–33.

5. The stories are "Der gliklekhster in kodny," (The happiest man in all kodny), "Konkurentn," (Competitors), "Stantsye baranovitsh" (Station Baranovitch), and "Tsvey antisemitn" (Two anti-Semites). For translations of the first three see Sholem Aleichem, *Tevye the Dairyman and the Railroad Stories*, trans. Hillel Halkin (New York: Schocken, 1987), 136–43; 143–52; 152–63. The fourth is translated by Miriam Waddington in *The Best of Sholem Aleichem*, ed. Irving Howe and Ruth R. Wisse (New York: New Republic, 1979), 115–21.

6. I. L. Peretz, "Bildung," in *Di yidishe bibliotek* (Warsaw: 1891). This translation: Sol Liptzin, "Education," in *Peretz* (New York: YIVO, 1947), 328. Subsequent translations from this article are mine.

7. I. L. Peretz, *Mayne zikhroynes, Ale verk*, 11:33–34. This translation: Seymour Levitan, in *The I. L. Peretz Reader*, ed. Ruth R. Wisse (New York: Schocken, 1990), 288.

8. Dokter shtitser (I. L. Peretz), "Unzer treyst un hofnung," in *Di treyst: a bletl af shabes nakhamu* (1894): 30. Reprinted in *Ale verk*, 8:70.

9. A. Rosenzweig, *Der radikaler period fun peretses shafn* (Peretz's radical period) (Kharkov and Kiev: State Publisher for National Minorities in the USSR, 1934), 31. Rosenzweig attempts a careful periodization of Peretz's opus to divide the periods of greater from lesser reaction.

10 Irving Howe, introduction to *A Treasury of Yiddish Stories* (New York: Schocken Books, 1958).

11. Shmuel Niger, *Y. L. Peretz, zayn lebn, zayn firendike perzenlikhkayt* (Buenos Aires: Alveltlekhn Yidisher Kultur-Kongres, 1952).

12. Nachman Meisel, *Yitskhok leybush perets un zayn dor shryaber* (New York: Yidisher kultur farband, 1951), 352–53.

13. I. L. Peretz, "Shma Yisroel; oder, der bas," in *Folkstimlekhe geshikhtn* (Stories in the folk manner) (New York: Congress for Jewish Culture, 1984): 119–33.

14. Isaac Rosenfeld, "Isaac Leib Peretz: The Prince of the Ghetto," in *Preserving the Hunger: An Isaac Rosenfeld Reader*, ed. Mark Shekhner (Detroit: Wayne State University Press, 1988), 137.

15. Steven A. Ascheim, "Nietzsche, Anti-Semitism and the Holocaust," in *Nietzsche and Jewish Culture*, ed. Jacob Golomb (London: Routledge, 1997), 15.

Chapter 10

1. David Aberbach, "Revolutionary Hebrew, Empire and Crisis: Toward a Sociological *Gestalt*," *British Journal of Sociology* 48, no. 1 (1997): 131–51.

2. This essay is part of a broader argument which I have made concerning Hebrew literature in its most original creative periods prior to 1948—notably in the prophetic age in the eighth to sixth centuries B.C.E, the tannaic era of the first two centuries C.E., and the "golden age" of Hebrew poetry in Muslim Spain in the eleventh and twelfth centuries C.E. Artistic breakthroughs in Hebrew appear to coincide and be connected with crises in the dominant empire, leading to heightened Jewish national identity. See David Aberbach, *Imperialism and Biblical Prophecy 750–500 BCE* (London: Routledge, 1993); David Aberbach, "Hebrew Poetry, Jewish Nationalism and the Empire of Islam 1031–1140" (London: London School of Economics, 1995); Aberbach, "Revolutionary Hebrew."

3. Mostly because it asserted Jewish national distinctiveness, Hebrew was banned under Soviet rule, and it is highly significant that many leading Soviet dissidents in the 1970s and 1980s, such as Anatoly Shcharansky, were teachers and students of Hebrew.

4. William Fuller, *Civil-Military Conflict in Imperial Russia 1881–1914* (Princeton: Princeton University Press, 1985); John Klier and Shlomo Lambroza, eds., *Pogroms: Anti-Jewish Violence in Modern Russian History* (Cambridge: Cambridge University Press, 1992).

5. Fuller, *Civil-Military Conflict.*

6. Jonathan Frankel, *Prophecy and Politics: Socialism, Nationalism, and the Russian Jews, 1862–1917* (Cambridge: Cambridge University Press, 1981), 49.

7. Robert Alter, *The Invention of Hebrew Prose: Modern Fiction and the Language of Realism* (Seattle: Washington University Press, 1988); David Aberbach, *Realism, Caricature and Bias: The Fiction of Mendele Mocher Sefarim* (Oxford: Littman Library, 1993).

8. Frankel, *Prophecy and Politics*; Eli Lederhendler, *The Road to Modern Jewish Politics: Political Tradition and Political Reconstruction in the Jewish Community of Tsarist Russia* (New York: Oxford University Press), 1989.

9. Mendele Mocher Sefarim means, in Hebrew, "Mendele the Bookpeddler," and is the name of the principal literary character of—and the pen name of—S. J. Abramowitz. On Mendele and his milieu, with literary and historical bibliography, see Aberbach, *Realism.* The most comprehensive recent history of Hebrew literature of the period 1881–1917 is Gershon Shaked, *Hebrew Narrative 1880–1970* (in Hebrew), vol. 1 (Tel Aviv: Hakibbutz Hame'uchad, 1977).

10. Sholem Aleichem means, in Hebrew, "How do you do?" and is the pen name of Sholem Rabinowitz.

11. On Mendele, see Aberbach, *Realism*, 45–46. On Bialik, see David Aberbach, "On Rereading Bialik: Paradoxes of a 'National Poet,'" *Encounter* 56, no. 6 (1981): 41–48, and *Bialik*, Jewish Thinkers Series (London: Peter Halban; New York: Grove Press, 1988). Ahad Ha'am, means, in Hebrew, "One of the People," and is the pen name of Asher Ginzberg. On Ahad Ha'am's rivalry with Herzl, see Steven Zipperstein, *Elusive Prophet: Ahad Ha'am and the Origins of Zionism* (London: Peter Halban, 1993).

12. David Aberbach, "Aggadah and Childhood Imagination in the Works of Mendele, Bialik and Agnon," in G. Abramson and T. V. Parfitt, eds., *Jewish Education and Learning* (Chur, Switzerland: Harwood Academic Publications, 1994).

13. Miroslav Hroch, *Social Preconditions of National Revival in Europe* (Cambridge: Cambridge University Press, 1985); John Hutchinson, *The Dynamics of Cultural Nationalism: The Gaelic Revival and the Creation of the Irish Nation State* (London: Allen & Unwin, 1987).

14. Hans Rogger, *Jewish Politics and Right-Wing Politics in Imperial Russia* (London: Macmillan, 1986); Heinz-Dietrich Löwe, *The Tsars and the Jews: Reform, Reaction and Antisemitism in Imperial Russia, 1772–1917* (Chur, Switzerland: Harwood Academic Publishers, 1993).

15. John Klier, *Imperial Russia's Jewish Question, 1855–1881* (Cambridge: Cambridge University Press, 1995), 455; Erich Haberer, *Jews and Revolution in Nineteenth-Century Russia* (Cambridge: Cambridge University Press, 1995).

16. Steven Zipperstein, *The Jews of Odessa: A Cultural History, 1794–1881* (Stanford: Stanford University Press, 1985).

17. Elie Kedourie, *Nationalism* (London: Hutchinson, 1960), 100–101.

18. Michael Stanislawski, *"For Whom Do I Toil?" J. L. Gordon and the Crisis of Russian Jewry* (New York: Oxford University Press, 1988); David Patterson, *The Hebrew Novel in Tsarist Russia* (Edinburgh: Edinburgh University Press, 1964).

19. Aberbach, *Realism*.

20. On the Hasidim as targets of satire, see Israel Davidson, *Parody in Jewish Literature* (New York: Columbia University Press, 1907). When the image of Hasidim in Hebrew literature began to change, one place in which the change was evident was Peretz's collection of stories, *Hasidut*, which portrayed them with glowing empathy.

21. Dan Miron, *When Loners Come Together: A Portrait of Hebrew Literature at the Turn of the Twentieth Century* (Hebrew) (Tel Aviv: Am Oved, 1987).

22. Letter of Tsar Nicholas II to his mother, quoted in Richard Pipes, *The Russian Revolution 1899–1919* (London: Collins Harvill, 1990), 48.

23. Quoted in Aberbach, *Bialik*.

24. Mordecai Zvi Feierberg, *Whither? And Other Stories*, trans. Hillel Halkin. (1899; rpt. Philadelphia: Jewish Publication Society, 1973), 214.

25. David Aberbach, *Charisma in Politics, Religion and the Media: Private Trauma, Public Ideals* (London: Macmillan, 1996).

26. Only one other major Hebrew writer—Agnon—followed Mendele in this ambiva-

lent, satiric mode of depiction of European Jews, which became the essence of his style. But in contrast with Mendele a generation earlier, Agnon was totally committed to Zionism, and he wrote most of his works in Jerusalem.

27. Mendele Mocher Sefarim, *Collected Works* (Hebrew) (Tel Aviv: Dvir, 1947), 1:259.

28. Ibid., 1:445.

29. Fyodor Dostoyevsky, *The House of the Dead*, trans. David McDuff (Harmondsworth: Penguin, 1985), 93.

30. David Goldstein, *Dostoievski et les Juifs* (Paris: Gallimard, 1976).

31. Nikolai Gogol, *Dead Souls*, trans. David Magarshack (Harmondsworth: Penguin Classics, 1976), 89.

32. Goldstein, *Dostoievski et les Juifs*.

33. Leo Tolstoy, *Anna Karenina*, trans. Rosemary Edmonds (Harmondsworth: Penguin, 1968), 775.

34. Ivan Turgenev, *Fathers and Sons*, trans. Rosemary Edmonds (Harmondsworth: Penguin, 1965), 116.

35. Gogol, *Dead Souls*, 99, 164, 208, 215, 307, 339.

36. Ibid., 169.

37. Erik Erikson, *Identity: Youth and Crisis* (London: Faber, 1974), 303.

38. Nikolai Chernyshevsky, quoted in Donald Treadgold, *The West in Russia and China*, vol. 1, *Russia, 1472–1917* (Cambridge: Cambridge University Press, 1973), 181.

39. Fyodor Dostoyevsky, *Crime and Punishment*, trans. David Magarshack (Harmondsworth: Penguin, 1966), 355.

40. Dostoyevsky, *The House of the Dead*, 31.

41. Fyodor Dostoyevsky, *The Possessed [The Devils]*, trans. Constance Garnett (London: Dent, 1952), 1:288.

42. In a letter of October 21, 1870, to A. N. Maikov, Dostoyevsky writes that *The Possessed* "describes how the devils entered into the herd of swine." Fyodor Dostoyevsky, *Selected Letters*, ed. Joseph Frank and David I. Goldstein, trans. Andrew R. MacAndrew. (New Brunswick: Rutgers University Press, 1987), 343.

43. Mikhail Saltykov-Shchedrin, *The Golovlovs*, trans. I. P. Foote. (New York: Oxford University Press, 1986), vii.

Chapter 11

1. Borvine Frenkel, *Mit Yidishe kinstler. Shmuesn un bamerkungen* (Paris: Yidisher kultur kongres, 1963), 109. Strikingly, Chagall's opinions in 1963 have changed little from his comments (in Yiddish) in "Bletlakh," *Shtrom*, Moscow, no. 1 (1922): 44–46. For an English translation, see Marc Chagall, "Leaves From My Notebook," in *Marc Chagall and the Jewish Theater* (New York: Guggenheim Museum, 1992), 173–74. Chagall has no difficulty with "Jewish artists" and even accepts Frenkel's suggestion that Pissarro, Modigliani, Soutine, and others are Jewish artists, but suggests that their "Jewish spirit" might have come to sharper focus if they were "closer to their people."

Since the death of Chagall, there has been a tendency to appropriate his accomplishment as the artistic expression of various states. France, Russia, Belarus, and Israel all claim him. See, among others, Susan Compton, "The Russian Background," *Chagall* (London: Royal Academy of Arts, 1985), 30–45; John E. Bowlt, "From the Pale of Settlement to the Reconstruction of the World," in *Tradition and Revolution: The Jewish Renaissance in Russian Avant-garde Art, 1912–1928*, ed. Ruth Apter-Gabriel (Jerusalem: The Israel Museum, 1987), 43–60; Aleksandr Kamensky, ed., *Chagall: The Russian Years, 1907–1922* (New York: Rizzoli, 1989); Christoph Vitali, ed., *Marc Chagall: The Russian Years, 1906–1922* (Frankfort: Schirn Kunsthalle, 1991); Alexandra Shatskikh, "Jewish Artists in the Russian Avant-garde," in *Russian Jewish Artists in a Century of Change, 1890–1990*, ed. Susan Tumarkin Goodman (Munich/New York: Prestel, 1996), 71–80.

The tendency to downplay Chagall's "Jewishness" within some erudition in order to "universalize" his art or link it unequivocally to some other culture tradition reflects, perhaps, either an unappreciation of what a distinctive holistic culture in the fullest anthropological sense the ordinary Eastern European Jews lived in the Pale of Settlement, in those market towns or *shtetlakh*, in spite of the secular modernization making constant inroads; or, it reflects earlier or atavistic thinking about the subject. Jewish painters as Artur Kolnik or Solomon Yudovin, lesser talents than Chagall, are not being claimed today by other cultures and states even though their own backgrounds, culturally and aesthetically, are hardly different from Chagall's. I am daring to say that a significant Jewish artist suddenly enters, as it were, the public domain when hegemonic powers lay claim to his/her accomplishment, whereas the lesser talented artist of Jewish origin can remain indisputably a representative of "Jewish art." The Einstein quip is still at play: "If E=mc squared is proven correct, the Germans will claim me as German and the French, as a citizen of the world; but if the formula is wrong, the French will say I am German and the Germans will say I'm a Jew." *Si non è vero, è ben trovato!*

2. See Linda Nochlin, "Starting with the Self: Jewish Identity and Its Representation," and Gale B. Murray, "Toulouse-Lautrec's Illustrations for Victor Joze and Georges Clemenceau and Their Relationship to French Anti-Semitism of the 1890's," in *The Jew in the Text: Modernity and the Construction of Identity*, ed. Linda Nochlin and Tamar Garb (London: Thames and Hudson, 1995), 7–19 and 57–82; Hillel Kasovsky, "Jewish Artists in Russia at the Turn of the Century: Issues of National Self-Identification in Art," *Jewish Art* 21–22 (1995–96): 20–39; and in the same issue: Elena I. Itkina, "The Jewish Theme in Russian Graphic Art of the Eighteenth and Nineteenth Centuries: A Survey of the Collection of the State Historical Museum, Moscow," 6–19.

3. Marek Rostworowski, ed., *Żydzi w Polsce, obraz i słowo* (Warsaw: Wydawnictwo Inter-press, 1993), 38, 42–43, 56, 154–56, 220–23. The Jew as Oriental or foreign was certainly developed by French painters who discovered the Algerian and Moroccan Jewry in the period of French imperialism, but in Europe, in general, a portraiture or a caricature of the indigenous Jew fit into elements of Orientalism. This is a complex subject not yet studied formally in terms of the Jews in Western arts but has an intelligent beginning in John M. MacKenzie, *Orientalism, History, Theory and the Arts* (Manchester: Manchester University Press, 1995).

4. There were earlier artists of Jewish origin but they were unique and circumstantial and did not attempt to aesthetically express a Jewish consciousness, with the exception of Moritz

Oppenheim (1800–1882) whose Jewish genre paintings are basically nostalgic re-creations. On the earliest manifestations of Jews in Polish art, see Yoysef Sendel, *Plastishe kunst bay poylishe Yidn in Poylen* (Warsaw: Yiddish Bukh, 1964), 7–9. On the influence of Jewish tombstone cutters, see Zalmen Gostynski, *Shteyner dertseyln* (Paris: Farband fun di mizrakh-eyropeyishe yidn in frankraykh, 1973); D. Goberman, *Jewish Tombstones in Ukraine and Moldavia* (Moscow: Image, 1993).

5. Ezra Mendelsohn, "Art and Jewish History: Maurycy Gottlieb's 'Christ Preaching at Capernaum'," *Tsyion* 63, no. 2 (1997): 191.

6. For various interpretations of the emergence of a Jewish national art see Seth L. Wolitz, "The Jewish National Art Renaissance in Russia " in *Tradition and Revolution*, ed. Ruth Apter-Gabriel, 21–42; Mirjam Rajner, "The Awakening of Jewish National Art in Russia," *Jewish Art* 16–17 (1990–91): 98–121; Ziva Amishai-Maisels, "The Jewish Awakening: A Search for National Identity," in Goodman, *Russian Jewish Artists*; Hillel Kasovsky, "Jewish Artists," 20–39.

7. Quoted in John A. Walker and Sarah Chaplin, *Visual Culture: An Introduction* (Manchester: Manchester University Press, 1997), 97–98.

8. Wagner stated, "The Jew is innately incapable of announcing himself to us artistically . . . Neither can we hold him capable of any sort of artistic utterance of purely human essence." Richard Wagner, "Das Judenthum in der Musik," *Neue Zeitschrift fuer Musik* 33, no. 1 (September 3, 1850) and no. 2 (September 6, 1850). For an English translation, see Paul Mendes-Flohr and Jehuda Reinharz, *The Jew in the Modern World*, *A Documentary History*, 2nd ed. (New York: Oxford University Press, 1995), 329.

9. The Lord Durham Report (1839) that described French-Canadians as "a people without a literature" reflects the same attitude and directly affected the course of Canadian history.

10. See Michael Berkowitz, *Zionist Culture and Western European Jewry before the First World War* (Cambridge: Cambridge University Press, 1993), 133. Noakh Prilutski in Warsaw, 1913, was no less offended by the refusal of Polish critics to mention Jewish artists in the Warsaw Art Salon and said: "the least talented Christians received a caress, and not one Jewish artist was acknowledged with a single word; boycott!—even in this domain." Noakh Prilutski, "Vegen natsionalisher kunst," (1913) in *Barg-aroyf* (Warsaw: Naye ferlag, 1917), 118–19. But his anger is directed also at Jews refusing to buy Jewish artwork and not supporting a national art that is part of building a national culture. Ibid., 119–29.

11. This historical recuperation was also suggested in other mediums, such as theater. Avrom Goldfaden's Yiddish melodrama *Bar Kokhba* (1881) for example, evoked a rich past, a bitter present, and instilled hope for a happier future.

12. After World War I, Jewish artists began writing short articles, introductions to catalogs, and even *manifesti*. See Moshe Boderzon, Manifest, *Yung-Yidish* 1 (1919): 2; Seth Wolitz, "Between Folk and Freedom: The Failure of the Yiddish Modernist Movement in Poland," *Yiddish* 8, no. 1 (1991): 26–51; Wolitz, "Modernizm in der Yidisher Literatur," *Yidishe Kultur* 2 (March–April 1980): 36–45.

13. Later, Third World cultures encountering the task of nation-building and cultural reconstruction would have similar preoccupations.

14. Berkowitz, *Zionist Culture*, 130.

15. Martin Buber, "Lesser Ury," in Davis [*sic*] Trietsch und Leo Winz, eds., *Ost und West* (Berlin: Verlag von S. Calvary & Co., 1901), Februar, Heft 2, 113.

16. Mark H. Gelber, "The Jungjuedische Bewegung: An Unexplored Chapter in German-Jewish Literary and Cultural History," in *Leo Baeck Institute, Year Book* 31 (London: Secker and Warburg, 1986), 113.

17. For the importance of the term *renaissance*, see Martin Buber, "Juedische Renaissance," *Ost und West* 1, no. 1 (1901): 7–10. It becomes the central motivic word for Jewish secular cultural undertakings down to the present in all ideological settings. Russian-speaking Jewish intellectuals used the term *vozrozhdenie*, rebirth, for national regeneration; a faction of former Poalei Tsiyon members published in Paris a journal with this name in 1904. See Jonathan Frankel, *Prophecy and Politics, Socialism, Nationalism, and the Russian Jews, 1862–1917* (Cambridge: Cambridge University Press, 1981), 279.

18. Berkowitz, *Zionist Culture*, 129.

19. Ibid., 119.

20. Gelber, "Jungjuedische Bewegung," 106

21. The old man is entrapped by a crown of thorns, a negative allusion to Christianity, not barbed wire, as Michael Berkowitz anachronistically maintains. Berkowitz, *Zionist Culture*, 128.

22. Stephen C. Hutchings, *Russian Modernism: The Transfiguration of the Everyday* (Cambridge: Cambridge University Press, 1997), 47. The Russian word *byt* is conceived here in its neutral sense: the everyday, routine. It is played off in the symbolist world against *zhizn'*, active life.

23. Milly Heyd, "Lilien and Beardsley," *Journal of Jewish Art* 7 (1980): 62–63.

24. Alfred Gold, *E. M. Lilien, Sonderabdruck aus Juedische Kuenstler* (Berlin: Juedischer Verlag, 1903), 86–87.

25. Ephraim Moses Lilien, *Jerusalem* (New York: Ktav, 1976).

26. Ran Shechori, *Art in Israel* (New York: Schocken, 1976), 12. See also: Moshe Zertal, *Omanim yehudim, hayim yehudiyim* (Tel Aviv: Sifriat poalim, 1970), 127–38.

27. Jerzy Malinowski, "Um eine juedische Nationalkunst, Ideen des Zionismus in der Kunst der polnischen Juden," in *Der Erste Zionistenkongress von 1897—Ursachen, Bedeutung, Actualitaet*, ed. Heiko Haumann (Basle: Karger, 1997), 516–19. This article underlines the "Polish-Jewish" contribution of Jewish artists to the Zionist national dream, citing Lilien, Hirszenberg, Ury, Wachtel, etc. The author appears to claim these artists as part of the patrimony of new Poland, not unlike Spain's contemporary use of the term, *convivencia*, in order to permit a reappropriation of Spanish Jews, like Maimonides or Yehuda Halevi, into the new national culture. See note 1 on new states claiming "native" Jewish artists as part of their national inheritance.

28. Nurit Shila-Cohen, ed., *"Betsalel" shel Shatz, 1906–1929* (Jerusalem: Israel Museum, 1995), 35. In Saint Petersburg, the Jewish artist, Mordecai Yoffe (1864–1941) initiated in 1908 the Jewish artistic society "Bezalel." This shows that support for a Jewish art institution in Jerusalem was not just a Western Jewish/Zionist interest. See *Proyekt ustava evreyskogo khudozhestvennogo obshchestva "Bezalel"* as cited in Kasovsky, "Jewish Artists," 37.

29. Alfred Werner, "The Tragedy of Ephraim Moses Lilien," *Herzl Year Book* II (New York: Herzl Press, 1959), 110.

30. Shechori, *Art in Israel*, 9.

31. Ezra Mendelsohn, *Class Struggle in the Pale* (Cambridge: Cambridge University Press, 1970), 116–25; Nathan Weinstock, *Le Pain De Misère, histoire du mouvement ouvrier juif en Europe* (Paris: Editions La Découverte, 1984) 1:227–29.

32. G. Kasovsky, *Artists From Vitebsk, Yehuda Pen and His Pupils* (Moscow: Image, n.d. [1991]), 27). It was called School of Drawing and Painting. Most of the students were Jews and it was closed on the Jewish Sabbath (ibid., 29). Vitebsk was a developed provincial city with a full cultural life in Russian and Yiddish. Fifty-two percent of the population was Jewish. But in this paper Vitebsk is used only in an onomastic function of representing the cultural / artistic aesthetic of Jewish Eastern European cultural uniqueness as an ideological underpinning of its plastic expression.

33. Frankel, *Prophecy and Politics*, 171. Simon Dubnov (1860–1941) argued for Jewish cultural autonomy with his unique vision of the Jews as a "spiritual nation." See his *Letters on the Old and New Judaism*. His friend and ideological opponent, Ahad Ha'am (Asher Ginzberg) (1856–1927), argued for cultural Zionism in Hebrew in a Jewish homeland in important essays collected in *Al pareshat derakhim* (1922). On the Hebrew / Yiddish debate, see Emanuel S. Goldsmith, *Modern Yiddish Culture, the Story of the Yiddish Language Movement*, 2nd ed. (New York: Fordham University Press, 1997).

34. David Guenzburg and Vladimir Stassof, eds. *L'Ornement Hébreu* (Berlin: Calvary, 1905). It has been republished and expanded with a long introduction: *Illuminations from Hebrew Bibles of Leningrad*, introduction and new descriptions by Bezalel Narkiss (Jerusalem: The Bialik Institute, 1990).

35. Avram Kampf, *Jewish Experience in the Art of the Twentieth Century* (Massachusetts: Bergin & Garvey Publishers, Inc., 1984), 15–16.

36. Seth Wolitz, "Chagall's Last Soviet Performance: The Graphics for *Troyer*, 1922," *Jewish Art* 21–22 (1995–96): 97–99.

37. Solomon Yudovin and M. Malkin, *Yidisher Folks-Ornament* (Vitebsk: Vitebsker I. L. Peretz gezelshaft, 1920). The folk elements also collected by Altman but then stylized can be found in Natan Altman, *Juedische Graphik*, text by Max Osborn (Berlin: Razum-Verlag, 1923). Further stylized folk motifs can be seen in Boris Aronson, *Sovremennaya evreiskaya grafika* (Berlin: Petropolis, 1924).

38. Buber, "Juedische Renaissance," 7.

39. Arthur Cohen, "From Eastern Europe to Paris and Beyond," in *The Circle of Montparnasse Jewish Artists in Paris: 1905–1945*, ed. Kenneth E. Silver and Romy Golan (New York: Universe Books, 1985), 60–79. Cohen treats Pen rather shabbily.

40. This book provides the first ordering of Yehuda Pen's production: *Materyialy da vystouki tvorau Iu. M. Pena. Kataloh vystauki tvorau Iuryia Moiseevicha Pena. 1854–1937* (Mensk: Dziarzhauny mastatski muzei RB, 1993). See also Yehuda Pen, "Zikhhroynes fun a kinstler," in *Vitebsk amol: geshikhte, zikhroynes, khurbn*, ed. Grigori Aronson, Yankev Leshtshinski, Avram Kahan (New York: Waldon Press, 1956), 363–90.

41. G. Kasovsky, *Artists From Vitebsk*, 57–61, notes the role of Yudovin's handling of streets and ethnographic depictions. Most of the celebrated woodcuts are from the series *Byloe* (The past) published in 1926.

42. Joseph Tchaikov, *Skulptur* (Kiev: Kultur-lige, 1921), quoted in Apter-Gabriel, *Tradition and Revolution*, 231.

43. Introduction to *Jewish Exhibition of Sculpture, Graphics and Drawings* (Kiev, February–March 1920), quoted in Apter-Gabriel, *Tradition and Revolution*, 230.

44. Boris Aronson, *Sovremmenaya evreiskaya grafika.* Quoted (in English translation) in Apter-Gabriel, *Tradition and Revolution*, 237.

45. Ibid., 236. I have changed the translation from "A Hebrew style has not been created" to a *Jewish* style, for the Russian word, *evreiskii*, means "Jewish" in this context although it does also mean Hebrew.

46. Issachar Rybak and Boris Aronson, "Di vegen fun der yidisher moleray," *Oyfgang*, (Kiev, 1919), 119–24. For English translation, see Apter-Gabriel, *Tradition and Revolution*, 229.

47. Kenneth E. Silver, "Jewish Artists in Paris, 1905–1945," in Silver and Golan, *The Circle of Montparnasse*, 26–33.

48. Seth Wolitz, "The Jewish National Art Renaissance in Russia," in *Tradition and Revolution*, 26–28.

49. Amishai-Maisels argues that the *Makhmadim* artists "had a strong effect on Chagall" because "he reacted with scorn to both their theories and art" and painted biblical themes "to show how a modern Jewish artist should render such themes" (Ziva Amishai-Maisels, "The Jewish Awakening: A Search for National Identity," in Goodman, *Russian Jewish Artists*, 55). But that was not their "strong effect on Chagall" for Chagall was light years ahead of them aesthetically and painterly. Rather, it was their essentialist attitudes to a unique Jewish art that was out of place in cosmopolitan reality.

50. Chagall, "Bletlakh."

51. Ziva Amishai-Maisels, "Chagall's 'Dedicated to Christ:' Sources and Meanings," *Jewish Art* 21–22 (1995–96): 68–94.

52. Marek Shvarts, "The National Element in Jewish Art," *Literarishe bleter* 1, no. 48 (April 3, 1925): 1.

53. Yitshok Likhtenshteyn, "Vitebsker kinstler," in Aronson, Leshtshinski, Kahan, *Vitebsk amol*, 447–48.

54. Leo Kenig, manuscript in the archives of the Jewish National and University Library, Jerusalem, no. 4- 1269 / 173.

55. Ziva Amishai-Maisels, "Chagall's Jewish In-Jokes," *Journal of Jewish Art* 5 (1978): 76–93. This article establishes in print what many already knew or suspected, that Chagall was making full use of his Jewish inheritance. See also Amishai-Maisels, "The Jewish Awakening," 54.

56. When Dina Halpern, (d. 1988), the famous Yiddish actress who appears in the Yiddish film version of An-sky's *Dybbuk*, was my guest of the University of Texas, Austin, in 1986, I showed her the first edition of the engravings of Chagall's *Mein lebn*. As she turned the leaves, she broke out in laughter or puzzled for a moment, and in each case, then blurted out with delight and sometimes in awe, the exact Yiddish idiom represented visually. Clearly, an intact Yiddish culture existed and could follow perfectly the aesthetic intentions of its plastic artists. I record this as testimony to what is disappearing before my eyes.

57. Edouard Roditi, *Dialogues on Art* (London: 1960), 60. Roditi, in a private conversation

[San Francisco, Spring, 1969], told me that Chagall resisted intensively any possible allusion to a Yiddish idiom or Jewish iconographic interpretation in his paintings. Only after continuous give and take with the painter did Chagall admit to a possible Yiddish idiom entering "by chance" in a work. Roditi, a poet and art connoisseur who lived in Paris, visited Chagall on and off at his apartment on Ile St. Louis, and is the first person to put into print the allusion to the visual puns of Chagall which Amishai-Maisels notes in "Chagall's Jewish In-Jokes," 84n25.

My own experiences with Chagall confirm Roditi's experience with Chagall's caution and shrewdness. In 1958 at the University of Chicago I helped Chagall with translations when he was in residence for two weeks. (Chagall did not know English even though he lived in New York during the war years. He spoke in heavily accented French. He always conversed in Russian with his second wife, Valentina.) One day Mircea Eliade, seemingly in a moment of euphoria, jumped up from his seat and shouted, "*Cher Maître, vous avez su trouver dans votre art la fusion du christianisme et du judaïsme.*" Everyone was terribly excited. Chagall stood up and repeated, "*Merci, merci!*" and everyone was awed by his humbleness. He sat down all smiles and whispered in my ear, "*Ikh hob keyn shum vort nit farshtanen.*" (I didn't understand a single word.) He used Yiddish to me as he spoke Russian to his wife; it was a private tongue—but not necessarily speaking the truth!

58. Many minority cultures or dominated ones must resort to Aesopian language and other subterfuges to maintain communication with their people. Marranism was rampant in South America among the slaves, where the *condomblé* tradition in Bahia, for example, uses the Catholic figures of saints to cover their own gods. A good example is Xango represented in homes by Saint George killing the dragon.

59. Mirjam Rajner, "Chagall: The Artist And The Poet," *Jewish Art* 21–22 (1995–96): 41–43.

60. Ziva Amishai-Maisels, "Chagall's Jewish In-Jokes," 83.

61. Ibid.

62. Louis Lozowick, *Arch of Titus* (*Titus harasha*), in Janet Flint, *The Prints of Louis Lozowick, A Catalogue Raisonné* (New York: Hudson Hills Press, 1982), 191–92, plate no. 264.

63. Joseph Tchaikov, *Skulptur* (Kiev: Kultur-lige, 1921). Quoted (in English translation) in Wolitz, "The Jewish National Art Renaissance," 231.

64. Dovid Bergelson, "Yosef Shur," in *Eygns* (Kiev, 1918). For English translation, see Irving Howe and Eliezer Greenberg, eds., *Ashes out of Hope, Fiction by Soviet-Yiddish Writers* (New York: Schocken, 1977), 67–70. Bergelson presents the first example of Jewish ekphrasis describing a Jewish painter's "masterpiece" of four horses. A Jewish Zionist poet looks at it and declares that the horse must be Jewish, given the mane hanging over its eyes.

Chapter 12

1. See, for example, Henry J. Tobias, *The Jewish Bund in Russia from Its Origins to 1905* (Stanford: Stanford University Press, 1972), 221–343; J. S. Hertz, ed., *Di geshikhte fun bund* vol. 2 (New York: Unzer Tsayt, 1962), 9–482.

2. On the Bund during the Russian revolution of 1917, see Arye Gelbard, *Ha-"Bund" ha-*

Rusi bi-shenat ha-mahpekhot 1917: te'udot ve-hahlatot/hehedir ve-hosif mavo ve-he'arot (Tel Aviv: Tel Aviv University, 1984); *Bi-se'arat ha-yamim, ha-Bund ha-rusi be-'itot mahapekha* (Tel Aviv: Tel Aviv University, 1987); J. S. Hertz, ed., *Di geshikhte fun bund* vol. 3 (New York: Unzer Tsayt, 1966), 81–188.

3. For the Bundist position in Poland during the late 1930s: Bernard K. Johnpoll, *The Politics of Futility: The General Jewish Workers Bund of Poland 1917–1943* (Ithaca, N.Y.: Cornell University Press, 1967), 204–24; Abraham Brumberg, "The Bund and the Polish Socialist Party in the Late 1930s," in *The Jews of Poland Between Two World Wars*, ed. Yisrael Gutman, Ezra Mendelsohn, Jehuda Reinharz, and Chone Shmeruk (Hanover, N.H.: University Press of New England, 1989), 75–94; Daniel Blatman, "The Bund in Poland, 1935–1939," *POLIN* 9 (1996): 58–82; Leonard Rowe, "Jewish Self-Defense: A Response to Violence," in Joshua A. Fishman, *Studies in Polish Jewry 1919–1939* (New York: YIVO, 1974), 105–49.

4. See, for example, Arcadius Kahan, "The Impact of Industrialization in Tsarist Russia on the Socioeconomic Conditions of the Jewish Population," in *Essays in Jewish Social and Economic History* (Chicago: University of Chicago Press, 1986), 1–69.

5. On the Jewish Socialist Federation, see Eugene Victor Orenstein, "The Jewish Socialist Federation of America 1912–1921: A Study of Integration and Particularism in the American Jewish Labor Movement" (Ph.D. diss., Columbia University, 1978); J. S. Hertz, *Di yidishe sotsyalistishe bavegung in amerike* (New York: Der Veker, 1954), 139–60; Melech Epstein, *Jewish Labor in U.S.A. An Industrial, Political and Cultural History of the Jewish Labor Movement*, 2 vols. (New York: Trade Union Sponsoring Committee, 1950), 1:350–51; Arthur Liebman, *Jews and the Left* (New York: Wiley, 1979), 482–85.

6. For an early analysis of socioeconomic mobility among the immigrant population, see Chaim Zhitlovsky, "Der antisemitizm un di yidishe parteyen," *Dos naye leben* (August 1912): 5–13.

7. On the initial development of the Jewish labor movement in the United States, see Eliyohu Cherikover, ed., *Geshikhte fun der yidisher arbeter bavegung in di fareynikte shtatn* vol. 2 (New York: 1945), 319–417; Gerald Sorin, *The Prophetic Minority: American Jewish Immigrant Radicals 1880–1920* (Bloomington, Ind.: Indiana University Press, 1985), 72–123; Epstein, *Jewish Labor in the U.S.A.* 1:132–91; 253–334.

8. On the Russian revolution of 1905, in general: Abraham Ascher, *The Revolution of 1905*, 2 vols. (Stanford: Stanford University Press, 1992); Sidney Harcave, *First Blood: The Russian Revolution of 1905* (New York: Macmillan: 1964); Howard D. Mehlinger and John M. Thompson, *Count Witte and the Tsarist Government in the 1905 Revolution* (Bloomington, Ind.: Indiana University Press, 1972); Walter Sablinsky, *The Road to Bloody Sunday: Father Gapon and the St. Petersburg Massacre of 1905* (Princeton: Princeton University Press, 1976). On the role of the Jewish parties, in particular: Yehuda Slutsky, "Shnat 1905 bekhayehem shel yehudei rusya," *He'avar* vol. 22 (1977): 3–23; Jonathan Frankel, *Prophecy and Politics: Socialism, Nationalism and the Russian Jews 1862–1917* (Cambridge: Cambridge University Press, 1981), 134–70.

9. For biographical details on Bundists and ex-Bundists, see, for example, J. S. Hertz, ed. *Doyres bundistn*, 3 vols. (New York: 1956–68); Shmuel Niger and Jacob Shatzky, eds., *Lek-*

sikon fun der nayer yidisher literature, 8 vols. (New York: Alveltlekher Yidishn Kultur Kongres, 1956–81).

10. See, for example, Max D. Danish, *The World of David Dubinsky* (Cleveland: The World Publishing Co., 1957) and Matthew Josephson, *Sidney Hillman: Statesman of American Labor* (New York: Doubleday, 1952).

11. David McCullough, *Truman* (New York: Simon and Schuster, 1993), 310, 330.

12. Zvi Gitelman, *Jewish Nationality and Soviet Politics: The Jewish Sections of the CPSU. 1917–1930* (Princeton: Princeton University Press, 1972), 226.

13. Melech Epstein, *The Jew and Communism: The Story of Early Communist Victories and Ultimate Defeats in the Jewish Community, U.S.A. 1919–1941* (New York: Trade Union Sponsoring Committee 1960), 388–94.

14. Danish, *The World of David Dubinsky,* 270–71; Yidisher arbeter komitet, *Kamf, retung, oyfboy: barikht fun land-tsuzamenfor fun yidishn arbeter komitet* (December 18–20, 1942): 25.

15. Epstein, *Jewish Labor in U.S.A.,* 1:335–420.

16. Nahman Syrkin, *Yidisher kongres in amerike* (New York: 1915).

17. On the Jewish Congress movement in the United States, see Oscar Janowsky, *Jews and Minority Rights (1898–1919)* (New York: Columbia University Press, 1933), 159–90; Jonathan Frankel, "The Jewish Socialists and the American Jewish Congress Movement," in *YIVO Annual of Jewish Social Science,* vol. 16, *Essays on the American Jewish Labor Movement,* ed. Ezra Mendelsohn (New York: YIVO, 1976), 202–341.

18. Ibid., 211–16.

19. Hertz, *Di yidishe sotsyalistishe,* 140, 163, 194.

20. Janowsky, *Jews and Minority Rights,* 179–90.

21. See Avrom Lesin: "To hobnob with the great men of the American Jewish Committee is easier, more pleasant . . . than to devote oneself to such banal subjects as simple Jewish workers." Fun an altn bundist, "Di natsyonale arbeter komitet," *Di tsukunft* (July 1916): 597.

22. "Di natsyonale arbeter konvenshon," editorial, *Di naye velt* 6, no. 118 (February 9, 1917): 2.

23. Frankel, "The Jewish Socialists," 291–94.

24. Shakhne Epstein, "Di natsyonale arbeter konvenshon," *Di naye velt* 7, no. 119 (February 16, 1917), 4–5.

25. Avrom Lesin, "An entfer tsu gen. Olgin," *Di tsukunft* (March 1917): 138–39.

26. On the antiwar movement generally, see H. C. Peterson and G. C. Fite, *Opponents of War 1917–18* (Madison: University of Wisconsin Press, 1957); on the war issue and the Jewish socialists, see Zosa Szajkowski, *Jews, War and Communism,* vol. 1 (New York: Ktav, 1972).

27. See, for example: Tali Tadmor-Shimony, "Sheelat hazehut haleumit shel hasotzyalizm hayehudi haamerikani 1917–1924" (Ph.D. diss., The Hebrew University of Jerusalem, 1995), 54–60, 85–90.

28. Epstein, *Jewish Labor in U.S.A.,* 2:108–12. For background, see Theodore Draper, *The Roots of American Communism* (New York: Viking, 1957), 303–95.

29. Hertz, *Di yidishe sotsyalistishe,* 277, 297. In 1927, Erlich held meetings in some fifty cities.

30. David Prudzon, "Hakomunizm vetnu'at hapo'alim hayehudit bearzot habrit" (Ph.D. diss., Tel-Aviv University, 1985), 50–96; Ruth Wisse, *A Little Love in Big Manhattan* (Cambridge, Mass.: Harvard University Press, 1988), 113–15; 162–64.

31. Wisse, *A Little Love*, 67–68; Sandra Parker, "An Educational Assessment of the Yiddish Secular School Movements in the United States," in *Never Say Die! A Thousand Years of Yiddish in Jewish Life and Letters*, ed. Joshua Fishman (The Hague, 1981), 496–503.

32. On subsidies paid by *Forverts* to the Farband, see Hertz, *Di yidishe sotsyalistishe*, 211, 273.

33. For the splits within, and final dissolution of, the Jewish socialist parties, see Gitelman, *Jewish Nationality*, 151–230.

34. Prominent among the returnees were Hillel Rogoff and Zivion (Ben-Tsiyen Hofman).

35. Tali Tadmor-Shimony, "Sheelat hazehut haleumit," 177–93.

36. "England shtitst di araber in Palestine," *Frayheyt*, August 24, 1929.

37. Headlines of August 27 and 30. (The reference is to veterans of the "Jewish Legion," the three Jewish battalions that fought within the British army in 1918.)

38. "Tsvantsig toyzent yiden in nyu york hoben zikh nekhten bateylikt in grosen demonstratsye," *Forverts*, August 27, 1929, p. 1.

39. "Tsionistn un klekoydesh firn durkh a mayofes demonstratsye," *Frayheyt*, August 24, 1929.

40. "Komunistishe miting in irving plaza efnt oyf di oygn fun di yidishe arbeter," *Frayheyt*, August 30, 1929.

41. Ibid.

42. "Di komunistishe tsaytungen in amerike hetsen itst gegen di yiden fun palestine," *Forverts*, August 28, 1929, p. 1.

43. "Di troyerike pasirungen in Palestine," *Der veker*, September 7, 1929, p. 1.

44. A. Muk. [Litvak], "Fun der zayt," *Der veker*, September 21, 1929, p. 7.

45. A. Shiplacoff, "Komunistishe printsipen un yidishe blut," *Der veker*, September 21, 1929, p. 14.

46. "Di troyerike pasirungen in palestine," *Der veker*, September 7, 1929, p. 1.

47. R. Abramovich, "Di palestiner gesheenishen un der tsienizm," *Der veker*, October 5, 1929, p. 5.

48. Epstein, *The Jew and Communism*, 224–33; Wisse, *A Little Love*, 190–98.

49. Zivion, "Yidishe interesn," *Forverts*, August 29, 1929, p. 3.

50. Frankel, *Prophecy and Politics*, 536; "Zionists Seek Aid of American Jews," *New York Times*, August 30, 1943, p. 6.

51. Frankel, *Prophecy and Politics*, 540–43; "Yidisher arbeter komitet kleybt oys 16 delegaten tsu algemeyner yidisher konferents," *Forverts*, August 28, 1943, p. 6.

52. Hertz, *Di yidishe sotsyalistishe*, 315–22.

53. On the Jewish Labor Committee, see Epstein, *Jewish Labor in U.S.A.*, 2:402–9.

54. Janowsky, *Jews and Minority Rights*, 264–390.

55. Isaac Neustadt-Noy, "The Unending Task: Efforts to Unite American Jewry from the American Jewish Congress to the American Jewish Conference" (Ph.D. diss., Brandeis University, 1976), 321, 336.

56. Stephen Wise warned in August 1943 that as many as four million Jews might already have been killed by the Nazis—a figure treated with skepticism by correspondents in *Forverts:* L. Fogelman, "Ken men zikh farlozn oyf ale barikhten vegn di shkhites of yiden in eyrope," *Forverts,* August 25, 1943, p. 1; Zivion, "Yidishe interesen," *Forverts,* August 28, 1943, p. 6.

57. "Folks komitet shikt briv tsu di delegatn fun yidisher konferents vegn eynikayt," *Morgn-Frayheyt,* August 12, 1943.

58. P. Novick, "Di konferents vegn palestine un di yidishe asembli," *Morgn-Frayheyt,* August 13, 1943.

59. The committee in exile ("Representation") of the Polish Bund issued a statement on August 9, 1943, calling for a boycott of the American Jewish Conference. Novick described the Representation as made up of "a number of sworn enemies of the Soviet Union" (ibid.). The leading figure on it at the time was Emmanuel Sherer. See Daniel Blatman, *Lema'an kherutenu vekheruthem: habund befolin 1939–1949* (Jerusalem: Yad Vashem, 1996), 201–16.

60. "Mit vos zol zikh farnemen di amerikaner yidishe konferents?" *Morgn-Frayheyt,* August 17, 1943.

61. N. Chanin, "Tsufil hoykh-politk un tsufil glaykhgiltikeyt," *Der veker,* September 1, 1943, p. 7.

62. *The American Jewish Conference: Its Organization and Proceedings of the First Session (August 29 to September 2, 1943)* (New York: 1944), 77–88; 115–29.

63. N. Chanin, "Di algemeyne yidishe konferents," *Der veker,* September 15, 1943, pp. 4–5.

64. Dovid Einhorn, "Di flamen vos baloykht di tsionistishe geule," *Der veker,* September 15, 1943, 10.

Chapter 13

1. Paula Hyman, *From Dreyfus to Vichy: The Remaking of French Jewry, 1906–1939* (New York: Columbia University Press, 1979). Also see Nancy Green, *The Pletzl of Paris: Jewish Immigrant Workers in the Belle Epoque* (New York: Holmes and Meier, 1986) and David H. Weinberg, *A Community on Trial: The Jews of Paris in the 1930s* (Chicago: University of Chicago Press, 1977).

2. David Weinberg, "France," in *The World Reacts to the Holocaust* ed. David S. Wyman (Baltimore: The Johns Hopkins University Press, 1996). Weinberg begins the project of situating the postwar years in the longer context of French Jewish history. See also Annette Wieviorka, "Les Juifs en France au lendemain de la guerre: État des lieux," *Archives juives: Revue d'histoire des juifs de France* 28, no. 1 (1995): 4–22; Wieviorka, *Déportation et génocide: Entre la mémoire et l'oubli* (Paris: Plon, 1992).

3. Hyman, *From Dreyfus to Vichy,* 236.

4. William Safran, "France and Her Jews: From 'Culte Israelite' to 'Lobby Juif'," *The Toqueville Review* 1 (Spring–Summer 1983): 104.

5. For example, seventeen consistorial rabbis were deported (approximately one-third of all such rabbis). See: *Activité des organisations juives en France sous l'occupation* (Paris: Centre de Documentation Juive Contemporaine, Série No. 4, Etudes et Monographies, 1947), 28.

6. Jacques Adler, *The Jews of Paris and the Final Solution: Communal Response and Internal Conflicts, 1940–44* (Oxford: Oxford University Press, 1985), 14, indicates that of the 76,000 Jews deported to concentration camps, 16,000 were of French descent, while 60,000 were either naturalized or immigrants.

7. Works on Jewish persecution in Vichy France abound, although the most important still remains Michael Marrus and Robert Paxton, *Vichy France and the Jews* (New York: Basic Books, 1981).

8. Doris Ben-Simon and Sergio della Pergola, *La Population juive de France: Socio-Démographie et identité* (Jerusalem: Hebrew University, 1984), 36.

9. *Tableau des organisations juives,* May 15, 1946, Consistoire israélite de Paris, cited in Annette Wieviorka, "Les Juifs en France," 9.

10. For a history on French Zionism prior to 1945, see Michel Abitol, *Les Deux terres promises: Les Juifs de France et le sionisme, 1897–1945* (Paris: O. Orban, 1989).

11. Between 1965 and 1971, for example, 6,852 French Jews emigrated from France to Israel, and since that time, Israel has received between 1,000–1,500 French Jews each year (due, in part, to the influx of North African Jews to France). Bensimon, *Les Juifs de France,* 171.

12. Guy de Rothschild, *The Whims of Fortune: The Memoirs of Guy de Rothschild* (New York: Random House, 1985), 306.

13. Weinberg, *A Community on Trial,* 53, 54.

14. Hyman, *From Dreyfus to Vichy,* 83–84.

15. Nadia Malinovich, "'Orientalism' and the Construction of Jewish Identity in France, 1915–1932" (paper presented at the annual meeting of the Association for Jewish Studies, Boston, Mass., December 21–23, 1997), argues that a new, more politically engaged Jewish identity was taking root as early as the late nineteenth and early twentieth century in the wake of the Dreyfus Affair.

16. Hyman, *From Dreyfus to Vichy,* chap. 6; Weinberg, *A Community on Trial,* 51–53.

17. Weinberg, *A Community on Trial,* 34.

18. Weinberg, *A Community on Trial,* chap. 5.

19. Richard Cohen, *The Burden of Conscience: French Jewish Leadership during the Holocaust* (Bloomington: Indiana University Press, 1987), 21–24. Similarly, in *The Jews of Paris and the Final Solution,* Jacques Adler has pointed out the inability, at least at first, of native Jews to understand what they were facing.

20. While the *Statut des Juifs* discriminated against all Jews, the position of foreign Jews was far more precarious. Special legislation gave police the right to intern foreign Jews or place them under police supervision in assigned residences. Cohen, *The Burden of Conscience,* 24.

21. Guy de Rothschild, letter to Mr. Fritz Baerwald, May 8, 1945, American Jewish Joint Distribution Committee [AJDC] archives, 311.

22. "Au lendemain de la défaite totale de l'Allemagne, le judaisme fait le bilan des 5 dernières années de persécutions," *Bulletin d'information,* May 1945, French Jewish Communities, 13 / 2-2, Jewish Theological Seminary [JTS].

23. Samuel René Kapel, *Au lendemain de la shoa: témoignage sur la renaissance du judaïsme de France et d'Afrique du Nord, 1945–1954* (Jerusalem: S. R. Kapel, 1991), 10–16.

24. Jean-Jacques Bernard, "Réflexions d'un français juives," *Revue juive de Genève* (October 1934): 23–27.

25. Bernard's conversion did not, in his mind, distance him from other Jews. This is quite clear in a biography of his father he published in 1955 when he noted that his baptism had not estranged him from his father. Despite such musings, Bernard could not help but speculate / hope that his father was on the verge of converting on his deathbed. Jean-Jacques Bernard, *Mon père: Tristan Bernard* (Paris: Albin Michel, 1955), 257–65.

26. Jean-Jacques Bernard, *Le camp de la mort lente: Compiègne 1941–1942* (Paris: Albin Michel, 1944). It should be noted that Bernard's experience in Compiègne were not typical of what most arrested Jews faced. See Wieviorka, *Déportation et génocide*, 447.

27. Jean-Jacques Bernard, "Autour du drame juif," *Le Figaro*, April 14, 1945, p. 2.

28. Ibid.

29. *Droit et Liberté*, April 27, 1945.

30. Jean Paul, "Une opinion sur le problème des juifs étrangers," *La Revue des Eclaireurs israélites de France*, April 1945.

31. Marc Jarblum, "En lissant J. J. Bernard: *Le camp de la mort lente*," *La Terre retrouvée*, February 1, 1945, p. 1.

32. The *Esprit* issue also included articles on the state of the catastrophe throughout Europe; the postwar position of French Jews; and a more lyrical piece describing one Jewish writer's disillusionment with his society.

33. André Spire, *Souvenirs à bâtons rompus* (Paris: Albin Michel, 1962), 239–47; *Encyclopedia Judaica*, 8:396–97.

34. His most explicit exploration of a Jewish "soul" can be found in Henri Hertz, "Ceux de job," in *Tragédies des temps volages: Contes et poèmes, 1906–1954* (Paris: 1955).

35. Henri Hertz, "Être ou ne pas être juif," *Esprit*, troisième année–nouvelle série (September 1945): 513.

36. Georges Wormser, letter to M. Feldmann, March 12, 1951, republished in Georges Wormser, *Français Israélites: Une doctrine-une tradition-une époque* (Paris: Les Editions de Minuit, 1963), 112.

37. Minutes, November 6, 1946, AA26, Consistoire de Paris.

38. *Bulletin du Centre israélite d'information*, October 1945, French Jewish Communities, 12/5, JTS.

39. *Encyclopedia Judaica*, 9:1287; Hyman, *From Dreyfus to Vichy*, 281.

40. Maurice P., letter to Terroine, May 5, 1945, AJ/38/1134, AN.

41. Zyzek M., letter to Commissaire de la République Limoges, November 29, 1944, AJ/38/1135, AN.

42. Jules C., letter to Ministre de l'intérieur, January 10, 1945, AJ/38/1138, AN.

43. Report, Association de defense des français israélites dépossedés par les Allemands, October 18, 1944, AJ/38/1134, AN [emphasis mine].

44. R&S S. to Sequestre de l'ex-Commissariat aux questions juives, March 8, 1945, Dossier no. 178, AJ/38/1137, AN.

45. Robert Gamzon, "The Fight for Survival Goes On," 1946, AJDC archives, 311.

46. As Annette Wieviorka, in *Déportation et génocide*, 347–52, has demonstrated, most of

the Consistorial leaders, whatever their position on postwar Jewish politics, also preferred to view the Vichy years "as a parenthesis which never encroached on the image that the Jews had forged of France since their emancipation." See also Henry Rousso, *The Vichy Syndrome*, trans. Arthur Goldhammer (Cambridge, Mass.: Harvard University Press, 1991).

47. "Réaction des milieux israélites après les évenements de Palestine," July 11, 1946, Dossier Palestine—Zionism, f/1a/3368, AN.

48. Report, "Réunion de protestation contre la politique britannique en Palestine, organisée par l'oganisations sioniste de France," July 5, 1946, Dossier Palestine—Zionism, f/1a/3368, AN. Another report in the same file calculated that over 3,000 participants attended, most of whom were Jewish youth.

49. "Appel aux autorités françaises!" by Irgoun Zvai Leoumi. Forwarded to Ministre de l'intérieur from Préfecture de Dobs, September 20, 1946, Dossier Palestine—Zionism, f/1a/3368, AN.

50. Georges Wormser, Report on Jewish community in France, Consultative Conference of the AIU, AJC, and AJA, June 1955, Anglo Jewish Association papers, AJ37/6/6/6/6, Parkes Library.

51. "Nos problèmes," *La Terre retrouvée*, September 18, 1944.

52. Conseil représentatif des Juifs de France, no date (but received at the Board of Deputies on December 18, 1944), C11/7/3b/1, Greater London Record Office [GLRO]. Also see, Jacques Fredj, "La Création du CRIF: 1943–1966," (mémoire de maitrise, Université de Paris IV, 1988).

53. According to both Jacques Adler, *The Jews of Paris and the Final Solution*, and Richard Cohen, *The Burden of Conscience*, the native Jewish leadership began shifting its position on these questions toward the end of the occupation, moving closer to those held by immigrant Jewish organizers. It is worth noting, however, that a more unified understanding of the problems did not necessarily translate into a more unified French Jewry.

54. Wieviorka, "Les Juifs en France," 9.

55. Examples of CRIF's restitution activities are detailed in a letter to Professor Terroine, October 17, 1945, B 10934, Ministry of Finance, in which the organization lobbies the French government to carry out its obligations to Jewish war victims. Evidence of CRIF's attempts to prevent the resurgence of anti-Semitism in Germany and elsewhere is found in "Mémoire concernant les revendications juives à l'égard de l'Allemagne," May 1951, Anglo Jewish Association papers, AJ37/6/6/5/2, Parkes Library.

56. Renée Poznanski, "Le Sionisme en France pendant la deuxième guerre mondiale: Développements institutionnels et impact idéologique," in *Les Juifs de France, le Sionisme et l'état d'Israel*, ed. Doris Bensimon and Benjamin Pinkus (Paris: Publications Langues'O, 1989), 212.

57. Dossiers non-inventoriés: Dossier généralites - Comité d'études des affaires juives, Archives du Ministère des relations extérieures, April and May 1945, Archives of the Ministère des relations extérieures, cited in Poznanski, "L'Héritage de la guerre," in *Les Juifs de France, le Sionisme et l'état d'Israel*, ed. Doris Bensimon and Benjamin Pinkus (Paris: Publications Langues'O, 1989), 247.

58. Central Zionist archives, Z. 4/10.300, cited in Poznanski, "L'Héritage de la guerre," 238.

59. "Traduction en langue française de la réunion de l'organisation des 'Sioniste revision-nistes unifiés,' tenue en langue yiddish le 20 Juin à la Maison de la mutualité," July 1, 1946, Dossier Palestine—Zionism, f/1a/3368, AN.

60. M. et L. Benaroya, "'Lève-toi et va dans la ville du massacre,'" *La Terre retrouvée*, February 1, 1945.

61. "Discours prononcé en Yiddish par trois orateurs juifs au cours de la réunion organisée le 12 juillet, salle Lancry, par l'Union juive de la résistance et de l'entr'aide," July 20, 1946, dossier Palestine—Zionism, f/1a/3368, AN; "Meeting de protestation contre les 'pogroms' de Pologne, organisée par l'Association des juifs polonais en France," July 12, 1946, same folder.

62. Report on "réunion de protestation contre la politique britannique en Palestine, organisée par l'organisations sioniste de France, July 5, 1946," Dossier Palestine—Zionism, f/1a/3368, AN.

63. Occasionally such divisions turned violent, as in cases when the Revisionists would interfere and attempt to disrupt other Zionist groups' rallies. "Réunion organisée par la Histadrouth (CGT Palestinienne), le 10 octobre," October 11, 1946, Dossier Palestine—Zionism, F/1a/3368, AN.

64. "Réunion organisée par l'Organisation sioniste," July 28, 1946, Dossier Palestine—Zionism, F/1a/3368, AN.

65. Cited in Poznanski, "Le Sionisme," 212.

66. "La propagande anti-britannique dans les milieux juifs de Paris," July 11, 1946, Dossier Palestine—Zionism, f/1a/3368, AN.

67. Simon Schwarzfuchs, *Napoleon, the Jews and the Sanhedrin* (London: Routledge & Kegan Paul, 1979).

68. Phyllis Cohen Albert, *The Modernization of French Jewry: Consistory and Community in the Nineteenth Century* (Hanover, N.H.: University Press of New England for Brandeis University Press, 1977), 45.

69. Cohen, *The Burden of Conscience*, 57; chap. 7.

70. Minutes, February 7, 1946, AA26, Consistoire de Paris.

71. Immigrant groups (Bundist, Zionist, and Communist) also de-emphasized Jewish particularity by constructing monuments that celebrated Jewish heroes fighting an antifascist war rather than Jewish deportees. Wieviorka, *Déportation et génocide*, 391–411.

72. M. Sachs, Consistoire Central, November 5, 1944, French Jewish Communities, 13/2-1, JTS.

73. Leon Meiss, Consistoire Central, November 5, 1944, French Jewish Communities, 13/2-1, JTS.

74. Minutes, December 2, 1947, AA27, Consistoire de Paris.

75. Minutes, May 26, 1948, AA27, Consistoire de Paris.

76. Cited in report by the President, "Position du Consistoire vis-à-vis de l'état d'Israel," Minutes, June 2, 1948, AA27, Consistoire de Paris.

77. Pierre Birnbaum, *Les Fous de la République: Histoire politique des juifs d'état, de Gambetta à Vichy* (Paris: Fayard, 1992), 341–44.

78. Report by the President, "Position du Consistoire vis-à-vis de l'état d'Israel."

79. Minutes, June 7, 1948, AA27, Consistoire de Paris.

80. Minutes, June 2, 1948, AA27, Consistoire de Paris.

81. Harry M. Rosen to Joseph J. Schwartz, "United Fund-Raising for French Jewish Community," June 30, 1948, 357, AJDC.

82. Rosen to Schwartz, "United Fund-Raising" 357, AJDC; Country Directors Conference Report: France, 1956, 309, AJDC archives, 309.

83. Weill Goudchaux, "Israel et la diaspora," *Journal des communautés,* April 28, 1961, p. 5, cited in Bensimon, *Les Juifs de France,* 164–65.

84. Malinovich, "'Orientalism' and the Construction of Jewish Identity."

CONTRIBUTORS

DAVID ABERBACH was educated at University College London and Oxford University. He is associate professor of Jewish studies at McGill University. In recent years he has published *The Roman Jewish Wars and Hebrew Cultural Nationalism; Revolutionary Hebrew, Empire and Crisis*; and *Realism, Caricature and Bias: The Fiction of Mendele Mocher Sefarim*.

GERSHON BACON is associate professor of Jewish history at Bar-Ilan University. He is the author of *The Politics of Tradition: Agudat Yisrael in Poland, 1916–1939* and *From Poland to Eastern Europe: Polish Jewry from the Partitions to World War One*, as well as studies of the political and social life of Polish Jewry in the nineteenth and twentieth centuries. His forthcoming book is entitled *The Jews of Modern Poland*.

DANIEL BLATMAN teaches history at the Institute of Contemporary Jewry at the Hebrew University of Jerusalem. His fields of research include East European Jewry, the Holocaust, and the history of the Jewish socialist movement. He has published numerous works, including *For Our Freedom and Yours, The Jewish Labor Bund in Poland, 1939–1949*.

DAVID E. FISHMAN is professor of Jewish history at the Jewish Theological Seminary and Senior Research Associate at the YIVO Institute for Jewish Research. He recently coedited (with Burton Visotzky) *From Mesopotamia to Modernity: Ten Introductions to Jewish History and Literature* and edited a volume of *Yivo-Bletter* on Yiddish folklore and popular culture. He is Director of Project Judaica, a joint academic program between JTS, YIVO, and the Russian State University for the Humanities in Moscow.

JONATHAN FRANKEL teaches modern Jewish and Russian history at the Hebrew University of Jerusalem, where he holds the Tamara and Saveli Grinberg Chair of Russian Studies. Among his books are *Prophecy and Politics: Socialism, Nationalism and the Russian Jews 1862–1917* and *The Damascus Affair: "Ritual Murder," Politics and the Jews in 1840*. He is coeditor of *Studies in Contemporary Jewry: An Annual*.

ZVI GITELMAN is professor of political science and Preston R. Tisch Professor of Judaic Studies at the University of Michigan. He is the author or editor of several books on Russian, East European, and Israeli politics, including, most recently, *A Century of Ambivalence: The Jews of Russia and the Soviet Union, 1881 to the Present*. He is currently working on ethnic identities of Russian and Ukrainian Jews and on oral histories of Soviet Jewish war veterans.

SAMUEL D. KASSOW is professor of history at Trinity College. He is the coeditor of *Between Tsar and People* and the author of *Students, Professors and the State in Tsarist Russia* and several articles on Russian and modern Jewish history. He is currently completing a study of Emanuel Ringelblum and the underground archive of the Warsaw ghetto.

MAUD MANDEL is the Dorot Assistant Professor of Judaic Studies and assistant professor of history at Brown University. She is the author of many articles and a forthcoming book called *In the Aftermath of Genocide: Armenians and Jews in Twentieth Century France.*

BENJAMIN NATHANS is Watkins Assistant Professor in the Humanities in the Department of History at the University of Pennsylvania. He is the author of *Beyond the Pale: The Jewish Encounter with Late Imperial Russia.*

ANTONY POLONSKY is Albert Abramson Professor of Holocaust Studies at Brandeis University and the United States Holocaust Memorial Museum. He is the author of *Politics in Independent Poland*; *The Little Dictators*; and *The Great Powers and the Polish Question* and coauthor of *A History of Modern Poland* and *The Beginnings of Communist Rule in Poland.* Most recently, he has edited, with Monika Grabowska, *Jewish Writing in the Contemporary World: Poland.* He is the chair of the editorial board of *POLIN: Studies in Polish Jewry.*

MICHAEL C. STEINLAUF is associate professor of history at Gratz College, Philadelphia. He has been to Poland as a Fulbright Fellow and as project director for the United States Holocaust Memorial Museum. He is the author of *Bondage to the Dead: Poland and the Memory of the Holocaust*, which has been recently published in Poland. He is currently working on a social and cultural history of Jewish theater in Poland and editing a special volume of *POLIN: Studies in Polish Jewry* devoted to Jewish popular culture in Poland and its afterlife.

RONALD GRIGOR SUNY is professor of political science at the University of Chicago. A specialist in the history and politics of the Soviet and post-Soviet world, his latest works include *The Revenge of the Past: Nationalism, Revolution, and the Collapse of the Soviet Union*; *The Soviet Experiment: Russia, the USSR, and the Successor States, Intellectuals and the Articulation of the Nation* (coedited with Michael D. Kennedy); and *A State of Nations: Empire and Nation-Making in the Age of Lenin and Stalin* (coedited with Terry Martin).

RUTH R. WISSE is Martin Peretz Professor of Yiddish Literature and Professor of Comparative Literature at Harvard University. Her books include *I. L. Peretz and the Making of Modern Jewish Culture; If I Am Not For Myself: The Liberal Betrayal of the Jews*; and *The Modern Jewish Canon: A Journey through Language and Culture.*

SETH L. WOLITZ holds the Gale Chair of Jewish Studies at the University of Texas, Austin, where he is also professor of French, Slavic, and comparative literatures. He specializes in twentieth-century Jewish literature and art. His works include *The Proustian Community; The Hidden Isaac Bashevis Singer;* and *The Renaissance in Kosher Cuisine: From Ethnicity to Universality.*

INDEX

Abramovich, Rafael, 181, 185, 192

Abramovich, Ze'ev, 81–83

Abramowitz, S. J., 249*n9*, see also Sefarim, Mendele Mocher

aggadah, 134–35

Agnon, Samuel Joseph, 136, 250*n26*

Aguda. See Agudat Yisrael

Agudat Yisrael, 5, 36–37, 43, 51–52, 85, 194, 240*n1*; and cooperation with Zionists, 93–94; and imitation of Zionism, 5, 85–92, 240*n6*, 241*n10*; and the *kehillot*, 93; and relationship with the Bund, 92–93; and view of Jewish nationalism, 89, 94

Ahad Ha'am, 9, 124, 134, 137, 154, 159, 250*n11*, 255*n33*

Akhdut Ha-Avodah, 72

Aleichem, Sholem, 107, 109, 112, 117, 127, 134, 140, 154, 250*n10*; and tragicomedy, 123–24, 248*n5*. *See also* Rabinowitz, Sholem

Alexander II, 20, 40

Alexander Rebbe, 243*n6*

Alliance Israelite Universelle, 24, 29

Alter, Rabbi Abraham Mordecai. *See* Gerer, Rebbe

Alter, Viktor, 61–62, 79

Amalgamated Clothing Workers of America, 185

American Communist Party, 184, 189

American Jewish Committee, 187, 193–94

American Jewish Conference of 1943, 192–95, 261*n56*, 261*n59*

American Jewish Congress, 189, 194

American Jewish Joint Distribution Committee, 64, 195, 202

Amishai-Maisels, Ziva, 169, 172, 256*n49*, 256*n55*

An-sky, Sh. (Sh.Z. Rappoport), 23, 96, 112, 160, 165, 176, 256*n56*

anti-Semitism: in Kingdom of Poland, 44–45, 52; and anti-Zionism in Poland, 44

Antokolsky, Mark, 152, 158

Arab uprising in Palestine of 1929, reactions to, 190–92

Arbeter Ring. *See* Workmen's Circle

Arbeter tsaytung, 75–77, 80, 83

Arbeter vort, 83

Aronson, Boris, 165–66, 168

art, nineteenth-century images of Jews in, 151–52, 252*n3*

artists: nineteenth-century Jewish, 152, 252*n4*; Jewish as representation of cultural *zeitgeist*, 153, 253*n11*

Asch, Sholem, 112, 117–18

Ashkenaz, 21

Askenazy, Szymon, 120–21

assimilation, 7, 23–24, 29, 31, 42

autonomists, 29. *See also* Jewish autonomy

Balfour Declaration, 46, 72, 75, 91, 188–89

Basel, Switzerland. *See* Basle, Switzerland

Basle, Switzerland, 4, 157–58

Belorussians, 40–41, 50

Ben-Gurion, David, 24, 72, 184, 209, 210, 213

Berdichevsky, M. Y., 134, 137–38

Berkowitz, I. D., 137, 140

Bernard, Jean Jacques, 204–8, 263nn25–26

Betar. *See* Betar youth movement; Zionist Revisionists

Betar youth movement, 99–100

Bezalel Academy. *See* Bezalel School of Jerusalem

Bezalel School of Jerusalem, 6, 151, 154, 158, 160, 164–65, 168–69, 172, 176, 254nn27–28, 257n64

Bezalel style. *See* Bezalel School of Jerusalem

Bialik, Chaim Nachman, 6, 128, 134–35, 137–40, 142–45

Bialystok, 29, 36, 66–67, 111

Birnbaum, Nathan, 109, 118

Birobidzhan, 79–83

Bittelman, Alexander, 184, 189

Blond, Dina, 68–69

Blondes, David, 27

Bolshevik Revolution, 58, 188

Bolsheviks, 4, 14

Borochov, Ber, 73–74, 77–80, 83–84, 118, 227n1, 243n18

Borochovism, 73–74, 76

Brenner, J. H., 137–39, 142

Buber, Martin, 154–55, 164, 176

Buchsbaum, Nathan, 73, 78, 83–84

Bulletin d'information, 202

Bulletin du Centre israélite d'information, 207–8

Bund: and Jewish associations, 117; and Yiddishism, 117–19; and allies, 43; and contributions, 18–19; and cultural and national autonomy in Poland, 62; and elections, 35–36, 84; failure of, 8–9; founding of, 4; national program, 228n14, 234n11; participation of women in, 16–17, 64–69, 236n46; in Poland, 4, 51–52, 55–62, 64–68; in Russia, 29, 56. *See also* Bundism; YAF

Bundism: and Jewish national-cultural autonomy, 113–15; and Yiddish language and culture, 5–6, 107, 109–11, 245n10, 245n16; and Yiddish literature, 5–6, 108, 111–13; and Yiddish schools, 115–16, 119

Bundist / folkist art. *See* Vitebsk school

byt, 156, 165, 254n22

Central-Verein deutscher Staatsbürger judischen Glaubens, 24, 29

Czernowitz conference on Yiddish language, 108–9, 117–18

Chagall, Marc, 6, 151–52, 160, 164, 168–69, 172–73, 176, 251n1, 256n57

Chaikov, Joseph. *See* Tchaikov, Joseph

Chanin, Nokhem, 189, 195

Charney, Vladek B., 113, 245n16

Chekov, Anton, 142–43, 149

citizenship, civic and ethnic, 32, 232n41

Clemenceau, Georges, 216

Comintern, 59, 190

Committee of Jewish Delegations to the Paris Peace Conference, 47–48

Compiègne, 204, 263n26

Congress Kingdom (Poland), 39, 41

Congress of Vienna, 39

Conseil Représentif Israélite de France (CRIF), 211–12, 217, 264n53, 264n55

Consistoire de Paris, 206–8, 210–11, 265n71; and support of Zionism, 213–19

Constitutional Democratic Party (Kadets), 20, 28–29

CYSHO (Central Yiddish School Organization), 68, 76–77

Defense Bureau, 27–28

Democratic Zionist bloc, 36

Der fraynd, 108–9, 111, 115
Der veker, 110, 190–93, 195
Der Yid (Dos Yidishe Togblat), 88–89
Der Yud, 111, 117–18
Dmowski, Roman, 42–43, 45
Dos yiddishe vort, 116, 247*n32*
Dostoyevsky, Fyodor, 142, 145–46, 148–49
double patriotism, 206–7
Dubinsky, David, 185, 190
Dubnov, Shimon, See Dubnow, Shimon
Dubnow, Shimon, 23, 37–38, 159, 176, 255*n33*

Edelshtat, Dovid, 9, 112
Einhorn, David, 185, 195
Epstein, Shakhne, 185, 187–88
Erlich, Henryk, 37, 58, 66, 184, 189
Esprit, 206, 263*n32*
Evsektsiia, 76, 80
Exodus, 217–18

February Revolution, 188
Fédération des sociétés juives de France (FSJF), 205, 212
Feierberg, M. Z., 137–38, 141, 145
Forverts, 184–85, 187–92, 194, 260*n34*
France: and assimilation debates in, 203–4; and Eastern European immigrants, 200–1; and key influence on Jewish politics in, 197–98. *See also* French Jews
French Jews: and immigration, 199, 262*n11*; impact of Holocaust on, 198, 207–8, 261*n5*, 262*n6*
Frayheyt, 185, 189–92, 195
Frumkin, Esther, 17, 116–18

Galicia, 36, 38–39, 42; and politics and elections, 43, 46. *See also* Zionists, in Galicia
Gamzon, Robert, 209
Gerer, Rebbe, 88, 91

Gessen, Valerii Iulevich, 20–21, 33
Gintsburg, Horace, 23, 25–26
Ginzberg, Asher, 250*n11*. *See also* Ahad Ha'am
Gnessin, Uri Nissan, 134, 137, 139, 142
Gogol, 142–44, 146–48
Goldfarb, Max, 185, 187. *See also* General Petrovskii
Goldshtain, Yosef, 15–16
Gordon, Judah Leib, 31, 135–36
Gordon, Yehuda Leib, See Gordon, Judah Leib
Gorky, Maxim, 140, 149
Grosser, Bronislaw, 58, 117
Grunbaum, Yitzhak, 50–51, 118
Gruzenberg, Oskar, 27, 32–33
Guenzburg, Baron David, 159–60

Haganah, 215, 217
Hashomer Hatsair, 98, 100
Hasidim, 13, 38
Haskalah, 135–36, 143–44, 148, 152; movement, 13, 21, 31, 136; Russian, 136
Hebrew language: and culture, 9–10, 72; and Jewish national identity, 150; and Palestine, 139; and Zionism, 138
Hebrew literature, 6, 42, 132,–33, 249*nn2–3*; and Hasidim, 139, 250*n20*; and Jewish liberation, 138–41; and Jewish stereotypes in Russian literature, 145–47; and pogroms, 136–38; pre-1881, 135–36; and relation to Russian literature, 141–45
He-Halutz, 73–76, 81–82
Helfand, Chaim. *See* Litvak, A.
Heller, Celia, 52
Helsingfors Conference, 29, 43, 118
Hertz, Henri, 206–7
Hertz, J. S., 56, 246*n17*
Herzl, Theodor, 13, 43, 45, 90, 155
Hillman, Sidney, 185
Hirszenberg, Samuel, 152, 254*n27*

Histadrut, 72–73, 75, 83–84, 190
Hitler, Adolph, 80, 82
Hochkultur, 53, 253*nn9–10*. *See also* Wagner, Richard

integration, 4, 23–33, 41–43, 60
International Ladies Garment Workers Union, 185, 189
Israel, Josef, 154–55
Israeli culture, 9

Jabotinsky, Vladimir. *See* Zhabotinsky, Vladimir
Jarblum, Marc, 205–7
Jean Christophe, 98, 243*n12*
Jewish autonomy, 4, 21, 29, 40, 42, 46, 59
Jewish Labor Bund. *See* Bund
Jewish Labor Committee, 36, 193–94
Jewish Literary Society, 116–17
Jewish politics, evolution of, 12–14, 17–18, 43, 45
Jewish Section of the Communist Party, 189, 191
Jewish Socialist Federation, 182, 184–89, 193
Jewish Socialist Workers Party (SERP), 15, 118
Jewish Socialist Farband, 189–95
Jewish Workers' Alliance. *See* Bund
Judicial Reform of 1864, 24
Juedische Kuenstler, 154, 253*n13*, 254*n17*
Jugendstil, 155, 165, 168–69, 176

Kamenev, Lev, 76, 184
Kapel, René, 203, 206–7
Katznelson, Berl, 72, 184
Kaunas, Lithuania, 46–48
Kazdan, Hayim-Shlomo, 68–69
kehilla, 19, 60; and Aguda, 51; and local elections, 8, 35; and politics, 13–14; and relationship to state, 22, 28, 47–48, 56. *See also* Law on *Kehillot*

Kenessia Gedola, 87
Kenig, Leo, 168, 172
khurbn, 6, 122, 126–27, 130–31
Kingdom of Poland, 38–39, 41–42; and emancipation of Jews, 41; and Jewish Politics, 40, 43
kinnus, 140
Kishinev pogrom, 140, 145
Kligsberg, Moishe, 98, 102–3, 244*n30*
Kosovsky, Vladimir, 56, 110, 185
Kossovskii, Vladimir. *See* Kosovsky, Vladimir
Kossovsky, Vladimir. *See* Kosovsky, Vladimir
Kulturkampf, Jewish, 153–54, 253*n12*

La Ruche, 168, 172
La Terre retrouvée, 205, 212
Law on *Kehillot*, 48–49
Lederhendler, Eli, 22–23, 25, 28
Left Poalei Tsiyon (LPZ), 5, 36, 71–72; and elections, 77, 84, 238*n18*; and ideology, 74–76; and internal ideological debates, 80–83, 240*n46*; and organizations, 76–77, 238*nn15–16*; and relationship with Bund, 76–80. *See also* Poalei Tsiyon
Lermontov, Mikhail, 146
Lesin, Avrom, 186, 188
Leskov, Nikolai, 143, 149
Lestchinsky, Jacob, 79
Lev, Yitzhak, 79, 82–83, 239*n43*
Levin, Emmanuel, 26
Liber, Mark. *See* Lieber, Mark
Lieber, Mark, 113, 181, 184
Lieberman, Max, 154
Likhtenshteyn, Yitshok, 164, 168, 172
Lilien, E. M. *See* Lilien, Ephraim
Lilien, Ephraim, 6, 154–57, 165, 168, 176, 254*n21*, 254*n27*
Lissitsky, El. *See* Lissitzky, El
Lissitzky, El, 6, 160, 164–65, 176

Literarishe monatshriftn, 108, 113
Lithuania and Jewish national autonomy, 46–50, 53
Lithuanians, 40–41, 43
Litvak, A., 110, 112–13, 185, 189, 245*n16*, 246*n17*
Lodz, 8, 35–36, 66–67, 77, 79, 109
L'Ornement Hébreu, 159–60
Lozowick, Louis, 173
Lublin, 36, 66–67
Lviv. *See* Lwow
Lwow, 36, 51, 58

Mahler, Raphael, 77, 79
Makhmadim, 168–69, 172, 176, 256*n49*
Manifesto of October 1905, 44
Mapai, 80, 83
Marranism, 172–73, 256*n56*, 257*n58*
Marshall, Louis, 46, 194
maskil, 9, 11, 13, 26, 43, 243*n17*
May Laws, 133
Medem, Vladimir, 13, 23, 56, 58–59, 110, 114, 119, 184–85
Mendele the Bookpeddler. *See* Sefarim, Mendele Mocher
Mendele. *See* Sefarim, Mendele Mocher
Mensheviks, 4, 14
Michalewicz, Beinish, 59–60, 66
Misnagdim, 13, 38, 47
Mizrachi. *See* Zionism, religious

National Council of Jewish Class Trade Unions (JCTU), 61
national-cultural autonomy, 13, 56, 58, 59–60
National Democratic movement, 42–43, 45, 51
National Minorities Bloc, 50–51
national-minorities policy, Poland, 54–55, 57
National Workmen's Committee, 187–88, 193

National Workmen's Committee on Jewish Rights in the Belligerent Lands. *See* National Workmen's Committee
Nazis, 52–53
Nicholas II. *See* Tsar Nicholas II
Niger, Shmuel, 113, 118, 128, 184
Nir-Rafalkes, Nahum, 82
Nossig, Alfred, 154–55
Novick, Pesach, 184–85, 194

Odessa, 24, 108
Odessa pogrom of May 1871, 24, 231*n9*
Olgin, Moishe. *See* Olgin, Moshe
Olgin, Moshe, 116, 184, 187, 189, 191, 247*n32*
Orshanskii, Ilya, 24–25
Orthodox Judaism, 7. *See also* Agudat Yisrael

Pale of Settlement, 16, 27, 39–40, 80, 109
Paris, 168, 172, 176
Pen, Yehuda, 6, 151, 158–59, 164–65, 169, 255*n40*
Peretz, I. L., 5–6, 103, 107, 109, 111–12, 117, 134, 137, 154; and circumcision scandal, 121–23; and Grzybowska vision, 120; and Jewish culture, 124–25, 130–31; and tragicomedy, 123–24
Peretz, Y. L. *See* Peretz, I. L.
Petrovskii, General, 185. *See also* Gold-farb, Max
Pilsudski, Jozef, 51, 60
Pine, Max, 188–89
Pinsker, Leon, 13, 23
Poalei Agudat Yisrael, 92
Poalei Tsiyon, 15, 118, 186–87, 193, 207; and split within party, 72–73. *See also* Left Poalei Tsiyon; Right Poalei Tsiyon; World Union of Poalei Tsiyon, Fifth Conference
pogroms: of 1881–1882, 26; of 1905–1906, 28

Poland: and Jewish national autonomy, 50–53, 60; and Jewish rights, 44; and Jewish trade unions, 60–64. *See also* Kingdom of Poland; Poles of the Mosaic faith, Polish

Poles of the Mosaic faith, 39–41, 99–100

Polish Communist Party (KPP), 58, 76–77, 83

Polish: Jewish youth movement, 97–104; as language of Jews, 100; nationality, 54–55; Sejm, 62, 85

Polish Socialist Party (PPS): and relationship with Bund, 8, 18, 35–36, 52, 57–58, 61–62, 65; and relationship with Left Poalei Tsiyon, 77

Polish-Lithuanian Commonwealth, 39, 41

Portnoi, Noakh, 185, 189

Rabinowitz, Sholem, 250*n10. See also* Aleichem, Sholem

Rafes, Moishe, 118–19

Raisin, Avrom, 192

Reform Judaism, 7, 89

Reich, Leon, 50–52

Reisin, Avrom, 111–12

Right Poalei Tsiyon, 72, 74, 76, 83

Ringelblum, Emanuel, 71, 77, 84, 238*n20*

Rola, 44

Rosenfeld, Morris, 9, 112

Rosenzweig, A., 127

Rothschild, Guy de, 199–200, 202

Russian Haskalah. *See* Haskalah, Russian

Russian literature, 147–49

Russian Social Democratic Labor Party, 18, 28

Saltykov-Shchedrin, Mikhail Evgrafovich, 136, 142, 144, 146, 149

Salutsky, Jacob, 187, 189

Schatz, Boris. *See* Shatz, Boris

Schwartz, Isaïe, 212

Second Jewish National Assembly, 46, 48

Sefarim, Mendele Mocher, 111, 134–37, 139–40, 142–49, 154, 249*n9*

Shatz, Boris, 6, 158

Sheftel, Mikhail, 23

Sherman, Bezalel, 82

Shoffman, Gershom, 134, 142

shtadlan, 13, 25–26, 30, 33

Shvarts, Marek, 168–69, 172

Shvartzbart, Dr. Ignacy (Yitzhak), 85–86

Sliozberg, Genrikh, 23–24, 26–27, 29–32, 43, 231*n20*, 232*n42*

Socialist Association of Artisans of the Republic of Poland, 63–64

Socialist Party of America, 182, 186, 188–89

Society for the Dissemination of Enlightenment, 20–21, 23, 25, 30, 33, 119

Soloveitchik, Dr. Max, 46–49

Stassov, V. V., 159–60

Stempowski, Jerzy, 120–21

Swietochowski, Alexander, 41, 44–45

Tchaikov, Joseph (Yosef), 172, 176

Tchernichovsky, Saul. *See* Tchernichowsky, Saul

Tchernichowsky, Saul, 137–38

territorialism, 7

Third All Russian Zionist Conference. *See* Helsingfors Conference

Tolstoy, Leo, 142, 146

Tomaszewski, Jerzy, 36, 52

Tönnies, Ferdinand, 32

Tsar Nicholas II, 137, 140

Turgenev, Ivan, 142–43, 146–48

Tzeirei Agudat Yisrael, 90–91

Ukrainians, 40–41, 57

Union for the Attainment of Equal Rights, 29, 33

United Hebrew Trades, 183, 187–88

Ury, Lesser, 154–55, 254*n27*

Versailles, 46

Vichy government and anti-Jewish
    statutes, 198–200, 202, 207–8,
    262n20, 263n46
Vilna, Lithuania, 4, 12, 36, 47, 50, 66–67,
    95, 108–11, 116, 118, 158
Vilnius, Lithuania. *See* Vilna, Lithuania
Vinaver, Maxim, 23–24, 27, 29–32
Vitebsk school, 6, 151, 154, 158–60, 164–65,
    168–69, 172, 176–77, 255n32
Vitebsk style. *See* Vitebsk school
Vladeck, Baruch, 184, 193

Wagner, Richard, 153–54, 253n8
Warsaw, 8, 36, 66–67, 77, 79, 108–9, 111,
    116–17
Weinreich, Max, 95–96, 246n17
Wielopolski, Alexander, 40–41
Wilno, Poland. *See* Vilna, Lithuania
Workers Party in America, 189
Workers Party in the Soviet Union, 190
Workmen's Circle, 183, 185, 187–88, 190
World Union of Poalei Tsiyon, Fifth Con-
    ference, 72
World Zionist Organization, 4, 46
Wormser, Georges, 206, 214, 216
Wygodzki, Dr. Jacob, 47

YAF (*Yidishe arbeter-froy-organizatsye*), 64,
    66–68. *See also* Bund, and participa-
    tion of women
Yehuda Pen's School of Drawing and
    Painting. *See* Vitebsk school
Yiddish: language, literature, and culture,
    5, 9–11, 42, 61, 72, 74, 77–79; publish-
    ing houses, 108, 115

Yiddish Scientific Institute (YIVO), 5, 77,
    95, 242n1, 242n3
Yiddishist ideology, 108
Yidisher Folks-Ornament, 160
Yontev bletlekh, 126
Yudovin, Salomon. *See* Yudovin, Shalom
Yudovin, Shalom, 6, 160, 164–65, 251n1,
    255n41
Yudovin, Solomon. *See* Yudovin, Shalom

Zadkine, Ossip, 164, 168, 172
Zagan, Shakhne, 83–84
Zerubavel, Jacob, 73–74, 80–84
Zhabotinsky, Vladimir (Zeev), 13, 24, 33,
    43, 52, 80, 227n1
zhargonishe komitetn, 111–12
Zhitlovsky, Chaim, 11, 109, 117–18
Zinberg, Israel, 118–19
Zinoviev, Grigori, 76, 184
Zionism: and allies, 43; and constituency,
    14–16; and contributions, 18–19; and
    elections, 35–36; founding of, 4; par-
    ticipation of women in, 16; in France,
    201–2, 209–13, 262n15, 265n63; in
    Poland, 44, 60; religious, 7–8, 85, 203,
    227n1; in Russia, 14; secular, 85; so-
    cialist, 7. *See also* Bezalel School of
    Jerusalem; World Zionist Organiza-
    tion; Zionist Revisionism; Zionists
Zionist art. *See* Bezalel School of
    Jerusalem
Zionist Revisionism, 7–8, 37, 194, 243n16
Zionists: in Galicia, 50; in Kingdom of
    Poland, 50
Zygielbojm, Szmuel, 61–62